Technical Analysis of the Futures Markets:

A Comprehensive Guide to Trading Methods and Applications

John J. Murphy

NEW YORK INSTITUTE OF FINANCE

NEW YORK • TORONTO • SYDNEY • TOKYO • SINGAPORE

Library of Congress Cataloging-in-Publication Data
Murphy, John J.
    Technical analysis of the futures markets.

    Bibliography: p. 548
    Includes index.
    1. Commodity exchanges.   I. Title.
HG6046.M87   1986   332.64'4   85-25958
ISBN 0-13-898008-X

This publication is designed to provide accurate and authoritative information in regard to the subject matter covered. It is sold with the understanding that the publisher is not engaged in rendering legal, accounting, or other professional service. If legal advice or other expert assistance is required, the services of a competent professional person should be sought.

From a Declaration of Principles Jointly Adopted by
a Committee of the American Bar Association and a
Committee of Publishers and Associations

Printed in the United States of America

20   19   18   17   16   15   14

NEW YORK INSTITUTE OF FINANCE
Englewood Cliffs, NJ 07632

A Simon & Schuster Company

*To my parents, Timothy and Margaret
and
to Patty, Clare, and Brian*

Contents

5
Major Reversal Patterns, 103

6
Continuation Patterns, 136

7
Volume and Open Interest, 176

8
Long-Term Charts and Commodity Indices, 207

9
Moving Averages, 234

13
Elliott Wave Theory, 371

14
Time Cycles, 414

15
Computers and Trading Systems, 456

16
Money Management and Trading Tactics, 487

Introduction

Why another book on the use of technical analysis in the commodity futures markets? The answer to that question goes back to the introduction of a course on that subject at the New York Institute of Finance several years ago.

In spring of 1981, I was asked to introduce a course on commodity technical analysis at the Institute. I had been a practicing technical analyst in the futures markets for over a dozen years and had done some lecturing on the subject. But the task of structuring a 15-week course was a challenge. At first, I wasn't sure there was enough material to fill an entire 15 weeks. In the process of outlining the subject matter I considered important, however, I began to realize that 15 weeks wasn't nearly enough time to do justice to such a complex subject.

Technical analysis is more than just a tight little body of specialized material. It is a combination of several different approaches and areas of specialization that combine to form the whole body of technical theory. To adequately cover the subject would require touching on at least a dozen different approaches in such a way that all would fit together into one coherent theory.

Having determined what should be included in the course, I set out to find a book that could be used as a suitable text. What I discovered in reviewing the available literature was that no such book existed. Certainly, there were enough good books around. However, those books that dealt adequately with the basics of charting were written for the stock market. I didn't want to use a stock market book in a commodity futures course.

Those books dealing with the futures markets fell into several categories. Virtually all began with the assumption that readers were already familiar with the basics of charting before proceeding to present some advanced theories or original work developed by the author. Such books weren't much use to people just beginning to learn the subject. Other books specialized in one area of technical analysis, such as bar or point and figure charting, Elliott Wave Theory, or cycles, which were too narrow for my purpose. Some dealt with the use of computers and the development of sophisticated systems and indicators. All good books, but too advanced or too specialized for a course on technical analysis.

It finally dawned on me that the book I needed for my course, a good solid text that began at the beginning and took the reader through most of the important areas of technical analysis as they applied to the futures markets in a logical, step-by-step fashion, simply did not exist. It became clear to me that a gap existed in the existing literature. Because all good technicians know that gaps should be filled, I concluded that, if I wanted such a book, I would have to write it myself.

Technical Analysis of the Futures Markets is not meant to be a definitive, all-encompassing book on technical analysis. No such book exists or ever will. Technical analysis is just too broad a topic, with so many subtleties and refinements, that any attempt to write the "definitive" book is not only presumptuous, but doomed to failure. Entire books have been written on just about every subject touched on in this book.

Neither is it meant as just a basic primer on the subject. It begins at the beginning and spends a fair amount of time on the basics of charting theory. This is partly because of my own strong conviction that most good technical analysis is nothing more than a sound application of those basics. Most of the more sophisticated indicators and systems in use today are just refinements of basic concepts. The book then moves in logical fashion into some of the more advanced areas. The subject matter is presented in such a way that a relative newcomer should be able to follow along. However, it is hoped that the intermediate technician, with a few years of experience, also finds much of the material helpful. The advanced chartist can use the book as a good review.

This last point is particularly significant. After all, aren't we all just students of technical analysis? One of the great masters, W. D. Gann, once said: "I have studied and improved my methods every year for the past forty years. I am still learning. I hope to make greater discoveries in the future." (*How to Make Profits in Commodities*, Pomeroy, WA: Lambert-Gann, 1976, p. 2).

The need for constant study and review cannot be overemphasized. One of the major benefits I have received from teaching technical theory has been the need to constantly go back and reread much of the literature I had read several years before. Each rereading has produced new insights, new subtleties that had escaped me previously. Even the most hardened veteran trader can benefit from a periodic review of the subject matter. On the shorter side of the experience spectrum, I can't help but feel amused when someone who has been in the business six months or a year informs me that he or she has already mastered the basics and is ready for the really "good stuff." Maybe I'm just jealous. After 15 years, I'm still trying to master them.

Chapter 1 covers much of the philosophy and rationale behind the technical analysis of futures. The subject is defined along with its basic premises. I have always felt that much of the confusion about technical analysis arises from a lack of understanding of what technical theory really is and the rationale or philosophy upon which it is based. The question of technical versus fundamental forecasting is discussed along with some of the advantages of charting. Since the question of how technical analysis of stocks compares with that of the futures markets is often raised, some of those similarities and differences are touched on. Two criticisms of technical analysis are treated briefly— Random Walk Theory and the self-fulfilling prophecy.

Chapter 2 covers the venerable Dow Theory from which most charting theory has developed. Many futures chartists seem unaware of how much of what they do can be traced back to the writings of Charles Dow around the turn of the century.

Chapter 3 explains how to construct the daily bar chart, the most commonly used type of chart, and introduces the concept of volume and open interest. The construction of weekly and monthly charts is also covered as a supplement to the daily charts.

Chapter 4 goes into the basic concepts of trend, or the building blocks of chart analysis. Subjects like trend, support and resistance, trendlines and channels, percentage retracements, gaps, and key reversal days are included.

Chapters 5 and 6 build on the previous concepts for a study of price patterns. Major reversal patterns, like the head and shoulders pattern and the double top or bottom, are explained in Chapter 5. Continuation patterns, such as the flag and pennant patterns and triangles, are treated in Chapter 6. The patterns are explained and illustrated. Measuring techniques are covered along with the role of volume in the formation and resolution of the price patterns.

Chapter 7 goes into volume and open interest in more depth. The discussion shows how both figures are used to confirm price action or to warn of impending trend changes. Some indicators that utilize volume, such as on-balance volume (OBV), are discussed. The usefulness of open interest figures in the Commitments of Traders Reports is also addressed.

Chapter 8 covers an important, but often overlooked area of charting—the use of weekly and monthly continuation charts. These longer-range charts provide a perspective on market trend that is impossible to achieve by using daily charts alone. The value of following general commodity indices, such as the Commodity Research Bureau Futures Price Index and the various group indices, is also stressed.

Chapter 9 deals with moving averages, one of the most widely used technical tools and the mainstay of most computerized technical trend-following systems.

That chapter also presents an alternative trend-following aproach— the weekly price channel, or the four-week rule.

Chapter 10 talks about oscillators and how they are used to determine overbought and oversold market conditions. Various types of oscillators are covered along with the important subject of how to spot divergences. Contrary Opinion is included as another method of determining market extremes.

Chapter 11 leaves bar charting for awhile and delves into the world of point and figure charting. While not as well-known, point and figure charts provide more precision and can be used as a valuable supplement to the bar chart.

Chapter 12 shows how some of the benefits of point and figure charting can be had without access to intra-day price data. The three-box reversal method is discussed along with optimized point and figure charts. With the increased use of computers and more sophisticated price reporting systems, point and figure charting appears to be staging a comeback in the futures arena.

Chapter 13 moves on to the Elliott Wave Theory and Fibonacci numbers. This theory was originally applied to the stock market averages, but has gained increased attention in the futures markets. If used properly, Elliott's principles provide a unique perspective on market movement that enables the analyst to anticipate market turns with greater insight and confidence.

Chapter 14 adds the dimension of time to the forecasting puzzle by the study of cycles. Annual seasonal patterns are also discussed here. Besides providing an overview of cycle theory, the chapter addresses the question of how other technical tools, such as the moving average and oscillator, can be improved if synchronized with underlying market cycles.

Chapter 15 pays tribute to the increased role of the computer in technical analysis and trading. Some of the advantages and disadvantages of using mechanical computer trading systems are treated. We'll take a look at some of the technical analysis routines available through the Compu Trac software. It is stressed, however, that computers are only a tool and not meant to be a substitute for good sound analysis. If the user does not understand the trading tools covered in Chapters 1 through 14, the computer won't be much help. A computer can make a good technician better. It won't make a bad technician better, and may even make him or her worse.

Chapter 16 discusses another much overlooked aspect of successful futures trading—money management. This chapter discusses what money management is and why it is so important to survival in the futures markets. Many traders consider money management to be the most important aspect of futures trading. The three stages of trading also are coordinated—forecasting, timing and money management. Forecasting helps the trader decide which side of the market to be trading from—the long or the short side. Market timing covers the specifics of entry and exit points—how and when to act. Money management helps determine how much to buy or sell. Different types of trading orders are discussed as well as the controversial subject of whether or not to use protective stops as part of a trading strategy.

Pulling It All Together pulls the preceding material together into one coherent theory, much like fitting together pieces in a giant jigsaw puzzle. It emphasizes the need to be familiar with all of the different approaches to technical analysis and how to blend them together. Many technicians specialize in one area of analysis, believing that area holds the key to successful trading. My own philosophy is that no one area holds all of the answers, but that they each hold part of the answer. In other words, each technical theory holds a piece of the puzzle. The more pieces the trader has under his or her command, the better the odds in solving the puzzle. A checklist is offered to aid the reader in that process.

Although the book deals primarily with the outright trading of commodity futures contracts, technical analysis has much application in the area of spread and options trading. These two important areas will be treated briefly in *Appendices 1 and 2*. Finally, no technical book would be complete without some mention of the legendary W. D. Gann. While an in-depth discussion of Gann's techniques isn't possible here, we'll touch on a couple of his simpler and, some believe, more useful trading tools in *Appendix 3*.

It is hoped that this book does indeed fill the gap perceived by the author, and that it contributes to a better understanding and appreciation of what technical analysis is all about. Technical analysis is certainly not for everyone. In fact, it would probably lose much of its value if everyone started to apply its principles. It is not the intention of this book to sell the technical approach to anyone. It is simply an attempt by one technical analyst to share his interpretation of this sometimes complex and intimidating subject with those wishing to learn more about it.

Technical analysis is much more than "tea leaf reading" or "crystal ball gazing," descriptions sometimes used by those who simply don't know any better. But neither is it the "Holy Grail," promising instant riches to its practitioners. Technical analysis is simply one approach to market forecasting based on a study of the past, human psychology, and the law of probabilities. It is certainly not infallible. But it is a technique that works more often than not, has stood the test of time in the real world of trading, and is worthy of study by any serious student of market behavior.

The overriding theme of this work is simplicity. There are those who insist on taking relatively simple concepts and making them more complicated. I prefer it the other way around. After experimenting with most of the technical tools available, from the very simple to the very sophisticated, I have come to the conclusion that, in most cases, the simpler techniques seem to work best. So, my advice throughout the book is to "keep it simple."

JOHN J. MURPHY

Acknowledgments

Any book that discusses all of the major theories in the field of technical analysis must of necessity draw on the ideas of many other analysts and authors. While the subject matter in this book represents my interpretation of those ideas, blended with my personal market experiences over a period of 15 years, I would like to acknowledge a debt of gratitude to those technical analysts who went before me and who put their ideas in writing. The hope is that some future technical writer will find this book helpful in his or her work.

Since technical analysis is a visual craft, it was necessary to include a large number of price charts to demonstrate the various points. Most of the charts were provided by the Commodity Research Bureau and were taken from their publication, the *CRB Futures Chart Service*. A special word of thanks is owed to that organization for permission to use its charts and to its production editor, Seymour Gaylinn, for their consistent high quality. Other services that contributed charts were *Chart Analysis, Ltd.*, *Chartcraft Commodity Service*, *Commodity Price Charts*, *Dunn & Hargitt*, *HAL Market Cycles*, *Quotron Futures Charts*, *Comtrend-Videcom*, *MarketVision*, and *Compu Trac*.

The Compu Trac software was especially invaluable for displaying many of the more sophisticated technical analysis routines and indicators. Chapter 15 relies heavily on the Compu Trac program to demonstrate what the computer is capable of doing in market analysis and trading. Special thanks goes out to that group and its president, Tim Slater.

Special mention is also owed to three experts, who took time from busy schedules to review particular chapters. Robert Prechter of the "Elliott Wave Theorist" not only spent several hours helping to polish Chapter 13, but also generously contributed several diagrams from his book, *The Elliott Wave Principle*. Walt Bressert of *HAL Market Cycles* and Jake Bernstein of *MBH Commodity Advisors* reviewed Chapter 14 on *Cycles*. That chapter draws heavily on the work of both of those cycles experts.

Ben Russell, president of the New York Institute of Finance, agreed on the need for a textbook in my course on *Commodity Technical Analysis*, and suggested making the book available to a broader audience. Without his gentle encouragement along the way, and continued patience at missed deadlines, I'm not sure the work would have been completed. I often wondered if the day would ever come when I would feel like thanking him for starting me on what seemed like an endless task. Well, that day has come. Thanks, Ben.

Thanks go also to Fred Dahl at the Institute for guiding me through the mechanics of preparing a manuscript for publication; and to my many students over the years at the Institute whose interest in technical analysis was a never-ending source of inspiration, and who kept asking those difficult questions that I've tried to answer in this book.

Finally, a book that's written over a three-year period—mainly on weekends at that—couldn't be done without the understanding and support of one's wife and family. Freedom from normal family responsibilities while writing is the only way it can be accomplished. To my wife, Patty, who carried more than her share of the burden during that period of time, I owe a deep debt of gratitude. To my two young children, Clare and Brian, both of whom were born during preparation of the manuscript, I hope I can make up for some lost time.

J.J.M.

1
Philosophy of
Technical Analysis

INTRODUCTION

Before beginning a study of the actual techniques and tools used in commodity technical analysis, it is necessary first to define what technical analysis is, to discuss the philosophical premises on which it is based, to draw some clear distinctions between technical and fundamental analysis and, finally, to address a couple of criticisms frequently raised against the technical approach.

The author's strong belief is that a full appreciation of the technical approach must begin with a clear understanding of what technical analysis claims to be able to do and, maybe even more importantly, the philosophy or rationale on which it bases those claims.

First, let's define the subject. *Technical analysis is the study of market action, primarily through the use of charts, for the purpose of forecasting future price trends.* The term "market action" includes the three principal sources of information available to the technician—price, volume, and open interest. The term "price action," which is often used, seems too narrow because most commodity technicians include volume and open interest as an integral part of their market analysis. With this distinction made, the terms "price action" and "market action" are used interchangeably throughout the remainder of this discussion.

PHILOSOPHY OR RATIONALE

There are three premises on which the technical approach is based:

1. Market action discounts everything.

2. Prices move in trends.

3. History repeats itself.

Market Action Discounts Everything

The statement "market action discounts everything" forms what is probably the cornerstone of technical analysis. Unless the full significance of this first premise is fully understood and accepted, nothing else that follows makes much sense. The technician believes that anything that can possibly affect the market price of a commodity futures contract—fundamental, political, psychological, or otherwise—is actually reflected in the price of that commodity. It follows, therefore, that a study of price action is all that is required. While this claim may seem presumptuous, it is hard to disagree with if one takes the time to consider its true meaning.

All the technician is really claiming is that price action should reflect shifts in supply and demand. If demand exceeds supply, prices should rise. If supply exceeds demand, prices should fall. This action is the basis of all economic and fundamental forecasting. The technician then turns this statement around to arrive at the conclusion that if prices are rising, for whatever the specific reasons, demand must exceed supply and the fundamentals must be bullish. If prices fall, the fundamentals must be bearish. If this last comment about fundamentals seems surprising in the context of a discussion of technical analysis, it shouldn't. After all, the technician is indirectly studying fundamentals. Most technicians would probably agree that it is the underlying forces of supply and demand, the economic fundamentals of a commodity, that cause bull and bear markets. The charts do not in themselves cause markets to move up or down. They simply reflect the bullish or bearish psychology of the marketplace.

As a rule, chartists do not concern themselves with the reasons why prices rise or fall. Very often, in the early stages of a price trend or at critical turning points, no one seems to know exactly why a market is performing a certain way. While the technical approach may sometimes seem overly simplistic in its claims, the logic behind this first premise—that markets discount everything—becomes more compelling the more market experience one gains.

It follows then that if everything that affects market price is ultimately reflected in market price, then the study of that market price is all that is necessary. By studying price charts and a host of supporting technical indicators, the chartist in effect lets the market tell him or her which way it is most likely to go. The chartist does not necessarily try to outsmart or outguess the market. All of the technical tools discussed later on are simply techniques used to aid the chartist in the process of studying market action. The chartist knows there are reasons why markets go up or down. He or she just doesn't believe that knowing what those reasons are is necessary in the forecasting process.

Prices Move in Trends

The concept of trend is absolutely essential to the technical approach. Here again, unless one accepts the premise that markets do in fact trend, there's no point in reading any further. The whole purpose of charting the price action of a futures market is to identify trends in early stages of their development for the purpose of trading in the direction of those trends. In fact, most of the techniques used in this approach are trend-following in nature, meaning that their intent is to identify and follow existing trends. (See Figure 1.1.)

There is a corollary to the premise that prices move in trends— *a trend in motion is more likely to continue than to reverse.* This corollary is, of course, an adaptation of Newton's first law of motion. Another way to state this corollary is that a trend in motion will continue in the same direction until it reverses. This is another one of those technical claims that seems almost circular. But the entire trend-following approach is predicated on riding an existing trend until it shows signs of reversing.

Figure 1.1 Example of an uptrend. Technical analysis is based on the premise that markets trend and that those trends tend to persist. (Chart courtesy of Commodity Research Bureau, a Knight-Ridder Business Information Service.)

History Repeats Itself

Much of the body of technical analysis and the study of market action has to do with the study of human psychology. Chart patterns, for example, which have been identified and categorized over the past one hundred years, reflect certain pictures that appear on price charts. These pictures reveal the bullish or bearish psychology of the market. Since these patterns have worked well in the past, it is assumed that they will continue to work well in the future. They are based on the study of human psychology, which tends not to change. Another way of saying this last premise—that history repeats itself—is that the key to understanding the future lies in a study of the past, or that the future is just a repetition of the past.

TECHNICAL VERSUS
FUNDAMENTAL FORECASTING

While technical analysis concentrates on the study of market action, fundamental analysis focuses on the economic forces of supply and demand that cause prices to move higher, lower, or stay the same. The fundamental approach examines all of the relevant factors affecting the price of a commodity in order to determine the intrinsic value of that commodity. The intrinsic value is what the fundamentals indicate a commodity is actually worth based on the law of supply and demand. If this intrinsic value is under the current market price, then the commodity is overpriced and should be sold. If market price is below the intrinsic value, then the market is undervalued and should be bought.

Both of these approaches to market forecasting attempt to solve the same problem, that is, to determine the direction prices are likely to move. They just approach the problem from different directions. *The fundamentalist studies the cause of market movement, while the technician studies the effect.* The technician, of course, believes that the effect is all that he or she wants or needs to know and that the reasons, or the causes, are unnecessary. The fundamentalist always has to know why.

Most futures traders classify themselves as either technicians or fundamentalists. In reality, there is a lot of overlap. Most fundamentalists have a working knowledge of the basic tenets of chart analysis. At the same time, most technicians have at least a passing awareness of the fundamentals. (Then, of course, there are those technicians, regarded as purists, who go to great lengths not to be contaminated with fundamental data). The problem is that the charts and fundamentals are often in conflict with each other. Usually at the beginning of important market moves, the fundamentals do not explain or support what the market seems to be doing. It is at these critical times in the trend that these two approaches seem to differ the most. Usually they come back into sync at some point, but often too late for the trader to act.

One explanation for these seeming discrepancies is that *market price tends to lead the known fundamentals.* Stated another way, *market price acts as a leading indicator of the fundamentals* or the conventional wisdom of the moment. While the known fundamentals have already been discounted and are already "in the market," prices are now reacting to the unknown fundamentals. Some of the most dramatic bull and bear markets in history have begun with little or no perceived change in the fundamentals. By the time those changes became known, the new trend was well underway.

After a while, the technician develops increased confidence in his or her ability to read the charts. The technician learns to be comfortable in a situation where market movement disagrees with the so-called conventional wisdom. A technician begins to like being in the minority. He or she knows that eventually the reasons for market action will become common knowledge. It is just that the technician isn't willing to wait for that added confirmation.

In accepting the premises of technical analysis, one can see why technicians believe their approach is superior to the fundamental. If a trader had to choose only one of the two approaches to use, the choice would logically have to be the technical. Because, by definition, the technical approach includes the fundamental. If the fundamentals are reflected in market price, then the study of those fundamentals becomes unnecessary. Chart reading becomes a short-cut form of fundamental analysis. The reverse, however, is not true. Fundamental analysis does not include a study of price action. It is possible to trade commodity futures markets using just the technical approach. It is doubtful that anyone could trade off the fundamentals alone with no consideration of the technical side of the market.

ANALYSIS VERSUS TIMING

This last point is made clearer if the decision-making process is broken down into two separate stages—analysis and timing. Because of the high leverage factor in the futures markets, timing is especially crucial to successful trading. It is quite possible to be correct on the general trend of the market and still lose money. Because margin requirements are so low in futures trading (usually less than 10%), a relatively small price move in the wrong direction can force the trader out of the market with the resulting loss of all or most of that margin. In stock market trading, by contrast, a trader who finds him or herself on the wrong side of the market can simply decide to hold onto the stock, hoping that it will stage a comeback at some point in the future. This is how many stock traders stop being traders and become investors.

Commodity traders don't have that luxury. A "buy and hold" strategy doesn't apply to the futures arena. Both the technical and the fundamental approach can be used in the first phase—the forecasting process. However, the question of timing, of determining specific entry and exit points, is almost purely technical. Therefore, considering the steps the trader must go through before making a market commitment, it can be seen that the correct application of technical principles becomes indispensable at some point in the process, even if fundamental analysis was applied in the earlier stages of the decision.

FLEXIBILITY AND ADAPTABILITY OF TECHNICAL ANALYSIS

One of the great strengths of technical analysis is its adaptability to virtually any trading medium and time dimension. There is no area of trading in either stocks or commodities where these principles do not apply.

In commodities, the chartist can easily follow as many markets as desired, which is generally not true of his or her fundamental counterpart. Because of the tremendous amount of data the latter must deal with, most fundamentalists tend to specialize in one commodity market or group of commodities, such as grains or metals. The advantages here should not be overlooked.

For one thing, markets go through active and dormant periods, trending and nontrending stages. The technician can concentrate his or her attention and resources in those markets that display strong trending tendencies and choose to ignore the rest. As a result, the chartist can rotate his or her attention and capital to take advantage of the rotational nature of the markets. At different times, certain markets become "hot" and experience important trends. Usually, those trending periods are followed by quiet and relatively trendless market conditions, while another market or group takes over. The technical trader is free to pick and choose. The fundamentalist, however, who tends to specialize in only one group, doesn't have that kind of flexibility. Even if he or she were free to switch groups, the fundamentalist would have a much more difficult time doing so than would the chartist.

Another advantage the technician has is the "big picture." By following all of the markets, he or she gets an excellent feel for what commodity markets are doing in general, and avoids the "tunnel vision" that can result from following only one group of markets. Also, because so many of the futures markets have built-in economic relationships and react to similar economic factors, price action in one market or group may give valuable clues to the future direction of another market or group of markets.

TECHNICAL ANALYSIS APPLIED TO DIFFERENT TRADING MEDIUMS

The principles of chart analysis apply to both *stocks* and *commodities*. Actually, technical analysis was first applied to the stock market and later adapted to commodities. With the successful introduction of *stock index futures*, the dividing line between these two areas is rapidly disappearing. *International stock markets* are also charted and analyzed according to technical principles. (See Figure 1.2.)

Financial futures, including *interest rate markets* and *foreign currencies*, have become enormously popular over the past decade and have proven to be excellent subjects for chart analysis.

Technical principles play a role in *spread trading* and *options trading*. Because price forecasting is one of the factors considered by the commercial hedger, technical forecasting can certainly be used to great advantage in the *hedging process*.

TECHNICAL ANALYSIS APPLIED TO DIFFERENT TIME DIMENSIONS

Another strength of the charting approach is its ability to handle different time dimensions. Whether the user is trading the intra-day tic-by-tic changes for *day trading purposes* or *trend trading* the intermediate trend, the same principles apply. A time dimension often overlooked is *longer-range technical forecasting*. The opinion expressed in some quarters that charting is useful only in the short term is simply not true. It has been suggested by some that fundamental analysis

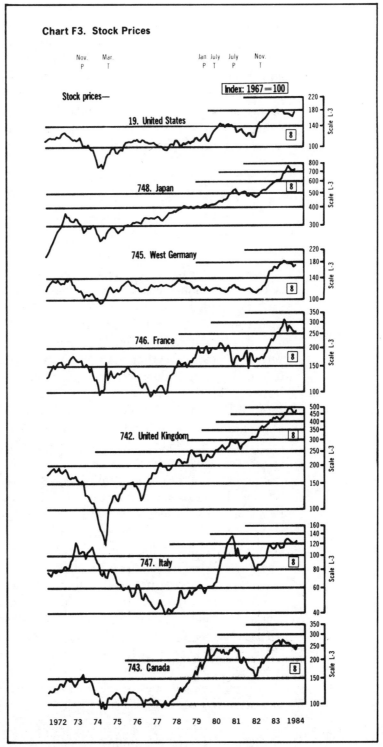

Figure 1.2 International stock markets. See *Business Conditions Digest,* August 1984, page 59. (Source: *Business Conditions Digest,* U.S. Department of Commerce.)

should be used for long-term forecasting with technical factors limited to short-term timing. The fact is that longer range forecasting, using weekly and monthly charts going back several years, has proven to be an extremely useful application of these techniques.

Once the technical principles discussed in this book are thoroughly understood, they will provide the user with tremendous flexibility as to how they can be applied, both from the standpoint of the medium to be analyzed and the time dimension to be studied.

ECONOMIC FORECASTING

Most of us tend to view technical analysis within a relatively narrow context. That is to say, it's something to use to forecast and trade the stock or futures markets. There's no reason why those same principles can't be applied to the broader field of economic forecasting—a use that seems to have been largely ignored.

Technical analysis is used to predict the course of financial markets. Do those predictions have any value in economic forecasting? Consider an article published a couple of years ago in the *Wall Street Journal* ("Bond Prices Rising Briskly of Late, Excel As Leading Indicator of Economy's Ups, Downs," September 28, 1982). The thrust of the article was that bond prices had a remarkable record in leading turns in the economy. The article stated: "Its record as a leading economic indicator outshines that of the stock market or, for that matter, of any of the government's widely followed leading indicators."

Notice the reference to the stock market. The Standard and Poor's 500 Stock Index is one of the twelve leading economic indicators tracked by the Commerce Department. The article makes reference to a study by the National Bureau of Economic Research in Cambridge, Mass. rating the stock market as the best of the 12 leading indicators. The point here is that there are futures contracts in both bonds and the Standard and Poor's 500 Index. *Because both of those contracts lend themselves quite well to technical forecasting, we're performing economic analysis whether we realize it or not.* The most dramatic example of this point is the tremendous bull market in the bond market and stock indices that began in the summer of 1982, signalling the end of the longest and deepest recession since World War II—a signal that was largely ignored by the economic community at the time.

The Coffee, Sugar, & Cocoa Exchange in New York has filed an application to establish futures contracts in four economic indices, including *Housing Starts* and the *Consumer Price Index for Wage Earners.* A new futures contract is anticipated on the Commodity Research Bureau Futures Price Index. The CRB Index has long been used as a barometer of inflationary pressures. But its usefulness as an economic indicator goes much beyond that. An article in the *1984 Commodity Year Book* (Commodity Research Bureau, Inc., Jersey City, N.J.) tracks the correlation between the CRB Index and various other economic indicators through four business cycles since 1970. (See Figure 1.3.)

One study, for example, showed a high correlation between the CRB Index and industrial production, and the tendency for commodity prices to lead movements in the latter index. To quote from the article: "The marked correlation between the CRB Index and industrial production best points up the reliability of the CRB Index as a broad economic indicator." (Stephen W. Cox, "The CRB Futures Price Index—A Basket of 27 Commodities That May Soon Be A Futures Contract," p. 46). I should add here that we have been charting and analyzing the CRB Index for years with considerable success.

Figure 1.3 Chart shows the strong correlation between the CRB Futures Price Index (solid line) and industrial production (dotted line). (Source: *Commodity Year Book 1984,* Commodity Research Bureau, Inc., Jersey City, N.J.)

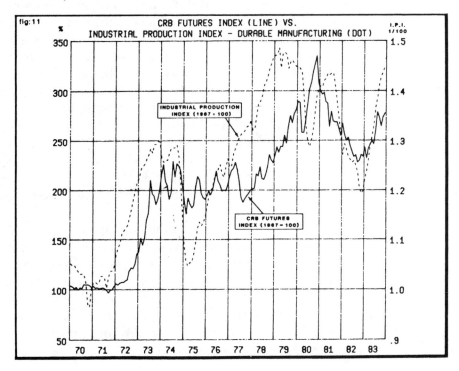

It seems clear, therefore, that the value of technical analysis as a forecasting technique extends far beyond the question of which way gold or soybean prices are moving. However, it also seems clear that the value of technical analysis as a forecaster of broader economic trends has yet to be fully explored. A futures contract on the Consumer Price Index (CPI-W) began trading on the CSCE, making that the first of these economic index contracts.

TECHNICIAN OR CHARTIST?

There are several different titles applied to practitioners of the technical approach: technical analyst, technician, chartist, market analyst. Up until recently, they all meant pretty much the same thing. However, with increased specialization in the field, it has become necessary to make some further distinctions and define the terms a bit more carefully. Because virtually all technical analysis was based on the use of charts up until the last decade, the terms "technician" and "chartist" meant the same thing. This is no longer necessarily true.

The broader area of technical analysis is being increasingly divided into two types of practitioners, the traditional chartist and, for want of a better term, statistical, or computer, technicians. Admittedly, there is a lot of overlap here too and most technicians combine both areas to some extent. But, as in the case of the technician versus the fundamentalist, most seem to fall into one category or the other.

Whether or not the traditional chartist uses computer technology to supplement his or her analysis, charts remain the primary working tool. Everything else is secondary. Charting, of necessity, remains somewhat subjective. The success of the approach depends, for the most part, on the skill of the individual chartist. The term "art charting" has been applied to this approach because chart reading is largely an art.

By contrast, the statistical, or computer, analyst takes these subjective principles, quantifies, tests, and optimizes them for the purpose of developing mechanical trading systems. These systems, or trading models, are then programmed into a computer that generates mechanical "buy" and "sell" signals. These systems range from the simple to the very complex. However, the intent is to reduce or completely eliminate the subjective human element in trading, to make it more scientific. These statisticians may or may not use price charts in their work. But they are considered technicians as long as their work is limited to the study of market action.

Even computer technicians can be subdivided further into those who favor mechanical systems, or the "black box" approach, and those who use computer technology to develop better technical indicators. The latter group maintains control over the interpretation of those indicators and also the decision-making process.

One way of distinguishing between the chartist and the statistician is to say that all chartists are technicians, but not all technicians are chartists. Although these terms are used interchangeably throughout this book, it should be remembered that charting represents only one area in the broader subject of technical analysis. Professional technical analysts prefer being referred to as technicians instead of chartists. It's much like the difference between a runner and a jogger. The former implies a higher level of expertise and dedication.

A BRIEF COMPARISON OF TECHNICAL ANALYSIS IN STOCKS AND FUTURES

A question often asked is whether technical analysis as applied to commodity futures is the same as the stock market. The answer is both yes and no. The basic principles are the same, but there are some significant differences. The principles of technical analysis were first applied to stock market forecasting and only later adapted to commodities. Most of the basic tools—bar charts, point and figure charts, price patterns, volume, trendlines, moving averages, and oscillators, for example—are used in both areas. Anyone who has learned these concepts in either stocks or commodities wouldn't have too much trouble making the adjustment to the other side. However, there are some general areas of difference having more to do with the different nature of stocks and commodity futures than with the actual tools themselves.

Pricing Structure

The pricing structure in commodities is much more complicated than in stocks. Each commodity is quoted in different units and increments. Grain markets, for example, are quoted in cents per bushel, livestock markets in cents per pound, gold and silver in dollars per ounce, and interest rates in basis points. The trader must learn the contract details of each market: which exchange it is traded on, how each contract is quoted, what the minimum and maximum price increments are, and what these price increments are worth.

Limited Life Span

Unlike stocks, commodity futures contracts have expiration dates. A March 1985 Treasury Bond contract, for example, expires in March of 1985. The typical futures contract trades for about a year and a half before expiration. Therefore, at any one time, at least a half dozen different contract months are trading in the same commodity at the same time. The trader must know which contracts to trade and which ones to avoid. (This is explained later in this book.) This limited life feature causes some problems for longer-range price forecasting. It necessitates the continuing need for obtaining new charts once old contracts stop trading. The chart of an expired contract isn't of much use. New charts must be obtained for the newer contracts along with their own technical indicators. This constant rotation makes the maintenance of an on-going chart library a good deal more difficult. For computer users, it also entails greater time and expense by making it necessary to be constantly obtaining new historical data as old contracts expire.

Lower Margin Requirements

This is probably the most important difference between stocks and commodity futures. All futures are traded on margin, which is usually less than 10% of the value of the contract. The result of these low margin requirements is tremendous leverage. Relatively small price moves in either direction tend to become magnified in their impact on overall trading results. For this reason, it is possible to make or lose large sums of money very quickly in futures. Because a trader puts up only 10% of the value of the contract as margin, then a 10% move in either direction will either double the trader's money or wipe it out. And if the position is put on just after breakfast, the whole process can easily be completed before lunch. By magnifying the impact of even minor market moves, the high leverage factor sometimes makes the futures markets seem more volatile than they actually are. When someone says, for example, that he or she was "wiped out" in the futures market, remember that he or she only committed 10% in the first place.

From the standpoint of technical analysis, the high leverage factor makes timing in the futures markets much more critical than it is in stocks. The correct timing of entry and exit points is crucial in futures trading and much more difficult and frustrating than market analysis. Largely for this reason, technical trading skills become indispensable to a successful futures trading program.

Time Frame Is Much Shorter

Because of the high leverage factor and the need for close monitoring of market positions, the time horizon of the commodity trader is much shorter of necessity. Stock market technicians tend to look more at the longer-range picture and talk in time frames that are beyond the concern of the average commodity trader. Stock technicians may talk about where the market will be in three or six months. Futures traders want to know where prices will be next week, tomorrow, or maybe even later this afternoon. This has necessitated the refinement of very short-term timing tools that are probably unknown to the stock technician. One example is the moving average. The most commonly watched average in stocks is 30 weeks, or 200 days. In commodities, most moving averages are under 40 days. A popular moving average combination in futures, for example, is 4, 9, and 18 days.

Greater Reliance on Timing

Timing is everything in futures trading. Determining the correct direction of the market only solves a portion of the trading problem. If the timing of the entry point is off by a day, or sometimes even minutes, it can mean the difference between a winner or a loser. It's bad enough to be on the wrong side of the market and lose money. Being on the right side of the market and still losing money is one of the most frustrating and unnerving aspects of futures trading. It goes without saying that timing is almost purely technical in nature, because the fundamentals rarely change on a day-to-day basis.

Less Use of
Broad Market Averages in Commodities

A tremendous amount of importance is placed on the movement of the stock market averages such as the Dow Jones Industrials or the Standard and Poor's 500 Stock Index. In fact, this is the starting point of all stock market analysis. This is generally not true in the commodity markets. While some indices that are used to gauge the direction of commodity prices in general, such as the Commodity Research Bureau Futures Price Index, are watched carefully and are taken into consideration, they are not given as much prominence as the stock market averages.

Less Use of
Broad Technical Indicators in Commodities

The broader technical market indicators that are given so much attention in the stock market—for example, the advance-decline line, new highs-new lows index, the short interest ratio—really don't apply much to commodities. This is not to say that some application of these principles would not be useful in the futures markets. Perhaps as the list of futures markets grows, the need for some broader gauges of market movement may become necessary. But, for now at least, these indicators have little use.

Specific Technical Tools

While most of the technical tools originally developed in the stock market have some application in commodity markets, they are not used in the exact same way. For example, chart patterns in futures often tend not to form as fully as they do in stocks, moving averages are much shorter in length, and traditional point and figure charting is less popular in futures. Because the intra-day data is much harder to obtain, intra-day point and figure charts are used mainly by floor traders. These points of difference and many others are discussed later in this book.

Finally, there is another area of major difference between stocks and futures. Technical analysis in stocks relies much more heavily on the use of *sentiment indicators* and *flow of funds* analysis. *Sentiment indicators* monitor the performance of different groups such as odd lotters, mutual funds, and floor specialists. Enormous importance is placed on sentiment indicators that measure the overall market bullishness and bearishness on the theory that the majority opinion is usually wrong. *Flow of funds* analysis refers to the cash position of different groups, such as mutual funds or large institutional accounts. The thinking here is that the larger the cash position, the more funds that are available for stock purchases. While these forms of analysis are generally considered of secondary importance, it often seems that stock market technicians place more reliance on them than on traditional market analysis.

Technical analysis in the futures markets is, in my opinion, a much purer form of price analysis. While contrary opinion theory is also used to some extent, much more emphasis is placed on basic trend analysis and the application of traditional technical indicators.

SOME CRITICISMS OF THE TECHNICAL APPROACH

A few questions generally crop up in any discussion of the technical approach. One of these concerns is the *self-fulfilling prophecy.* Another is the question of whether or not past price data can really be used to forecast future price direction. The critic usually says something like: "Charts tell us where the market has been, but can't tell us where it is going." For the moment, we'll put aside the obvious answer that a chart won't tell you anything if you don't know how to read it. The Random Walk Theory questions whether prices trend at all and doubts that any forecasting technique can beat a simple *buy and hold* strategy. These questions deserve a response.

The Self-Fulfilling Prophecy

The question of whether there is a self-fulfilling prophecy at work seems to bother most people because it is raised so often. It is certainly a valid concern, but of much less importance than most people realize. Perhaps the best way to address this question is to quote from a text on the subject of commodity trading that discusses some of the disadvantages of using chart patterns:

> a. The use of most chart patterns has been widely publicized in the last several years. Many traders are quite familiar with these patterns and often act on them in concert. This creates a "self-fulfilling prophecy," as waves of buying or selling are created in response to "bullish" or "bearish" patterns. . .
> b. Chart patterns are almost completely subjective. No study has yet succeeded in mathematically quantifying any of them. They are literally in the mind of the beholder. . . . (Richard J. Teweles, Charles V. Harlow, Herbert L. Stone, *The Commodity Futures Game,* McGraw-Hill, 1977, p. 176.)

These two criticisms contradict one another and the second point actually cancels out the first. If chart patterns are "completely subjective" and "in the mind of the beholder," then it is hard to imagine how everyone could see the same thing at the same time, which is the basis of the self-fulfilling prophecy. Critics of charting can't have it both ways. They can't, on the one hand, criticize charting for being so objective and obvious that everyone will act in the same way at the same time (thereby causing the price pattern to be fulfilled), and then also criticize charting for being too subjective.

The truth of the matter is that charting is very subjective. Chart reading is an art. (Possibly the word "skill" would be more to the point.) Chart patterns are seldom so clear that even experienced chartists always agree on their interpretation. There is always an element of doubt and disagreement. As this book demonstrates, there are many different approaches to technical analysis that often disagree with one another.

Even if most technicians did agree on a market forecast, they would not all necessarily enter the market at the same time and in the same way. Some would try to anticipate the chart signal and enter the market early. Others would buy or sell the "breakout" from a given pattern or indicator. Still others would wait for the pullback after the breakout before taking action. Some traders are aggressive; others are conservative. Some use stops to enter the market, while others like to use market orders or resting limit orders. Some are trading for the long pull, while others are day trading. Therefore, the possibility of all technicians acting at the same time and in the same way is actually quite remote.

Even if the self-fulfilling prophecy were of major concern, it would probably be "self-correcting" in nature. In other words, traders would rely heavily on charts until their concerted actions started to affect or distort the markets. Once traders realized this was happening, they would either stop using the charts or adjust their trading tactics. For example, they would either try to act before the crowd or wait longer for greater confirmation. So, even if the self-fulfilling prophecy did become a problem over the near term, it would tend to correct itself.

It must be kept in mind that bull and bear markets only occur and are maintained when they are justified by the law of supply and demand. Technicians could not possibly cause a major market move just by the sheer power of their buying and selling. If this were the case, technicians would all become wealthy very quickly.

Of much more concern than the chartists is the tremendous

growth in the use of computerized technical trading systems by large trading interests. These systems are mainly trend-following in nature, which means that they are all programmed to identify and trade major trends. With the explosion in professionally managed money over the past decade in the futures industry, and the proliferation of multi-million dollar public and private funds, most of which are using these technical systems, tremendous concentrations of money are chasing only a handful of existing trends. Because the universe of futures markets is still quite small, the potential for these systems distorting short-term price action is growing. However, even in cases where distortions do occur, they are generally short term in nature and do not cause major moves. *

Here again, even the problem of concentrated sums of money using technical systems is probably self-correcting. If all of the systems started doing the same thing at the same time, traders would make adjustments by making their systems either more or less sensitive.

The self-fulfilling prophecy is generally listed as a criticism of charting. It might be more appropriate to label it as a compliment. After all, for any forecasting technique to become so popular that it begins to influence events, it would have to be pretty good. We can only speculate as to why this concern is seldom raised regarding the use of fundamental analysis.

Can the Past
Be Used to Predict the Future?

Another question often raised concerns the validity of using past price data to predict the future. It is surprising how often critics of the technical approach bring up this point because every known method of forecasting, from weather predicting to fundamental analysis, is based completely on the study of past data. What other kind of data is there to work with?

The field of statistics makes a distinction between *descriptive statistics* and *inductive statistics*. *Descriptive statistics* refers to the graph-

---

*As an aside here, for many years the term "chart buying or selling" was used in the reporting media to explain any surprising market move not easily explained by fundamental factors. More recently, terms like "computer chart buying" have become more common. I'd hate to think of where the financial press would be without the technicians to fall back on whenever they're stumped by not being able to explain the reasons behind a market move.

ical presentation of data, such as the price data on a standard bar chart. *Inductive statistics* refers to generalizations, predictions, or extrapolations that are inferred from that data. Therefore, the price chart itself comes under the heading of the descriptive, while the analysis technicians perform on that price data falls into the realm of the inductive.

As one statistical text puts it: "The first step in forecasting the business or economic future consists, thus, of gathering observations from the past." (John E. Freund and Frank J. Williams, *Modern Business Statistics*, Prentice-Hall, 1969, p. 383). Chart analysis is just another form of *time series analysis*, based on a study of the past, which is exactly what is done in all forms of time series analysis. The only type of data anyone has to go on is past data. We can only estimate the future by projecting past experiences into that future. Quoting again from the same text:

> Population forecasts, industry forecasts, and the like are based in large part on what has happened in the past. In business and in science, as well as in everyday life, we project our experience of the past in an effort to predict what may happen in the uncertain future. (*Modern Business Statistics*, p. 383.)

So it seems that the use of past price data to predict the future in technical analysis is grounded in sound statistical concepts. If anyone were to seriously question this aspect of technical forecasting, he or she would have to also question the validity of every other form of forecasting based on historical data, which includes all economic and fundamental analysis.

RANDOM WALK THEORY

The *Random Walk Theory*, developed and nurtured in the academic community, claims that price changes are "serially independent" and that price history is not a reliable indicator of future price direction. In a nutshell, price movement is random and unpredictable. The book that popularized the theory was *The Random Character of Stock Market Prices* by Paul H. Cootner (ed.), published by MIT Press, 1964. Since then, much has been written on both sides of the issue. The theory is based on the *efficient market hypothesis*, which holds that prices fluctuate randomly about their intrinsic value. It also holds that the best market strategy to follow would be a simple "buy and hold" strategy as opposed to any attempt to "beat the market."

While there seems little doubt that a certain amount of randomness or "noise" does exist in all markets, it's just unrealistic to believe that *all* price movement is random. This may be one of those areas where empirical observation and practical experience prove more useful than sophisticated statistical techniques, which seem capable of proving anything the user has in mind or incapable of disproving anything. It might be useful to keep in mind that randomness can only be defined in the negative sense of an inability to uncover systematic patterns in price action. The fact that many academics have not been able to discover the presence of these patterns does not prove that they do not exist. (See Figure 1.4.)

The academic debate as to whether markets trend is of little interest to the average market analyst or trader who is forced to deal in the real world where market trends are clearly visible. If the reader has any doubts on this point, a casual glance through any chart book (randomly selected) will demonstrate the presence of trends in a very graphic way. How do the "random walkers" explain the persistence of these trends if prices are serially independent, meaning that what happened yesterday, or last week, has no bearing on what may happen today or tomorrow? How do they explain the profitable "real life" track records of many trend-following systems?

How, for example, would a buy and hold strategy fare in the commodity futures markets where timing is so crucial? Would those long positions be held during bear markets? How would traders even know the difference between bull and bear markets if prices are unpredictable and don't trend? In fact, how could a bear market even exist in the first place because that would imply a trend?

It seems doubtful that statistical evidence will ever totally prove or disprove the Random Walk Theory. However, the idea that markets are random is totally rejected by the technical community. If the markets were truly random, no forecasting technique would work. Far from disproving the validity of the technical approach, the *efficient market hypothesis* is very close to the technical premise that *markets discount everything*. The academics, however, feel that because markets quickly discount all information, there's no way to take advantage of that information. The basis of technical forecasting, already touched upon, is that important market information is discounted in the market price long before it becomes known. Without meaning to, the academics have very eloquently stated the need for closely monitoring

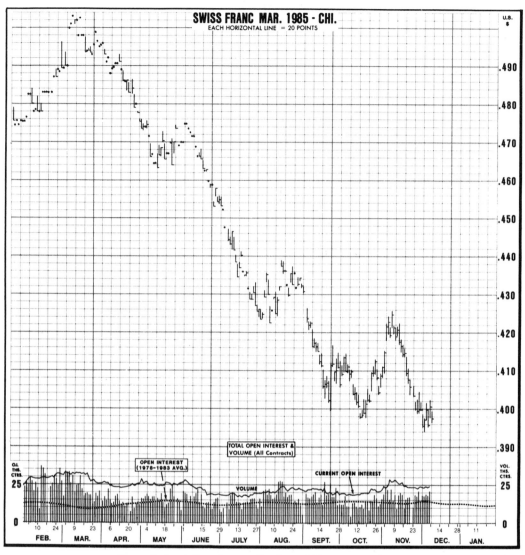

Figure 1.4 A "random walker" would have a tough time convincing a trader in the Swiss franc that trends don't really exist. (Chart courtesy of Commodity Research Bureau, a Knight-Ridder Business Information Service.)

price action and the futility of trying to profit from fundamental information, at least over the short term.

Finally, it seems only fair to observe that any process appears random and unpredictable to those who do not understand the rules under which that process operates. An electrocardiogram printout, for example, might appear like a lot of random noise to a layperson. But to a trained medical person, all those little blips make a lot of sense and are certainly not random. The working of the futures markets may appear random to those who have not taken the time to study the rules of market behavior. *The illusion of randomness gradually disappears as the skill in chart reading improves.* Hopefully, that is exactly what will happen as the reader progresses through the various sections of this book.

For those who might like to read more on the Random Walk Theory, a summary of research done since the early 1970s in the commodity futures markets is available in "Issues in Futures Markets: A Survey," by Avraham Kamara in the Fall 1982 issue of *The Journal of Futures Markets,* pages 275-278, published by John Wiley & Sons in affiliation with the Columbia University Center for the Study of Futures Markets. Kamara cites several research studies that claim continuity in futures markets, rejecting the random hypothesis. However, evidence on the other side is also presented, leaving the academic debate alive and well. Because that publication has a strong academic bias, other articles on randomness occasionally appear. Another book on the subject is *A Random Walk Down Wall Street* by Burton G. Malkiel, published by W.W. Norton & Co., New York, 1973.

I'd like to conclude the discussion on the Random Walk Theory by quoting from the "President's Comments" to the membership of the Market Technicians Association concerning recent contacts by academic research teams desiring greater interaction with practicing technicians.

> I detect a significant attitude change as academic researchers now realize that analysts and investors have been very successful in spite of all the adverse academic publicity in years gone by. (Fred Dickson, President, February 1984 issue of *MTA Newsletter.*)

CONCLUSION

Having laid a philosophical foundation on which technical theory rests, and having addressed some of the questions often raised about technical analysis, it's time to begin looking at some of that theory. There's no better place to start than with the oldest and best known technical theory, the venerable Dow Theory.

2

Dow Theory

INTRODUCTION

An article appeared in the July 3, 1984 issue of the *Wall Street Journal* entitled "The Centennial of Charles Dow's Captivating Index." During the same week, the *Journal's* sister publication, *Barron's*, carried a story, "For a Century Dow Theory Has Served Investors Well." The reason for the two articles was to commemorate the one hundredth anniversary of the first publication of a stock market average by Charles H. Dow on July 3, 1884. That first average included only 11 stocks, of which nine were railroad companies. It wasn't until 1897 that the original index was split into two indices, a 12-stock industrial index and a 20-stock rail index. In 1928, the industrial index was increased to 30 and in 1929 a utility index was included. But it all started in 1884 with Dow's first index.

To further commemorate Dow's work, the Market Technicians Association presented a Gorham silver bowl to Dow Jones & Co., the organization that Dow founded along with Edward Jones in 1882.

According to the MTA, "The award recognizes the lasting contribution that Charles Dow made to the field of investment analysis. His index, the forerunner of what today is regarded as the leading barometer of stock market activity, remains a vital tool for market technicians 80 years after his death."

Unfortunately for us, Dow never wrote a book on his theory. He set down his ideas of stock market behavior in a series of *Wall Street Journal* editorials around the turn of the century. It wasn't until after his death in 1902 that his editorials were reprinted in a 1903 work by S.A. Nelson, *The ABC of Stock Speculation* (available in a 1978 reprint by Fraser Publishing Company, Burlington, Vermont). It was in that work that the term "Dow's Theory" was first used. In the introduction, Richard Russell compares Dow's contribution to stock market theory with Freud's contribution to psychiatry.

Why all the fuss about Dow's work and why is it considered so important? The reason is that much of what is generally accepted today under the broad heading of technical analysis actually derives from the Dow Theory, in one form or another. Dow Theory is considered the granddaddy of technical analysis. Even in today's world of computer technology, with the proliferation of newer and supposedly better technical indicators, Dow's ideas still have application. Most futures technicians are probably unaware of how much their "modern" tools depend on the principles laid down by Dow. This is why I believe it is important to begin the study of technical analysis with at least a brief glance at the Dow Theory.

We've already mentioned that Dow's tenets were written in a series of editorials. These tenets were later categorized and published in a more organized fashion by Dow's associate and successor at the *Journal,* William Peter Hamilton, in his 1922 book, *The Stock Market Barometer* (New York: Harper Brothers). Robert Rhea developed the theory even further in the *Dow Theory* (New York: Barron's), published in 1932.

While Dow's work was applied to the stock market averages that he created, the Industrials and the Rails, most of the analytical concepts are quite applicable to the commodity futures markets. In this chapter, we'll point out the general tenets of the theory and, while we're doing that, begin to show how those ideas relate to much of the data covered in later chapters. We'll mention six basic tenets, most of which should sound familiar to the futures technician. We'll leave a more in-depth discussion of each of these points, however, to later chapters.

BASIC TENETS

1. The Averages Discount Everything.   Sound familiar? This is, of course, one of the basic premises of technical theory mentioned in Chapter 1, except with reference to the averages in this case instead of the individual markets. The theory states that every possible factor affecting supply and demand must be reflected in the market averages. Allowance is even made for "acts of God"—earthquakes and various other natural calamities. While these obviously cannot be anticipated by the markets, they are quickly discounted and assimilated into the price action.

2. The Market Has Three Trends.   Dow's definition of a trend was that an uptrend existed as long as each successive rally high and each successive rally low was higher than the one before. In other words, an uptrend had to have a pattern of rising peaks and troughs. A downtrend would be just the opposite with successively lower peaks and troughs. As we'll see in Chapter 4, this is still the basic definition of a trend and the starting point of all trend analysis.

Dow divided the trend into three different categories—*the primary, secondary, and minor.* His main concern was with the *primary,* or *major trend,* which usually lasted for more than a year and possibly for several years. It was his belief that most stock market investors were concerned with the major direction of the market. Dow compared the three categories of trend to the tide, waves, and ripples of the sea.

The primary trend was like the tide. The secondary, or intermediate, trend was compared to the waves that made up the tide. The minor trends were just like ripples on the waves. By using stakes to measure the highest point on the beach reached by each successive wave, the direction of the tide could be measured. If each successive wave moved further inland than the preceding one, the tide was still in. Only when the waves began to recede would the observer know that the tide of the ocean had turned out.

The *secondary,* or *intermediate, trend* represents corrections in the primary trend and usually lasts for three weeks to three months. These intermediate corrections usually retrace one-third to two-thirds of the previous trend. Often the retracement will be about half, or 50%.

The *minor,* or *near-term, trend* usually lasts less than three weeks and represents shorter term fluctuations in the intermediate trend. During our coverage of trend concepts in Chapter 4, we'll use pretty much the same terminology as well as similar percentage retracement parameters.

3. Major Trends Have Three Phases. The major trend usually takes place in three distinct phases. The first phase, called the accumulation phase, represents informed buying by the most astute investors as all the so-called bad economic news has finally been discounted by the market. The second phase, where most technical trend-followers begin to participate, takes place as prices begin to advance rapidly and business news improves. The third and final phase is characterized by increased public participation as newspapers begin to print increasingly bullish stories, economic news is better than ever, and speculative volume increases. It is during this last phase that the informed investors who began to "accumulate" near the bear market bottom, when no one else wanted to buy, now begin to "distribute" when no one else seems to be selling.

Students of the Elliott Wave Theory will recognize this particular division of the major bull market into three distinct phases. R.N. Elliott built on the foundation of Rhea's work in *Dow Theory* in the 1930s while formulating his own theory. Elliott also recognized three major upward moves in a bull market. In our chapter on Elliott Wave Theory, we'll show the close similarity between Dow's three phases of a bull market and the various wave personalities under the wave principle. One major difference between Elliott's and Dow's work is the principle of confirmation, which is the next basic tenet.

4. The Averages Must Confirm Each Other. In this point, Dow was referring to the Industrial and Rail Averages. He meant that no important bull or bear market signal could take place unless both averages gave the same signal. In other words, both averages had to exceed a previous secondary peak in order for a bull market to begin. If only one average gave the signal, then there was no bull market. The signals did not have to occur simultaneously, but the closer together the better. When the two averages diverged from one another, the prior trend was assumed to be still in effect. (See Figure 2.1.) Elliott Wave Theory differs from Dow Theory on this point by only requiring signals in a single average. We'll have a lot more to say on the principles of *confirmation* and *divergence* later on. (See Figure 2.2.)

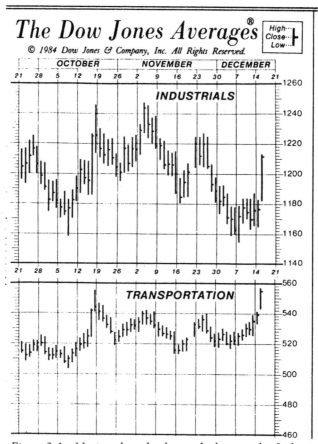

Figure 2.1 Notice that the latest decline in the Industrials below the late November lows was not confirmed by a similar violation in the Transportation index. That lack of downside confirmation was a warning that the short-term "sell" signal in the Industrials was suspect. Now, the Industrials must overcome resistance to confirm the upside breakout in the Transportation. Source: *Wall Street Journal*, (December 19, 1984).

5. Volume Must Confirm the Trend. Dow recognized the importance of volume as a secondary but important factor in confirming the signals generated on the price charts. To state this tenet simply, *volume should expand in the direction of the major trend.* If the major trend is up, volume should expand or increase as prices move higher. Conversely, volume should diminish as prices dip. In a downtrend, the opposite should take place. Volume should be heavier as prices drop and should diminish as prices rally in the downtrend. It should be stressed, however, that volume is only a secondary indicator. The actual Dow

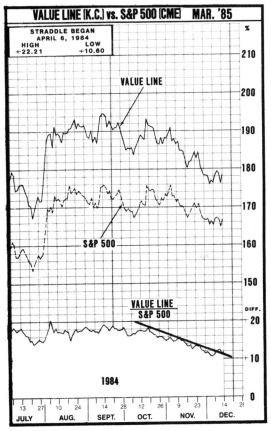

VALUE LINE (K.C.) vs. S&P 500 (CME)   MAR. '85

STRADDLE BEGAN
APRIL 6, 1984
HIGH   LOW
+22.21   +10.60

VALUE LINE

S&P 500

VALUE LINE
S&P 500

1984

13	27	10	24	14	28	12	26	9	23	14	21
JULY		AUG.		SEPT.		OCT.		NOV.		DEC.	

Figure 2.2 The principle of confirmation can be applied to any two markets or indices. This chart shows the spread (difference) between the Value Line and S&P 500 futures indices. Notice that the S&P 500 has just now violated its October low, barely confirming the earlier breakdown in the Value Line. The spread chart along the bottom shows that Value Line has been consistently weaker, usually an indicator of market weakness. Notice, however, that the spread has begun to strengthen (breaking the down trendline), signalling a possible market turn to the upside. In other words, the Value Line index has begun to outperform the S&P, usually a sign of market strength. (Chart courtesy of Commodity Research Bureau, a Knight-Ridder Business Information Service.)

Theory buy and sell signals are based entirely on closing prices. In Chapter 7, we'll cover the question of volume in much more depth. But you'll see at that time that the principles are still the same. Even the more sophisticated volume indicators are used to help determinine in which direction the heavier volume is flowing. This information is then compared to price action.

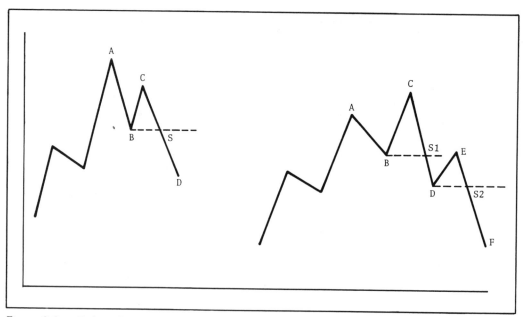

Figure 2.3a Failure Swing. The failure of the peak at C to overcome A, followed by the violation of the low at B, constitutes a "sell" signal at S.

Figure 2.3b Nonfailure Swing. Notice that C exceeds A before falling below B. Some Dow Theorists would see a "sell" signal at S1, while others would need to see a lower high at E before turning bearish at S2.

6. A Trend Is Assumed to Be in Effect Until It Gives Definite Signals That It Has Reversed. This tenet, which we touched upon in Chapter 1, forms much of the basis of the trend-following approach as it is used today. It is another way of saying that a trend in motion tends to continue in motion. Of course, being able to spot reversal signals isn't as easy as it sounds. The study of support and resistance levels, price patterns, trendlines, and moving averages are among several technical tools available that indicate when an existing trend may be in the process of changing. The use of oscillators helps to provide an even earlier warning signal of loss of momentum. The odds usually favor the trend continuing. By following that simple premise, you'll be right more often than wrong. (See Figures 2.3a and 2.3b.)

The most difficult task for a Dow Theorist, and any trend-follower for that matter, is being able to distinguish between a normal secondary correction in an existing trend and the first leg of a new trend in the opposite direction. There is some disagreement among users of the theory as to when an actual reversal signal is given. Figures 2.3a and 2.3b show two different market scenarios. In Figure 2.3a, notice that

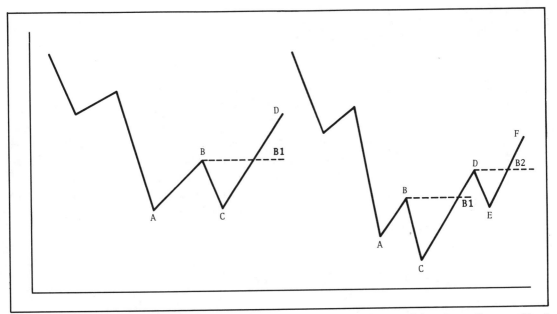

Figure 2.4a Failure Swing Bottom. The "buy" signal takes place when point B is exceeded (at B1).

Figure 2.4b Nonfailure Swing Bottom. "Buy" signals occur at points B1 or B2.

the rally at point C is unable to clear the previous peak at A before declining below point B. In this case, two lower peaks and two lower troughs now exist, giving a clearcut sell signal at the point where the low at B is broken (point S). This reversal pattern is sometimes referred to as a "failure swing."

In Figure 2.3b, notice that the rally top at C actually exceeds the previous peak at A, before declining below point B. While a violation of support clearly takes place at S1, some Dow Theorists would not consider that a bona fide sell signal. The reason is that only lower lows now exist, not lower highs. They would prefer to see a rally to E, falling short of C, then another new low below point D. To them, the actual sell signal would be given at S2, at which point two lower highs and two lower lows are now present. The reversal pattern shown in Figure 2.3b is referred to as a "nonfailure swing." A failure swing (shown in Figure 2.3a) is a much weaker pattern than the nonfailure swing in Figure 2.3b. Figures 2.4a and 2.4b show the same scenarios at a market bottom. (See Figures 2.4a and 2.4b.)

THE USE OF CLOSING PRICES
AND THE PRESENCE OF LINES

Dow relied exclusively on closing prices. Therefore, the averages had to actually close beyond a previous peak or trough. Intra-day penetrations were not considered valid penetrations. *Lines* in the averages refer to horizontal trading bands that occur on the charts. These sideways trading ranges often take the place of corrective phases. These phases are usually referred to as consolidations. They can also take place at tops and bottoms. In more modern terms, we might refer to such lateral patterns as "rectangles."

SOME CRITICISMS OF DOW THEORY

Despite the fact that the Dow Theory has performed well over the years in identifying major bull and bear markets, it has not escaped some criticism. Probably the most frequently heard is that its signals are too late. Usually a Dow Theory buy signal takes place in the second phase of an uptrend as a previous intermediate peak is penetrated. On average, about 20 to 25% of the move is missed before a signal is given. This is also, incidentally, about where most trend-following technical systems begin to identify and participate in existing trends.

This criticism should sound familiar to users of trend-following techniques. It must be remembered that the Dow Theory was never intended to anticipate trends. Its purpose was to signal the emergence of major bull and bear markets. Available records of its performance suggest that it has performed that function reasonably well. The article mentioned earlier in *Barron's* quoted some statistics showing that between 1920 and 1975, Dow Theory signals captured 68% of the moves in the Industrial and Transportation Averages and 67% of those in the S&P 500 Composite Index.

As in the case of most trend-following systems, the intent is to capture the major middle portion of important market moves. So the criticism is valid in one sense. But, at the same time, the criticism shows a lack of understanding of the trend-following philosophy. Virtually no trend-following system attempts to catch the actual top or bottom. Those that try seldom succeed.

One other criticism of the theory over the years has been that a person could not buy or sell the averages, that the theory does not tell the trader which stocks to buy or sell. With the successful introduction of stock index futures, however, a trader is now able to "buy the averages" and not even be concerned with individual stocks. Possibly with increased attention now being given to the averages themselves, the Dow Theory will prove to be an even more useful forecasting device for commodity technicians.

The theory is certainly not infallible. It's had its share of bad signals over the years. But that's generally true of any good system. Dow apparently never even intended to use his theory to forecast the direction of the stock market. He felt its real value was to use stock market direction as a barometer of general business conditions. We can only marvel at the vision of Dow since, in addition to formulating so much of what is used today in price forecasting, he recognized long ago the usefulness of stock market averages as a leading economic indicator.

SUMMARY

This chapter presented a relatively quick review of the more important aspects of the Dow Theory. It will become clear, as you proceed through this book, that an understanding and appreciation of the Dow Theory provides a solid foundation for any study of technical analysis. It will also become increasingly obvious that much of what is covered in later chapters represents some adaptation of Dow's original theory. The standard definition of a trend, the classifying of a trend into three categories and phases, the principles of confirmation and divergence, the interpretation of volume, and the use of percentage retracements, to name a few, are all derived in one way or another from the Dow Theory.

CONCLUSION

Before concluding our treatment of the Dow Theory, it should be made clear that while most of the original work has some application to commodity futures, there are some important differences. For one thing, Dow assumed that most investors only traded the major trend. The intermediate correction might be used only for timing purposes. The near-term trend was considered unimportant. Obviously, this is not the case in futures trading.

Most trend traders trade the intermediate instead of the major trend. Minor swings are extremely important for timing purposes. That is to say, in an intermediate uptrend that is expected to last for a couple of months, the trend trader would use short-term dips for purchases. Minor bounces would be used for short sales in an intermediate downtrend. The minor trend, therefore, becomes extremely important in futures trading. Many short-term traders deal only in the very near term and try to capture even intra-day moves.

In addition to the sources already cited in this chapter, an excellent review of the principles of the Dow Theory can be found in *Technical Analysis of Stock Trends* by Robert D. Edwards and John Magee, published by John Magee, Inc., Springfield, Mass., 1966.

3
Chart Construction

INTRODUCTION

This chapter is primarily intended for those readers who are unfamiliar with bar chart construction. We'll begin by discussing the different types of charts available and then turn our focus to the most commonly used chart—*the daily bar chart*. We'll look at how the price data is read and plotted on the chart. *Volume and open interest* are also included in addition to price. We'll then look at other variations of the bar chart, including *longer range weekly and monthly charts* as well as the shorter-term *intra-day chart*. Once that has been completed, we'll be ready to start looking at some of the analytical tools applied to that chart in the following chapter. Those readers already familiar with the charts themselves might find this chapter too basic. Feel free to move on to the next chapter.

TYPES OF CHARTS AVAILABLE

The daily bar chart has already been acknowledged as the most widely used type of chart in commodity futures trading. There are, however, other types of charts also used by technicians. The two we'll discuss here are the point and figure chart and the line chart. Figure 3.1 shows a standard daily bar chart. The reason it's called a bar chart is because each day's action is represented by a vertical bar. The bar chart usually shows only the high, low, and closing prices. The tic to the right of the vertical bar is the closing price. Some technicians also have begun plotting the opening price, shown here by a tic to the left of the bar.

Figure 3.1 A daily bar chart of a gold contract. Each vertical bar represents one day's price action. The most commonly used prices are the high, low, and close. The tic to the right of the bar is the close. Some chartists plot the opening price with a small tic to the left of the vertical bar.

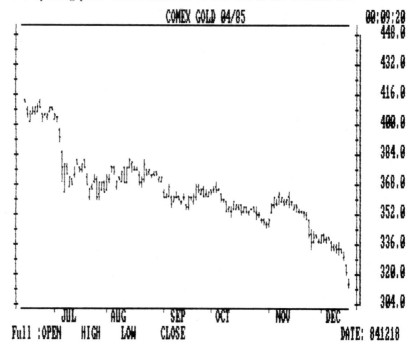

Figure 3.2 shows what the same futures contract looks like on a line chart. In the line chart, only the closing price is plotted for each successive day. Many chartists believe that because the closing price is the most critical price of the trading day, a line (or close-only) chart is a more valid measure of price activity. Depending on what the technician is looking for, certain techniques used in chart analysis are easier to perform on the line chart than on the bar chart.

Chart Construction

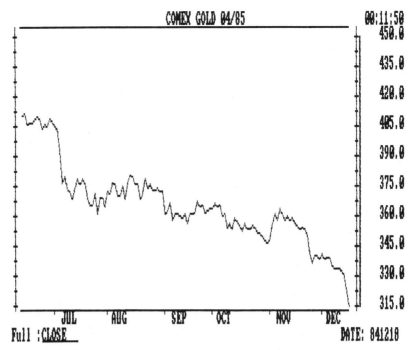

Figure 3.2 A line chart of the same gold contract. This type of chart produces a solid line by connecting only the closing prices.

A third type of chart, the point and figure chart, is shown in Figure 3.3. Two later chapters take an in-depth look at this type of chart analysis. Notice here that the point and figure chart shows the same price action but in a more compressed format. Notice the alternating column of x's and o's. The x columns show rising prices and the o columns, declining prices. Buy and sell signals are more precise and easier to spot on the point and figure chart than on the bar chart. This type of chart also has a lot more flexibility. The point and figure chart in Figure 3.3 uses only the high and low prices and can be constructed right from the newspaper.

The types of charts shown so far focus primarily on the high, low, and closing prices, and even sometimes include the opening price. However, there is an enormous amount of trading activity that takes place on the floor of the Exchange that is lost on these charts. For those that have access to more sophisticated equipment, such as *ADP Comtrend's Videcom retrieval system,* intra-day bar charts, line charts, and point and figure charts can also be obtained to capture that intra-day activity. Bar charts, for example, can be obtained for time periods of 5 minutes, 15 minutes, and 1 hour. For shorter-term trading purposes, this intra-day data becomes extremely useful. We'll come back

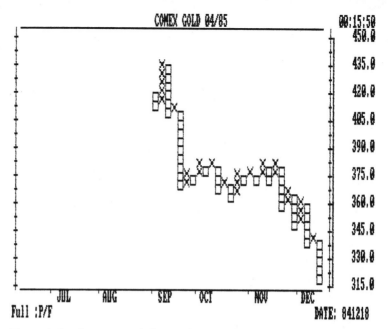

Figure 3.3 A point and figure chart of the same gold contract shown in Figures 3.1 and 3.2. Notice the alternating columns of x's and o's. The x column shows rising prices. The o column shows falling prices. Buy and sell signals are more precise on this type of chart. Notice also how much the price data has been compressed.

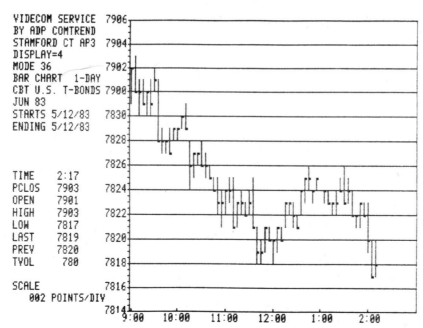

Figure 3.4 An intra-day bar chart of a Treasury bond contract. Each bar shows the high, low, and last prices for every five-minute interval. This chart shows only one day's price action. (Chart courtesy of Automatic Data Processing, Inc., Comtrend Division, Stamford, CT.)

to intra-day charts in later chapters. We'll also be spending more time on the line and point and figure charts as we go through the book. For now, let's confine our discussion to the more popular inter-day bar chart. (See Figures 3.4 and 3.5a and b.)

Figure 3.5a   The chart is an intra-day point and figure chart of a gold contract. An enormous amount of price data can be found on such a chart, including hidden support and resistance levels. (Chart courtesy of Automatic Data Processing, Inc., Comtrend Division, Stamford, CT.)

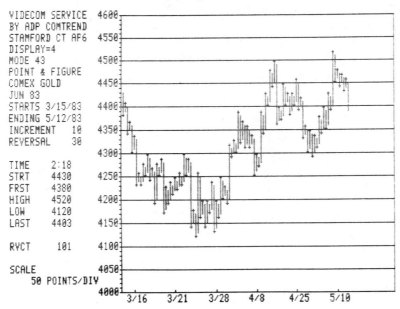

Figure 3.5b   This price data shows the actual intra-day prices for a Swiss franc contract. Intra-day charting necessitates having access to intra-day price data. (Data courtesy of Automatic Data Processing, Inc., Comtrend Division, Stamford, CT.)

VIDECOM SERVICE
BY ADP COMTREND
STAMFORD CT AF5
DISPLAY=4
MODE 45
POINT & FIGURE
CME SWISS FRANCS
JUN 83
STARTS 4/29/83
ENDING 5/12/83
INCREMENT   5
REVERSAL   5

TIME   2:16
STRT   4875
FRST   4875
HIGH   4975
LOW   4850
LAST   4963

RVCT   114

4/29	4875	4880	4860	4865	4850	4860	4855	
5/2	4870	4860	4865	4855	4860	4855	4860	4855
	4860	4855	4865	4855				
5/3	4870	4865	4870	4860	4865	4860	4870	4865
5/4	4885	4880	4890	4885	4890	4875		
5/5	4905	4900	4905	4900	4905			
5/6	4885	4900	4890	4930	4920	4930	4925	4930
	4925							
5/9	4950	4925	4930	4925	4930	4925	4935	4925
	4930	4925	4935	4930	4940	4935		
5/10	4940	4915	4920	4905	4925	4920	4930	4925
	4935	4930	4940	4935	4940			
5/11	4935	4950	4945	4950	4935	4940	4935	4945
	4940	4965	4960	4965	4955	4960	4955	4965
	4960	4970						
5/12	4940	4960	4955	4960	4950	4970	4965	4970
	4965	4975	4970	4975	4965	4970	4960	4965
	4955	4965	4960	4970	4960	4965		

ARITHMETIC VERSUS LOGARITHMIC SCALE

In the futures industry, virtually all commercially available charts use arithmetic price scales. For some types of analysis, however, particularly for very long-range trend analysis, there may be some advantage to using logarithmic charts. (See Figures 3.6 and 3.7.) Figure 3.6 shows what the different scales would look like. On the arithmetic scale, the vertical price scale shows an equal distance for each price unit of change. For example, a move from 5 to 10 on an arithmetic scale would be be the same distance as a move from 50 to 55, even though the former represents a doubling in price, while the latter is a price increase of only 10%. Prices plotted on ratio or log scales show equal distances for similar percentage moves. For example, a move

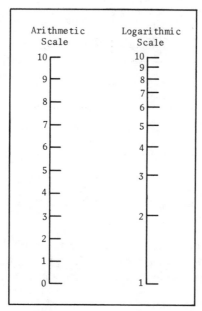

Figure 3.6   A comparison of an arithmetic and logarithmic scale. Notice the equal spacing on the scale to the left. The log scale shows percentage changes (right scale).

from 10 to 20 (a 100% increase) would be the same distance on a log chart as a move from 20 to 40 or 40 to 80. Notice in this example that each point on the arithmetic scale is equidistant. On the log scale, however, note that the percentage increases get smaller as the price scale increases. The distance from points 1 to 2 is the same as the distance from points 5 to 10 because they both represent the same doubling in price. Despite the possible advantanges of having access to log charts for longer-range trend analysis, that type of chart is not

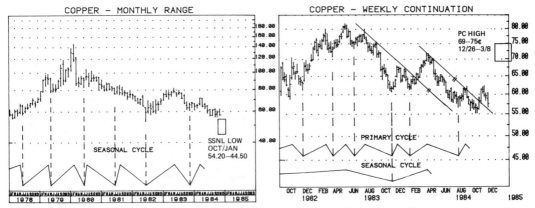

Figure 3.7 These two charts are monthly and weekly continuation charts of copper plotted on a logarithmic scale. Notice how the scale expands as prices drop and contracts at higher prices. The drawing of trendlines and channels can be greatly affected by using a log scale, particularly on long-term charts. (Charts courtesy of HAL Market Cycles, Tucson, AZ.)

readily available at this time. Because most of us have little choice but to use the more traditional arithmetic charts, we'll concentrate on that type of chart throughout this book.

CONSTRUCTION OF THE DAILY BAR CHART: PRICE, VOLUME, AND OPEN INTEREST

The construction of the daily bar chart is extremely simple. The bar chart is both a price and a time chart. The vertical axis (the y axis) shows a scale representing the price of the contract. The horizontal axis (the x axis) records the passage of time. Dates are marked along the bottom of chart. All the user has to do is plot a vertical bar in the appropriate day from the day's high to the day's low (called the range). Then, place a small horizontal tic to the right of the vertical bar identifying the daily closing price. (See Figure 3.8.)

The reason for placing the tic to the right of the bar is to distinguish it from the opening price, which some chartists record to the left of the bar. Traditionally, only the high, low, and closing prices were recorded. However, more shorter-term traders are beginning to record and use the opening price. Once that day's activity has been plotted, the user moves one day to the right to plot the next day's action. Most chart services use five-day weeks. Weekends are not shown on the chart. Whenever an exchange is closed during the trading week, that day's space is left blank.

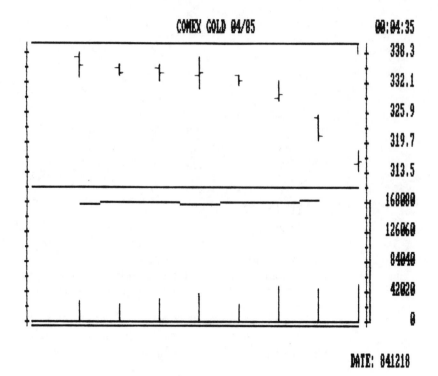

COMEX GOLD 04/85

DATE	OPEN	HIGH	LOW	CLOSE	VOL	OI
841207	337.5	338.3	333.0	335.5	28823	163480
841210	335.0	336.0	333.5	334.1	23318	164270
841211	335.0	336.1	332.5	334.0	31287	166100
841212	333.7	337.5	331.0	334.1	37666	164140
841213	333.7	333.7	331.7	332.4	22242	165050
841214	328.8	332.5	328.5	329.8	48486	166040
841217	324.8	325.2	320.0	321.1	46688	168080
841218	315.0	318.0	313.5	315.4	51000	0

(est)

Figure 3.8 The top chart shows eight days of price action. The tic to the right of the bar is the close. The tic to the left is the open. The lower chart shows total volume (vertical bars) and total open interest (solid line). The table at the bottom shows the actual data. The last day's volume is estimated. No open interest is available for the last day because it is reported a day late.

VOLUME AND OPEN INTEREST

Two other pieces of important information should be included on the bar chart—volume and open interest. *Volume* represents the total amount of trading activity in that commodity market for that day. It is the total number of contracts traded during the day. It is similar to the number of common stock shares that change hands on a given day in the stock market. The volume is recorded by a vertical bar at the bottom of the chart under that day's price bar. A higher volume bar means the volume was heavier for that day. A smaller bar represents lighter volume. A vertical scale along the bottom of the chart is provided to help plot the data. (See Figure 3.9.)

Figure 3.9 A standard daily bar chart. The price scale is shown along the right vertical side of the chart. Notice the time scale along the bottom. Total volume is shown by the vertical bars along the bottom. Total open interest is the solid line just above the volume. The scales for volume and open interest are along the bottom right and left. The dotted line along the bottom is the five-year average open interest number. This line is used to spot seasonal open interest patterns. (Chart courtesy of Commodity Research Bureau, a Knight-Ridder Business Information Service.)

Open interest is the total number of outstanding contracts that are held by market participants at the end of the day. Open interest is the number of outstanding contracts held by the longs or the shorts, not the total of both. Remember, because we're dealing with trading contracts, for every long there must also be a short. Therefore, we only have to know the totals on one side. Open interest is marked on the chart with a solid line along the bottom, usually just above the volume but below the price. Many chart services also include a dotted five-year average line of open interest, which is used to identify its seasonal tendency.

Total Versus Individual Volume and Open Interest Numbers

Most commercial chart services, along with most futures technicians, use only the total volume and open interest figures. Although figures are available for each individual delivery month, the total figures for each commodity market are the ones that are used for forecasting purposes. There is a good reason for this.

In the early stages of a futures contract's life, volume and open interest are usually quite small. The figures build up as the contract reaches maturity. In the last couple of months before expiration, however, the numbers begin to drop again. Obviously, traders have to liquidate open positions as the contract approaches expiration. Therefore, the increase in the numbers in the first few months of life and the decline near the end of trading have nothing to do with market direction and are just a function of the limited life feature of a commodity futures contract. To provide the necessary continuity in volume and open interest numbers, and to give them forecasting value, the total numbers are generally used. I use the word "generally" because, during the middle months of a contract's life, some chartists believe that the individual contract's volume and open interest numbers do have some forecasting value.

Volume and Open Interest Reported a Day Late

Official volume and open interest numbers are reported a day late. Therefore, the chartist must be content with a day's lag in obtaining and interpreting the figures. The numbers are usually reported during the following day's trading hours, but too late for publication in the day's financial newspapers. Estimated volume figures are available, however, after the markets close and are included in the following morning's paper. Estimated volume numbers are just that, but they do at least give the technician some idea of whether trading activity was heavier or lighter the previous day. In the morning paper, therefore, what the reader gets is the last day's prices along with an estimated volume figure. Official volume and open interest numbers, however, are given for the previous day. For example, a Wednesday morning paper will have prices and estimated volume for Tuesday, but official volume and open interest numbers for Monday. While the one-day lag in those numbers is a bit of a handicap to those who place importance on day-to-day changes, the inconvenience is a relatively minor one. (See Figure 3.10.)

Figure 3.10 is taken from the futures page in the *Wall Street Journal*. All of the information needed to plot the bar chart is included. Notice that under the heading for each commodity market, prices are reported for each delivery month. The delivery months are listed in the column to the far left. The open, high, low, and settlement (closing) prices from the last trading day are shown in that order from left to right. The column to the far right shows the open interest for each individual contract. Along the bottom of each market, the estimated volume for the last trading day is shown, followed by the official volume and open interest for the previous day. The volume and open interest figures along that bottom line are the total numbers. The plus or minus sign after the open interest is the increase or decrease in the number of contracts at the end of the last day reported. For reasons discussed in Chapter 7, the direction of those numbers is what gives open interest its forecasting value.

The Value of Individual Volume and Open Interest Numbers

While the individual open interest numbers are not that useful for the study of market direction, they do provide valuable information. They tell us which contracts are the most liquid for trading purposes. *As a general rule, trading activity should be limited to those delivery months with the highest open interest. Months with low open interest numbers should be avoided.* As the term implies, higher open interest means that there is more interest in certain delivery months. Some traders prefer to use individual volume figures to measure activity. I believe the open interest figures have more validity for that purpose. Individual contract volume figures are published daily in the *Journal of Commerce*.

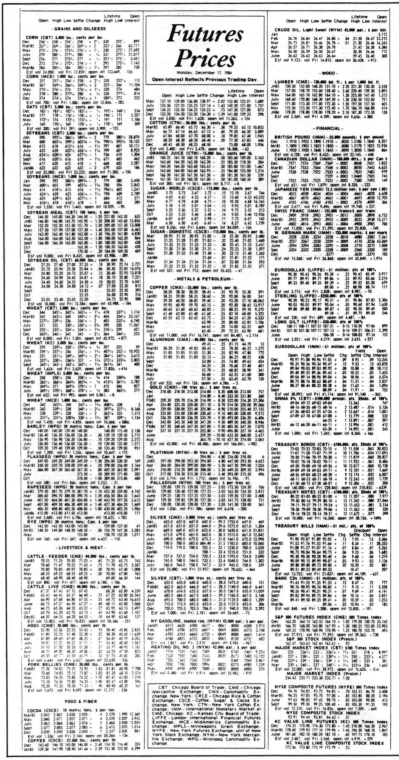

Figure 3.10   Source: *Wall Street Journal*.

HOW TO PLOT VOLUME
AND
OPEN INTEREST IN GRAIN MARKETS

There's one final point that needs to be mentioned concerning the plotting of volume and open interest figures in the grain and soybean markets. The figures are reported in some newspapers by contracts. However, chart services use scales plotted in thousands or millions of bushels. There are 5,000 bushels per contract. Therefore, before plotting the numbers printed in the paper, they must first be multiplied by five to make them compatible with the chart. (See Figure 3.11.)

Figure 3.11   A bar chart of soybeans. Notice that the scale along the bottom of the right and left vertical borders is in millions of bushels. To plot volume and open interest numbers from the *Wall Street Journal* and the *New York Times,* the number of contracts published must be multiplied by five to convert into numbers of bushels. (Chart courtesy of Commodity Research Bureau, a Knight-Ridder Business Information Service.)

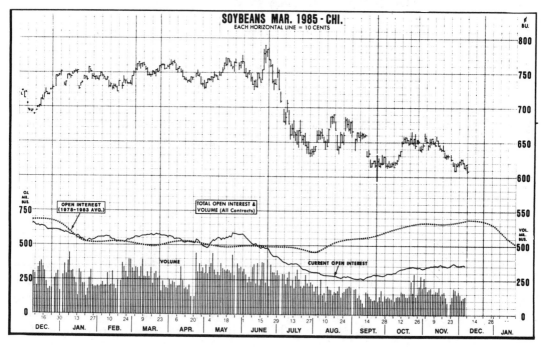

PERSONAL CHARTS VERSUS A CHART SERVICE

We're not going to concern ourselves here with the interpretation of volume and open interest. We'll cover that subject in Chapter 7. All we want to accomplish here is to make sure that you know where to find the data and how to plot it on the chart. I don't recommend that you actually construct your own charts. Aside from the amount of time involved, there's an easier way. Subscribe to one of the chart services that are commercially available. The relatively low cost is more than offset by the benefits. New, updated charts are sent out each week. Much useful supplementary technical information is included to assist in the analytical process. Most services also provide some analysis of the charts that should prove helpful, especially in the early going. The idea is to spend your time studying the charts, not constructing and updating them. Once you've mastered the pricing structure of each market and practised updating the charts, an entire futures portfolio can be updated each day in less than half an hour.

WEEKLY AND MONTHLY BAR CHARTS

We've focused so far on the daily bar chart. However, be aware that a bar chart can be constructed for any time period. We've already mentioned the intra-day bar chart, which measures the high, low, and last prices for periods as short as five minutes. The average daily bar chart covers from six to nine months of price action. For longer-range trend analysis, however, weekly and monthly bar charts must be used. The value of using these longer range charts is covered in Chapter 8. But the method of constructing and updating the charts is essentially the same. (See Figures 3.12 and 3.13.)

On the weekly chart, one bar represents the price activity for the entire week. On the monthly chart, each bar shows the entire month's price action. Obviously, weekly and monthly charts compress the price action to allow for much longer-range trend analysis. By constructing continuation charts, a weekly chart can go back as much as five years and a monthly chart over 20 years. A continuation chart is constructed by simply using the prices of the nearest expiring contracts. It's a simple technique that helps the chartist study the markets from a longer range perspective—a valuable perspective that is often lost in the futures markets.

Figure 3.12 An example of a weekly continuation chart of gold. Each bar represents one week's price action of the nearest expiring contract. Up to five years of price information can be viewed and analyzed with this type of chart. (Chart courtesy of Commodity Research Bureau, a Knight-Ridder Business Information Service.)

CONCLUSION

Now that we know how to plot a daily bar chart, and having introduced the three basic sources of information—price, volume, and open interest—we're ready to look at how that data is interpreted. Remember that the chart only records the data. In itself, it has little value. It's much like a paint brush and canvas. By themselves, they have no value. In the hands of a talented artist, however, they can help create beautiful images. Perhaps an even better comparison is a scalpel. In the hands of a gifted surgeon, it can help save lives. In the hands of most of us, however, a scalpel is not only useless, but might even be

Figure 3.13 An example of a monthly continuation chart of gold. Each bar represents one month's data. This chart allows the viewing of over 20 years of price history. (Chart courtesy of Commodity Research Bureau, a Knight-Ridder Business Information Service.)

dangerous. A chart can become an extremely useful tool in the art or skill of market forecasting once the rules are understood. Let's begin the process. In the next chapter, we'll look at some of the basic concepts of trend and what I consider to be the building blocks of chart analysis.

For those not familiar with the contract details in the various futures markets, a guide entitled "Futures Trading Facts" is provided at the end of this chapter. (See Figure 3.14.) Such things as how different markets are quoted, minimum and maximum moves, the

FUTURES TRADING FACTS

COMMODITY	NAME OF EXCHANGE	TRADING HOURS N.Y. Time Mon. thru Fri.	CONTRACT	MINIMUM FLUCTUATION Per Lb., etc.	Per Contract	DAILY TRADING LIMITS* (From Previous Close)
ALUMINUM	Commodity Exch., Inc., N.Y.	9:30 A.M. - 2:15 P.M.	40,000 Lbs.	5/100¢	$20.00	5¢
CATTLE (Feeder)	Chicago Mercantile Exchange	10:05 A.M. - 2:00 P.M.	44,000 Lbs.	2½/100¢	$11.00	1½¢
CATTLE (Live Beef)	Chicago Mercantile Exchange	10:05 A.M. - 2:00 P.M.	40,000 Lbs.	2½/100¢	$10.00	1½¢
COCOA	Coffee, Sugar & Cocoa Ex.	9:30 A.M. - 3:00 P.M.	10 Tonnes	$1.00 Tonne	$10.00	$88.00
COFFEE "C"	Coffee, Sugar & Cocoa Ex.	9:45 A.M. - 2:28 P.M.	37,500 Lbs.	1/100¢	$3.75	No Limit Spot Others 4¢
COPPER	Commodity Exch., Inc., N.Y.	9:50 A.M. - 2:00 P.M.	25,000 Lbs.	5/100¢	$12.50	5¢
COTTON #2	New York Cotton Exchange	10:30 A.M. - 3:00 P.M.	50,000 Lbs.	1/100¢	$5.00	2¢
Currencies BRITISH POUND	International Monetary Market of the Chicago Mercantile Exchange	8:30 A.M. - 2:24 P.M.	25,000 BP	$.0005	$12.50	$.0500
CANADIAN DOLLAR		8:30 A.M. - 2:26 P.M.	100,000 CD	$.0001	$10.00	$.0075
DEUTSCHE MARK		8:30 A.M. - 2:20 P.M.	125,000 DM	$.0001	$12.50	$.0100
JAPANESE YEN		8:30 A.M. - 2:22 P.M.	12.5 Mil. JY	$.000001	$12.50	$.0001
MEXICAN PESO		8:30 A.M. - 2:18 P.M.	1,000,000 MP	$.00001	$10.00	$.00150
SWISS FRANC		8:30 A.M. - 2:16 P.M.	125,000 SF	$.0001	$12.50	$.0150
CDs (Domestic Bank)	IMM—Chicago Merc. Ex.	8:30 A.M. - 3:00 P.M.	$1,000,000	.01	$25.00	.80
CRUDE OIL	N.Y. Mercantile Exchange	9:45 A.M. - 3:10 P.M.	1,000 Barrels	1¢/barrel	$10.00	$1.00
	Chicago Board of Trade	9:30 A.M. - 3:30 P.M.	1,000 Barrels	1¢/barrel	$10.00	$1.00
EURODOLLAR	IMM—Chicago Merc. Ex.	8:30 A.M. - 3:00 P.M.	$1,000,000	.01	$25.00	1.00
GASOLINE (Leaded)	N.Y. Mercantile Exchange	9:55 A.M. - 3:00 P.M.	42,000 Gals.	1/100¢ Gal.	$4.20	2¢
GNMA MTGES (CDR)	Chicago Board of Trade	9:00 A.M. - 3:00 P.M.	$100,000@8%	1/32 pt.	$31.25	64/32
GOLD	IMM—Chicago Merc. Ex.	9:00 A.M. - 2:30 P.M.	100 Troy Oz.	$.10 Oz.	$10.00	$50.00
	Chicago Board of Trade	9:00 A.M. - 2:40 P.M.	32.15 Troy Oz.	10¢/Troy Oz.	$3.22	$50/Troy Oz.
	Commodity Exch. Inc., N.Y.	9:00 A.M. - 2:30 P.M.	100 Troy Oz.	$.10/Oz.	$10.00	$25.00
	MidAmerica Com. Ex., Chi.	9:00 A.M. - 2:40 P.M.	33.2 Troy Oz.	$.025/Oz.	$ 0.83	$50.00
	Winnipeg Commodity Exch.	9:25 A.M. - 2:30 P.M.	20 Troy Oz.	$.10/Oz.	$ 2.00	$25.00 (U.S.)
Grains — Chicago WHEAT SOYBEANS, CORN, OATS	Chicago Board of Trade	10:30 A.M. - 2:15 P.M.	5,000 Bus.	1/4¢	$12.50	Wheat 20¢ Soybeans 30¢
	MidAmerica Com. Ex., Chi.	10:30 A.M. - 2:30 P.M.	1,000 Bus.	1/8¢	$ 1.25	Corn 10¢, Oats 10¢
Grains — Minneapolis WHEAT	Minneapolis Grain Exchange	10:30 A.M. - 2:15 P.M.	5,000 Bus.	1/8¢	$ 6.25	20¢
Grains — Kansas City WHEAT	Kansas City Board of Trade	10:30 A.M. - 2:15 P.M.	5,000 Bus.	1/4¢	$12.50	25¢
Grains — Winnipeg BARLEY, OATS, RYE, RAPESEED, FLAXSEED	Winnipeg Commodity Ex.	10:30 A.M. - 2:15 P.M.	20 Tonnes	10¢/Tonne	$ 2.00	Barley, Oats, Rye $5.00/Tonne (Cdn.) Rapeseed & Flaxseed $10.00/Tonne (Cdn.)
HOGS (Live)	Chicago Mercantile Exchange	10:10 A.M. - 2:00 P.M.	30,000 Lbs.	2½/100¢	$ 7.50	1½¢
LUMBER (Random Lengths)	IOM—Chicago Merc. Ex.	10:00 A.M. - 2:05 P.M.	130,000 Bd. Ft.	10¢/1000 Board Ft.	$13.00	$5.00
OIL HEATING #2 N.Y.	N.Y. Mercantile Exchange	9:50 A.M. - 3:05 P.M.	42,000 Gals.	1/100¢/Gal.	$ 4.20	2¢
ORANGE JUICE (FCOJ)	New York Cotton Exchange	10:15 A.M. - 2:45 P.M.	15,000 Lbs.	5/100¢	$ 7.50	5¢
PALLADIUM	N.Y. Mercantile Exchange	8:50 A.M. - 2:20 P.M.	100 Troy Oz.	$.05/Oz.	$ 5.00	$6.00
PLATINUM	N.Y. Mercantile Exchange	9:00 A.M. - 2:30 P.M.	50 Troy Oz.	$.10/Oz.	$ 5.00	$25.00
PORK BELLIES	Chicago Mercantile Exchange	10:10 A.M. - 2:00 P.M.	38,000 Lbs.	2½/100¢	$ 9.50	2¢
POTATOES	N.Y. Mercantile Exchange	9:45 A.M. - 2:00 P.M.	50,000 Lbs.	1¢/50 Lbs.	$10.00	40¢
SILVER	Commodity Exch., Inc., N.Y.	9:05 A.M. - 2:25 P.M.	5,000 Troy Oz.	10/100¢	$ 5.00	50¢
	Chicago Board of Trade	9:05 A.M. - 2:25 P.M.	1,000 Troy Oz.	10/100¢	$ 1.00	50¢
	Winnipeg Commodity Exch.	9:30 A.M. - 2:35 P.M.	200 Troy Oz.	1¢	$ 2.00	50¢ (U.S.)
SOYBEAN MEAL	Chicago Board of Trade	10:30 A.M. - 2:15 P.M.	100 Tons	10¢/Ton	$10.00	$10.00
SOYBEAN OIL	Chicago Board of Trade	10:30 A.M. - 2:15 P.M.	60,000 Lbs.	1/100¢	$ 6.00	1¢
Stock Index Futures N.Y.S.E. COMP. INDEX	N.Y. Futures Exchange	10:00 A.M. - 4:15 P.M.	$500 x Idex	.05	$25.00	No Limit
S & P 500 INDEX	IOM—Chicago Merc. Ex.	10:00 A.M. - 4:15 P.M.	$500 x Index	.05	$25.00	No Limit
VALUE LINE INDEX	Kansas City Board of Trade	10:00 A.M. - 4:15 P.M.	$500 x Index	.05	$25.00	No Limit
SUGAR world #11 domestic #12	Coffee, Sugar & Cocoa Ex.	10:00 A.M. - 1:43 P.M.	112,000 Lbs.	1/100¢	$11.20	No Limit 1st 2 Contracts Others ½¢
T - BILLS (13 weeks)	IMM—Chicago Merc. Exch.	9:00 A.M. - 3:00 P.M.	$1,000,000	.01	$25.00	.60
T - BONDS (Long Term)	Chicago Board of Trade	9:00 A.M. - 3:00 P.M.	$100,000@8%	1/32 Pt.	$31.25	64/32
T - NOTES (10 year)	Chicago Board of Trade	9:00 A.M. - 3:00 P.M.	$100,000@8%	1/32 Pt.	$31.25	64/32

*Expanded limits go into effect under certain conditions except for C.M.E. Livestock and Lumber and K.C. Wheat.

Commissions and Margins: CONTACT YOUR BROKER FOR ALL INFORMATION.

All statements made herein, while not guaranteed, are based on information we consider reliable and accurate as of 11/1/84.

Commodity Research Bureau   75 Montgomery Street, Jersey City, N.J. 07302

Figure 3.14   Courtesy of Commodity Research Bureau, a Knight-Ridder Business Information Service.

dollar value of those moves, which exchange they're traded on, and the trading hours are necessary information. This guide is provided only as a reference source to help familiarize you with the different futures markets. Be advised, however, that these facts are changed periodically. Make sure whatever guide you're using is the most current one available.

4
Basic Concepts of Trend

DEFINITION OF TREND

The concept of *trend* is absolutely essential to the technical approach to market analysis. All of the tools used by the chartist—support and resistance levels, price patterns, moving averages, trendlines, etc.—have the sole purpose of helping to measure the trend of the market for the purpose of participating in that trend. We often hear such familiar expressions as "always trade in the direction of the trend," "never buck the trend," or "the trend is your friend." So let's spend a little time to define what a trend is and classify it into a few categories.

In a general sense, the trend is simply the direction of the market, which way it's moving. But we need a more precise definition with which to work. First of all, markets don't generally move in a straight line in any direction. Market moves are characterized by a series of zigzags. These zigzags resemble a series of successive waves with fairly obvious peaks and troughs. *It is the direction of those peaks and troughs that constitutes market trend.* Whether those peaks and troughs are

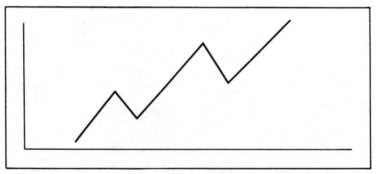

Figure 4.1a   Example of an uptrend with ascending peaks and troughs.

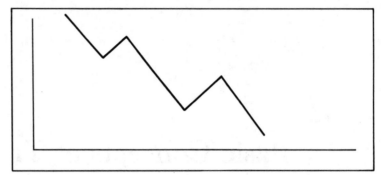

Figure 4.1b   Example of a downtrend with descending peaks and troughs.

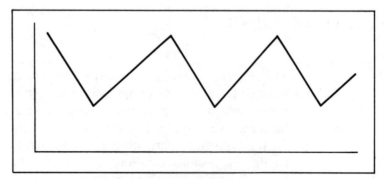

Figure 4.1c   Example of a sideways trend with horizontal peaks and troughs. This type of market is often referred to as "trendless."

moving up, down, or sideways tells us the trend of the market. An uptrend would be defined as a series of successively higher peaks and troughs; a downtrend is just the opposite, a series of declining peaks and troughs; horizontal peaks and troughs would identify a sideways price trend. (See Figures 4.1a to d.)

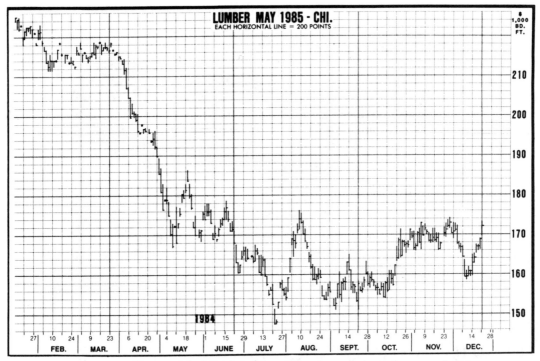

LUMBER MAY 1985 - CHI.
EACH HORIZONTAL LINE = 200 POINTS

$
1,000
BD.
FT.

Figure 4.1d The left side of the chart shows a downtrend. Prices are now in a sideways trend. A decisive penetration of the November/August highs would initiate a new uptrend. A close under July/September lows would resume the downtrend. (Chart courtesy of Commodity Research Bureau, a Knight-Ridder Business Information Service.)

TREND HAS THREE DIRECTIONS

We've mentioned an uptrend, downtrend, and sideways trend for a very good reason. Most people tend to think of markets as being always in either an uptrend or a downtrend. The fact of the matter is that markets actually move in three directions—up, down, and sideways. It is important to be aware of this distinction because for at least a third of the time, by a conservative estimate, prices move in a flat, horizontal pattern that is referred to as a "trading range." This type of sideways action reflects a period of equilibrium in the price level where the forces of supply and demand are in a state of relative balance. (If you'll recall, Dow Theory refers to this type of pattern as a *line.*) Although we've defined a flat market as having a sideways trend, it is more commonly referred to as being "trendless."

Most technical tools and systems are trend-following in nature, which means that they are primarily designed for markets that are moving up or down. They usually work very poorly, or not at all, when markets enter these lateral or "trendless" phases. It is during these periods of sideways market movement that technical traders experience their greatest frustration, and systems traders their greatest equity losses. A trend-following system, by its very definition, needs a trend in order to do its stuff. The failure here lies not with the system. Rather, the failure lies with the trader who is attempting to apply a system designed for trending markets into a nontrending market environment.

There are three decisions confronting the futures trader—whether to buy a market (go long), sell a market (go short), or do nothing (stand aside). When a market is rising, the buying strategy is preferable. When it is falling, the second approach would be correct. *However, when the market is moving sideways, the third choice—to stay out of the market—is usually the wisest.*

TREND HAS THREE CLASSIFICATIONS

In addition to having three directions, trend is usually broken down into the three categories mentioned in the previous chapter. Those three categories are the major, intermediate, and near-term trends. In reality, there are almost an infinite number of trends interacting with one another, from the very short-term trends covering minutes and hours to super-long trends lasting 50 or 100 years. Most technicians, however, limit trend classifications to three. There is a certain amount of ambiguity, however, as to how different analysts define each trend.

Dow Theory, for example, classifies the major trend as being in effect for longer than a year. Because futures traders operate in a shorter time dimension than do stock investors, I would be inclined to shorten the major trend to anything over six months in the commodity markets. Dow defined the intermediate, or secondary, trend as three weeks to as many months, which also appears about right for the futures markets. The near-term trend is usually defined as anything less than two or three weeks.

Each trend becomes a portion of its next larger trend. For example, the intermediate trend would be a correction in the major

Basic Concepts of Trend

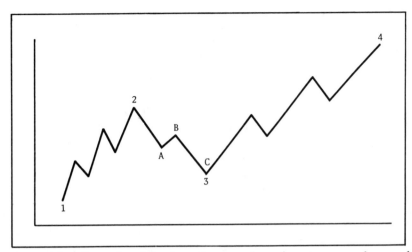

Figure 4.2a Example of the three degrees of trend: major, secondary, and near-term. Points 1, 2, 3, and 4 show the major uptrend. Wave 2-3 represents a secondary correction within the major uptrend. Each secondary wave in turn divides into near-term trends. For example, secondary wave 2-3 divides into minor waves A-B-C.

Figure 4.2b If someone were to ask the trend in cotton, it could be stated that the major trend is down, the intermediate trend (the last six weeks) is sideways, and the near-term trend (past two weeks) is up. It's always necessary to define which trend is being addressed. (Chart courtesy of Commodity Research Bureau, a Knight-Ridder Business Information Service.)

trend. In a long-term uptrend, the market pauses to correct itself for a couple of months before resuming its upward path. That secondary correction would itself consist of shorter waves that would be identified as near-term dips and rallies. This theme recurs many times—that each trend is part of the next larger trend and is itself comprised of smaller trends. (See Figures 4.2a and b.)

In Figure 4.2a, the major trend is up as reflected by the rising peaks and troughs (points 1, 2, 3, 4). The corrective phase (2-3) represents an intermediate correction within the major uptrend. But notice that the wave 2-3 also breaks down into three smaller waves (A, B, C). At point C, the analyst would say that the major trend was still up, but the intermediate and near-term trends were down. At point 4, all three trends would be up. It is important to understand the distinction between the various degrees of trend. When someone asks what the trend is in a given market, it is difficult, if not impossible, to respond until you know which trend the person is inquiring about. You may have to respond in the manner previously discussed by defining the three different trend classifications.

Quite a bit of misunderstanding arises because of different traders' perceptions as to what is meant by a trend. To long-term position traders, a few days' to a few weeks' price action might be insignificant. To a day trader, a two- or three-day advance might constitute a major uptrend. It's especially important, then, to understand the different degrees of trend and to make sure that all involved in a transaction are talking about the same ones.

As a general statement, most trend-following approaches in the futures markets actually focus on the intermediate trend, which may last for several months. The near-term trend is used primarily for timing purposes. In an intermediate uptrend, short-term setbacks would be used to initiate long positions. In intermediate downtrends, short-term bounces would be used for short positions.

SUPPORT AND RESISTANCE

In the previous discussion of trend, it was stated that prices move in a series of peaks and troughs, and that the direction of those peaks and troughs determined the trend of the market. Let's now give those peaks and troughs their appropriate names and, at the same time, introduce the concepts of *support and resistance.*

Basic Concepts of Trend

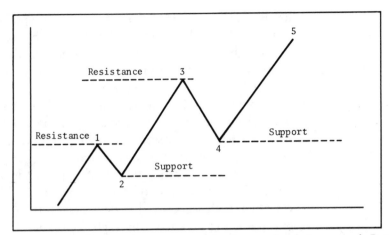

Figure 4.3a Shows rising support and resistance levels in uptrend. Points 2 and 4 are support levels which are usually previous reaction lows. Points 1 and 3 are resistance levels, usually marked by previous peaks.

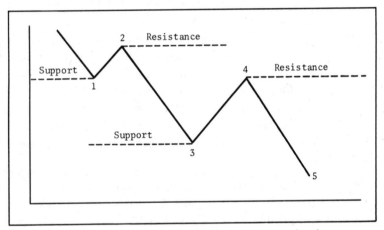

Figure 4.3b Shows support and resistance in a downtrend.

The troughs, or reaction lows, are called *support*. The term is self-explanatory and indicates that support is a level or area on the chart *under the market* where buying interest is sufficiently strong to overcome selling pressure. As a result, a decline is halted and prices turn back up again. Usually a support level is identified beforehand by a previous reaction low. In Figure 4.3a, points 2 and 4 represent support levels in an uptrend. (See Figures 4.3a and b.)

Resistance is the opposite of support and represents a price level or area *over the market* where selling pressure overcomes buying pressure and a price advance is turned back. Usually a resistance level is identified by a previous peak. In Figure 4.3a, points 1 and 3 are resistance levels. Figure 4.3a shows an uptrend. In an uptrend, the support and resistance levels show an ascending pattern. Figure 4.3b shows a downtrend with descending peaks and troughs. In the downtrend, points 1 and 3 are support levels under the market and points 2 and 4 are resistance levels over the market.

In an uptrend, the resistance levels represent pauses in that uptrend and are usually exceeded at some point. In a downtrend, support levels are not sufficient to stop the decline permanently, but are able to check it at least temporarily.

A solid grasp of the concepts of support and resistance is necessary for a full understanding of the concept of trend. For an uptrend to continue, each successive low (support level) must be higher than the one preceding it. Each rally high (resistance level) must be higher than the one before it. If the corrective dip in an uptrend comes all the way down to the previous low, it may be an early warning that the uptrend is ending or at least moving from an uptrend to a sideways trend. If the support level is violated, then a trend reversal from up to down is likely.

Each time a previous resistance peak is being tested, the uptrend is in an especially critical phase. Failure to exceed a previous peak in an uptrend, or the inability of prices to violate the previous support low in a downtrend, is usually the first warning that the existing trend is changing. Chapters 5 and 6 on *price patterns* show how the testing of these support and resistance levels form pictures on the charts that suggest either a trend reversal in progress or merely a pause in the

Figure 4.4a Example of a trend reversal. The failure of prices at point 5 to exceed the previous peak at point 3 followed by a downside violation of the previous low at point 4 constitutes a downside trend reversal. This type of pattern is called a "double top."

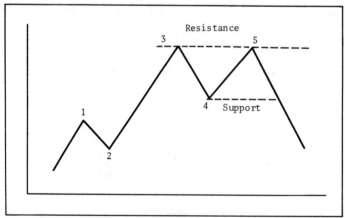

Basic Concepts of Trend

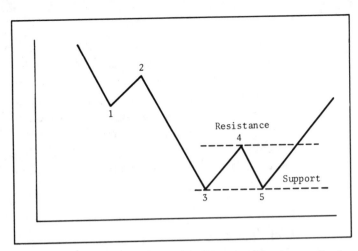

Figure 4.4b Example of a bottom reversal pattern. Usually the first sign of a bottom is the ability of prices at point 5 to hold above the previous low at point 3. The bottom is confirmed when the peak at 4 is overcome.

Figure 4.4c A classic example of a bottom reversal. Notice the low point in late June holding above the low of late May. The trend turned up when the mid-June peak was penetrated. (Chart courtesy of Commodity Research Bureau, a Knight-Ridder Business Information Service.)

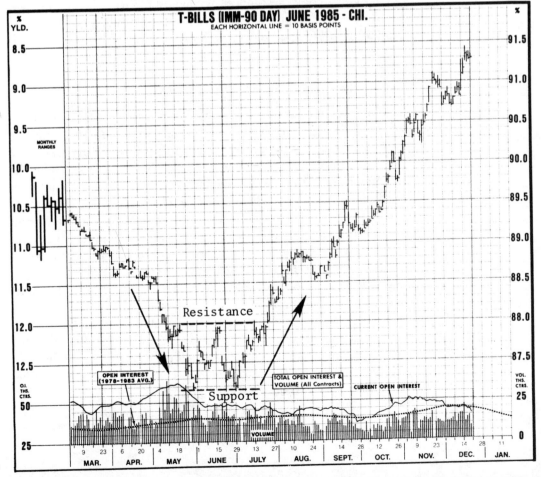

existing trend. But the basic building blocks on which those price patterns are based are support and resistance levels.

Figures 4.4a to c are examples of a classic trend reversal. Notice, in Figure 4.4a, that at point 5 prices failed to exceed the previous peak (point 3) before turning down to violate the previous low at point 4. This trend reversal could have been identified simply by watching the support and resistance levels. In our later coverage of price patterns, this type of reversal pattern will be identified as a *double top*.

How Support and Resistance Levels Reverse Their Roles

So far we've defined "support" as a previous low and "resistance" as a previous high. However, this is not always the case. This leads us to one of the more interesting and lesser known aspects of support and resistance—their reversal of roles. *Whenever a support or resistance level is penetrated by a significant amount, they reverse their roles and become the opposite.* In other words, a resistance level becomes a support level and support becomes resistance. To understand why this occurs, perhaps it would be helpful to discuss some of the psychology behind the creation of support and resistance levels.

The Psychology of Support and Resistance

To illustrate, let's divide the market participants into three categories—the longs, the shorts, and the uncommitted. The longs are those traders who have already purchased contracts; the shorts are those who have already committed themselves to the sell side; the uncommitted are those who have either gotten out of the market or remain undecided as to which side to enter.

Let's assume that a market starts to move higher from a support area where prices have been fluctuating for some time. The longs (those who bought near the support area) are delighted, but regret not having bought more. If only the market would dip back near that support area again so they could add to their long positions. The shorts now realize (or strongly suspect) that they are on the wrong side of the market. (How far the market has moved away from that support area will greatly influence these decisions, but we'll come back to that point a bit later.) The shorts are hoping (and praying) for a dip back to that area where they went short so they can get out of the market where they got in (their breakeven point).

Those sitting on the sidelines can be divided into two groups—those who never had a position and those who, for one reason or another, liquidated previously held long positions in the support area. The latter group are, of course, mad at themselves for liquidating their longs prematurely and are hoping for another chance to reinstate those longs near where they sold them.

The final group, the undecided, now realize that prices are going higher and resolve to enter the market on the long side on the next good buying opportunity. All four groups are resolved to "buy the next dip." They all have a "vested interest" in that support area under the market. Naturally, if prices do decline near that support, renewed buying by all four groups will materialize to push prices up.

The more trading that takes place in that support area, the more significant it becomes because more participants have a vested interest in that area. The amount of trading in a given support or resistance area can be determined in three ways: the amount of time spent there, volume, and how recent the trading took place.

The longer the period of time that prices trade in a support or resistance area, the more significant that area becomes. For example, if prices trade sideways for three weeks in a congestion area before moving higher, that support area would be more important than if only three days of trading had occurred.

Volume is another way to measure the significance of support and resistance. If a support level is formed on heavy volume, this would indicate that a large number of contracts changed hands, and would mark that support level as more important than if very little trading had taken place. Point and figure charts that measure the intra-day trading activity are especially useful in identifying these price levels where most of the trading took place and, consequently, where support and resistance will be most likely to function.

A third way to determine the significance of a support or resistance area is how recently the trading took place. Because we are dealing with the reaction of traders to market movement and to positions that they have already taken or failed to take, it stands to reason that the more recent the activity, the more potent it becomes.

Now let's turn the tables and imagine that, instead of moving higher, prices move lower. In the previous example, because prices advanced, the combined reaction of the market participants caused each downside reaction to be met with additional buying (thereby creating new support). However, if prices start to drop and move below the previous support area, the reaction becomes just the opposite. All those who bought in the support area now realize that they made a mistake. To make matters worse, their brokers are now calling frantically for more margin money. Because of the highly leveraged nature of futures trading, traders cannot sit with losses very long. They must put up additional margin money or liquidate their losing positions.

What created the previous support in the first place was the predominance of buy orders under the market. Now, however, all of the previous buy orders under the market have become sell orders over the market. *Support has become resistance.* And the more significant that previous support area was—that is, the more recent and the more trading that took place there—the more potent it now becomes as a resistance area. All of the factors that created support by the three categories of participants—the longs, the shorts, and the uncommitted—will now function to put a ceiling over prices on subsequent rallies or bounces.

It is useful once in a while to pause and reflect on why the price patterns used by chartists and concepts like support and resistance actually do work. It's not because of some magic produced by the charts or some lines drawn on those charts. These tools work because they provide pictures of what the market participants are actually doing and enable us to determine their reactions to market events. Chart analysis is actually a study of human psychology and the reactions of traders to changing market conditions. Unfortunately, because we live in the fast-paced world of commodity futures markets, we tend to rely heavily on chart terminology and short-cut expressions that overlook the underlying forces that created the pictures on the charts in the first place. There are sound psychological reasons why support and resistance levels can be identified on price charts and why they can be used to help predict market movements.

Support Becoming Resistance and Vice Versa: Degree of Penetration

A support level, penetrated by a significant margin, becomes a resistance level and vice versa. Figures 4.5a to c are similar to Figures 4.3a and b but with one added refinement. Notice that as prices are rising in Figure 4.5a the reaction at point 4 stops at or above the top of the peak at point 1. That previous peak at point 1 had been a resistance level. But once it was decisively penetrated by wave 3, that previous resistance peak became a support level. All of the previous selling near the top of wave 1 (creating the resistance level) has now become buying under the market. In Figure 4.5b, showing declining prices,

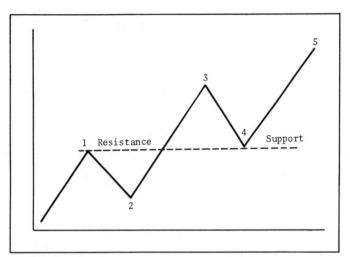

Figure 4.5a In an uptrend, resistance levels that have been broken by a significant margin become support levels. Notice that once resistance at point 1 is exceeded, it provides support at point 4. Previous peaks function as support on subsequent corrections.

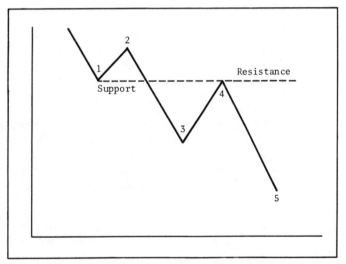

Figure 4.5b In a downtrend, violated support levels become resistance levels on subsequent bounces. Notice how previous support at point 1 became resistance at point 4.

point 1 (which had been a previous support level under the market) has now become a resistance level over the market acting as a ceiling at point 4.

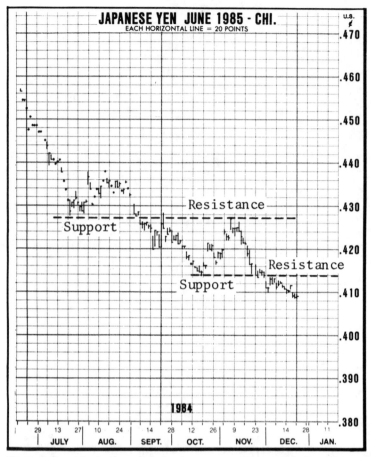

Figure 4.5c Notice how the previous support low in July became a resistance barrier in November. The support became resistance. The October low also became resistance in December. (Chart courtesy of Commodity Research Bureau, a Knight-Ridder Business Information Service.)

It was mentioned earlier that the distance prices travelled away from support or resistance increased the significance of that support or resistance. This is particularly true when support and resistance levels are penetrated and reverse roles. For example, it was stated that support and resistance levels reverse roles only after a significant penetration. But what constitutes significant? There is quite a bit of subjectivity involved here in determining whether a penetration is significant or not. As a benchmark, some chartists use a 10% penetration as a criteria, particularly for major support and resistance levels. Shorter-term support and resistance areas would probably require a much smaller number, such as 3 to 5%. In reality, each analyst must decide for himself or herself what constitutes a significant penetration. It's important to remember, however, that support and resistance areas only reverse roles when the market moves far enough away to convince the market participants that they have made a mistake. The farther away the market moves, the more convinced they become.

The Importance of Round Numbers as Support and Resistance

There is a tendency for round numbers to stop advances or declines. Traders tend to think in terms of important round numbers, such as 10, 20, 25, 50, 75, 100 (and multiples of 100), as price objectives and act accordingly. These round numbers, therefore, will often act as "psychological" support or resistance levels. A trader can use this information to begin taking profits as an important round number is approached.

The gold market is an excellent example of this phenomenon. The 1982 bear market low was right at $300. The market then rallied to just above $500 in the first quarter of 1983 before falling to $400. Here prices stabilized for about six months. After prices broke under $400 at the end of 1983, the market tried unsuccessfully three times over the next six months to break back above $400 (which had now become a resistance level). As of this writing, prices are now bearing down on the $300 support area again. The $450 and $350 levels were also significant support and resistance areas. Below $300, the next long-term support area is near $250. The 1974 bull market high was just below $200 and the 1976 bear market low at $100.

Another application of this principle is *to avoid placing trading orders right at these obvious round numbers*. For example, if the trader is trying to buy into a short-term market dip in an uptrend, it would make sense to place limit orders just above an important round number. Because others are trying to buy the market at the round number, the market may never get there. Traders looking to sell short on a bounce would place resting sell orders just below round numbers. The opposite would be true when placing protective stops on existing positions. As a general rule, *avoid placing protective stops at obvious round numbers*. A trader on the short side, for example, instead of putting a protective buy stop at $4.00, would put it at $4.01. Or, on the opposite side, a long position would be protected at $3.49 instead of $3.50.

In other words, protective stops on long positions should be placed below round numbers and on short positions, above such numbers. The tendency for markets to respect round numbers, and especially the more important round numbers previously referred to, is one of those peculiar market characteristics that can prove most helpful in futures trading and should be kept in mind by the technically-oriented futures trader.

TRENDLINES

Now that we understand support and resistance, let's add another building block to our arsenal of technical tools—*the trendline.* (See Figures 4.6a to c.) The basic trendline is one of the simplest of the technical tools employed by the chartist, but is also one of the most valuable in futures trading. An *up trendline* is a straight line drawn up to the right along successive reaction lows as shown by the solid line in Figure 4.6a. A *down trendline* is drawn down to the right along successive rally peaks as shown in Figure 4.6b.

Figure 4.6a Example of an up trendline. The up trendline is drawn under the rising reaction lows. A tentative trendline is first drawn under two successively higher lows (points 1 and 3), but needs a third test to confirm the validity of the trendline (point 5).

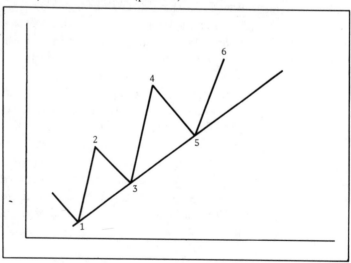

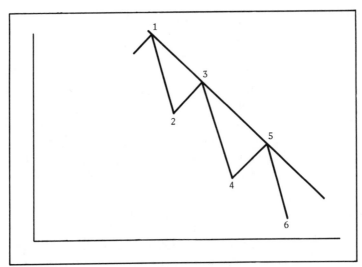

Figure 4.6b A down trendline is drawn over the successively lower rally highs. The tentative down trendline needs two points (1 and 3) to be drawn and a third test (5) to confirm its validity.

Figure 4.6c Example of a down trendline. The rally in December confirmed the validity of the trendline drawn over the October/November highs. (Chart courtesy of Commodity Research Bureau, a Knight-Ridder Business Information Service.)

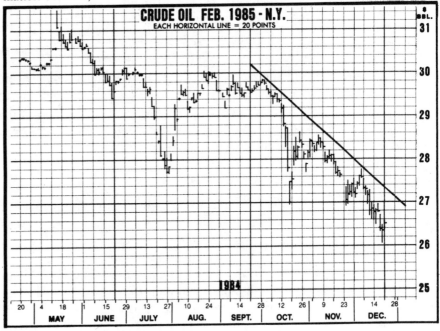

Drawing a Trendline

The correct drawing of trendlines is an art like every other aspect of charting and some experimenting with different lines is usually necessary to find the correct one. Sometimes a trendline that looks correct may have to be redrawn. But there are some useful guidelines in the search for that correct line.

First of all, there must be evidence of a trend. This means that, for an up trendline to be drawn, there must be at least two reaction lows with the second low higher than the first. Of course, it always takes two points to draw any straight line. In Figure 4.6a, for example, only after prices have begun to move higher from point 3 is the chartist reasonably confident that a reaction low has been formed, and only then can a tentative up trendline be drawn under points 1 and 3.

Some chartists require that the peak at point 2 be penetrated to confirm the uptrend before drawing the trendline. Others only require a 50% retracement of wave 2-3, or that prices approach the top of wave 2. While the criteria may differ, the main point to remember is that the chartist wants to be reasonably sure that a reaction low has been formed before identifying a valid reaction low. Once two ascending lows have been identified, a straight line is drawn connecting the lows and projected up and to the right.

Tentative Versus the Valid Trendline

So far, all we have is a "tentative" trendline. In order to confirm the validity of a trendline, however, that line should be touched a third time with prices bouncing off of it. Therefore, in Figure 4.6a, the successful test of the up trendline at point 5 confirmed the validity of that line. Figure 4.6b shows a downtrend, but the rules are the same. The successful test of the trendline occurs at point 5. To summarize, two points are needed to draw the trendline, and a third point to confirm its validity.

How to Use the Trendline

Once the third point has been confirmed and the trend proceeds in its original direction, that trendline becomes very useful in a variety of ways. One of the basic concepts of trend is that a trend in motion will tend to remain in motion. As a corollary to that, once a trend assumes a certain slope or rate of speed, as identified by the trendline, it will usually maintain the same slope. The trendline then helps not only to determine the extremities of the corrective phases, but maybe even more importantly, tells us when that trend is changing.

In an uptrend, for example, the inevitable corrective dip will often touch or come very close to the up trendline. Because the intent of the futures trader is to buy dips in an uptrend, that trendline provides a support boundary under the market that can be used as a buying area. A down trendline can be used as a resistance area for selling purposes. (See Figures 4.7a and b.)

Figure 4.7a Once the up trendline has been established, subsequent dips near the line can be used as buying areas. Points 5 and 7 in this example could have been used for new or additional longs. The breaking of the trendline at point 9 called for liquidation of all longs by signalling a downside trend reversal.

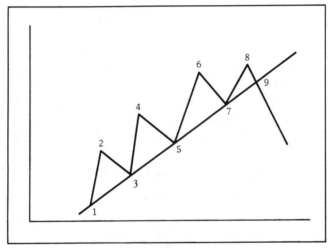

Figure 4.7b Points 5 and 7 could have been used as selling areas. The breaking of the trendline at point 9 signalled an upside trend reversal.

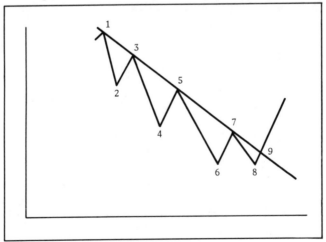

As long as the trendline is not violated, it can be used to determine buying and selling areas. However, at point 9 in Figures 4.7a and 4.7b, the violation of the trendline signals a trend change, calling for liquidation of all positions in the direction of the previous trend. Very often, *the breaking of the trendline is one of the best early warnings of a change in trend.*

How to Determine
The Significance of a Trendline

Let's discuss some of the refinements of the trendline. First, what determines the significance of a trendline? The answer to that question is twofold—*the longer it has been intact and the number of times it has been tested.* A trendline that has been successfully tested eight times, for example, that has continually demonstrated its validity, is obviously a more significant trendline than one that has only been touched three times. Also, a trendline that has been in effect for nine months is of more importance than one that has been in effect for nine weeks or nine days. The more significant the trendline, the more confidence it inspires and the more important is its penetration.

Trendlines Should Include All Price Action

Trendlines on bar charts should be drawn over or under the entire day's price range. Some chartists prefer to draw the trendline by connecting only the closing prices, but that is not the more standard

Figure 4.8 The correct drawing of a trendline should include the entire day's trading range.

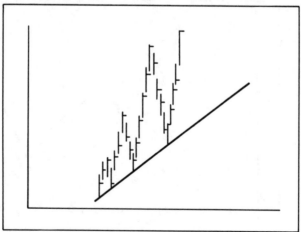

Basic Concepts of Trend

procedure. The closing price may very well be the most important price of the day, but it still represents only a small sample of that day's activity. The technique of including the day's price range takes into account all of the activity and is the more common usage. (See Figure 4.8.)

How to Handle Small Trendline Penetrations

Sometimes prices will violate a trendline on an intra-day basis, but then close in the direction of the original trend, leaving the analyst in some doubt as to whether or not the trendline has actually been broken. (See Figure 4.9.) If it turns out that the minor breaking of the trendline was only temporary, should a new trendline be drawn to include the new data? Figure 4.9 shows how such a situation might look. Prices did dip under the trendline during the day, but closed back above the up trendline. Should the trendline be redrawn?

Unfortunately, there's no hard and fast rule to follow in such a situation. Sometimes it is best to ignore the minor breach, especially if subsequent market action proves that the original line is still valid. Sometimes a compromise is called for where a revised, but tentative, new trendline is drawn as shown by the dotted line in Figure 4.9.

Figure 4.9 Sometimes an intra-day violation of a trendline will leave the chartist in doubt as to whether the original trendline is still valid or if a new line should be drawn. A compromise is to keep the original trendline, but draw a new dotted line until it can be better determined which is the truer line.

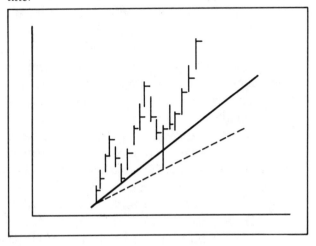

This way the chartist has both the original line (solid line) and new line (dotted line) for future reference. As a general rule of thumb, if the violation of the line is relatively minor, is only on an intra-day basis, and prices close back above the trendline, then it is probably best to stay with the original line and pay no attention to the violation. As in so many other areas of market analysis, experience and judgment must play the deciding role in such ambiguous cases.

What Constitutes
a Valid Breaking of a Trendline?

To answer this question a certain amount of subjectivity is involved. As a general rule, *a close beyond the trendline is more significant than just an intra-day penetration.* To go a step further, sometimes even a closing penetration is not enough. Most technicians employ a variety of time and price filters in an attempt to isolate valid trendline penetrations and eliminate bad signals or "whipsaws." One example of a price filter is the 3% *penetration criteria.* This price filter is used mainly for the breaking of longer-term trendlines, but requires that the trendline be broken, on a closing basis, by at least 3%. (The 3% rule doesn't apply to some financial futures, such as the interest rate markets.)

If, for example, gold prices broke a major up trendline at $400, prices would have to close below that line by 3% of the price level where the line was broken (in this case, prices would have to close $12 below the trendline, or at $388). Obviously, a $12 penetration criteria would not be appropriate for shorter-term trading. Perhaps a 1% criterion would serve better in such cases. The 3% rule represents just one type of price filter. Some chartists use a multiple of the minimum fluctuation allowed in each market. Others use no price filter at all. There is trade-off involved in the use of any type of filter. If the filter is too small, it won't be very useful in reducing the impact of whipsaws. If it's too big, then much of the initial move will be missed before a valid signal is given. Here again, the trader must determine what type of filter is best suited to the degree of trend being followed, always making allowances for the differences in the individual markets.

An alternative to a price filter (requiring that a trendline be broken by some predetermined price increment or percentage amount) is a *time filter.* A very common time filter is the *two-day rule.* In other words, to have a valid breaking of a trendline, prices must close beyond the trendline for two successive days. To break an up trendline, therefore, prices must close under the trendline two days in a row. A one-day violation would not count. It should also be mentioned here that the 3% rule and the two-day rule are also applied to the breaking of important support and resistance levels, not just to major trendlines.

How Trendlines Reverse Roles

It was mentioned earlier that support and resistance levels became the opposite once violated. The same principle holds true of trendlines. (See Figures 4.10a to c.) In other words, an up trendline (a support line) will usually become a resistance line once it's decisively broken.

Figure 4.10a Example of a rising support line becoming resistance. Usually a support line will function as a resistance barrier on subsequent rallies, after it has been broken on the downside.

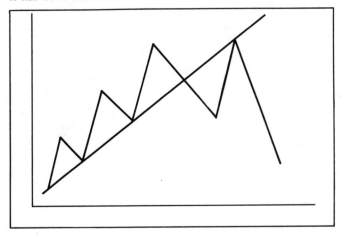

Figure 4.10b Very often a down trendline will become a support line once it's been broken on the upside.

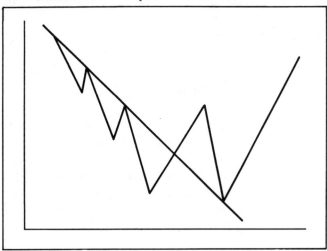

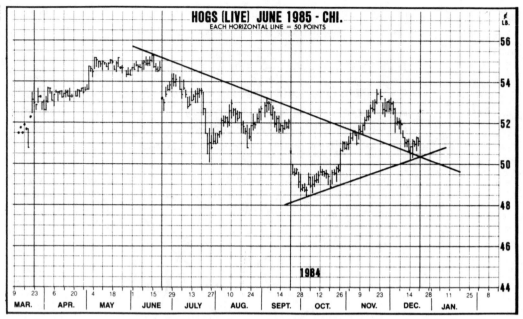

Figure 4.10c Notice that the major down trendline along the June/September highs became a support line in December once it had been broken on the upside. Also notice how well the up trendline along the October lows checked the price decline in December. (Chart courtesy of Commodity Research Bureau, a Knight-Ridder Business Information Service.)

A down trendline (a resistance line) will often become a support line once it's decisively broken. This is why it's usually a good idea to project all trendlines as far out to the right on the chart as possible even after they've been broken. It's surprising how often old trendlines act as support and resistance lines again in the future, but in the opposite role.

Measuring Implications of Trendlines

Trendlines can be used to help determine price objectives. We'll have a lot more to say about price objectives in the next two chapters on price patterns. In fact, some of the price objectives addressed that are derived from various price patterns are similar to the one we'll cover here with trendlines. Stated briefly, once a trendline is broken, prices will usually move a distance beyond the trendline equal to the vertical

Basic Concepts of Trend

distance that prices achieved on the other side of the line, prior to the trend reversal.

In other words, if in the prior uptrend, prices moved $50 above the up trendline (measured vertically), then prices would be expected to drop that same $50 below the trendline after it's broken. In the next chapter, for example, we'll see that this measuring rule using the trendline is similar to that used for the well-known *head and shoulders* reversal pattern, where the distance from the "head" to the "neckline" is projected beyond that line once it's broken.

THE FAN PRINCIPLE

This brings us to another interesting use of the trendline—the *fan principle*. (See Figures 4.11a to c.) Sometimes after the violation of an up trendline, prices will decline a bit before rallying back to the bottom of the old up trendline (now a resistance line). In Figure 4.11a, notice how prices rallied to but failed to penetrate line 1. A second trendline (line 2) can now be drawn, which is also broken. After another failed rally attempt, a third line is drawn (line 3). *The breaking of that third trendline is usually an indication that prices are headed lower.*

Figure 4.11a Example of the fan principle. The breaking of the third trendline signals the reversal of a trend. Notice also that the broken trendlines 1 and 2 often become resistance lines.

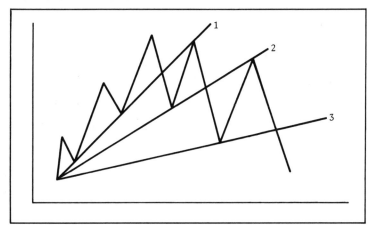

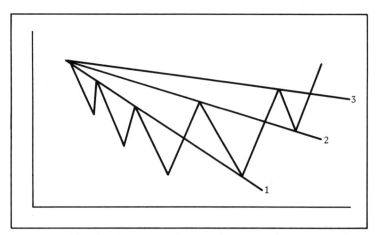

Figure 4.11b The fan principle at a bottom. The breaking of the third trendline signals the upside trend reversal. The previously broken trendlines (1 and 2) often become support levels.

Figure 4.11c The fan principle in action. The downside secondary correction from the April peak formed three successive fan lines. The upside penetration of line 3 signalled that the uptrend was resuming. Notice how the three lines became support once they were penetrated on the upside. Notice also how well the down trendline from the November peak contained the bear trend on the left of the chart. The up trendline from the February/March bottom also contained the new uptrend quite well. (Chart courtesy of Commodity Research Bureau, a Knight-Ridder Business Information Service.)

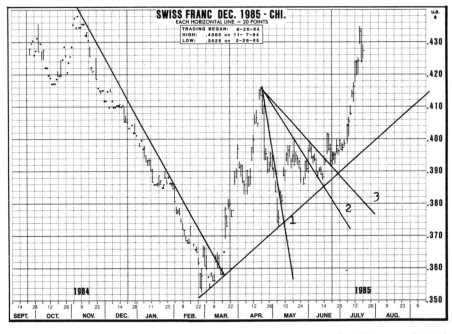

Basic Concepts of Trend

In Figure 4.11b, the breaking of the third down trendline (line 3) constitutes a new uptrend signal. Notice in these examples how previously broken support lines became resistance and resistance lines became support. The term "fan principle" derives from the appearance of the lines that gradually flatten out, resembling a fan. *The important point to remember here is that the breaking of the third line is the valid trend reversal signal.*

THE IMPORTANCE OF THE NUMBER THREE

In examining the three lines in the fan principle, it's interesting to note how often the number three shows up in the study of technical analysis and the important role it plays in so many technical approaches. For example, the fan principle uses three lines; major bull and bear markets usually have three major phases (Dow Theory and Elliott Wave Theory); there are three kinds of *gaps* (to be covered shortly); some of the more commonly known reversal patterns, such as the *triple top* and the *head and shoulders,* have three prominent peaks; there are three different classifications of trend (major, secondary, and minor) and three trend directions (up, down, and sideways); among the generally accepted continuation patterns, there are three types of *triangles*—the symmetrical, ascending, and descending; there are three principle sources of information—price, volume, and open interest. For whatever the reason, the number three plays a very prominent role throughout the entire field of technical analysis.

THE RELATIVE STEEPNESS OF THE TRENDLINE

The relative steepness of the trendline is also important. In general, most important up trendlines tend to approximate an average slope of about 45 degrees. Some chartists simply draw a 45-degree line on the chart from a prominent high or low and use this as a major trendline. The 45-degree line was one of the techniques favored by W.D. Gann. Such a line reflects a situation where prices are advancing or declining at such a rate that price and time are in perfect balance. (Gann relied heavily on geometric angles of which the 45-degree line was the most important. The subject of Gann's geometric angles is treated in more depth in Appendix 3.)

If a trendline is too steep (see line 1 in Figure 4.12), it usually indicates that prices are advancing too rapidly and that the current steep ascent will not be sustained. The breaking of that steep trendline may be just a reaction back to a more sustainable slope closer to the 45-degree line (line 2). If a trendline is too flat (see line 3), it may indicate that the uptrend is too weak and not to be trusted. In addition to the later coverage of Gann analysis, the 45-degree line is mentioned again during the discussion of three-point reversal and optimized point and figure charts.

Figure 4.12 Most valid trendlines rise at an angle approximating 45 degrees (see line 2). If the trendline is too steep (line 1), it usually indicates that the rate of ascent is not sustainable. A trendline that is too flat (line 3) suggests that the uptrend is too weak and probably suspect. Many technicians use 45-degree lines from previous tops or bottoms as major trendlines.

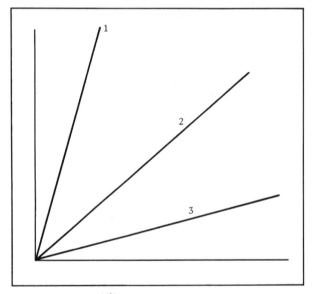

How to Adjust Trendlines

Sometimes trendlines have to be adjusted to fit a slowing or an accelerating trend. (See Figure 4.13 and Figures 4.14a and b.) For example, as shown in the previous case, if a steep trendline is broken, a slower trendline might have to be drawn. If the original trendline is too flat, it may have to be redrawn at a steeper angle. Figure 4.13 shows a situation where the breaking of the steeper trendline (line 1) necessitated the drawing of a slower line (line 2). In Figure 4.14, the

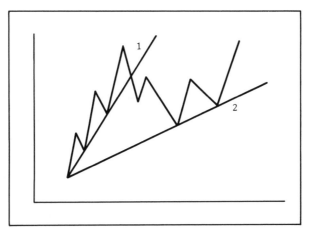

Figure 4.13   Example of a trendline that is too steep (line 1). The original up trendline proved too steep. Often the breaking of a steep trendline is only an adjustment to a slower and more sustainable up trendline (line 2).

original trendline (line 1) is too flat and has to be redrawn at a steeper angle (line 2). The uptrend accelerated, requiring a steeper line. A trendline that is too far away from the price action is obviously of little use in tracking the trend.

Figure 4.14a   Example of an up trendline that is too flat (line 1). Line 1 proved too slow as the uptrend accelerated. In this case, a second and steeper trendline (line 2) should be drawn to more closely track the rising trend.

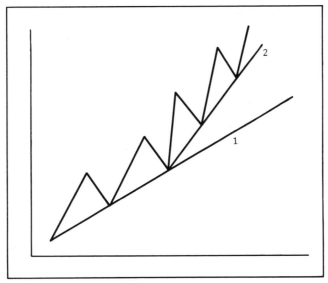

Figure 4.14b Example of how an accelerating uptrend requires the drawing of a steeper up trendline. Even in such cases, however, it is a good idea to continue all trendlines. They may become useful at some point in the future. (Chart courtesy of Commodity Research Bureau, a Knight-Ridder Business Information Service.)

In the case of an accelerating trend, sometimes several trendlines may have to be drawn at increasingly steeper angles. Some chartists advocate the use of a curving trendline in such cases. In my experience, however, where steeper trendlines become necessary, it is best to resort to another tool—the moving average—which is the same as a curvilinear trendline. One of the advantages of having access to several different types of technical indicators is being able to choose the one most appropriate for a given situation. All of the techniques covered in this book work well in certain situations, but not so well in others. By having an arsenal of tools to fall back on, the technician can quickly switch from one tool to another that might work better in a given situation. An accelerated trend is one of those cases where a moving average would be more useful than a series of steeper and steeper trendlines.

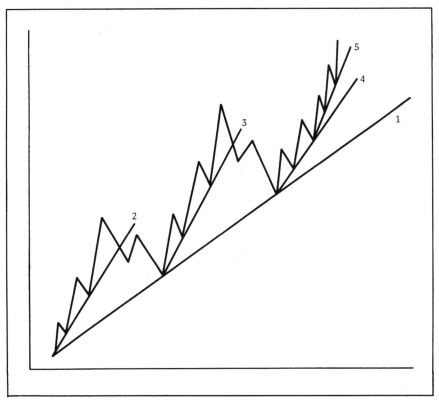

Figure 4.15 Different trendlines are used to define the different degrees of trend. Line 1 in the above example is the major up trendline, defining the major uptrend. Lines 2, 3, and 4 define the intermediate uptrends. Finally, line 5 defines a shorter-term advance within the last intermediate uptrend. Technicians use many different trendlines on the same chart.

Just as there are several different degrees of trend in effect at any one time, so is there a need for different trendlines to measure those various trends. A major up trendline, for example, would connect the low points of the major uptrend, while a shorter and more sensitive line might be used for secondary swings. An even shorter line can measure the short-term movements. (See Figure 4.15.)

THE CHANNEL LINE

The *channel line,* or the *return line* as it is sometimes called, is another useful variation of the trendline technique. Sometimes prices trend between two parallel lines—the basic trendline and the channel line.

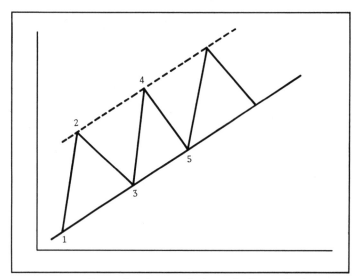

Figure 4.16a Example of a trend channel. Once the basic up trendline is drawn (below points 1 and 3) a channel, or return, line (dotted line) can be projected over the first peak at 2, which is parallel to the basic up trendline.

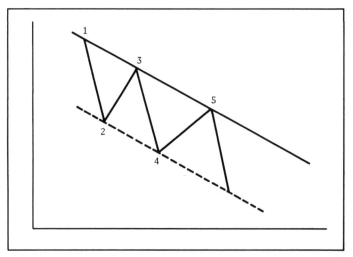

Figure 4.16b A trend channel in a downtrend. The channel is projected downward from the first low at point 2, parallel to the down trendline along the 1 and 3 peaks. Prices will often remain within such a trend channel.

Obviously, when this is the case and when the analyst recognizes that a channel exists, this knowledge can be used to profitable advantage.

The drawing of the channel line is relatively simple. In an up-trend (see Figure 4.16a), first draw the basic up trendline along the lows. Then draw a dotted line from the first prominent peak (point 2), which is parallel to the basic up trendline. Both lines move up to

       Basic Concepts of Trend

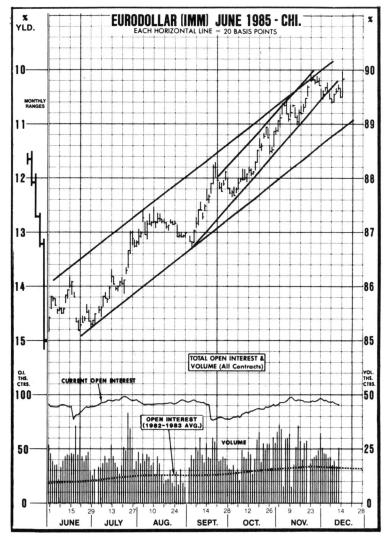

Figure 4.16c Notice how the entire uptrend was enclosed within parallel up trendlines. Notice that a second trend channel developed within the larger channel. The basic up trendlines (the lower lines) are always the more important. However, channel lines in uptrends can help identify overhead resistance areas. (Chart courtesy of Commodity Research Bureau, a Knight-Ridder Business Information Service.)

the right, forming a channel. If the next rally reaches and backs off from the channel line (at point 4), then a channel may exist. If prices then drop back to the original trendline (at point 5), then a channel probably does exist. The same holds true for a downtrend (Figure 4.16b), but of course in the opposite direction.

The reader should immediately see the value of such a situation. The basic up trendline can be used for the initiation of new long positions. The channel line can be used for short-term profit-taking. More aggressive traders might even use the channel line to initiate a countertrend short position, although trading in the opposite direction of the prevailing trend can be a dangerous and usually costly tactic. As in the case of the basic trendline, the longer the channel remains intact and the more often it is successfully tested, the more important and reliable it becomes.

The breaking of the major trendline indicates an important change in trend. But the breaking of a rising channel line has exactly the opposite meaning, and signals an acceleration of the existing trend. Some traders view the clearing of the upper line in an uptrend as a reason to add to long positions.

Another way to use the channel technique is to spot failures to reach the channel line, usually a sign of a weakening trend. In Figure 4.17, the failure of prices to reach the top of the channel (at point 5) may be an early warning that the trend is turning, and increases the odds that the other line (the basic up trendline) will be broken.

Figure 4.17   The failure to reach the upper end of the channel is often an early warning that the lower line will be broken. Notice the failure to reach the upper line at point 5 is followed by the breaking of the basic up trendline at point 6.

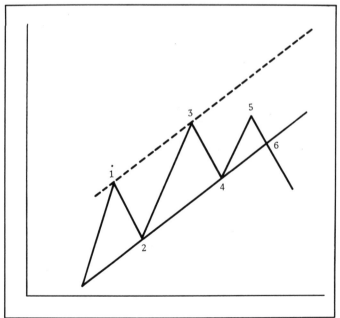

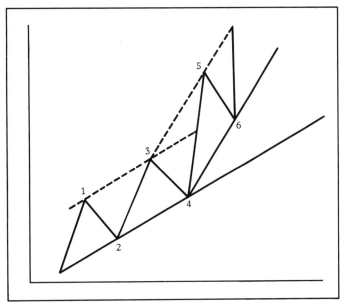

Figure 4.18 When the upper channel line is broken (as in wave 5), many chartists will redraw the basic up trendline parallel to the new upper channel line. In other words, line 4-6 is drawn parallel to line 3-5. Because the uptrend is accelerating, it stands to reason that the basic up trendline will do likewise.

As a general rule of thumb, the failure of any move within an established price channel to reach one side of the channel usually indicates that the trend is shifting, and increases the likelihood that the other side of the channel will be broken.

The channel can also be used to adjust the basic trendline. (See Figures 4.18 and 4.19.) If prices move above a projected rising channel line by a significant amount, it usually indicates a strengthening trend. Some chartists then draw a steeper basic up trendline from the last reaction low parallel to the new channel line (as demonstrated in Figure 4.18). Often, the new steeper support line functions better than the old flatter line. Similarly, the failure of an uptrend to reach the upper end of a channel justifies the drawing of a new support line under the last reaction low parallel to the new resistance line over the past two peaks (as shown in Figure 4.19).

Channel lines have measuring implications. *Once a breakout occurs from an existing price channel, prices usually travel a distance equal to the width of the channel.* Therefore, the user has to simply measure the width of the channel and then project that amount from the point at which either trendline is broken.

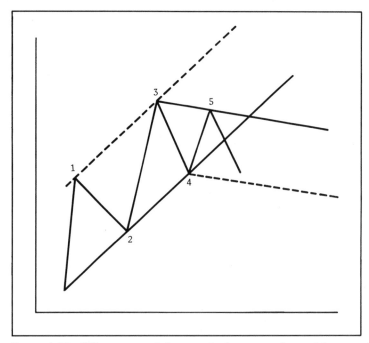

Figure 4.19 When prices fail to reach the upper channel line, and a down trendline is drawn over the two declining peaks (line 3-5), a tentative channel line can be drawn from the low at point 4 parallel to line 3-5. The lower channel line sometimes indicates where initial support will be evident.

It should always be kept in mind, however, that of the two lines, the basic trendline is by far the more important and the more reliable. The channel line is a secondary use of the trendline technique. But the use of the channel line works often enough to justify its inclusion in the chartist's toolkit.

PERCENTAGE-RETRACEMENTS

In all of the previous examples of uptrends and downtrends, the reader has no doubt noticed that after a particular market move, prices retrace a portion of the previous trend before resuming the move in the original direction. These countertrend moves tend to fall into certain pre-dictable percentage parameters. The best known application of the phenomenon is the *50% retracement*. Let's say, for example, that a market is trending higher and travels from the 100 level to the 200

Basic Concepts of Trend

level. Very often, the subsequent reaction retraces about half of the prior move, to about the 150 level, before upward momentum is regained. This is a very well-known market tendency and happens quite frequently in the futures markets. Also, these percentage retracements apply to any degree of trend—major, secondary, and near-term.

Besides the 50% retracement, which is more of a tendency than a precise hard and fast rule, there are minimum and maximum percentage parameters that are also widely recognized—*the one-third and the two-thirds retracements*. In other words, the price trend can be divided into thirds. Usually, a minimum retracement is about 33% and a maximum about 66%. What this means is that, in a correction of a strong trend, the market usually retraces at least a third of the previous move. This is very useful information for a number of reasons. If a trader is looking for a buying area under the market, he or she can just compute a 33%-50% zone on the chart and use that price zone as a general frame of reference for buying opportunities. (See Figures 4.20a and b.)

The maximum retracement parameter is 66%, which becomes an especially critical area. If the prior trend is to be maintained, the correction must stop at the two-thirds point. This then becomes a relatively low risk buying area in an uptrend or selling area in a

Figure 4.20a   Prices often retrace about half of the prior trend before resuming in the original direction. This example shows a 50% retracement. The minimum retracement is a third and the maximum, two-thirds of the prior trend.

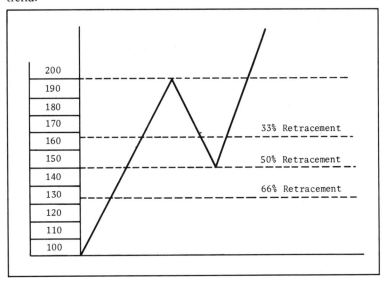

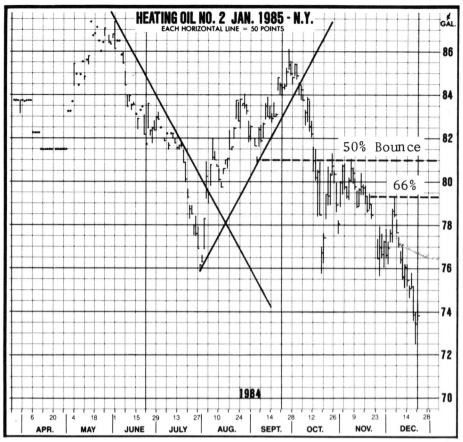

Figure 4.20b Notice the bounce in October retraced half of the October price collapse from 86¢ to 76¢ (prices recovered 5¢ to 81¢). The second bounce in early December recovered almost exactly two-thirds of the decline from the November high. Notice also how the early September low near 81¢ became resistance in the Oct./Nov. period. Look at how well trendlines have called some of the market turns. They don't always work that well, but sometimes they're the best warning of a market reversal. (Chart courtesy of Commodity Research Bureau, a Knight-Ridder Business Information Service.)

downtrend. If prices move beyond the two-thirds point, the odds then favor a trend reversal rather than just a retracement. The move usually then retraces the entire 100% of the prior trend.

You may have noticed that the three percentage retracement parameters we've mentioned so far—50%, 33%, and 66%—are taken right from the original Dow Theory. When we get to the Elliott Wave Theory and Fibonacci ratios, we will see that followers of that approach use percentage retracements of 38% and 62%. I prefer to combine both approaches for a minimum retracement zone of 33% to 38% and a maximum zone of 62% to 66%. Some technicians round off these numbers even further to arrive a 40% to 60% retracement zone.

Students of W.D. Gann are aware that he broke down the trend structure into eighths—$^1/_8$, $^2/_8$, $^3/_8$, $^4/_8$, $^5/_8$, $^6/_8$, $^7/_8$, $^8/_8$. However, even Gann attached special importance to the $^3/_8$ (38%), $^4/_8$ (50%), and $^5/_8$ (62%) retracement numbers and also felt it was important to divide the trend into thirds—$^1/_3$ (33%) and $^2/_3$ (66%).

SPEED RESISTANCE LINES

Speaking of thirds, let's touch on another technique that combines the trendline with percentage retracements—*speedlines*. This technique, developed by Edson Gould of Anametrics, is actually an adaptation of the idea of dividing the trend into thirds. The main difference from the percentage retracement concept is that the speed resistance lines (or speedlines) measure the rate of ascent or descent of a trend (in other words, its speed).

To construct a bullish *speedline*, find the highest point in the current uptrend. (See Figure 4.21.) From that high point on the chart, a vertical line is drawn toward the bottom of the chart to where the trend began. That vertical line is then divided into thirds. A trendline is then drawn from the beginning of the trend through the two points marked off on the vertical line, representing the one-third and two-thirds points. In a downtrend, just reverse the process. Measure the vertical distance from the low point in the downtrend to the beginning of the trend, and draw two lines from the beginning of the trend through the one-third and two-thirds points on the vertical line. (See Figures 4.21b and c.)

Each time a new high is set in an uptrend or a new low in a downtrend, a new set of lines must be drawn (because there is now a new high or low point). Because the *speedlines* are drawn from the beginning of the trend to the one-third and two-thirds points, those trendlines may sometimes move through some of the price action. This is one case where trendlines are not drawn under lows or over highs, but actually through the price action.

The theory behind the speedline approach is similar to that already mentioned for the 33% and 66% retracements. If an uptrend is in the process of correcting itself, the downside correction will usually stop at the higher speedline (the $^2/_3$ speedline). If not, prices

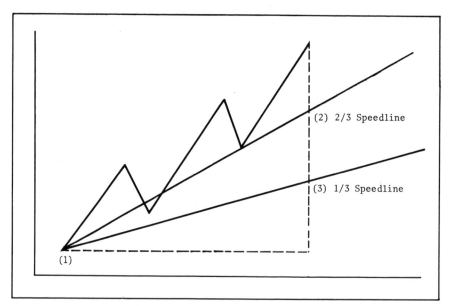

Figure 4.21a Examples of speed resistance lines in an uptrend. The vertical distance from the peak to the beginning of the trend is divided into thirds. Two trendlines are then drawn from point 1 through points 2 and 3. The upper line is the ²/₃ speedline and the lower, the ¹/₃. The lines should act as support during market corrections. When they're broken, they revert to resistance lines on bounces. Sometimes these speedlines intersect price action.

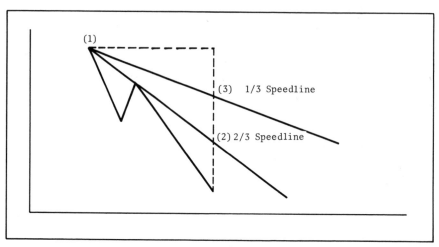

Figure 4.21b Speedlines in a downtrend.

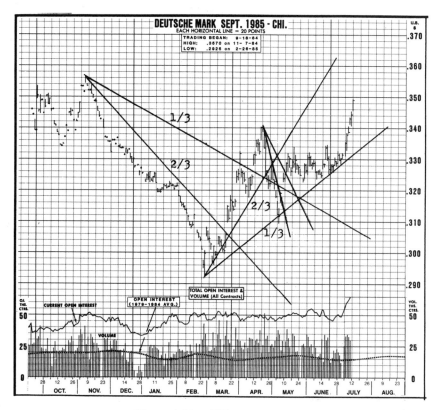

Figure 4.21c What speedlines look like in both uptrends and downtrends. The end of the bear trend in March was signalled by the breaking of the $^2/_3$ speedline drawn from the November peak. The upside breaking of the $^1/_3$ line confirmed that a new uptrend was underway. The secondary correction from the April peak stopped at the $^1/_3$ rising speedline from the February/March bottom. That downside move from the spring high was completed when the two declining speedlines from the April high were broken on the upside. (Chart courtesy of Commodity Research Bureau, a Knight-Ridder Business Information Service.)

will drop the lower speedline (the $^1/_3$ speedline). If the lower line is also broken, prices will probably continue all the way to the beginning of the prior trend. In a downtrend, the breaking of the lower line indicates a probable rally to the higher line. If that is broken, a rally to the top of the prior trend would be indicated.

As with all trendlines, speedlines reverse roles once they are broken. Therefore, during the correction of an uptrend, if the upper line ($^2/_3$ line) is broken and prices fall to the $^1/_3$ line and rally from there, that upper line becomes a resistance barrier. Only when that upper line is broken would a signal be given that the old highs will probably be challenged. The same principle holds true in downtrends.

Another important building block is the *reversal day*. This particular chart formation goes by many names—the top reversal day, the bottom reversal day, the buying or selling climax, and the key reversal day. Sometimes it forms a *two-day reversal*. By itself, this formation is not of major importance. But, taken in the context of other technical information, it can sometimes be very important. Let's first define what a *reversal day* is.

A *reversal day* takes place either at a top or a bottom. The generally accepted definition of a *top reversal day* is the setting of a new high in an uptrend, followed by a lower close on the same day. In other words, prices set a new high for a given upmove at some point during the day (usually at or near the opening) then weaken and actually close lower than the previous day's closing. A *bottom reversal day* would be a new low during the day followed by a higher close.

The wider the range for the day and the heavier the volume, the more significant is the signal for a possible near-term trend reversal. Figures 4.22a to c show what both would look like on a bar chart.

Figure 4.22a Example of a top reversal day. The heavier the volume on the reversal day and the wider the range, the more important it becomes.

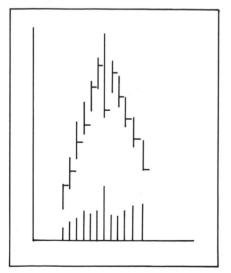

Figure 4.22b Example of a bottom reversal day. If volume is especially heavy, bottom reversals are often referred to as "selling climaxes."

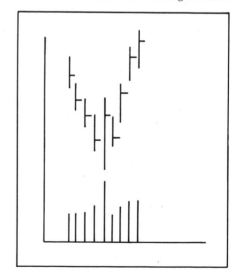

Basic Concepts of Trend

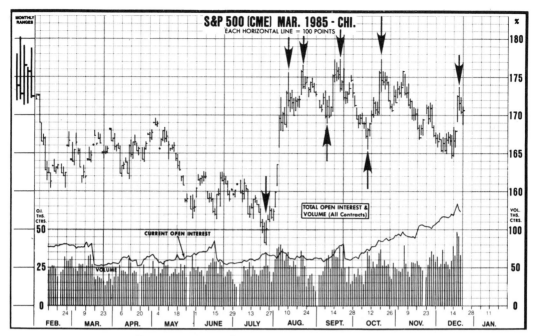

Figure 4.22c In this S&P 500 contract, notice that just about every significant market turn took place on a "reversal day." (Chart courtesy of Commodity Research Bureau, a Knight-Ridder Business Information Service.)

Note the heavier volume on the reversal day. Also notice that both the high and low on the reversal day exceed the range of the previous day, forming an *outside day*. While an outside day is not a requirement for a reversal day, it does carry more significance.

The bottom reversal day is sometimes referred to as a *selling climax*. This is usually a dramatic turnaround at the bottom of a bear market where all the discouraged longs have finally been forced out of the market on heavy volume. The subsequent absence of selling pressure creates a vacuum over the market, which prices quickly rally to fill. The selling climax is one of the more dramatic examples of the reversal day and, while it may not mark the final bottom of a bear market, it usually signals that a significant low has been seen.

The Key Reversal Day

The term "key reversal day" is widely misunderstood. All one-day reversals are potential key reversal days, but only a few actually become key reversal days. Many of the one-day reversals represent nothing more than temporary pauses in the existing trend after which the trend resumes its course. The true *key reversal day* marks an important turning point, but cannot be correctly identified as such until well after the fact—that is, after prices have moved significantly in the opposite direction of the prior trend.

The Two-Day Reversal

Sometimes a reversal will take two days to form and is appropriately called a *two-day reversal.* This is a situation where, in an uptrend, prices set a new high for a move and close near the day's high. The next day, however, instead of continuing higher, prices open about unchanged and then close near the previous day's low. The opposite picture would occur at bottoms of course. Here again, the wider the swings during the two days and the heavier the volume, the more significance is attached to the reversal. (See Figures 4.23a and b.)

As stated earlier, the reversal day itself was not a major pattern, but it could be given the right circumstances. The reader must understand that markets have to be viewed in the light of all technical evidence. If a market has been rising steeply for some time without correcting itself, has exceeded all technical objectives, is near a historically important resistance area, and is dangerously overbought, then a downside reversal would be worth paying close attention to.

Figure 4.23a Example of a two-day top reversal on heavy volume.

Figure 4.23b Example of a two-day reversal bottom on heavy volume.

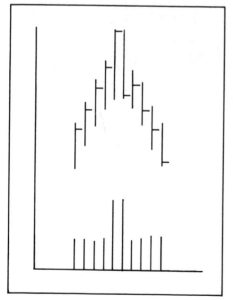

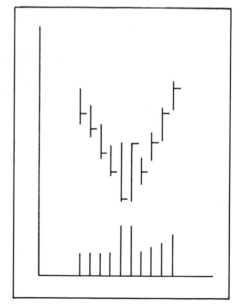

Most major turning points in the futures markets are accompanied by some variation of the reversal day, but that reversal day is usually part of a larger and more important chart pattern. The top of the "head" in a *head and shoulders* topping pattern may be a reversal day. That doesn't mean, however, that the reversal day is in itself responsible for turning the entire trend.

The secret is being able to determine when a reversal day is important and when it's not. This judgment can only be made, however, when all other technical evidence has been reviewed. While the reversal day by itself is considered a relatively minor price signal, the trader would be well-advised to learn to recognize its occurrence and to be on the alert for possible market turns.

Weekly and Monthly Reversals

This type of reversal pattern can show up on any kind of bar chart, particularly on weekly and monthly bar charts, and with much greater significance. On a weekly chart, each bar represents the entire week's range with the close registered on Friday. An *upside weekly reversal*, therefore, would occur when the market trades lower during the week, makes a new low for the move, but on Friday closes above the previous Friday's close. (Milton Jiler, the septuagenarian founder of the Commodity Research Bureau, informs me that in the old days an upside weekly reversal was called a "whammy." I made the mistake one day of asking him what a downside weekly reversal was called and he replied: "Why, a reverse whammy, of course.")

Weekly reversals are much more significant than daily reversals for obvious reasons and are watched closely by chartists as signalling important turning points. By the same token, monthly reversals are even more important. One last form of reversal is the *island reversal* pattern. But to treat that adequately requires a more extensive introduction to the use of price gaps.

PRICE GAPS

Price *gaps* are simply areas on the bar chart where no trading has taken place. In an uptrend, for example, prices open above the highest price of the previous day, leaving a gap or open space on the chart that is not filled during the day. In a downtrend, the day's highest price is below the previous day's low. Upside gaps are signs of market strength, while downside gaps are usually signs of weakness. Gaps can appear on long-term weekly and monthly charts and, when they do, are usually very significant. But they are more commonly seen on daily bar charts.

Several cliches exist concerning the interpretation of gaps. One of the maxims often heard is that "gaps are always filled." This is simply not true. Let's spend a little time here and try to clear up some of the mystery. We'll see that some gaps are important while others are not. Some should be filled and others shouldn't. We'll also see that gaps have different forecasting implications depending on which types they are and where they occur.

Four Types of Gaps

There are four general types of gaps—the *common, breakaway, runaway (or measuring), and exhaustion gaps.*

The Common Gap.   The *common gap* is the least important for forecasting purposes. It usually occurs in very thinly traded markets or in the middle of horizontal trading ranges. It is more a symptom of lack of interest than anything else, when relatively small trading orders can create gaps on the chart. Most chartists generally ignore common gaps.

The Breakaway Gap.   The *breakaway gap* usually occurs at the completion of an important price pattern, and usually signals the beginning of a significant market move. After a market has completed a major basing pattern, such as an inverse head and shoulders bottom, the breaking of the neckline often occurs on a breakaway gap. Major breakouts from topping or basing areas are breeding grounds for this type of gap. The breaking of a major trendline, signalling a reversal of trend, might also see a breakaway gap.

Breakaway gaps usually occur on heavy volume. More often than not, breakaway gaps are not filled. Prices may return to the upper end of the gap (in the case of a bullish breakout), and may even close a portion of the gap, but some portion of the gap is usually left unfilled. As a rule, the heavier the volume after such a gap appears, the less likely it is to be filled. In fact, if the gap is completely filled, with prices moving back below the gap area, that may actually be an indication of a false breakout. Upside gaps usually act as support areas on subsequent market corrections, and downside gaps as resistance areas on subsequent bounces. (See Figures 4.24a to c.)

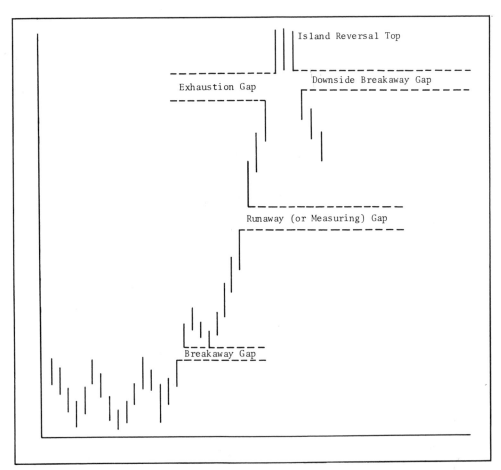

Figure 4.24a The three types of gaps. The breakaway gap signalled the completion of the basing pattern. The runaway occurred at about the midway point (which is why it is also called the measuring gap). An exhaustion gap to the upside, followed within a week by a breakaway gap to the downside, left an island reversal top. Notice that the breakaway and runaway gaps were not filled on the way up, which is usually the case.

Runaway or Measuring Gaps. After the move has been underway for awhile, somewhere around the middle of the move, prices will leap forward to form a second type of gap (or a series of gaps) called the *runaway gap.* This type of gap reveals a situation where the market is moving effortlessly on moderate volume. In an uptrend, it's a sign of market strength; in a downtrend, a sign of weakness. Here again, runaway gaps act as support under the market on subsequent corrections and are usually not filled. As in the case of the breakaway, a move below the runaway gap is a negative sign in an uptrend.

This variety of gap is also called a *measuring gap* because it usually occurs at about the halfway point in a trend. By measuring the distance the trend has already travelled, from the original trend signal or break-out, an estimate of the probable extent of the remaining move can be determined by doubling the amount already achieved.

Figure 4.24b The three downside gaps can be seen during the Aug./Oct. decline. The breakaway began the decline, the measuring was about midway, and the exhaustion was within a week of the bottom. Notice that the first two downside gaps were not closed. The complete closing of the exhaustion gap usually indicates a reversal of some magnitude. (Chart courtesy of Commodity Research Bureau, a Knight-Ridder Business Information Service.)

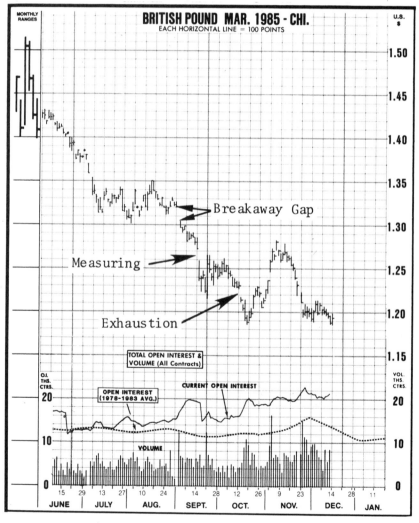

Basic Concepts of Trend

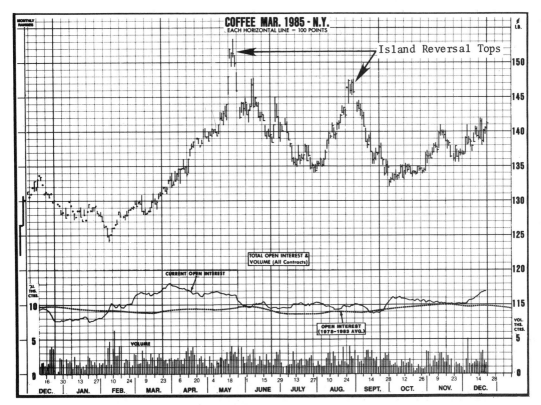

Figure 4.24c The two tops in May and August in the coffee market took place on obvious island reversals. Notice in both cases that a week's price activity stands out alone, with gaps on both sides. (Chart courtesy of Commodity Research Bureau, a Knight-Ridder Business Information Service.)

The Exhaustion Gap. The final type of gap appears near the end of a market move. After all objectives have been achieved and the other two types of gaps (breakaway and runaway) have been identified, the analyst should begin to expect the *exhaustion gap.* Near the end of an uptrend, prices leap forward in a last gasp, so to speak. However, that upward leap quickly fades and prices turn lower within a couple of days or within a week. When prices close under that last gap, it is usually a dead giveaway that the exhaustion gap has made its appearance. This is a classic example where the filling of a gap in an uptrend has very bearish implications.

The Island Reversal

This takes us back to the point that began our discussion of gaps— *the island reversal pattern.* Sometimes after the upward exhaustion gap has formed, prices will trade in a narrow range for a couple of days or a week before gapping to the downside. Such a situation leaves the few days of price action looking like an "island" surrounded by space or water. The exhaustion gap to the upside followed by a breakaway gap to the downside completes the island reversal pattern and usually indicates a trend reversal of some magnitude. Of course, the major significance of the reversal depends on where prices are in the general trend structure.

Intra-Day Price Gaps

Before leaving the subject of *gaps*, we should note that the discussion has centered primarily on inter-day price gaps, the kind that show up on daily bar charts. Many other gaps, however, also occur on an intra-day basis, that is, during the trading day that are not visible on the daily bar chart. Intra-day gaps can be seen on bar charts covering shorter time periods during the day. A five-minute bar chart, for example, will reveal many gaps that occur intra-day. There's no reason why the interpretation of these "hidden gaps" should differ from the inter-day variety. The user who has access to intra-day data can spot these hidden gaps and put this information to good use.

SUMMARY

This chapter introduced a number of introductory technical tools that I consider to be the building blocks of chart analysis—support and resistance, trendlines and channels, percentage retracements, speed resistance lines, reversal days, and gaps. Every technical approach covered in subsequent chapters uses these concepts and tools in one form or another. Armed with a better understanding of these concepts, we're now ready to begin a study of price patterns.

5

Major Reversal Patterns

INTRODUCTION

So far we've touched on Dow Theory, which is the basis of most trend-following work being used today. We've examined the basic concepts of trend, such as support, resistance, and trendlines. And we've introduced volume and open interest. We're now ready to take the next step, which is a study of chart patterns. You'll quickly see that these patterns build on the previous concepts.

In the previous chapter, the definition of a trend was given as a series of ascending or descending peaks and troughs. As long as they were ascending, the trend was up; if they were descending, the trend was down. It was stressed, however, that markets also move sideways for a certain portion of the time. It is these periods of sideways market movement that will concern us most in these next two chapters.

It would be a mistake to assume that most changes in trend are very abrupt affairs. The fact is that important changes in trend usually require a period of transition. The problem is that these periods of transition do not always signal a trend reversal. Sometimes these periods just indicate a pause or consolidation in the existing trend after which the original trend is resumed.

PRICE PATTERNS

The study of these transition periods and their forecasting implications leads us to the question of price patterns. First of all, what are price patterns? Price patterns are pictures or formations, which appear on price charts of stocks or commodities, that can be classified into different categories, and that have predictive value.

TWO TYPES OF PATTERNS: REVERSAL AND CONTINUATION

There are two major categories of price patterns—reversal and continuation. As these names imply, reversal patterns indicate that an important reversal in trend is taking place. The continuation patterns, on the other hand, suggest that the market is only pausing for awhile, possibly to correct a near-term overbought or oversold condition, after which the existing trend will be resumed. The trick is to distinguish between the two types of patterns as early as possible during the formation of the pattern.

In this chapter, we'll be examining the five most commonly used major reversal patterns: the head and shoulders, triple tops and bottoms, double tops and bottoms, spike (or V) tops and bottoms, and the rounding (or saucer) pattern. We will examine the price formation itself, how it is formed on the chart, and how it can be identified. We will then look at the other important considerations—the accompanying *volume pattern* and *measuring implications*.

Volume plays an important confirming role in all of these price patterns. In times of doubt (and there are lots of those), a study of the volume pattern accompanying the price data can be the deciding factor as to whether or not the pattern can be trusted.

Most price patterns also have certain *measuring techniques* that help the analyst to determine minimum price objectives. While these objectives are only an approximation of the size of the subsequent move, they are helpful in assisting the trader to determine his or her reward to risk ratio.

In the next chapter, we'll look at a second category of patterns—the continuation variety. There we will examine triangles, flags, pennants, wedges, and rectangles. These patterns usually reflect pauses in the existing trend rather than trend reversals, and are usually classified as intermediate and minor as opposed to major.

Preliminary Points
Common to All Reversal Patterns

Before beginning our discussion of the individual major reversal patterns, there are a few preliminary points to be considered that are common to all of these reversal patterns.

1. A prerequisite for any reversal pattern is the existence of a prior trend.
2. The first signal of an impending trend reversal is often the breaking of an important trendline.
3. The larger the pattern, the greater the subsequent move.
4. Topping patterns are usually shorter in duration and more volatile than bottoms.
5. Bottoms usually have smaller price ranges and take longer to build.
6. Volume is usually more important on the upside.

The Need for a Prior Trend. The existence of a prior major trend is an important prerequisite for any reversal pattern. A market must obviously have something to reverse. A formation occasionally appears on the charts, resembling one of the reversal patterns. If that pattern, however, has not been preceded by a trend, there is nothing to reverse and the pattern is suspect. Knowing where certain patterns are most apt to occur in the trend structure is one of the key elements in pattern recognition.

A corollary to this point of having a prior trend to reverse is the matter of measuring implications. It was stated earlier that most of the measuring techniques give only *minimum* price objectives. The *maximum* objective would be the total extent of the prior move. If a major bull market has occurred and a major topping pattern is being formed, the maximum implication for the potential move to the downside would be a 100% retracement of the bull market, or the point at which it all began.

The Breaking of Important Trendlines. The first sign of an impending trend reversal is often the breaking of an important trendline. Remember, however, that the violation of a major trendline does not necessarily signal a trend reversal. What is being signalled is a *change* in trend. The breaking of a major up trendline might signal the beginning of a sideways price pattern, which later would be identified as either the reversal or consolidation type. Sometimes the breaking of the major trendline coincides with the completion of the price pattern.

The Larger the Pattern, the Greater the Potential. When we use the term "larger," we are referring to the height and the width of the price pattern. The height measures the volatility of the pattern. The width is the amount of time required to build and complete the pattern. The greater the size of the pattern—that is, the wider the price swings within the pattern (the volatility) and the longer it takes to build— the more important the pattern becomes and the greater the potential for the ensuing price move.

Virtually all of the measuring techniques in these two chapters are based on the *height* of the pattern. This is the method applied primarily to bar charts, which use a *vertical* measuring criteria. The practice of measuring the *horizontal* width of a price pattern usually is reserved for point and figure charting. That method of charting uses a device known as the *count*, which assumes an almost one-to-one relationship between the width of a top or bottom and the subsequent price target.

Differences Between Tops and Bottoms. Topping patterns are usually shorter in duration and are more volatile than bottoms. Price swings within the tops are wider and more violent. Tops usually take less time to form. Bottoms usually have smaller price ranges, but take longer to build. For this reason it is usually easier and less costly to identify and trade bottoms than to catch market tops. One consoling factor, which makes the more treacherous topping patterns worthwhile, is that *prices tend to decline faster than they go up.* Therefore, the trader can usually make more money a lot faster by catching the short side of a bear market than by trading the long side of a bull market. Everything in life is a trade-off between reward and risk. The greater risks are compensated for by greater rewards and vice versa. Topping patterns are harder to catch, but are worth the effort.

Volume is More Important on the Upside. Volume should generally increase in the direction of the market trend and is an important confirming factor in the completion of all price patterns. The completion of each pattern should be accompanied by a noticeable increase in volume. However, in the early stages of a trend reversal, *volume is not as important at market tops.* Markets have a way of "falling of their own weight" once a bear move gets underway. Chartists like to see an increase in trading activity as prices drop, but it is not critical. At bottoms, however, the volume pick-up is absolutely essential. If the volume pattern does not show a significant increase during the upside price *breakout,* the entire price pattern should be questioned. We will be taking a more in-depth look at volume in Chapter 7.

THE HEAD AND SHOULDERS REVERSAL PATTERN

Let's take a close look now at what is probably the best known and most reliable of all major reversal patterns—*the head and shoulders reversal.* We'll spend more time on this pattern because it is important and also to explain all the nuances involved. Most of the other reversal patterns are just variations of the head and shoulders and will not require as extensive a treatment.

This major reversal pattern, like all of the others, is just a further refinement of the concepts of trend covered in the previous chapter. Picture a situation in a major uptrend, where a series of ascending peaks and troughs gradually begin to lose momentum. The uptrend then levels off for awhile. During this time the forces of supply and demand are in relative balance. Once this distribution phase has been completed, support levels along the bottom of the horizontal trading range are broken and a new downtrend has been established. That new downtrend now has descending peaks and troughs.

Let's see how this scenario would look on a *head and shoulders top.* (See Figures 5.1a and b.) At point A, the uptrend is proceeding as expected with no signs of a top. Volume expands on the price move into new highs, which is normal. The corrective dip to point B is on lighter volume, which is also to be expected. At point C, however, the alert chartist might notice that the volume on the upside breakout through point A is a bit lighter than on the previous rally. This change is not in itself of major importance, but a little yellow caution light goes on in the back of the analyst's head.

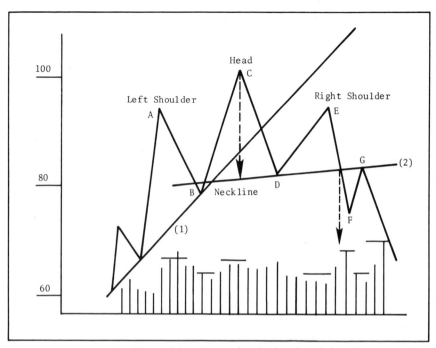

Figure 5.1a Example of a head and shoulders top. The left and right shoulders (A and E) are at about the same height. The head (C) is higher than either shoulder. Notice the lighter volume on each peak. The pattern is completed on a close under the neckline (line 2). The minimum objective is the vertical distance from the head to the neckline projected downward from the breaking of the neckline. A return move will often occur back to the neckline, which should not recross the neckline once it has been broken.

Prices then begin to decline to point D and something even more disturbing happens. The decline carries below the top of the previous peak at point A. Remember that, in an uptrend, a penetrated peak should function as support on subsequent corrections. The decline well under point A, almost to the previous reaction low at point B, is another warning that something may be going wrong with the uptrend.

The market rallies again to point E, this time on even lighter volume, and isn't able to reach the top of the previous peak at point C. (That last rally at point E will often retrace a half to two-thirds of the decline from points C to D.) To continue an uptrend, each high point must exceed the high point of the rally preceding it. The failure of the rally at point E to reach the previous peak at point C fulfills half of the requirement for a new downtrend—namely, descending peaks.

By this time, the major up trendline (line 1) has already been broken, usually at point D, constituting another danger signal. But, despite all of these warnings, all that we know at this point is that the trend has shifted from up to sideways. This might be sufficient cause to liquidate long positions, but not necessarily enough to justify new short sales.

The Breaking of
the Neckline Completes the Pattern

By this time, a flatter trendline can be drawn under the last two reaction lows (points B and D), which is called a *neckline* (see line

Figure 5.1b A head and shoulders top. Notice the three peaks with the head higher than either shoulder. See how the major up trendline was broken before the right shoulder formed. Note the return move back to the neckline after the downside reversal is given. The distance from the head to the neckline projected downward from the point where the neckline was broken gives the minimum price target. (Chart courtesy of Commodity Research Bureau, a Knight-Ridder Business Information Service.)

2). This line generally has a slight upward slope at tops (although it's sometimes horizontal and, less often, tilts downward). *The deciding factor in the resolution of the head and shoulders top is a decisive closing violation of that neckline.* The market has now violated the trendline along the bottom of points B and D, has broken under support at point D, and has completed the requirement for a new downtrend—descending peaks and troughs. The new downtrend is now identified by the declining highs and lows at points C, D, E, and F. Volume should increase on the breaking of the neckline. A sharp increase in downside volume, however, is not critically important in the initial stages of a market top.

The Return Move

Usually a *return move* develops which is a bounce back to the bottom of the neckline or to the previous reaction low at point D (see point G), both of which have now become overhead resistance. The return move does not always occur or is sometimes only a very minor bounce. Volume may help determine the size of the bounce. If the initial breaking of the neckline is on very heavy trading, the odds for a return move are diminished because the increased activity reflects greater downside pressure. Lighter volume on the initial break of the neckline increases the likelihood of a return move. That bounce, however, should be on light volume and the subsequent resumption of the new downtrend should be accompanied by noticeably heavier trading activity.

Summary

Let's review the basic ingredients for a head and shoulders top.

1. A prior uptrend.

2. A left shoulder on heavier volume (point A) followed by a corrective dip to point B.

3. A rally into new highs but on lighter volume (point C).

4. A decline that moves below the previous peak (at A) and approaches the previous reaction low (point D).

5. A third rally (point E) on noticeably light volume that fails to reach the top of the head (at point C).

6. A close below the neckline.

7. A return move back to the neckline (point G) followed by new lows.

What has become evident is three well-defined peaks. The middle peak (the head) is slighter higher than either of the two shoulders (points A and E). The pattern, however, is not complete until the neckline is decisively broken on a closing basis. Here again, the 3% penetration criterion (or some variation thereof) or the requirement of two successive closes below the neckline (the two-day rule) can be used for added confirmation. Until that downside violation takes place, however, there is always the possibility that the pattern is not really a head and shoulders top and that the uptrend may resume at some point.

THE IMPORTANCE OF VOLUME

The accompanying volume pattern plays an important role in the development of the head and shoulders top as it does in all price patterns. As a general rule, the second peak (the head) should take place on lighter volume than the left shoulder. This is not a requirement, but a strong tendency and an early warning of diminishing buying pressure. The most important volume signal takes place during the third peak (the right shoulder). Volume should be noticeably lighter than on the previous two peaks. Volume should then expand on the breaking of the neckline, decline during the return move, and then expand again once the return move is over.

As mentioned earlier, volume is less critical during the completion of market tops. But, at some point, volume should begin to increase if the new downtrend is to be continued. Volume plays a much more decisive role at market bottoms, a subject to be discussed shortly. Before doing so, however, let's discuss the measuring implications of the head and shoulders pattern.

FINDING A PRICE OBJECTIVE

The method of arriving at a price objective is based on the *height* of the pattern. Take the vertical distance from the head (point C) to the neckline. Then project that distance from the point where the neckline is broken. Assume, for example, that the top of the head is at 100 and the neckline is at 80. The vertical distance, therefore, would be the difference, which is 20. That 20 points would be measured downward from the level at which the neckline is broken. If the neckline in Figure 5.1a is at 82 when broken, a downside objective would be projected to the 62 level $(82 - 20 = 62)$.

Another technique that accomplishes about the same task, but is a bit easier, is to simply measure the length of the first wave of the decline (points C to D) and then double it. In either case, the greater the height or volatility of the pattern, the greater the objective. Chapter 4 stated that the measurement taken from a trendline penetration was similar to that used in the head and shoulders pattern. You should be able to see that now. Prices travel roughly the same distance below the broken neckline as they do above it. You'll see throughout our entire study of price patterns that *most price targets on bar charts are based on the height or volatility of the various patterns*. The theme of measuring the height of the pattern and then projecting that distance from a breakout point will be constantly repeated.

It's important to remember that the objective arrived at is only a minimum target. Prices will often move well beyond the objective. Having a minimum target to work with, however, is very helpful in determining beforehand whether there is enough potential in a market move to warrant taking a position. If the market exceeds the price objective, that's just icing on the cake. The *maximum* objective is the size of the prior move. If the previous bull market went from 30 to 100, then the maximum downside objective from a topping pattern would be a complete retracement of the entire upmove all the way down to 30. Reversal patterns can only be expected to reverse or retrace what has gone before them.

Adjusting Price Objectives

A number of other factors should be considered while trying to arrive at a price objective. The measuring techniques from price patterns, such as the one just mentioned for the head and shoulders top, are only the first step. There are other technical factors to take into consideration. For example, where are the prominent support levels left by the reaction lows during the previous bull move? Bear markets often pause at these levels. What about percentage retracements? The maximum objective would be a 100% retracement of the previous bull market. But where are the 50% and 66% retracement levels? Those levels often provide significant support under the market. What about any prominent gaps underneath? They often function as support areas. Are there any long-term trendlines visible below the market?

The technician must consider other technical data in trying to pinpoint price targets taken from price patterns. If a downside price measurement, for example, projects a target to 30, and there is a prominent support level at 32, then the chartist would be wise to adjust the downside measurement to 32 instead of 30. As a general rule, when a slight discrepancy exists between a projected price target and a clearcut support or resistance level, it's usually safe to adjust the price target to that support or resistance level. It is often necessary to adjust the measured targets from price patterns to take into account additional technical information. The analyst has many different tools at his or her disposal. The most skillful technical analysts are those who learn to blend all of those tools together properly.

THE INVERSE HEAD AND SHOULDERS

The head and shoulders bottom, or the *inverse head and shoulders* as it is sometimes called, is pretty much a mirror image of the topping pattern. As Figure 5.2a shows, there are three distinct bottoms with the head (middle trough) a bit lower than either of the two shoulders. A decisive close through the neckline is also necessary to complete the pattern, and the measuring technique is the same. One slight difference at the bottom is the greater tendency for the return move back to the neckline to occur after the bullish breakout.

The most important difference between the top and bottom pattern is the volume sequence. Volume plays a much more critical role in the identification and completion of a head and shoulders bottom. This point is generally true of all bottom patterns. It was stated earlier that markets have a tendency to "fall of their own weight." At bottoms, however, markets require a significant increase in buying pressure, reflected in greater volume, to launch a new bull market.

Think of this difference as the market versus the law of gravity. We all know that an object falls to the floor very quickly with no further effort on our part if we just let go of it. Lifting something is a different matter and does require effort on our part. For those more athletically inclined, think of the effort required to run a race where there are hills on the course. Running on hills is easy as long as you're going downhill. It's the uphill portion that'll test your endurance. If "heartbreak hill" near the end of the Boston Marathon were downhill instead of uphill, it would probably be known as "happiness hill" or something like that.

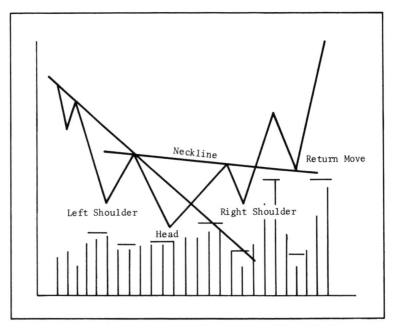

Figure 5.2a Example of an inverse head and shoulders. The bottom version of this pattern is a mirror image of the top. The only significant difference is the volume pattern in the second half of the pattern. The rally from the head should see heavier volume and the breaking of the neckline should see a burst of trading activity. The return move back to the neckline is more common at bottoms.

    A more technical way of looking at this difference is that a market can fall just from inertia. Lack of demand or buying interest on the part of traders is often enough to push a market lower; but a market does not go up on inertia. Prices only rise when demand exceeds supply and buyers are more aggressive than sellers.

    The volume pattern at the bottom is very similar to that at the top for the first half of the pattern. That is, the volume at the head is a bit lighter than that at the left shoulder. The rally from the head, however, should begin to show not only an increase in trading activity, but the level of volume often exceeds that registered on the rally from the left shoulder. The dip to the right shoulder should be on very light volume. The critical point occurs at the rally through the neckline. This signal must be accompanied by a sharp burst of trading volume if the breakout is for real.

    This point is where the bottom differs the most from the top. At the bottom, heavy volume is an absolutely essential ingredient in the completion of the basing pattern. The return move is more common at bottoms than at tops and should occur on light volume. Following that, the new uptrend should resume on heavier volume. The measuring technique is the same as at the top.

The Slope of the Neckline

The neckline at the top usually slopes slightly upward. Sometimes, however, it is horizontal. In either case, it doesn't make too much of a difference. Once in a while, however, a top neckline slopes downward. This slope is a sign of market weakness and is usually accompanied by an weak right shoulder. However, this is a mixed blessing.

Figure 5.2b Example of a *head and shoulders* bottom. The *left shoulder* was formed in October and the *right shoulder* in May. The *head*, which was formed in February and March, looks like a *V-reversal* botttom. The CRB Currency Futures Index closed above the 8-month *neckline* in July, giving a major bullish signal for foreign currency markets. (Chart courtesy of Commodity Research Bureau, a Knight-Ridder Business Information Service.)

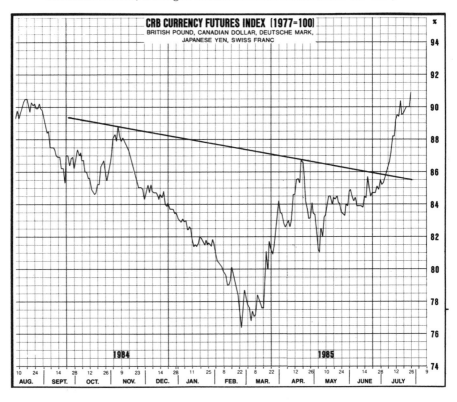

The analyst waiting for the breaking of the neckline to initiate a short position has to wait a bit longer, because the signal from the down-sloping neckline occurs much later and only after much of the move has already taken place. For basing patterns, most necklines have a slight downward tilt. A rising neckline is a sign of greater market strength, but with the same drawback of giving a later signal.

COMPLEX HEAD AND SHOULDERS PATTERNS

A variation of the head and shoulders pattern sometimes occurs which is called the *complex head and shoulders pattern*. These are patterns where two heads may appear or a double left and right shoulder. These patterns are not that common, but have the same forecasting implications. A helpful hint in this regard is the strong tendency toward symmetry in the head and shoulders pattern. This means that a single left shoulder usually indicates a single right shoulder. A double left shoulder increases the odds of a double right shoulder.

TACTICS

The question of market tactics plays an important role in all futures trading and is treated in more detail in later chapters. Not all technical traders like to wait for the breaking of the neckline before initiating a new position. As Figure 5.3 shows, more aggressive traders, believing that they have correctly identified a head and shoulders bottom, will begin to probe the long side during the formation of the right shoulder. Or they will buy the first technical signal that the decline into the right shoulder has ended.

Some will measure the distance of the rally from the bottom of the head (points C to D) and then buy a 50% or 66% retracement of that rally. Others will look to see if a support gap exists below the market and use that as a buying point. Still others would draw a tight down trendline along the decline from points D to E and buy the first upside break of that trendline. Because these patterns are reasonably symmetrical, some will buy into the right shoulder as it approaches the same level as the bottom of the left shoulder. The point being demonstrated is that a lot of anticipatory buying takes place during the formation of the right shoulder. If the initial long probe proves to be profitable, additional positions can be added on the actual penetration of the neckline or on the return move back to the neckline after the breakout.

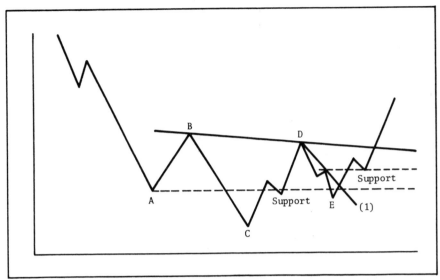

Figure 5.3 Tactics for a head and shoulders bottom. Many technical traders will begin to initiate long positions while the right shoulder (E) is still being formed. A half to two-thirds pullback of the rally from points C to D, a dip into a near-term support level or a support gap, a decline to the same level as the left shoulder at point A, or the breaking of a short-term down trendline (line 1) all provide early opportunities for market entry. More positions can be added on the breaking of the neckline or the return move back to the neckline.

THE FAILED
HEAD AND SHOULDERS PATTERN

Once prices have moved through the neckline and completed a head and shoulders pattern, *prices should not recross the neckline again.* At a top, once the neckline has been broken on the downside, any subsequent close back above the neckline is a serious warning that the initial breakdown was probably a bad signal, and creates what is often called, for obvious reasons, a *failed head and shoulders.* This type of pattern starts out looking like a classic head and shoulders reversal, but at some point in its development (either prior to the breaking of the neckline or just after it), prices resume their original trend.

There are two important lessons here. The first is that none of these chart patterns are infallible. They work most of the time, but not always. The second lesson is that technical traders must always be on the alert for chart signs that their analysis is incorrect. One of the keys to survival in the futures markets (which is covered in Chapter 16 on money management and tactics) is to keep one's trading losses small and to exit a losing trade as quickly as possible. This might be an appropriate place to add that one of the greatest advantages of chart analysis is its ability to quickly alert the trader to the fact that he or she is on the wrong side of the market. The ability and willingness to quickly recognize and admit one's trading errors and to take defensive action immediately are qualities not to be taken lightly in the futures markets.

THE HEAD AND SHOULDERS AS A CONSOLIDATION PATTERN

Before moving on to the next price pattern, there's one final point to be made on the head and shoulders. We started this discussion by listing it as the best known and most reliable of the major reversal patterns. You should be warned, however, that this formation can, on occasion, act as a consolidation rather than a reversal pattern. When this does happen, it's the exception rather than the rule. We'll talk more about this in Chapter 6 on continuation patterns.

TRIPLE TOPS AND BOTTOMS

Most of the points covered in the treatment of the head and shoulders pattern are also applicable to other types of reversal patterns. (See Figures 5.4a through c.) The *triple top or bottom*, which is much rarer in occurrence, is just a slight variation of that pattern. The main difference is that the three peaks or troughs in the *triple top or bottom* are at about the same level. (See Figure 5.4a.) Chartists often disagree as to whether a reversal pattern is a head and shoulders or a triple top. The argument is academic, because both patterns imply the exact same thing.

The volume tends to decline with each successive peak at the top and should increase at the breakdown point. The triple top is not complete until support levels along both of the intervening lows have

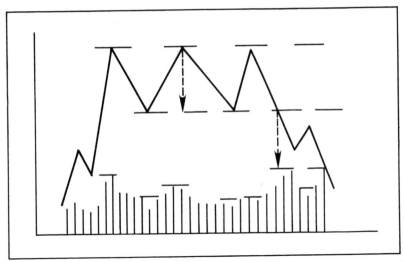

Figure 5.4a A triple top. Similar to the head and shoulders except that all peaks are at the same level. Each rally peak should be on lighter volume. The pattern is complete when both troughs have been broken on heavier volume. The measuring technique is the height of the pattern projected downward from the breakdown point. Return moves back to the lower line are not unusual.

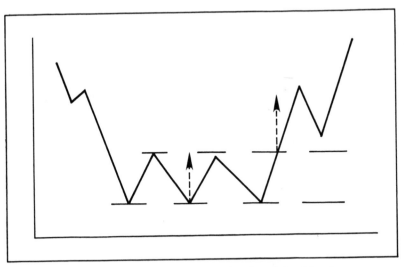

Figure 5.4b A triple bottom. Similar to a head and shoulders bottom except that each low is at the same level. A mirror image of the triple top except that volume is more important on the upside breakout.

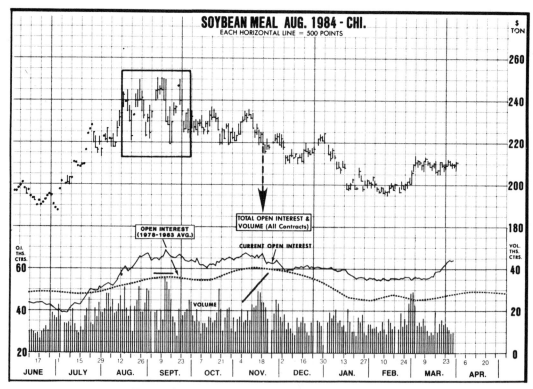

Figure 5.4c A triple top reversal. Notice the three peaks formed at 250 during August and September. Notice how the support area around 220 became resistance once it was broken on the downside. Notice also how close prices came to the downside target. If you look closely, you'll see heavier downside volume during the topping pattern and noticeably heavier trading activity during the downside breakout in November. (Courtesy of Commodity Research Bureau, a Knight-Ridder Business Information Service.)

been broken. Conversely, prices must close through the two inter-vening peaks at the bottom to complete a triple bottom. (As an alternate strategy, the breaking of the nearest peak or trough can also be used as a reversal signal.) Heavy upside volume on the completion of the bottom is also essential.

The measuring implication is also similar to the head and shoulders, and is based on the height of the pattern. Prices will usually move a minimum distance from the breakout point at least equal to the height of the pattern. Once the breakout occurs, a return move to the breakout point is not unusual. Because the triple top or bottom represents only a minor variation of the head and shoulders pattern, we won't say much more about it here.

DOUBLE TOPS AND BOTTOMS

A much more common reversal pattern is the *double top or bottom.* Next to the *head and shoulders,* it is the most frequently seen and the most easily recognized. (See Figures 5.5a through e.) Figures 5.5a and 5.5b show both the top and bottom variety. For obvious reasons, the top is often referred to as an "M" and the bottom as a "W." The general characteristics of a *double top* are similar to that of the head and shoulders and triple top except that only two peaks appear instead of three. The volume pattern is similar as is the measuring rule.

In an uptrend (as shown in Figure 5.5a), the market sets a new high at point A, usually on increased volume, and then declines to point B on declining volume. So far, everything is proceeding as expected in a normal uptrend. The next rally to point C, however, is unable to penetrate the previous peak at A on a closing basis and begins to fall back again. A potential *double top* has been set up. I use the word "potential" because, as is the case with all reversal patterns, the reversal is not complete until the previous support point at B is violated on a closing basis. Until that happens, prices could be in just a sideways consolidation phase, preparing for a resumption of the original uptrend.

Figure 5.5a Example of a double top. This pattern has two peaks (A and C) at about the same level. The pattern is complete when the middle trough at point B is broken on a closing basis. Volume is usually lighter on the second peak (C) and picks up on the breakdown (D). A return move back to the lower line is not unusual. The minimum measuring target is the height of the top projected downward from the breakdown point.

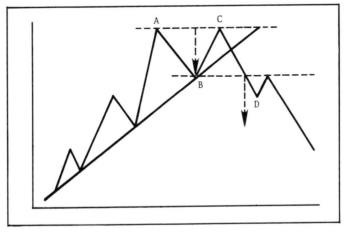

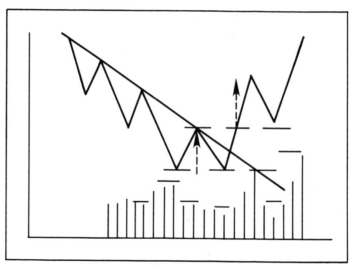

Figure 5.5b Example of a double bottom. A mirror image of the double top. Volume is more important on the upside breakout. Return moves back to the breakout point are more common at bottoms.

Figure 5.5c Example of a double bottom. Notice the clear double bottom near 5800 formed during May through June. The close above 6116 completed the bottom and turned the trend higher. Notice at the top right that prices have backed away from the previous peak at 72. That type of action is not unusual in an uptrend. A close below the low point at 6916 is needed, however, to complete a double top. (Chart courtesy of Commodity Research Bureau, a Knight-Ridder Business Information Service.)

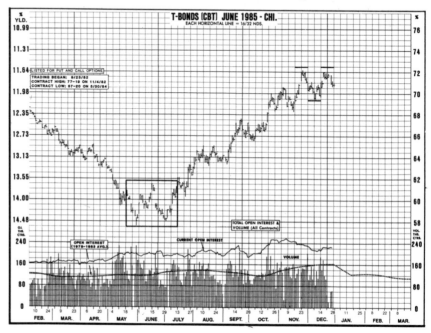

The ideal top has two prominent peaks at about the same price level. Volume tends to be heavier during the first peak and lighter on the second. A decisive close under the middle trough at point B on heavier volume completes the pattern and signals a reversal of trend to the downside. A return move to the breakout point is not unusual prior to resumption of the downtrend.

Measuring Technique for the Double Top

The measuring technique for the double top is the height of the pattern projected from the breakdown point (the point where the middle trough at point B is broken). As an alternative, measure the height of the first downleg (points A to B) and project that length downward from the middle trough at point B. Measurements at the bottom are the same, but in the other direction.

Figure 5.5d Examples of a double top and bottom. Note the classic double top just above 30 during May and June. The two bottoms in July and September might also qualify as a double bottom. (Chart courtesy of Commodity Research Bureau, a Knight-Ridder Business Information Service.)

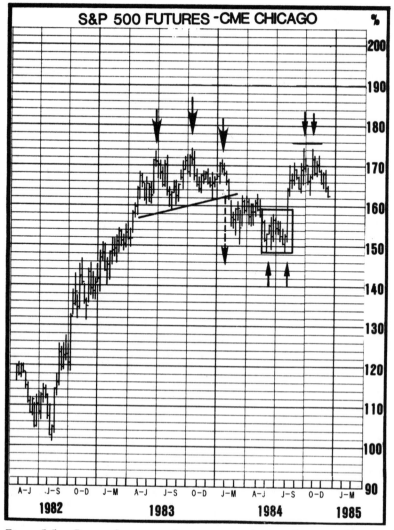

Figure 5.5e Reversal patterns show up quite frequently on weekly continuation charts. Note the head and shoulders top during the second half of 1983. See how well the downside target worked. Notice the smaller double bottom near 150 and the potential double top near 174. One possible view of this chart is that the late 1984 high could be the second peak in a major double top. A close under 148, however, would be needed to justify that bearish interpretation. It's not unusual for prices to back off from important resistance. (Chart courtesy of Commodity Research Bureau, a Knight-Ridder Business Information Service.)

VARIATIONS FROM THE IDEAL PATTERN

As in most other areas of market analysis, real-life examples are usually some variation of the ideal. For one thing, sometimes the two peaks are not at exactly the same price level. On occasion, the second peak will not quite reach the level of the first peak, which is not too problematical. What does cause some problems is when the second peak actually exceeds the first peak by a slight margin. What at first may appear to be a valid upside breakout and resumption of the uptrend may turn out to be part of the topping process. To help resolve this dilemma, some of the filtering criteria already mentioned may come in handy.

Filters

Most chartists require a close beyond a previous resistance peak instead of just an intra-day penetration. Second, a price filter of some type might be used. One such example is a percentage penetration criterion (such as 1% or 3%). Third, the two-day penetration rule could be used as an example of a time filter. In other words, prices would have to close beyond the top of the first peak for two consecutive days to signal a valid penetration.

Figure 5.6a Example of a false breakout, usually called a "bull trap." Sometimes near the end of a major uptrend, prices will exceed a previous peak before failing. Chartists use various time and price filters to reduce such whipsaws. This topping pattern would probably qualify as a double top.

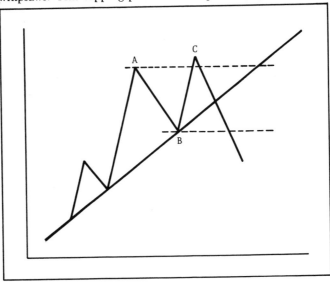

Figure 5.6b Example of a false breakout before failing. Notice at the top that prices cleared the previous peak, giving a bad signal. Prices then reversed direction, completing a variation of the double top. Note, however, that prices did not stay above the previous peak for two successive days. The use of the two-day time filter might have prevented a losing trade in this instance. (Chart courtesy of Commodity Research Bureau, a Knight-Ridder Business Information Service.)

These filters are certainly not infallible, but do serve to reduce the number of false signals (or whipsaws) that often occur. Sometimes these filters are helpful, and sometimes they're not. The analyst must face the realization that he or she is dealing with percentages and probabilities, and that there will be times when bad signals occur. That's simply a fact of trading life.

It's not that unusual for the final leg or wave of a bull market to set a new high before reversing direction. In such a case, the final upside breakout would become a "bull trap." (See Figures 5.6a and b.) But it is comforting to know that most trend signals do follow through. Otherwise, the entire trend-following approach would lose much of its value and validity.

The Term "Double Top" Greatly Overused

The terms "double top and bottom" are greatly overused in the futures markets. Most potential double tops or bottoms wind up being something else. The reason for this is that prices have a strong tendency to back off from a previous peak or bounce off a previous low. These price changes are a natural reaction and do not in themselves constitute a reversal pattern. Remember that, at a top, prices must actually violate the previous reaction low before the double top exists.

Notice in Figure 5.7a that the price at point C backs off from the previous peak at point A. This is perfectly normal action in an uptrend. Many futures traders, however, will immediately identify this pattern as a double top as soon as prices fail to clear the first peak on the first attempt. Figure 5.7b shows the same situation in a downtrend. It is very difficult for the chartist to determine whether the pullback from the previous peak or the bounce from the previous low is just a temporary setback in the existing trend or the start of a double top or bottom reversal pattern. Because the technical odds usually favor continuation of the present trend, it is usually wise to await completion of the pattern before taking action.

Time Between Peaks or Troughs Is Important

Finally, the size of the pattern is always important. The longer the time period between the two peaks and the greater the height of the pattern, the greater the potential impending reversal. This is true of all chart patterns. In general, most valid double tops or bottoms should

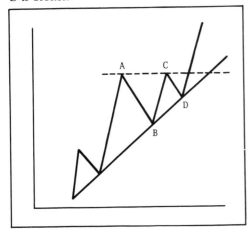

Figure 5.7a Example of a normal pullback from a previous peak before resumption of the uptrend. This is normal market action and not to be confused with a double top. The double top only occurs when support at point B is broken.

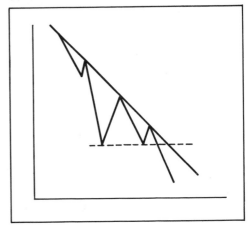

Figure 5.7b Example of a normal bounce off a previous low. This is normal market action and not to be confused with a double bottom. Prices will normally bounce off a previous low at least once, causing premature calls for a double bottom.

have at least a month between the two peaks or troughs. Some will even be two or three months apart. (On longer-range monthly and weekly charts, these patterns can span several years.) Most of the examples used in this discussion have described market tops. The reader should be aware by now that bottoming patterns are mirror images of tops except for some of the general differences already touched upon at the beginning of the chapter.

SAUCERS OR
ROUNDING TOPS AND BOTTOMS

The next reversal pattern is much less frequent than the ones already mentioned. It is called by various names—the *saucer*, the *rounding top or bottom*, or the *bowl*. The term "inverted" is usually used at market tops. This pattern represents a very slow and gradual change in trend. Figures 5.8a and b illustrate these chart patterns.

Notice the very gradual shift from up to down or from down to up. Note also the volume pattern along the bottom of each chart that tends to form a saucer of its own. At both tops and bottoms, volume diminishes as the market makes its gradual turn, and then gradually increases as the new direction begins to take hold.

Figure 5.8a Example of a saucer top. The uptrend gradually begins to lose upside momentum and begins to roll over into a new downtrend. Notice that the volume tends to form a saucer of its own. The topping pattern is also called an inverted saucer.

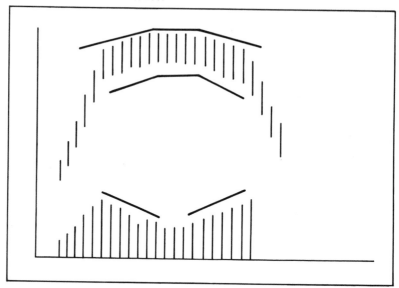

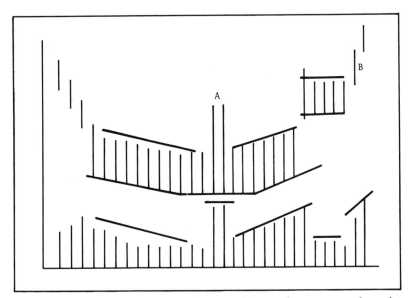

Figure 5.8b Example of a saucer bottom. Notice the saucer in the volume pattern. Sometimes a burst of activity will occur just beyond the midpoint of the bottom. A platform will often form to the right. Bottoms are more common than tops. The bottom is completed either on the break of the peak at point A or the upside breakout of the platform at point B.

Figure 5.8c This coffee chart shows an example of a saucer or rounding bottom. Notice the gradual change in trend from September to November. This type of market bottom is usually slow and dull. (Chart courtesy of Commodity Research Bureau, a Knight-Ridder Business Information Service.)

Sometimes just after the midpoint of the bottom (see Figure 5.8b), a sudden spurt in prices on uncharacteristically heavy volume occurs after which prices return to the slow rounding process. A *handle* or *platform* sometimes appears toward the end of the base, followed by resumption of the new uptrend. Notice the saucer bottom in the volume, the sudden increase in volume just after the midpoint, the gradual increase in activity as prices turn higher, the decline in volume during formation of the *platform*, and the heavier trading activity on the subsequent upside breakout.

It's hard to say exactly when a *saucer* has been completed. If the midpoint rally at point A took place, then an upside penetration of that rally might be considered a bullish signal. As a second possibility, the upside breakout from the platform could be used to signal completion of the base.

There are no precise measuring rules for the *saucer bottom*. However, the technician has at his or her disposal an arsenal of other technical tools to help measure the significance of the new trend. For example, the size of the prior trend is important, and gives the analyst some idea of how much price action must be retraced. The amount of time that the saucer pattern has been forming is also significant. The longer it takes to complete the rounding process, the greater the potential for the subsequent move. The technician also has other criteria to consider—such as previous support and resistance levels, percentage retracements, gaps, or long-term trendlines—to name a few.

As previously stated, saucers, or rounding patterns, are relatively infrequent. The reason the bottom pattern has been emphasized here is due to my own experience that, when these rare patterns do make their appearance, it's usually at market bottoms. I suspect that one of the reasons for the rarity of this type of pattern over the past decade has been due to the types of markets we've experienced. The 1970s were characterized by dramatic bull markets and the 1980s by bear markets. These are not the types of environment that breed saucer bottoms. Possibly, when commodity markets again stabilize and show signs of major bottoming formations, we'll see a recurrence of the saucer, or *rounding* bottom.

V FORMATIONS, OR SPIKES

The final reversal pattern that we will look at is the most difficult to identify at the time of its occurrence, but is not an uncommon pattern. In reality, the *V top or bottom* (or the *spike*) is so hard to identify because it is actually a nonpattern. All of the reversal patterns examined represent gradual changes in trend. The existing trend gradually slows to a point where the forces of supply and demand are in relative balance and a tug-of-war then develops between buyers and sellers to determine whether the old trend will be reversed or resumed.

Prices move sideways for a while during which time the analyst has time to study the market action and to look for clues to future direction. Prices are said to be in a transition phase. This is the way it is with most reversal patterns.

The V pattern, however, represents a radical departure from the tendency of markets to gradually change direction. What happens instead is an abrupt reversal of trend with little or no warning, followed by a sudden and swift move in the opposite direction. It is a nonpattern because no pattern actually exists except in hindsight. Most often these moves are marked by key reversal days or island reversals (covered in Chapter 4). How then does the trader anticipate such patterns, recognize (or at least suspect) when they are occurring, and take appropriate action? To answer these questions, let's look at the V top more closely. (See Figures 5.9a to c.)

Figure 5.9a Example of a V, or spike, top. This type of pattern usually occurs after a runaway bull trend where the market gets too overextended on the upside. The turnaround is usually accomplished by a key reversal day or island reversal. The market "turns on a dime" and abruptly reverses direction.

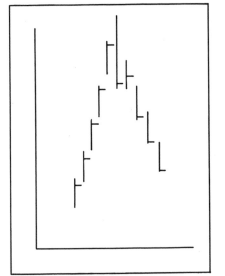

Figure 5.9b Example of a V, or spike, bottom. The downtrend quickly reverses to an uptrend with no warning or period of transition. This is probably the most difficult price pattern to spot and trade.

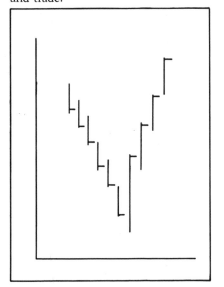

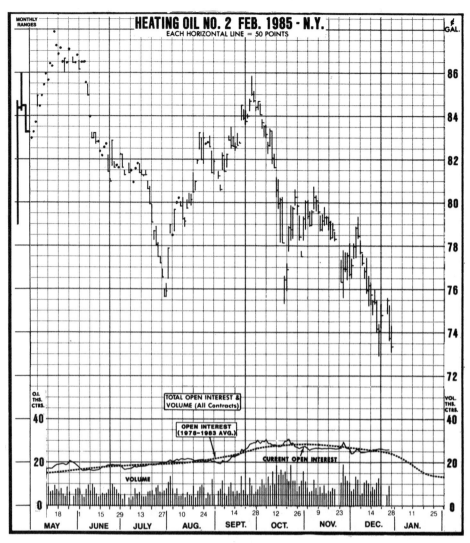

Figure 5.9c Example of V reversals. The heating oil market has a history of sudden reversals resembling Vs or spikes. The absence of transition periods makes for more difficult trading. Notice the number of key reversal days and island reversals. (Chart courtesy of Commodity Research Bureau, a Knight-Ridder Business Information Service.)

First of all, there is the prior trend. Most often, the trend preceding the V reversal is a runaway situation with few and generally minor corrections along the way. Usually, several gaps have been left behind. It is a situation where things appear to have gotten out of control, and a market that seems to have run well beyond most normal expectations. Most professional traders have learned to be wary of such situations.

Of course, as you can imagine, it is a trader's dream to be aboard for the ride in such a runaway market situation. But, at some point, even the most experienced trader starts to feel uneasy as the move continues. It's much like the analogy of "riding a tiger." It's one thing to catch the tiger and climb safely on its back. The trickier question becomes how or when to make your exit with your dignity and most of your skin still intact.

The reason for the concern is that runaway markets have a nasty habit of becoming so overextended in one direction that they will often snap back in the opposite direction like a rubber band that has been stretched too far. These snap-backs usually occur with little or no warning and are usually characterized by a series of limit moves in the opposite direction.

Preconditions for a V Reversal

The main precondition for a V or spike reversal is a steep or runaway trend. The actual turn is characterized by a *key reversal day* on very heavy volume or an *island reversal* pattern. Sometimes the only valid trend signal that accompanies such a reversal is the breaking of a very steep up trendline. Moving averages aren't that useful in this situation because of their natural tendency to lag behind the runaway price action.

The subsequent decline usually retraces a significant portion of the prior uptrend (as much as a third to 50%) in a very short period of time. One of the reasons for the sudden move in the opposite direction is the absence of support and resistance levels during the prior trend and the presence of "air" left behind by the large number of gaps.

The decline is further fueled by those who have been trapped near the top of the market who are now scrambling to liquidate losing positions. An unusually high open interest figure is another danger signal, particularly if a significant amount of the increase took place during the latter stages of the prior advance. (We'll talk more about open interest in Chapter 7.)

The dilemma facing the trader is how long to stay with a strongly trending market. He or she can always "let profits run" by the use of trailing protective stops. This is one common way of letting profits accumulate while protecting against a sudden adverse trend reversal.

The problem with runaway situations and the sudden V reversals that often terminate such trends is that limit moves in the opposite direction make it unusually difficult to exit the market, even with open stops on the books. If the trader tries to anticipate such tops by taking profits, the usual result is to exit the profitable trade too early. But, then again, no one ever said getting rich would be easy. We've been referring here mainly to market tops as opposed to bottoms. While this type of pattern occurs in both situations, the most dramatic examples take place at tops.

Extended V Reversal Patterns

A variation of the V reversal pattern is the *extended V*. This pattern is basically the same as the V pattern except that a small platform forms shortly after the market turns. The platform usually forms on the right-hand side of the chart as shown in Figure 5.10a. The platform slopes slightly against the new trend much like the flag pattern (covered in Chapter 6).

Figure 5.10a Example of an extended V top. A small platform forms just after the market turn and usually slopes slightly against the new downtrend. The breakdown from the platform completes the trend reversal. A bottom reversal looks the same, but turned upside down.

Figure 5.10b Example of a left-handed extended V top. This type of pattern, which is fairly rare, is similar to the normal extended V except that the platform precedes the market turn.

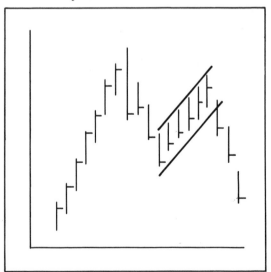

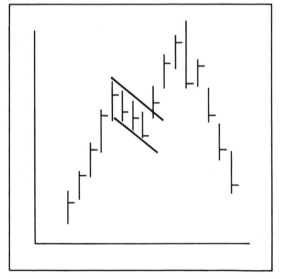

At a top, the platform slopes upward and at a bottom will tend to slope downward. The platform also takes place on declining volume, which then picks up once the new trend resumes. The pattern is considered to be complete once the platform has been cleared. The *extended* V reversal pattern is rarer than the true V pattern, but does provide the chartist with a greater opportunity to take action, either to exit an old position or initiate a new position in the direction of the new trend.

The Left-Handed Extended V

An even rarer variety of the extended V occurs when the platform falls on the left-hand side of the chart pattern, prior to the market turn (see Figure 5.10b). While this pattern is not of much use to the trader after the market turns, it does provide a reference point on the chart at a previous reaction low which, when violated, completes the topping reversal pattern. That previous reaction low may also provide some temporary support under the market which can slow the decline and give the trader more time to react.

CONCLUSION

We've discussed the five most commonly used major reversal patterns—the head and shoulders, double and triple tops and bottoms, the saucer, and the V, or spike. Of those, the most common are the head and shoulders, double tops and bottoms, and the V reversal. These patterns usually signal important trend reversals in progress and are classified as major reversal patterns. There is another class of patterns, however, which are shorter-term in nature and usually suggest trend consolidations rather than reversals. They are aptly called *continuation* patterns. Let's look at this other type of pattern in the next chapter.

6

Continuation Patterns

INTRODUCTION

The chart patterns covered in this chapter are called *continuation* patterns. These patterns usually indicate that the sideways price action on the chart is nothing more than a pause in the prevailing trend, and that the next move will be in the same direction as the trend that preceded the formation. This distinguishes this group of patterns from those in the previous chapter, which usually indicate that a major trend reversal is in progress.

Another difference between reversal and continuation patterns is their time duration. Reversal patterns usually take much longer to build and represent major trend changes. Continuation patterns, on the other hand, are usually shorter-term in duration and are more accurately classified as near-term or intermediate patterns.

Notice the constant use of the term "usually." The treatment of all chart patterns deals of necessity with general tendencies as opposed to rigid rules. There are always exceptions. Even the grouping of price patterns into different categories sometimes becomes tenuous. Triangles are usually continuation patterns, but sometimes act as reversal patterns. Although triangles are usually considered intermediate patterns, they may occasionally appear on long-term charts and take on major trend significance. A variation of the triangle—the inverted variety—usually signals a major market top. Even the head and shoulders pattern, the best known of the major reversal patterns, will on occasion be seen as a consolidation pattern.

Even with allowances for a certain amount of ambiguity and the occasional exception, chart patterns do generally fall into the above two categories and, if properly interpreted, can help the chartist determine what the market will probably do most of the time.

TRIANGLES

Let's begin our treatment of continuation patterns with the triangle. There are three types of triangles—*symmetrical, ascending,* and *descending.* (Some chartists include a fourth type of triangle known as an *expanding triangle,* or *broadening formation.* This is treated as a separate pattern later.) Each type of triangle has a slightly different shape and has different forecasting implications.

Figures 6.1a to c show examples of what each triangle looks like. The symmetrical triangle (see Figure 6.1a) shows two converging trendlines, the upper line descending and the lower line ascending.

Figure 6.1a Example of a bullish symmetrical triangle. Notice the two converging trendlines. A close outside either trendline completes the pattern. The vertical line at the left is the base. The point at the right where the two lines meet is the apex.

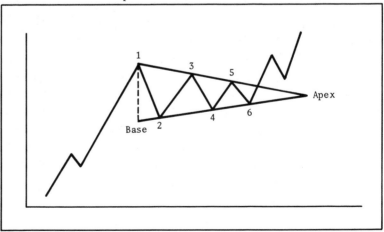

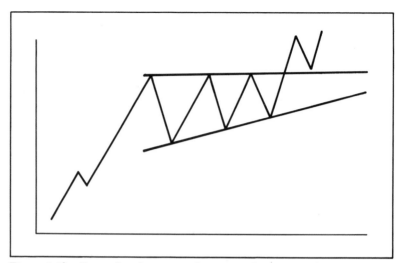

Figure 6.1b Example of an ascending triangle. Notice the flat upper line and the rising lower line. This is generally a bullish pattern.

The vertical line at the left, measuring the height of the pattern, is called the *base*. The point of intersection at the right, where the two lines meet, is called the *apex*. For obvious reasons, the symmetrical triangle is also called a *coil*.

The ascending triangle has a rising lower line with a flat or horizontal upper line (see Figure 6.1b). The descending triangle (Figure 6.1c), by contrast, has the upper line declining with a flat or horizontal bottom line. Let's see how each one is interpreted.

Figure 6.1c Example of a descending triangle. Notice the flat bottom line and the declining upper line. This is usually a bearish pattern.

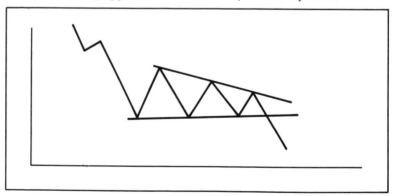

THE SYMMETRICAL TRIANGLE

The *symmetrical triangle* (or the *coil*) is usually a continuation pattern. It represents a pause in the existing trend after which the original trend is resumed. In the example in Figure 6.1a, the prior trend was up, so that the percentages favor resolution of the triangular consolidation on the upside. If the trend had been down, then the symmetrical triangle would have bearish implications.

The minimum requirement for a triangle is four reversal points. Remember that it always takes two points to draw a trendline. Therefore, in order to draw two converging trendlines, each line must be touched at least twice. In Figure 6.1a, the triangle actually begins at point 1, which is where the consolidation in the uptrend begins. Prices pull back to point 2 and then rally to point 3. Point 3, however, is lower than point 1. The upper trendline can only be drawn once prices have declined from point 3.

Notice that point 4 is higher than point 2. Only when prices have rallied from point 4 can the lower upslanting line be drawn. It is at this point that the analyst begins to suspect the he or she is dealing with the symmetrical triangle. Now there are four reversal points (1, 2, 3, and 4) and two converging trendlines.

While the minimum requirement is four reversal points, in reality most triangles usually have six reversal points as shown in Figure 6.1a. This means that there are actually three peaks and three troughs that combine to form five waves within the triangle before the uptrend resumes. (When we get to the Elliott Wave Theory, we'll have more to say about the five-wave tendency within triangles.)

Time Limit for Triangle Resolution

There is a time limit for the resolution of the pattern, and that is the point where the two lines meet—at the apex. As a general rule, prices should break out in the direction of the prior trend somewhere between the one-half to three-quarters point of the horizontal width of the triangle. That is, the distance from the vertical base on the left of the pattern to the apex at the far right. Because the two lines must meet at some point, that time distance can be measured once the two converging lines are drawn. An upside breakout is signalled by a penetration of the upper trendline. If prices remain within the triangle beyond the three-quarters point, the triangle begins to lose its potency, and usually means that prices will continue to drift out to the apex and beyond.

The triangle, therefore, provides an interesting combination of price and time. The converging trendlines give the price boundaries of the pattern, and indicate at what point the pattern has been completed and the trend resumed by the penetration of the upper trendline (in the case of an uptrend). But these trendlines also provide a time target by measuring the width of the pattern. If the width, for example, were twenty weeks long, then the breakout should take place sometime between the tenth and the fifteenth week.

The actual trend signal is given by a closing penetration of one of the trendlines. Sometimes a *return move* will occur back to the penetrated trendline after the breakout. In an uptrend, that line has become a support line. In a downtrend, the lower line becomes a resistance line once it's broken. The apex also acts as an important support or resistance level after the breakout occurs. Various penetration criteria can be applied to the breakout, similar to those covered in the previous two chapters. A minimum penetration criterion would be a closing price outside the trendline and not just an intra-day penetration.

The Occasional False Signal

For some strange reason, bullish triangles sometimes flash a false bear signal just prior to resuming an uptrend. This signal usually occurs during the fifth and last leg of the triangle. This phenomenon often occurs very close to the apex, which means that the trend has progressed too far to the right. It is characterized by a two- or three-day break to the downside on heavy volume after which prices will then just as sharply turn higher and resume the uptrend.

Importance of Volume

Volume should diminish as the price swings narrow within the triangle. This tendency for volume to contract is true of all consolidation patterns. But the volume should pick up noticeably at the penetration of the trendline that completes the pattern. The return move should be on light volume with heavier activity again as the trend resumes.

Two other points should be mentioned about volume. As is the case with reversal patterns, volume is more important on the upside than on the downside. An increase in volume is essential to the resumption of an uptrend in all consolidation patterns. It is also important on the downside, but not so in the first couple of days. In fact, a big jump in volume on the downside breakout, especially if prices have moved close to the apex, is one warning signal of the false bear signal referred to earlier.

The second point about volume is that, even though trading activity diminishes during formation of the pattern, a close inspection of the volume usually gives a clue as to whether the heavier volume is occurring during the upmoves or downmoves. In an uptrend, for example, there should be a slight tendency for volume to be heavier during the bounces and lighter on the price dips.

Measuring Technique

Triangles have measuring techniques. In the case of the symmetrical triangle, there are a couple of techniques generally used. The simplest technique is to measure the height of the vertical line at the widest part of the triangle (the base) and measure that distance from either the breakout point or the apex. Figure 6.2a shows the distance projected from the breakout point, which is the technique I prefer.

Figure 6.2a There are two ways to take a measurement from a symmetrical triangle. One is to measure the height of the base (AB); project that vertical distance from the breakout point at C or the apex. Another method is to draw a parallel line upward from the top of the baseline (A) parallel to the lower line in the triangle.

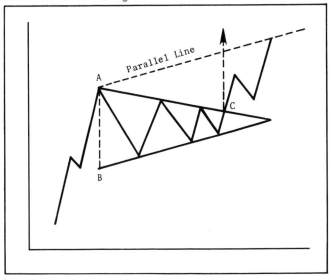

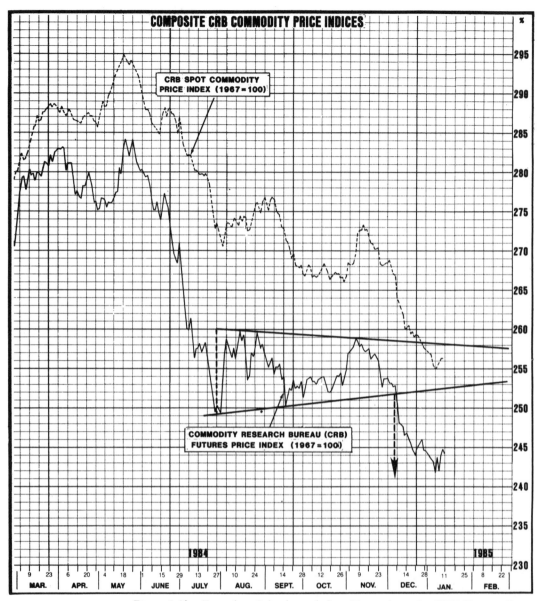

Figure 6.2b From late July through late November, the CRB Futures Price Index (lower line) formed a bearish symmetrical triangle. If you measure the height of the triangle and project it downward, you'll see that the downside target to 242 has been fulfilled. (Courtesy of Commodity Research Bureau, a Knight-Ridder Business Information Service.)

The second method is to draw a trendline from the top of the base (at point A) parallel to the lower trendline. This upper channel line then becomes the upside target in an uptrend. Because there is

Continuation Patterns

also a tendency for the new upleg to roughly approximate the slope or angle of the previous upleg (before the triangle formed), it is also possible to arrive at a rough time target for prices to meet the upper channel line as well as a price target.

Figure 6.2c An example of a symmetrical triangle that acted as a reversal pattern. The breaking of the lower line in October 1983 gave a major bear signal. Notice to the far right another smaller symmetrical triangle between 7.00 and 8.00. The second triangle was a bearish continuation pattern. (Courtesy of Commodity Research Bureau, a Knight-Ridder Business Information Service.)

THE ASCENDING TRIANGLE

The ascending and descending triangles are variations of the symmetrical, but have different forecasting implications. Figures 6.3a and b show examples of an *ascending triangle*. Notice that the upper trendline is flat, while the lower line is rising. This pattern indicates that buyers are more aggressive than sellers. It is considered a bullish pattern and is usually resolved with a breakout to the upside.

Both the ascending and descending triangles differ from the symmetrical in a very important sense. No matter where in the trend structure the ascending or descending triangles appear, they have very definite forecasting implications. The ascending triangle is bullish and the descending triangle is bearish. The symmetrical triangle, by contrast, is inherently a neutral pattern. This does not mean, however, that the symmetrical triangle does not have forecasting value. On the contrary, because the symmetrical triangle is a continuation pattern, the analyst must simply look to see the direction of the previous trend and then make the assumption that that previous trend will continue.

It has been claimed by some that because the symmetrical triangle has no inherent bias, that it therefore has no forecasting value. This statement is somewhat misleading because this type of triangle usually results in a continuation of the prior trend. Clearly, then, the symmetrical triangle does have forecasting value.

Figure 6.3a   An ascending triangle. The pattern is completed on a decisive close above the upper line. This breakout should see a sharp increase in volume. That upper resistance line should act as support on subsequent dips after the breakout. The minimum price objective is obtained by measuring the height of the triangle (AB) and projecting that distance upward from the breakout point at C.

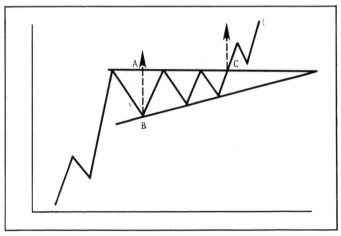

Continuation Patterns

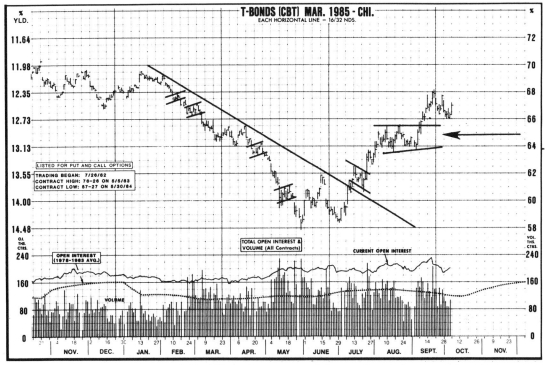

Figure 6.3b The sideways consolidation during the uptrend in August is an ascending triangle. Note the flat upper line and the rising lower line. Note also the declining flag during July. During the downtrend from February to May, notice the number of rising flags. (Courtesy of Commodity Research Bureau, a Knight-Ridder Business Information Service.)

Let's get back to the ascending triangle. As already stated, more often than not, the ascending triangle is bullish. The bullish breakout is signalled by a decisive closing above the flat upper trendline. As in the case of all valid upside breakouts, volume should see a noticeable increase on the breakout. A return move back to the support line (the flat upper line) is not unusual and should take place on light volume.

Measuring Technique

The measuring technique for the ascending triangle is relatively simple. Simply measure the height of the pattern at its widest point and project that vertical distance from the breakout point. This is just another example of using the volatility of a price pattern to determine a minimum price objective.

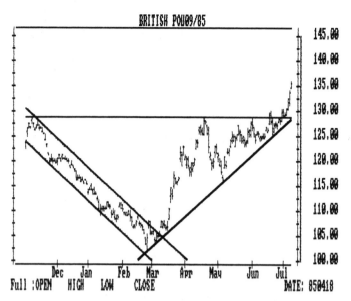

Figure 6.3c The consolidation from April through June in the British pound is an excellent example of an *ascending triangle*, which is normally a bullish pattern. Notice in this example that the rising line is also the major up trendline from the bottom. The flat upper line is the *neckline* of a major *head and shoulders* bottom. Take note of the well defined channel from November to February.

Figure 6.3d A closer look at the same British pound chart in the previous example. Notice the three upside *gaps*. Notice also the *key reversal* low day, which has the appearance of a *selling climax* and *V reversal* bottom. See how the down trendline at the left became a support line once it was passed over. The failure of the uptrend in April to reach the upper channel line warned of a downside correction.

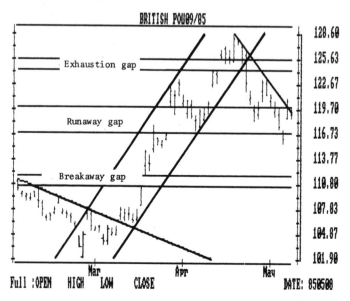

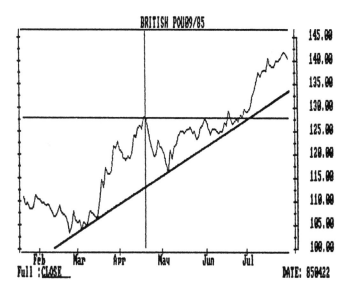

BRITISH POU09/85

145.00
140.00
135.00
130.00
125.00
120.00
115.00
110.00
105.00
100.00

Feb   Mar   Apr   May   Jun   Jul
Full :CLOSE   DATE: 850422

```
          % Retracement for CLOSE - <esc> to Exit
                      Base:  .01

Base Start:         103.50
Base End  :         128.05
Retrace to:         116.40
% Retrace :   47.454

33-1/3%   :         119.87
40%       :         118.23
50%       :         115.78
60%       :         113.32
66-2/3%   :         111.68

<rtn> to Continue:
```

Figure 6.3e Continuing with the same British pound contract, *the ascending triangle* is easier to spot here. The upside measurement has been completed, which is the height of the triangle projected from the upside breakout point. The numbers under the chart provide various percentage retracement parameters. The April downside correction retraced 47.4% of the previous advance, using closing prices. Intra-day prices retraced almost exactly 50%. This chart and the previous two examples show how the various technical patterns and tools can be combined into one analysis.

THE ASCENDING TRIANGLE AS A BOTTOM

While the ascending triangle most often appears in an uptrend and is considered a continuation pattern, it sometimes appears as a bottoming pattern. It is not unusual toward the end of a downtrend to see an ascending triangle develop. However, even in this situation, the interpretation of the pattern is bullish. The breaking of the upper line signals completion of the base and is considered a bullish signal. Both the ascending and descending triangles are sometimes also referred to as *right angle* triangles.

THE DESCENDING TRIANGLE

The *descending triangle* is just a mirror image of the ascending, and is generally considered a bearish pattern. Notice in Figures 6.4a and b the descending upper line and the flat lower line. This pattern indicates that sellers are more aggressive than buyers, and is usually resolved on the downside. The downside signal is registered by a decisive close under the lower trendline, usually on increased volume. A return move sometimes occurs which should encounter resistance at the lower trendline.

The measuring technique is exactly the same as the ascending triangle in the sense that the analyst must measure the height of the pattern at the base to the left and then project that distance down from the breakdown point.

Figure 6.4a A descending triangle. The bearish pattern is completed with a decisive close under the lower flat line. The measuring technique is the height of the triangle (AB) projected down from the breakout at point C.

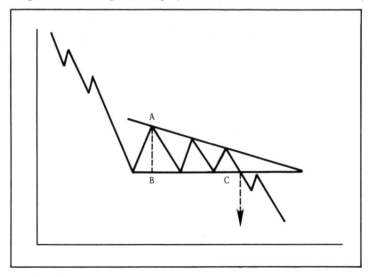

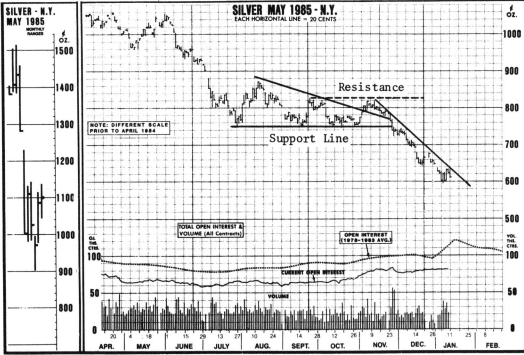

SILVER MAY 1985 - N.Y.
EACH HORIZONTAL LINE = 20 CENTS

Resistance

NOTE: DIFFERENT SCALE
PRIOR TO APRIL 1984

Support Line

TOTAL OPEN INTEREST &
VOLUME (All Contracts)

OPEN INTEREST
(1978-1983 AVG.)

CURRENT OPEN INTEREST

VOLUME

Figure 6.4b Example of a bearish descending triangle. Notice here that the last peak broke the upper line, but failed to exceed resistance at the September high. The downside objective has been fulfilled and prices are finding some "psychological" support near the round number at $6.00. Notice how the down trendline since November has contained the bounces. (Courtesy of Commodity Research Bureau, a Knight-Ridder Business Information Service.)

The Descending Triangle as a Top

While the descending triangle is a continuation pattern and usually is found within downtrends, it is not unusual on occasion for the descending triangle to be found at market tops. This type of pattern is not that difficult to recognize when it does appear in the top setting. In that case, a close below the flat lower line would signal a major trend reversal to the downside.

The Volume Pattern

The volume pattern in both the ascending and descending triangles is very similar in that the volume diminishes as the pattern works itself out and then increases on the breakout. As in the case of the symmetrical triangle, during the formation the chartist can detect slight shifts in the volume pattern coinciding with the swings in the price action. This means that in the ascending pattern, the volume tends to be slightly heavier on bounces and lighter on dips. In the descending formation, volume should be heavier on the downside and lighter during the bounces.

The Time Factor in Triangles

One final factor to be considered on the subject of triangles is that of the time dimension. The triangle is considered an intermediate pattern, meaning that it usually takes longer than a month to form, but generally less than three months. A triangle that lasts less than a month is probably a different pattern, such as a *pennant*, which will be covered shortly. As mentioned earlier, triangles sometimes appear on long-term price charts, but their natural habitat is on the daily charts.

THE BROADENING FORMATION

This next price pattern is an unusual variation of the triangle and is relatively rare. It is actually an inverted triangle or a triangle turned backwards. All of the triangular patterns examined so far show converging trendlines. The *broadening formation*, as the name implies, is just the opposite. As the pattern in Figure 6.5a shows, the trendlines actually diverge in the broadening formation, creating a picture that looks like an expanding triangle.

The volume pattern also differs in this formation. In the other triangular patterns, volume tends to diminish as the price swings grow narrower. Just the opposite happens in the broadening formation. *The volume tends to expand along with the wider price swings.* This situation represents a market that is out of control and unusually emotional. Because this pattern also represents an unusual amount of public participation, it most often occurs at major market tops. *The expanding pattern, therefore, is usually a bearish formation.*

How the Broadening Top Is Formed

The most common shape of this pattern can be seen in Figure 6.5a. That figure shows three successively higher peaks (points 1, 3, and 5) and two troughs (points 2 and 4) with the second trough (point 4)

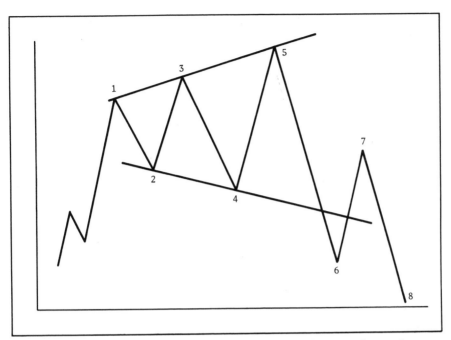

Figure 6.5a   A broadening top. This type of expanding triangle usually occurs at major tops. It shows three successively higher peaks and two declining troughs. The violation of the second trough completes the pattern. This is an unusually difficult pattern to trade and fortunately is relatively rare.

lower than the first. It is obviously an extremely difficult pattern to trade because a number of false signals take place during its formation. This pattern also contradicts much of what has already been said about the trend-following approach in the sense that the penetration of a previous peak usually indicates resumption of an uptrend, while the violation of a previous low normally signals either the beginning or the continuation of a downtrend. The trader who is using upside and downside breakouts as action signals will be subjected to a series of bad signals.

Completion of the Pattern

The pattern is completed and the major bear signal given when the reaction from the third peak violates the bottom of the second trough (see point 6). As in all important penetrations, various filters can be applied to minimize false signals. Because the pattern has three peaks and two troughs, it is sometimes referred to as a *five-point reversal pattern*. Notice again the recurrence of the number five, which was mentioned in our treatment of the symmetrical triangle.

Figure 6.5b Example of a broadening top. A relatively rare reversal pattern that usually occurs at major tops. (Courtesy of Commodity Research Bureau, a Knight-Ridder Business Information Service.)

It is not unusual in this type of topping formation for a return move to occur after the bear signal is given, which may retrace as much as 50% of the prior downleg before the new bear trend is resumed. While the third peak usually moves higher than the first two peaks, the last peak will on occasion either stop at the top of the second peak or not quite reach it. In such a situation, the analyst is given some additional early warning of market failure, and the pattern actually begins to resemble a head and shoulders top with a declining neckline.

Summary of the Broadening Formation

First of all, the broadening formation is a relatively rare pattern. When it does appear, however, it's usually at an important market top. It looks like an expanding triangle with three successively higher peaks and two declining troughs. The wider price swings are accompanied by gradually increased trading activity. The resolution of the formation is signalled by the violation of the second low after the completion of the third peak.

Continuation Patterns

THE DIAMOND FORMATION

The *diamond formation* is another relatively rare pattern that usually shows up at market tops. This pattern is peculiar in that it is actually a combination of two different types of triangles—the *expanding* and the *symmetrical.* If you take a look at Figure 6.6a, you see that the first half of the diamond resembles an expanding triangle and the second half, a symmetrical. The volume pattern conforms to the price action by expanding during the first half of the pattern and then gradually declining as the price swings narrow in the second half of the formation.

The diverging trendlines followed by converging trendlines form a chart picture resembling a diamond. Hence, its name. It is a relatively rare pattern, but *is most often seen at market tops.* More often than not, it is a reversal rather than a continuation pattern. The diamond is completed when the uptrend line along the second half of the formation is broken on the downside. Normally the breakdown will see an increase in trading activity.

Figure 6.6a   Example of a diamond. This is usually a topping reversal pattern. It resembles first an expanding triangle and then a symmetrical triangle. The pattern is completed when the lower upslanting trendline is broken. Measure the height of the pattern at its widest point and then project that distance down from the breakout point.

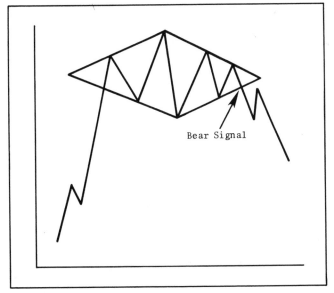

Bear Signal

How to Measure from a Diamond

The measuring technique for the diamond is similar to that already given for the triangular patterns. The vertical distance is measured from the widest part of the pattern, which is then projected down from the breakout point. Sometimes a return move takes place that approaches the lower resistance line, after which the new downtrend should resume.

Figure 6.6b Example of a diamond top. Note the expanding triangle to the left and the symmetrical triangle to the right. The breaking of the rising line to the right signals the reversal. Measure the vertical width of the diamond and project it downward from the breakdown point. (Courtesy of Commodity Research Bureau, a Knight-Ridder Business Information Service.)

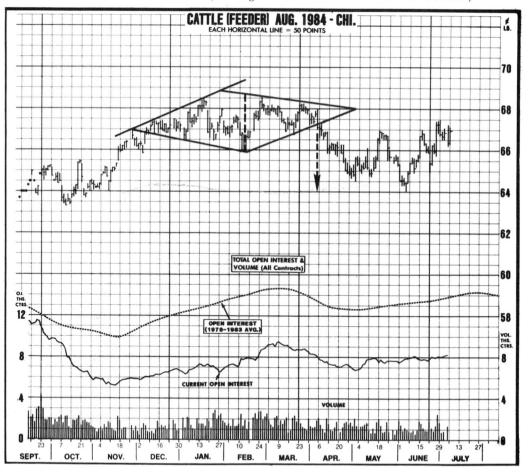

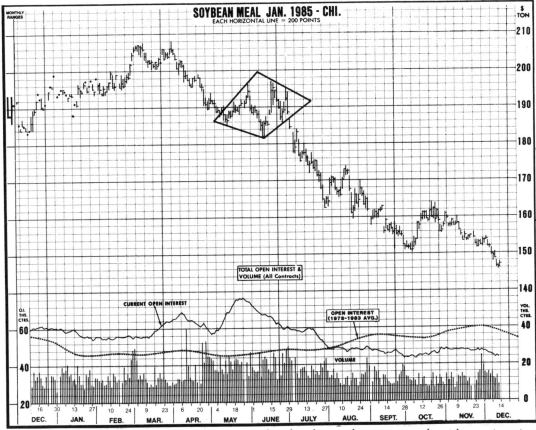

Figure 6.6c An example of a diamond acting as a bearish continuation pattern. (Courtesy of Commodity Research Bureau, a Knight-Ridder Business Information Service.)

CONCLUSION

The discussion of the diamond pattern completes the treatment of the entire subject of triangles. Triangles, in the context of technical chart patterns, normally refer to the symmetrical, ascending, and descending varieties. The broadening and diamond formations represent unusual variations of the triangle. Let's move on now to some of the other commonly used continuation patterns.

FLAGS AND PENNANTS

While the broadening and diamond formations are relatively rare, the *flag* and *pennant* formations are quite common in the futures markets. They are usually treated together because they are very similar in appearance, tend to show up at about the same place in an existing trend, and have the same volume and measuring criteria.

The *flag* and *pennant* represent brief pauses in a dynamic market move. In fact, one of the requirements for both the flag and the pennant is that they be preceded by a sharp and almost straight line move. They represent situations where a steep advance or decline has gotten ahead of itself, and where the market pauses briefly to "catch its breath" before running off again in the same direction.

Flags and pennants are among the most reliable of continuation patterns and only rarely produce a trend reversal. Figures 6.7a and b show what these two patterns look like. To begin with, notice the steep price advance preceding the formations on heavy volume. Notice

Figure 6.7a Example of a bullish flag. The flag usually occurs after a sharp move and represents a brief pause in the trend. The flag should slope against the trend. Volume should dry up during the formation and build again on the breakout. The flag usually occurs near the midpoint of the move.

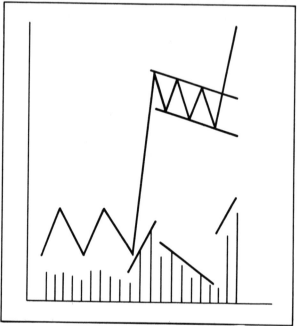

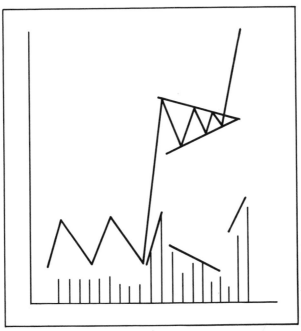

Figure 6.7b A bullish pennant. Resembles a small symmetrical triangle, but usually lasts no longer than three weeks. Volume should be light during its formation. The move after the pennant is completed should duplicate the size of the move preceding it.

also the dramatic drop-off in activity as the consolidation patterns form and then the sudden burst of activity on the upside breakout.

Construction of Flags and Pennants

The construction of the two patterns differs slightly. The flag resembles a parallelogram or rectangle marked by two parallel trendlines that tend to slope against the prevailing trend. In a downtrend, the flag would have a slight upward slope.

The pennant is identified by two converging trendlines and is more horizontal. It very closely resembles a small symmetrical triangle. An important requirement is that volume should dry up noticeably while each of the patterns is forming.

Both patterns are relatively short term and should be completed within one to three weeks. Pennants and flags in downtrends tend to take even less time to develop, and often last no longer than one or two weeks. Both patterns are completed on the penetration of the upper trendline in an uptrend. The breaking of the lower trendline

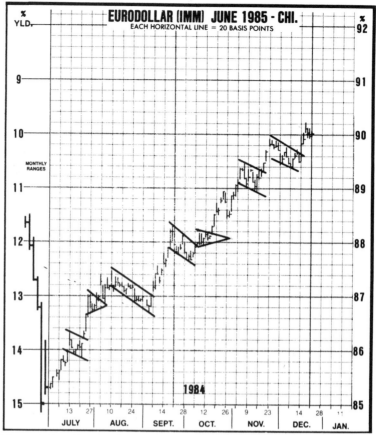

Figure 6.7c Flags and pennants are symptomatic of dynamic market moves. Both patterns are brief pauses in the trend. Note the number of flags and pennants in the Eurodollar advance. (Courtesy of Commodity Research Bureau, a Knight-Ridder Business Information Service.)

would signal resumption of downtrends. The breaking of those trendlines should take place on heavier volume. As usual, upside volume is more critically important than downside volume.

Measuring Implications

The measuring implications are similar for both patterns. Flags and pennants are said to "fly at half-mast" from a *flagpole*. The flagpole is the prior sharp advance or decline. The term "half-mast" suggests that these minor continuation patterns tend to appear at about the halfway

Continuation Patterns

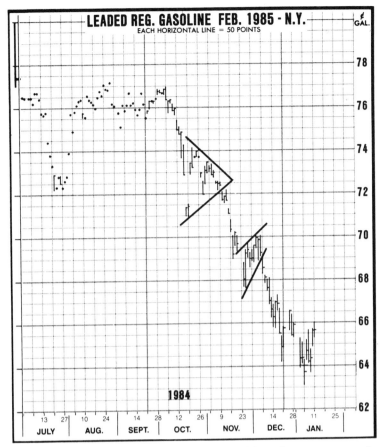

Figure 6.7d The first pattern to the left could be either a symmetrical triangle or a pennant. The second formation looks more like a rising flag. These pauses rarely last longer than a couple of weeks in a downtrend. (Courtesy of Commodity Research Bureau, a Knight-Ridder Business Information Service.)

point of the move. In general, the move after the trend has resumed will duplicate the flagpole or the move just prior to the formation of the pattern.

To be more precise, measure the distance of the preceding move from the original breakout point. That is to say, the point at which the original trend signal was given, either by the penetration of a support or resistance level or an important trendline. That vertical distance of the preceding move is then measured from the breakout point of the flag or pennant—that is, the point at which the upper line is broken in an uptrend or the lower line in a downtrend.

Summary

Let's summarize the more important points of both patterns.

1. They are both preceded by an almost straight line move (called a flagpole) on heavy volume.

2. Prices then pause for about one to three weeks on very light volume.

3. The trend resumes on a burst of trading activity.

4. Both patterns occur at about the midpoint of the market move.

5. The pennant resembles a small horizontal symmetrical triangle.

6. The flag resembles a small parallelogram that slopes against the prevailing trend.

7. Both patterns take less time to develop in downtrends.

8. Both patterns are very common in the futures markets.

THE WEDGE FORMATION

The *wedge* formation is similar to a symmetrical triangle both in terms of its shape and the amount of time it takes to form. Like the symmetrical triangle, it is identified by two converging trendlines that come together at an *apex.* In terms of the amount of time it takes to form, the wedge usually lasts more than a month but not more than three months, putting it into the intermediate category.

What distinguishes the *wedge* is its noticeable slant. The wedge pattern has a noticeable slant either to the upside or the downside. As a rule, like the flag pattern, the wedge slants against the prevailing trend. Therefore, a *falling wedge is considered bullish and a rising wedge is bearish.* Notice in Figure 6.8a that the bullish wedge slants downward between two converging trendlines. In the downtrend in Figure 6.8b, the converging trendlines have an unmistakable upward slant.

Wedges as Tops
and Bottom Reversal Patterns

Wedges show up most often within the existing trend and usually constitute continuation patterns. The wedge can appear at tops or

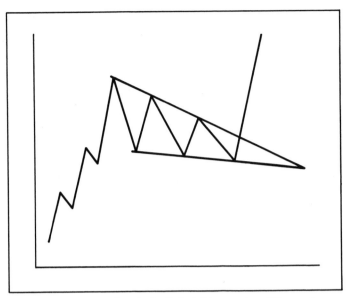

Figure 6.8a Example of a bullish falling wedge. The wedge pattern has two converging trendlines, but slopes against the prevailing trend. A falling wedge is usually bullish.

bottoms and signal a trend reversal. But that type of situation is much less common. Near the end of an uptrend, the chartist may observe a clearcut rising wedge. Because a continuation wedge in an uptrend should slope downward against the prevailing trend, the rising wedge is a clue to the chartist that this is a bearish and not a bullish pattern. At bottoms, a falling wedge would be a tip-off of a possible end of a bear trend.

Figure 6.8b Example of a bearish wedge. A bearish wedge should slope upward against the prevailing downtrend.

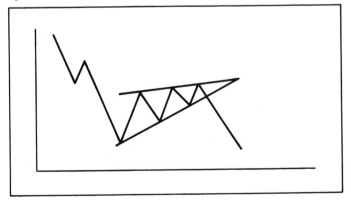

Whether the wedge appears in the middle or the end of a market move, the market analyst should always be guided by the general maxim that *a rising wedge is bearish and a falling wedge is bullish.*

The wedge pattern usually moves at least two-thirds of the way to the apex before breaking out, and will sometimes move all the way to the apex before resolving itself. (The tendency to sometimes move all the way to the apex is another difference from the symmetrical triangle.) The volume should contract during the formation of the wedge and increase on the breakout. Wedges also take less time to form in downtrends than in uptrends.

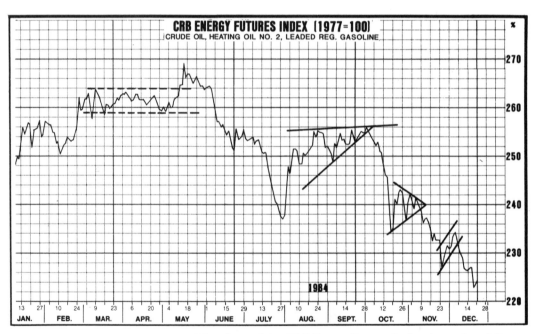

Figure 6.8c This chart of the CRB Energy Futures Index shows four different patterns. The first to the upper left shows a rectangular consolidation in the uptrend. The second pattern in August through September shows a bearish rising wedge. The third is a bearish pennant during October and November. The fourth is a rising flag into December. (Courtesy of Commodity Research Bureau, a Knight-Ridder Business Information Service.)

Continuation Patterns

Figure 6.8d A case could be made for the October to November rally in heating oil being a rising wedge. The lines are converging and slanting upward. The rally into December looks like a rising flag. This chart is similar to the Energy Index in the previous example. (Courtesy of Commodity Research Bureau, a Knight-Ridder Business Information Service.)

THE RECTANGLE FORMATION

The *rectangle formation* often goes by other names, but is usually easy to spot on a price chart. It represents a pause in the trend during which prices move sideways between two parallel horizontal lines. (See Figures 6.9a through c.)

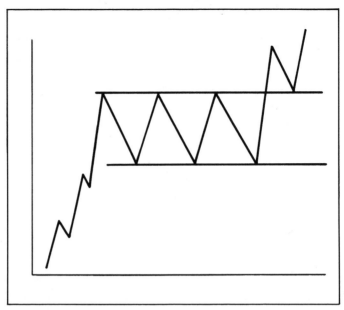

Figure 6.9a Example of a bullish rectangle in an uptrend. This pattern is also called a trading range, and shows prices trading between two horizontal trendlines. It is also called a congestion area.

The rectangle is sometimes referred to as a *trading range* or a *congestion area*. In Dow Theory parlance, it is referred to as a *line*. Whatever it is called, it usually represents just a consolidation period

Figure 6.9b Example of a bearish rectangle. While rectangles are usually considered continuation patterns, the trader must always be alert for signs that it may turn into a reversal pattern, such as a triple bottom.

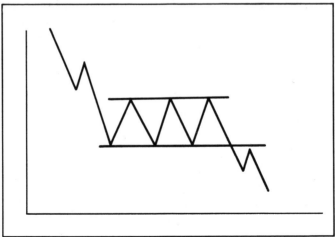

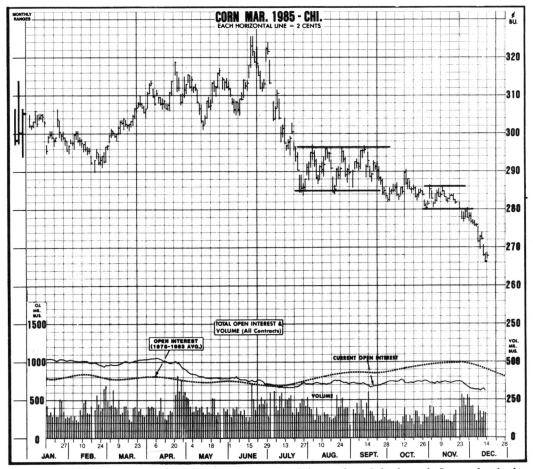

Figure 6.9c The sideways consolidation from July through September looks like a rectangular pattern. In this type of pattern, prices trade sideways between two horizontal trendlines. A smaller range also appears during November. (Courtesy of Commodity Research Bureau, a Knight-Ridder Business Information Service.)

in the existing trend, and is usually resolved in the direction of the market trend that preceded its occurrence. In terms of forecasting value, it can be viewed as being similar to the symmetrical triangle but with flat instead of converging trendlines.

A decisive close outside either the upper or lower boundary signals completion of the rectangle and points the direction of the trend. The market analyst must always be on the alert, however, that the rectangular consolidation does not turn into a reversal pattern. In the uptrend shown in Figure 6.9a, for example, notice that the three peaks might possibly be viewed as a triple top reversal pattern.

The Importance of the Volume Pattern

One important clue to watch for is the volume pattern. Because the price swings in both directions are fairly broad, the analyst should keep a close eye on which moves have the heavier volume. If the rallies are on heavier and the setbacks on lighter volume, then the formation is probably a continuation in the uptrend. If the heavier volume is on the downside, then it can be considered a warning of a possible trend reversal in the works.

Swings Within the Range Can Be Traded

Some chartists trade the swings within such a pattern by buying dips near the bottom and selling rallies near the top of the range. This technique enables the short-term trader to take advantage of the well-defined price boundaries, and profit from an otherwise trendless market. Because the positions are being taken at the extremes of the range, the risks are relatively small and well defined. If the trading range remains intact, this countertrend trading approach works quite well. When a breakout does occur, the trader not only exits the last losing trade immediately, but can reverse the previous position by initiating a new trade in the direction of the new trend. *Oscillators* are especially useful in sideways trading markets, but less useful once the breakout has occurred for reasons discussed in Chapter 10.

Other traders assume the rectangle is a continuation pattern and take long positions near the lower end of the price band in an uptrend, or initiate short positions near the top of the range in downtrends. Others avoid such trendless markets altogether and await a clearcut breakout before committing their funds. Chapter 15 addresses the problems encountered by mechanical trend-following systems during such choppy and indecisive market periods. Suffice it to say here that most trend-following systems perform very poorly during such times of sideways and trendless market action.

Other Similarities and Differences

In terms of duration, the rectangle usually falls into the one- to three-month category, similar to triangles and wedges. The volume pattern differs from other continuation patterns in the sense that the broad price swings prevent the usual drop-off in activity seen in other such patterns.

The most common measuring technique applied to the rectangle is based on the height of the price range. Measure the height of the trading range, from top to bottom, and then project that vertical distance from the breakout point. This method is similar to the other vertical measuring techniques already mentioned, and is based on the volatility of the market. When we cover the *count* in point and figure charting, we'll say more on the question of horizontal price measurements.

Everything mentioned so far concerning volume on breakouts and the probability of return moves applies here as well. Because the upper and lower boundaries are horizontal and so well defined in the rectangle, support and resistance levels are more clearly evident. This means that, on upside breakouts, the top of the former price band should now provide solid support on any selloffs. After a downside breakout in downtrends, the bottom of the trading range (the previous support area) should now provide a solid ceiling over the market on any rally attempts.

THE MEASURED MOVE

The *measured move*, or the *swing* measurement as it is also sometimes called, describes the phenomenon where a major market advance or decline is divided into two equal and parallel moves as shown in Figure 6.10a. For this approach to work, the market moves should be fairly orderly and well defined. The measured move is really just a variation of some of the techniques we've already touched on. We've seen that some of the consolidation patterns, such as flags and pennants, usually occur at about the halfway point of a market move. We've also mentioned the tendency of markets to retrace about a third to a half of a prior trend before resuming that trend.

In the measured move, when the chartist sees a well-defined situation, such as in Figure 6.10a, with a rally from point A to point B followed by a countertrend swing from point B to point C (which retraces a third to a half of wave AB), it is assumed that the next leg in the uptrend (CD) will come close to duplicating the first leg (AB). The height of wave (AB), therefore, is simply measured upward from the bottom of the correction at point C. This duplication implies the size of the move and its slope. There is a strong tendency for the second major upmove to not only travel the same distance as the first,

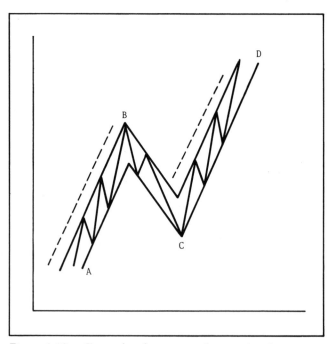

Figure 6.10a Example of a measured move (or the swing measurement) in an uptrend. This theory holds that the second leg in the advance (CD) duplicates the size and slope of the first upleg (AB). The corrective wave (BC) often retraces a third to a half of AB before the uptrend is resumed.

but also to parallel the slope or angle of that first upmove. It should be mentioned here in closing that there are other more sophisticated measuring techniques that build on the measured move that will be taken up in later sections.

THE CONTINUATION HEAD AND SHOULDERS PATTERN

In the previous chapter, we treated the head and shoulders pattern at some length and described it as the best known and most trustworthy of all reversal patterns. Just in case the reader is beginning to feel complacent about how easy all of this looks, let's inject a new note of doubt into the process by stating that the head and shoulders pattern can sometimes appear as a continuation instead of a reversal pattern.

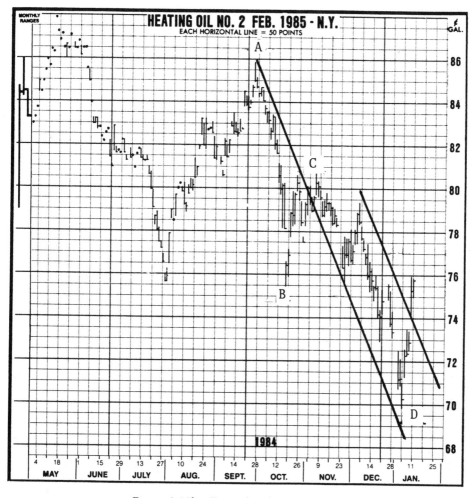

Figure 6.10b Example of a measured move or the swing measurement in a downtrend. Notice that the second downleg (CD) is exactly the same length and slope as the first downleg (AB). The rally phase in between the two downlegs (BC) retraced one half of the first downleg. (Courtesy of Commodity Research Bureau, a Knight-Ridder Business Information Service.)

(We might also mention at this point that chart patterns used as examples in books and articles are chosen very carefully and are always crystal clear, tending to produce a false sense of security in the aspiring chartist. Real-life situations aren't always so clear.)

In the continuation head and shoulders pattern, prices trace out a pattern that looks very similar to a sideways rectangular pattern except that the middle trough in an uptrend (see Figure 6.11a) tends to be lower than either of the two shoulders. In a downtrend (see

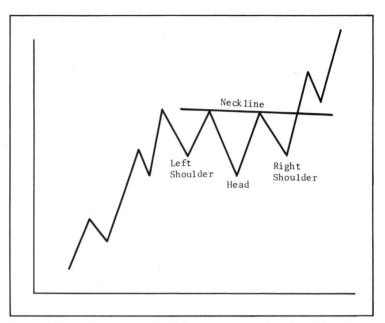

Figure 6.11a Example of a bullish continuation head and shoulder pattern.

Figure 6.11b), the middle peak in the consolidation exceeds the other two peaks. The result in both cases is a head and shoulders pattern turned upside down. Because it is turned upside down, there is no chance of confusing it with the reversal pattern. (Having read this last statement, perhaps the reader can go back to feeling a bit more complacent again.)

Figure 6.11b Example of a bearish continuation head and shoulders pattern.

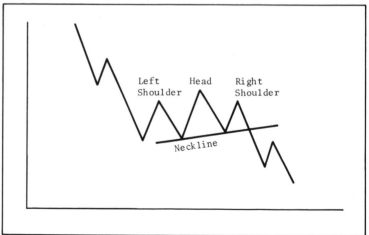

Continuation Patterns

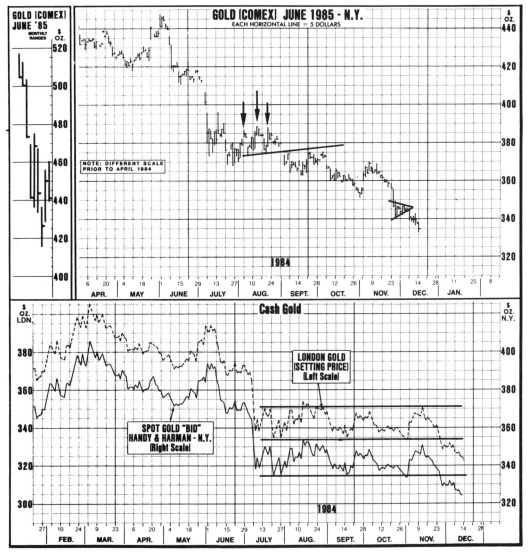

Figure 6.11c If you look closely at the June gold chart (top chart), you'll see a small head and shoulders continuation pattern. Note the three peaks and the neckline. Notice also the return move after the breaking of the neckline. A small pennant is visible to the bottom right during December. The bottom chart shows rectangular consolidation patterns on the gold cash chart. (Courtesy of Commodity Research Bureau, a Knight-Ridder Business Information Service.)

Once the continuation head and shoulders pattern is recognized, the neckline can be drawn as usual. From that point on, the interpretation of the pattern is the same as that covered in the previous chapter (except for the very important distinction that the trend is likely to be continued instead of reversed). The trend is resumed with the breaking of the neckline, and the volume and measuring criteria are similar. The only real distinction between the continuation and reversal versions of the head and shoulders pattern is that in the former, the measuring reliability is somewhat diminished and the volume requirement not as rigidly applied.

THE PRINCIPLE OF CHARACTERIZATION

In general, all of the chart patterns described in these two chapters can be applied to virtually any market. One oft-stated claim of technical analysts is that it is not even necessary to know the name of the stock or commodity being analyzed in order to apply the principles of chart analysis. The statement that "a chart is a chart" is often heard.

While these claims are generally quite true, as usual there is a need for some further qualification and clarification. While the principles of chart analysis can be universally applied to most markets, it does not necessarily follow that all markets behave in identical fashion. There is considerable evidence that individual markets do in fact possess a personality of their own, which should be taken into consideration in the analytical process.

Computer testing of various technical indicators, such as moving averages, has revealed that while certain moving averages work well in most markets, each market tends to have its own moving average that works best. This may seem like a contradictory statement at first, but it really isn't. Certain moving averages, like chart patterns, do a good job of identifying and tracking market trends when applied to all markets. However, what works well in most cases may not be the best in each individual case. The process of *optimization*, through the use of computer simulations, has revealed that each market does seem to possess its own unique character or personality, and that various technical indicators, including chart patterns, can be tailored or customized to each individual market.

We'll come back to the question of optimizing moving averages in Chapter 9. Let's confine our comments here to the subject of chart patterns. Most experienced traders and chartists are at least intuitively aware of each market's individuality. There is a world of difference between the pork belly and the copper markets, or between wheat and the Japanese yen. Because these markets represent different industries and financial areas, the difference in their behavior is not surprising.

Chartists are also aware that some markets chart better than others. Copper and gold are considered good charting markets. Wheat and soybeans are another two examples of markets that chart well. Pork bellies and orange juice, however, are much more difficult to trade based on standard charting techniques.

Very little has been published on the character or personality of various markets. A booklet entitled "How Charts Are Used in Commodity Price Forecasting," by William L. Jiler (New York: Commodity Research Bureau, 1982, p. 8), addresses the question of characterization.

Generally speaking, charts of the same commodity tend to have similar pattern sequences which may be different from those of another commodity. In other words, charts of one particular commodity may appear to have an identity or a character peculiar to that commodity. For example, cotton charts display many round tops and bottoms, and even a series of these constructions which are seldom observed in soybeans or wheat. The examination of soybeans charts over the years reveals that triangles are especially favored. Head and shoulders formations abound throughout the wheat charts. All commodities seem to favor certain behavior patterns.

An article by Robert Joel Taylor in the August 1972 issue of *Commodities* (now *Futures*) *Magazine*, entitled "Technical Personalities of Major Commodities," discusses the same point. Taylor makes the case that each market does have its own personality and addresses chart patterns from the standpoint of the frequency of occurrence and the price forecasting reliability of certain technical formations in different commodities. Taylor developed a Technical Reliability Index to measure the frequency and reliability of a number of commonly used chart patterns as applied to different markets.

Some chartists still use a Technical Reliability Index, which measures the percentage of times that a given chart pattern actually does what it is supposed to do. In using this type of an index, a 70% reliability rating is usually required before a given chart pattern is trusted in a given situation.

While little has been written in recent years to aid the chartist in this area, experience is still the best teacher. Working with the various commodity markets over the years has the effect of sensitizing the technician to the personalities and quirks of the different markets. These differences should be considered when applying all charting principles.

CONFIRMATION AND DIVERGENCE

The principle of *confirmation* is one of the common themes running throughout the entire subject of market analysis, and is used in conjunction with its counterpart—*divergence*. We'll introduce both concepts here and explain their meaning, but we'll return to them again and again throughout the book because their impact is so important. We're disussing confirmation here in the context of chart patterns, but it applies to virtually every aspect of technical analysis. *Confirmation* refers to the comparison of all technical signals and indicators to ensure that most of those indicators are pointing in the same direction and are confirming one another.

Within the context of price patterns, confirmation means comparing chart patterns of all delivery months of the market being analyzed to make sure they agree. A bullish or bearish pattern in one delivery month should be confirmed by similar readings in other delivery months. It doesn't stop there, though. It also means looking at all related markets as well. Groups of related markets tend to move together. Check to see what the other markets in the same group are doing. If a metals market is being analyzed, what are the other metals markets doing?

As an added incentive, the analysis of a related market often provides clues to the market under analysis. Go a step further and check the general direction of the broad commodity indices to see if your analysis fits with the direction of most commodity markets. A bullish analysis of any one market would carry less weight if commodity markets in general are in downtrends. Find out if the general environment for commodity markets is bullish or bearish.

Look at the patterns on the weekly and monthly continuation charts for further confirmation. See if they agree. Then look at all of the technical indicators at your disposal. Check out the moving averages, oscillators, trendlines, and volume and open interest to make sure they agree.

The principle of confirmation simply holds that the more technical evidence that the analyst has to support his or her conclusions in a given market, the more confidence that analysis inspires and the better the odds of making the correct decision.

Divergence is the opposite of confirmation and refers to a situation where different delivery months or related markets or technical indicators fail to confirm one another. While it is being used here in a negative sense, divergence is a valuable concept in market analysis, and one of the best early warning signals of impending trend reversals. We'll discuss the principle of divergence at greater length in Chapter 10 on oscillators.

This concludes our treatment of price patterns. It was stated earlier that the three pieces of raw data used by the technical analyst were *price, volume,* and *open interest.* Most of what we've said so far has focused on price. Let's take a closer look now at volume and open interest and how they are incorporated into the analytical process.

7

Volume and
Open Interest

INTRODUCTION

Most technicians in the futures markets use a three-dimensional approach to market analysis by tracking the movement of three sets of figures—*price, volume,* and *open interest.* Chapter 3 discussed the construction of the daily bar chart and showed how the three figures were plotted on that type of chart. It was stated then that even though volume and open interest figures are available for each delivery month in commodity markets, the *total* figures are the ones generally used for forecasting purposes. The reader was advised, however, to keep an eye on the open interest figures in the individual delivery months in order to concentrate trading activity in the most actively traded (or the most liquid) contracts.

Most of the discussion of charting theory to this point has concentrated mainly on price action with some mention of volume. In this chapter, we'll round out the three-dimensional approach by taking a closer look at the role played by volume and open interest in the forecasting process.

VOLUME AND OPEN INTEREST
AS SECONDARY INDICATORS

Let's begin by placing volume and open interest in their proper perspective. *Price* is by far the most important. *Volume* and *open interest* are secondary in importance and are used primarily as confirming indicators. Of those two, volume is the more important. Open interest is a distant third. In ranking the three pieces of information in order of importance on a scale of 1 to 10, price is a 5, volume is a 3, and open interest is a 2. While some technicians might disagree with that ranking, I can only say that it is based on my own personal market experiences.

Some practitioners totally ignore volume and open interest, while others give them more weight than they deserve. My own experience places me somewhere in between those two extremes. I have found that the tracking of volume and open interest along with the price action sometimes yields important clues to market direction, and at other times, they are of little use. The thorough technical analyst should, however, include these figures in his or her checklist of things to watch, and always be on the alert for those situations where important messages are being sent.

Volume

Let's define both terms again. *Volume* is the number of contracts traded during the time period under study. Because we'll be dealing primarily with daily bar charts, our main concern is with *daily* volume. That daily volume is plotted by a vertical bar at the bottom of the chart under the day's price action. Notice in Figure 7.1 the scale for volume at the right of the chart under the price scale.

Volume can be plotted for *weekly* bar charts as well. In that case, total volume for the week would simply be plotted under the bar representing that week's price action. Volume is usually not used, however, on *monthly* bar charts. Remember that only the *total* volume and open interest numbers are used for forecasting purposes.

Open Interest

The total number of outstanding or unliquidated contracts at the end of the day is *open interest*. In Figure 7.1, notice the vertical scale along the bottom left of the bar chart. Open interest is plotted on the chart

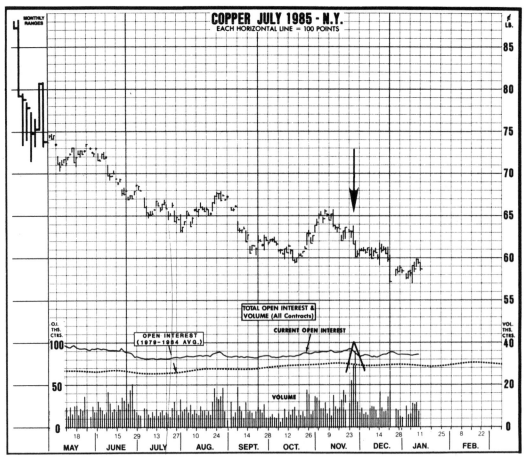

Figure 7.1 Notice the volume scale along the bottom right. Open interest is plotted using the scale along the bottom left. The dotted line is the five-year average of open interest and is used to show seasonal tendencies.

Notice in late November how the volume expanded as prices weakened. That was clearly a bearish indication. Heavier volume should be in the same direction as the price trend. (Courtesy of Commodity Research Bureau, a Knight-Ridder Business Information Service.)

under its corresponding price data for the day, but above the volume bars. Remember that official volume and open interest figures are reported a day late in the commodity markets and are, therefore, plotted with a one-day lag. (Only estimated volume figures are available for the last trading day.) That means that each day the chartist plots the high, low, and closing price bar for the last day of trading, but plots the official volume and open interest figures for the previous day.

Open interest represents the total number of outstanding longs or shorts in the market, *not the sum of both*. Open interest is the number of contracts. A contract must have both a buyer and a seller. Therefore, two market participants—a buyer and a seller—combine to create only one contract. The open interest figure reported each day is followed by either a positive or negative number showing the increase or decrease in the number of contracts for that day. It is those changes in the open interest levels, either up or down, that give the chartist clues as to the changing character of market participation and give open interest its forecasting value.

Seasonality in Open Interest.   Let's explain one more piece of information in the example in Figure 7.1. So far we have the price and volume bars and the total open interest line. The dotted (almost horizontal) line along the bottom of the chart shows the five-year average of open interest. This average is used to show the *seasonal tendency* for the open interest. Like the price action, open interest has very definite seasonal tendencies that should be taken into consideration.

An increase in open interest, for example, is only significant if that increase exceeds the seasonal tendency. By visually netting out the seasonal tendency, the increase or decrease in the actual open interest takes on much more validity. It is the difference between what the open interest is actually doing (solid line) and what it normally does (dotted line) at certain times of the year (season) that gives significance to the changes in the open interest line.

How Changes in Open Interest Occur.   In order to grasp the significance of how changes in the open interest numbers are interpreted, the reader must first understand how each trade produces a change in those numbers.

Every time a trade is completed on the floor of the exchange, the open interest is affected in one of three ways—it increases, decreases, or stays unchanged. Let's see how those changes occur.

Buyer	Seller	Change in Open Interest
1. Buys new long	Sells new short	Increases
2. Buys new long	Sells old long	No change
3. Buys old short	Sells new short	No change
4. Buys old short	Sells old long	Decreases

In the first case, both the buyer and seller are initiating a new position and a new contract is established. In case 2, the buyer is initiating a new long position, but the seller is merely liquidating an old long. One is entering and the other exiting a trade. The result is a standoff and no change takes place in the number of contracts. In case 3, the same thing happens except this time it is the seller who is initiating a new short and the buyer who is only covering an old short. Because one of the traders is entering and the other exiting a trade, again no change is produced. In case 4, both traders are liquidating an old position and the open interest decreases accordingly.

To sum up, if both participants in a trade are initiating a new position, the open interest will increase. If both are liquidating an old position, the open interest will decline. If, however, one is initiating a new trade while the other is liquidating an old trade, open interest will remain unchanged. By looking at the net change in the total open interest at the end of the day, the chartist is able to determine whether money is flowing into or out of the market. This information enables the analyst to draw some conclusions about the strength or weakness of the current price trend.

General Rule for Interpreting Volume and Open Interest

The market technician incorporates volume and open interest information into market analysis. The rules for the interpretation of volume and open interest are generally combined because they are so similar. There are, however, some distinctions between the two that should be addressed. We'll begin here with a statement of the general rule for both. Having done that, we'll then treat each one separately before combining them again at the end.

Price	Volume	Open Interest	Market
Rising	Up	Up	Strong
Rising	Down	Down	Weak
Declining	Up	Up	Weak
Declining	Down	Down	Strong

If volume and open interest are both increasing, then the current price trend will probably continue in its present direction (either up or down). If, however, volume and open interest are declining, the action can be viewed as a warning that the current price trend may be nearing an end. Having said that, let's now take a look at volume and open interest separately. (See Figure 7.2.)

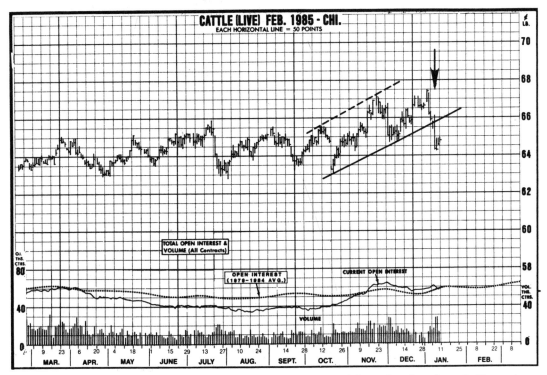

Figure 7.2 The open interest increased from October through November, confirming the price uptrend. Open interest then leveled off reflecting profit-taking and giving an early warning of a possible top. Notice that the second peak in January had lower open interest than the first price peak in late November.

Note also the lighter volume on the second price peak and the heavy downside volume on the January price selloff. These were all bearish indications. (Courtesy of Commodity Research Bureau, a Knight-Ridder Business Information Service.)

INTERPRETATION OF VOLUME

The level of volume measures the intensity or urgency behind the price move. Heavier volume reflects a higher degree of intensity or pressure. By monitoring the level of volume along with price action, the technician is better able to gauge the buying or selling pressure behind market moves. This information can then be used to confirm price movement or warn that a price move is not to be trusted. (See Figures 7.3 and 7.4.)

To state the rule more concisely, *volume should increase or expand in the direction of the existing price trend.* In an uptrend, volume should be heavier as the price moves higher, and should decrease or contract on price dips. As long as this pattern continues, volume is said to be confirming the price trend.

The chartist is also watching for signs of *divergence* (there's that word again). Divergence occurs if the penetration of a previous high by the price trend takes place on declining volume. This action alerts the chartist to diminishing buying pressure. If the volume also shows

Figure 7.3 Notice that the heavier volume tends to take place in the direction of the price trend. Prior to the market top in June, heavier volume was on the upside. During the subsequent bear market, volume was heavier on the downside. Notice, for example, the heavy downside volume in November. (Courtesy of Commodity Research Bureau, a Knight-Ridder Business Information Service.)

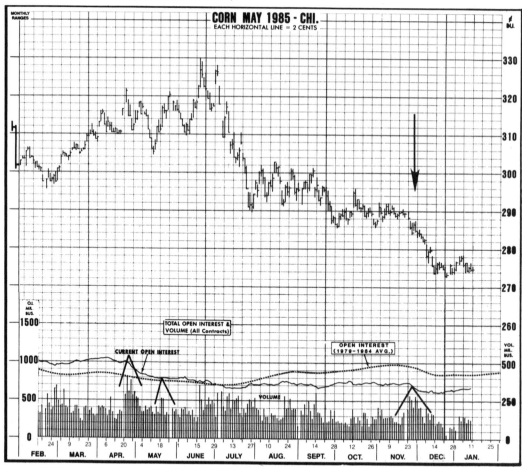

Volume and Open Interest

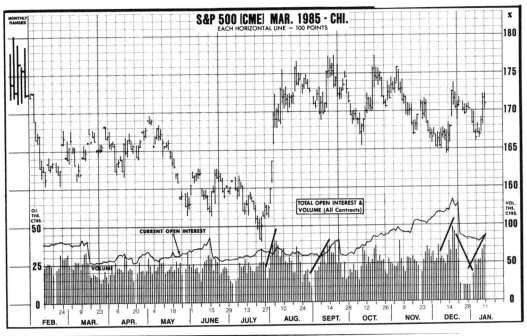

Figure 7.4 Here is another example of volume following the trend. On this chart, the period from late July shows a definite bullish tendency. Notice, in particular, the surge in volume in mid-December on the rally, light volume on the correction, and heavier upside volume. This shows that volume pressure is confirming higher prices. (Courtesy of Commodity Research Bureau, a Knight-Ridder Business Information Service.)

a tendency to pick up on price dips, the analyst begins to worry that the uptrend is in trouble.

Volume as Confirmation in Price Patterns

During our treatment of price patterns in Chapters 5 and 6, volume was mentioned several times as an important confirming indicator. One of the first signs of a *head and shoulders* top occurred when prices moved into new highs during the formation of the *head* on light volume with heavier activity on the subsequent decline to the *neckline*. The *double* and *triple tops* saw lighter volume on each successive peak followed by heavier downside activity. Continuation patterns, like the *triangle*, should be accompanied by a gradual drop off in volume. As a rule, the resolution of all price patterns (the breakout point) should be accompanied by heavier trading activity if the signal given by that breakout is real. (See Figure 7.5.)

Figure 7.5 Heavy volume should confirm the resolution of price patterns. This chart shows a descending triangle. Note the heavy volume as the lower trendline is broken.

Notice also the large buildup in open interest through October and November, while prices were still consolidating. An increase in open interest during a consolidation intensifies the market move following the breakout. (Courtesy of Commodity Research Bureau, a Knight-Ridder Business Information Service.)

In a downtrend, the volume should be heavier during down moves and lighter on bounces. As long as that pattern continues, the selling pressure is greater than buying pressure and the downtrend should continue. It's only when that pattern begins to change that the chartist starts looking for signs of a bottom.

Volume Precedes Price

By monitoring the price and volume together, we're actually using two different tools to measure the same thing—pressure. By the mere fact that prices are trending higher, we can see that there is more buying than selling pressure. It stands to reason then that the greater volume should take place in the same direction as the prevailing trend.

Technicians believe that *volume precedes price,* meaning that the loss of upside pressure in an uptrend or downside pressure in a downtrend actually shows up in the volume figures before it is manifested in a reversal of the price trend.

On Balance Volume

Technicians have experimented with many volume indicators to help quantify buying or selling pressure. (See Figures 7.6a to 7.8b.) Trying to "eyeball" the vertical volume bars along the bottom of the chart is not always precise enough to detect significant shifts in the volume flow. The simplest and best known of these volume indicators is *on balance volume* or *OBV.* Developed and popularized by Joseph Granville in his 1963 book, *Granville's New Key to Stock Market Profits* (Prentice Hall, Englewood Cliffs, N.J.), OBV actually produces a volume line or curve along the bottom of the price chart. This line or curve can be used either to confirm the quality of the current price trend or warn of an impending reversal by diverging from the price action.

Figure 7.6a shows a standard daily bar chart with price and volume bars. An analyst might have been able to detect shifts in the volume flow by careful scrutiny of the price bars. Figure 7.6b shows the same price chart with the OBV line along the bottom of the chart instead of the volume bars. Notice how much easier it is to follow the volume trend with the OBV line.

The construction of the OBV line is simplicity itself. The total volume for each day is assigned a plus or minus value depending on whether prices close higher or lower for that day. A higher close causes the volume for that day to be given a plus value, while a lower close counts for negative volume. A running cumulative total is then maintained by adding or subtracting each day's volume based on the direction of the market close.

It is the direction of the OBV line (its trend) that is important and not the actual level of the numbers themselves. However, instead of beginning the OBV line at zero and allowing its value to slip into negative territory, a large whole number is generally used as the starting point. This is just to keep the value of the OBV line positive and its plotting simpler. A number like 10,000 is generally employed as the starting value. In reality, whether the actual value of the OBV line is positive or negative means very little.

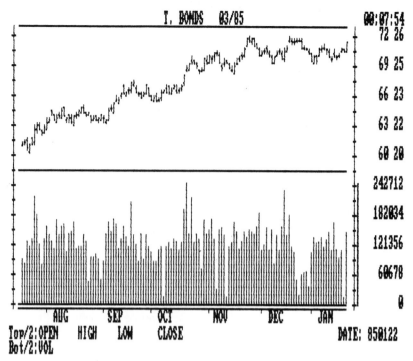

T. BONDS   03/85
00:07:54
72 26
69 25
66 23
63 22
60 20
242712
182034
121356
60678
0
AUG   SEP   OCT   NOV   DEC   JAN
Top/2:OPEN   HIGH   LOW   CLOSE
Bot/2:VOL
DATE: 850122

Figure 7.6a   In this bar chart of Treasury Bonds with volume bars, it's not that easy to tell which way the volume is flowing by just "eyeballing" the vertical volume bars.

Figure 7.6b   The lower line is the on balance volume line, or (OBV). Notice how much easier it is to follow the volume flow.

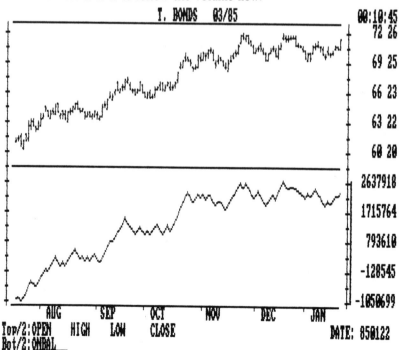

T. BONDS   03/85
00:10:45
72 26
69 25
66 23
63 22
60 20
2637918
1715764
793610
-128545
-1050699
AUG   SEP   OCT   NOV   DEC   JAN
Top/2:OPEN   HIGH   LOW   CLOSE
Bot/2:ONBAL
DATE: 850122

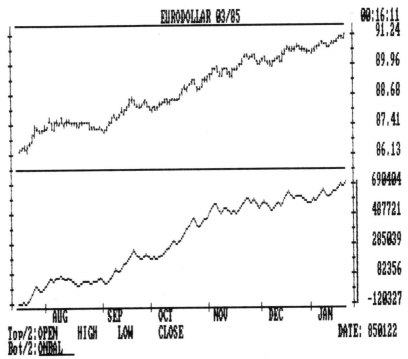

Figure 7.7a The bottom line is another example of OBV. Notice that the OBV line is trending higher and confirming the bull trend in prices.

Figure 7.7b Notice in this example that the OBV line is moving sideways and is not confirming the lower price trend. This might be a warning signal not to be too bearish at this point in the downtrend.

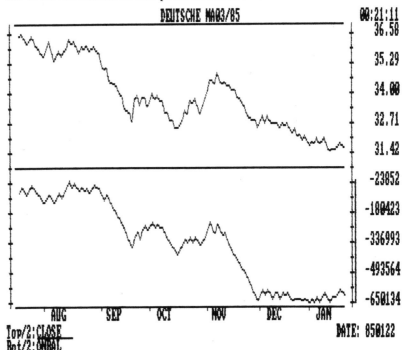

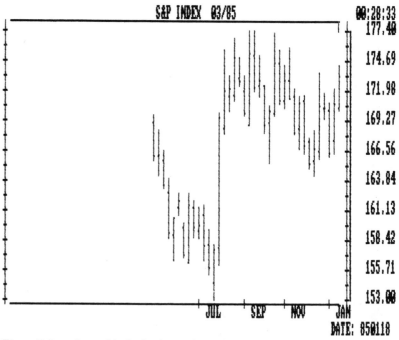

Figure 7.8a A weekly high, low, close chart of an S&P futures contract.

Figure 7.8b On balance volume can be plotted on weekly charts as well. Notice in this example that the OBV line is already in new highs, and is giving off bullish readings.

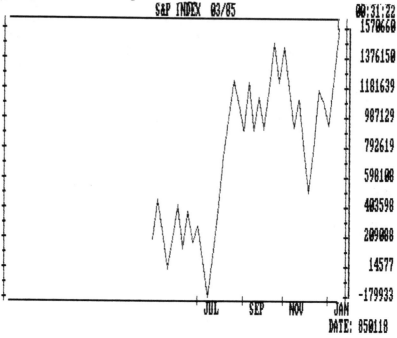

The *on balance volume* line should follow in the same direction as the price trend. If prices show a series of higher peaks and troughs (an uptrend), the OBV line should do the same. If prices are trending lower, so should the OBV line. It's when the volume line fails to move in the same direction as prices that a divergence exists and warns of a possible trend reversal.

Various technical indicators can be applied to the OBV line in the exact same fashion as the price trend. Peaks (resistance) and troughs (support) are readily seen on the volume line. In addition, *trendline* analysis and the use of *moving averages* can be applied to spot trend reversals in the OBV. There's no reason why oscillator analysis couldn't also be applied to the volume line. A few examples are shown of the OBV line in action in the accompanying charts.

Volume Accumulation: An Alternative to OBV

The *on balance volume* line does its job reasonably well, but it has some shortcomings. For one thing, it seems unrealistic to assign an entire day's volume a plus or minus value. Suppose a market closes up on the day by some minimal amount such as one or two tics. Is it reasonable to assign all of that day's activity a positive value? Or consider a situation where the market spends most of the day on the upside, but then closes slightly lower. Should all of that day's volume be given a negative value? To resolve these questions, technicians have experimented with many variations of OBV in an attempt to discover the true upside and downside volume.

One variation is to give greater weight to those days where the trend is the strongest. On an up day, for example, the volume is multiplied by the amount of the price gain. This technique still assigns positive and negative values, but gives greater weight to those days with greater price movement and reduces the impact of those days where the actual price change is minimal.

Another alternative to Granville's *on balance volume* is an indicator devised by Marc Chaikin of Drexel Burnham Lambert in New York City called *volume accumulation (VA)*. Chaikin's volume accumulation is a more sensitive intra-day measure of volume in relation to price action. It is considered more useful in stocks, but can also be applied to commodity futures (particularly those markets with large public participation). Whereas the OBV line assigns all of the day's volume a positive or negative value, *volume accumulation* counts only a percentage of the volume as plus or minus, depending on where the close is in relation to its mean (or average) price for the day. In other words, if prices close above the daily mean (or midpoint in the range), a percentage of that day's volume is given a positive value. If prices close below the midpoint, a percentage of the day's value is assigned a negative value. (See Figures 7.9a to 7.10b.)

The only time the entire day's volume is assigned a positive value is when the close is the same as the day's high. When the opposite occurs, and prices close right at the day's low, all the day's volume is counted as negative. To construct the line, assume a starting value of 10,000 and use the following formula:

$$VA = \{[(C-L) - (H-C)]/(H-L)\} \times V$$

where H = High, C = Close, L = Low, and V = Volume.

The volume accumulation line is used along with price action in the exact same way as the OBV line and either moves with or diverges from the price action. Various technical tools can be applied to the VA line to help track its trend. The VA line can also be turned into an oscillator, which is discussed in Chapter 10.

There are other more complicated formulas that incorporate volume with the price action. *The Demand Index* developed by James Sibbet of Sibbet Publications in Pasadena, Calif. is an example of such. Computer software is now available for all three of the volume indicators mentioned here, eliminating the tedious chore of constructing and maintaining them. The Compu Trac group in New Orleans includes all three in their technical analysis software. Many other Compu Trac routines are used in later chapters.

Even with the more sophisticated variations of OBV, however, the intent is always the same—to determine whether the heavier volume is taking place on the upside (bullish) or the downside (bearish). For all of its simplicity, the OBV line still does a pretty good job of tracking the volume curve of a market. It can be used as a coincident (confirming indicator) or as a leading indicator of a price move, depending on the situation. Because it presents the volume curve in more graphic form that can be viewed and analyzed more easily, the OBV line (or some variation thereof) can be a very useful addition to the chartist's weaponry.

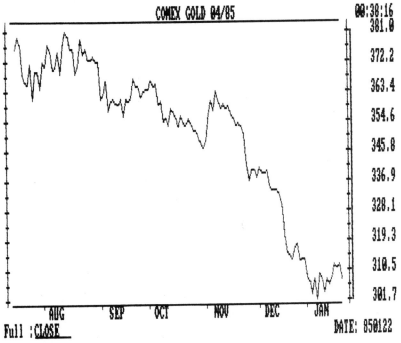

Figure 7.9a A close-only chart of a gold contract.

Figure 7.9b A comparison of the OBV line (upper line) and volume accumulation (lower line). In this case, the VA line appears more sensitive. The sharp rise in the VA line in November has to be viewed as a false signal.

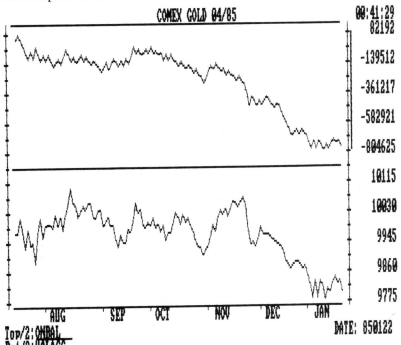

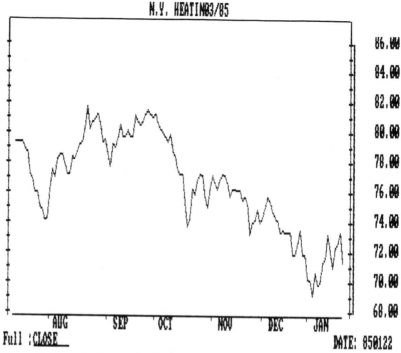

Figure 7.10a   A close-only chart of a heating oil contract.

Figure 7.10b   Another comparison of the OBV and the volume accumulation line. The OBV (upper) line has bounced sharply, while the VA (lower) line has continued into new lows. Subsequent market action suggests the VA line was the better performer here. Prices sold off sharply after this chart was constructed.

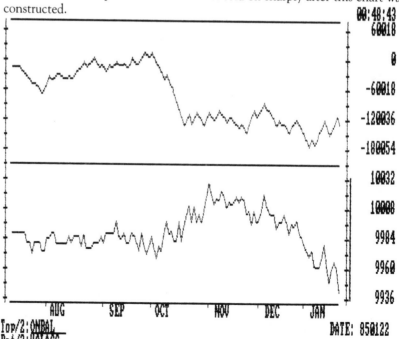

Volume Analysis Not as Useful in Commodity Futures

Volume analysis is not considered as useful in commodity futures as in stocks. For one thing, there is the problem of the one-day lag in reporting the numbers. For another, there is the relatively awkward practice of using total volume numbers to analyze individual contracts instead of each contract's actual volume. There are good reasons for using total volume. But how does one deal with situations when some contracts close higher and others lower in the same commodity market on the same day? *Limit* days produce other problems. Days when markets are locked *limit up* usually produce very light volume. This is a sign of strength as the numbers of buyers so overwhelm the sellers that prices reach the maximum trading limit and cease trading. According to the traditional rules of interpretation, light volume on a rally is bearish. The light volume on *limit* days is a violation of that principle and can distort OBV numbers.

Another problem is the absence of upside-downside volume, available in the stock market averages, and the number of shares traded on upticks versus downticks in individual common stocks. This useful information is not available in commodity futures. Even with these limitations, however, volume analysis can still be used to great advantage in the futures markets, and the technical trader would be well-advised to keep a watchful eye on these volume indications.

INTERPRETATION OF OPEN INTEREST

The rules for interpreting open interest changes are similar to those for volume, but require additional explanation.

1. With prices advancing in an uptrend, if total open interest increases more than its seasonal average (the five-year average), *new money is flowing into the market reflecting aggressive new buying, and is considered bullish.*

2. If, however, prices are rising and open interest declines more than seasonally, *the rally is being caused primarily by short covering* (holders of losing short positions being forced to cover those positions). *Money is leaving rather than entering the market.* This action is considered bearish because the uptrend will probably run out of steam once the necessary short covering has been completed.

3. With prices in a downtrend and open interest rising more than seasonally, the technician knows that *new money is flowing into the market, reflecting aggressive new short selling*. This action increases the odds that the downtrend will continue and is considered bearish.

4. If, however, total open interest is declining more than seasonally along with declining prices, *the price decline is being caused by discouraged or losing longs being forced to liquidate their positions*. This action is believed to indicate a strengthening technical situation because the downtrend will probably end once open interest has declined sufficiently to show that most losing longs have completed their selling.

Let's summarize these four points:

1. *Rising open interest in an uptrend is bullish.*

2. *Declining open interest in an uptrend is bearish.*

3. *Rising open interest in a downtrend is bearish.*

4. *Declining open interest in a downtrend is bullish.*

Other Situations
Where Open Interest Is Important

In addition to the preceding tendencies, there are other market situations where a study of open interest can prove useful.

1. Toward the end of major market moves, where open interest has been increasing throughout the price trend, *a leveling off or decline in open interest is often an early warning of a change in trend.* (See Figure 7.11.)

2. *A high open interest figure at market tops can be considered bearish if the price drop is very sudden.* This means that all of the new longs established near the end of the uptrend now have losing positions. Their forced liquidation will keep prices under pressure until the open interest has declined sufficiently. As an example, let's assume that an uptrend has been in effect for some time. Over the past month, open interest has increased noticeably. Remember that every new open interest contract has one new long and one new short. Suddenly, prices begin to drop sharply and fall below the lowest price set over the past month. Every single new long established during that month now has a loss.

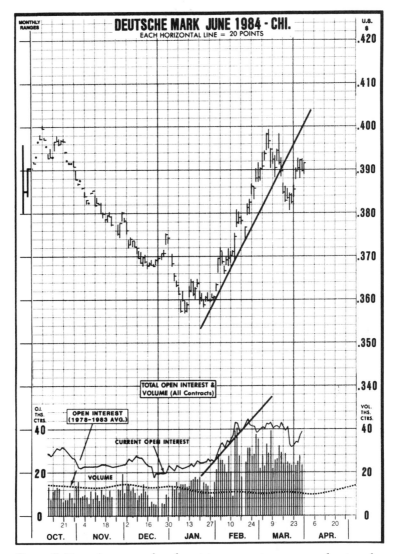

Figure 7.11a An example of a rising open interest confirming the rally. Note, however, that the leveling off of open interest beginning in late February warned of a market top. Prices dropped sharply from that point. (Courtesy of Commodity Research Bureau, a Knight-Ridder Business Information Service.)

The forced liquidation of those longs keeps prices under pressure until they have all been liquidated. Worse still, their forced selling often begins to feed on itself and, as prices are pushed even lower, causes additional margin selling by other longs and intensifies the new

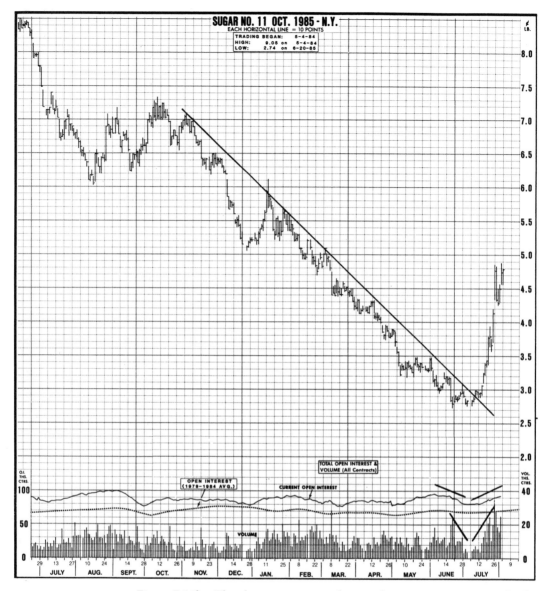

Figure 7.11b The dramatic turn to the upside in sugar prices can also be seen in the volume and open interest numbers. Notice the sharp dip in both volume and open interest just prior to the steep rally in July. Note the rising volume and open interest during July showing a significant shift in market sentiment from bearish to bullish, enhancing the probability that an important bottom has been seen. (Courtesy of Commodity Research Bureau, a Knight-Ridder Business Information Service.)

price decline. One of the most striking examples of this phenomenon took place toward the end of 1980 when commodity markets peaked and began a five-year tumble. Several markets got caught with historically high open interest figures that helped fuel the ensuing price collapse. As a corollary to the preceding point, *an unusually high open interest in a bull market is a danger signal.* (See Figure 7.12.)

3. *If open interest builds up noticeably during a sideways consolidation or a horizontal trading range, the ensuing price move intensifies once the breakout occurs.* This only stands to reason. The market is in a period

Figure 7.12 A classic example of how very high open interest can be a bearish factor if prices begin to drop. Prices dropped $2.00 in two weeks. All of the longs established since late August had losing positions. Prices remained in a downtrend until those losing longs were liquidated. Notice the subsequent sharp drop in the open interest line. (Courtesy of Commodity Research Bureau, a Knight-Ridder Business Information Service.)

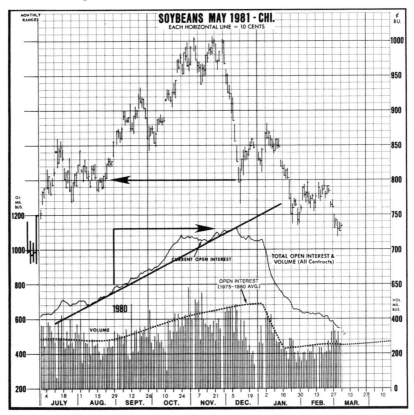

of indecision. No one is sure which direction the trend breakout will take. The increase in open interest, however, tells us that a lot of traders are taking positions in anticipation of the breakout. Once that breakout does occur, a lot of traders are going to be caught on the wrong side of the market. (Check back to Figure 7.5 where this phenomenon is illustrated by the breakdown in the silver market.)

Let's assume we've had a three-month trading range and that the open interest has jumped by 10,000 contracts. This means that 10,000 new long positions and 10,000 new short positions have been taken. Prices then break out on the upside and new three-month highs are established. Because prices are trading at the highest point in three months, every single short position (all 10,000 of them) initiated during the previous three months now shows a loss. The scramble to cover those losing shorts naturally causes additional upside pressure on prices, producing even more panic. Prices remain strong until all or most of those 10,000 short positions have been offset by buying into the market strength. If the breakout had been to the downside, then it would have been the longs doing the scrambling and the shorts the smiling.

The early stages of any new trend immediately following a break-out are usually fueled by panic liquidation by those caught on the wrong side of the market. The more traders caught on the wrong side (manifested in the high open interest), the more severe the response to a sudden adverse market move. On a more pleasant note, the new trend is further aided by those on the right side of the market (the smart or the lucky ones) whose judgment has been vindicated, and who are now using accumulated paper profits to finance additional positions. (A sobering thought to ponder is that for every new open interest contract created, someone is making a mistake.) It can be seen why *the greater the increase in open interest during a trading range (or any price formation for that matter), the greater the potential for the subsequent price move.*

4. *Increasing open interest at the completion of a price pattern is viewed as added confirmation of a reliable trend signal.* The breaking of the *neckline*, for example, of a *head and shoulders* bottom is more convincing if the breakout occurs on increasing open interest along with the heavier volume. The analyst has to be careful here. Because the impetus following the initial trend signal is often caused by those on the wrong side of the market, *sometimes the open interest dips slightly at the beginning of a new trend.* This initial dip in the open interest can mislead the unwary chart reader, and argues against focusing too much attention on the open interest changes over the very short term.

SUMMARY OF
VOLUME AND OPEN INTEREST RULES

Let's summarize some of the more important elements of price, volume, and open interest.

1. Only the *total* volume and open interest are used for forecasting.

2. Open interest must be seasonally adjusted.

3. Increasing volume and open interest indicate that the current price trend will probably continue.

4. Declining volume and open interest suggest that the price trend may be changing.

5. Volume precedes price. Changes in buying or selling pressure are often detected in volume before price.

6. On balance volume (OBV), or some variation thereof, can be used to more accurately measure the direction of volume pressure.

7. Within an uptrend, a sudden leveling off or decline in open interest often warns of a change in trend.

8. Very high open interest at market tops is dangerous and can intensify downside pressure.

9. A buildup in open interest during consolidation periods intensifies the ensuing breakout.

10. Increases in volume and open interest help confirm the resolution of price patterns or any other significant chart developments that signal the beginning of a new trend.

BLOWOFFS AND SELLING CLIMAXES

One final situation not covered so far that deserves mention is the type of dramatic market action that often takes places at tops and bottoms—*blowoffs* and *selling climaxes*. *Blowoffs* occur at major market tops and *selling climaxes* at bottoms. In the case of a blowoff at market tops, prices suddenly begin to rally sharply after a long advance, accompanied by a large jump in trading activity and a sizeable decline in the open interest. In a selling climax, after a long decline, prices suddenly drop sharply on heavy trading activity with a large decline in open interest. (See Figure 7.13.)

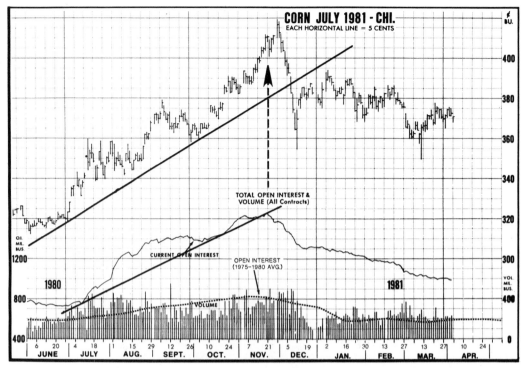

Figure 7.13 Example of a blowoff. Notice the heavy volume during the last stages of the uptrend. Of more significance, notice that the open interest began to drop sharply the week before the prices topped. A drop in open interest after a sharp price advance is bearish. (Courtesy of Commodity Research Bureau, a Knight-Ridder Business Information Service.)

The two things to watch for in each case are a sudden spurt in volume and a sharp drop in open interest. These two factors together after an extended price move reveal significant liquidation in progress and are warning signals of an impending and often sudden change of trend.

COMMITMENTS OF TRADERS REPORT

Our treatment of open interest would not be complete without mentioning the *Commitments of Traders Report* and how it is used by technicians as a forecasting tool. The report is released by the Commodity Futures Trading Commission (CFTC) on the eleventh day of each month and shows open interest statistics as of the end of the previous month. The monthly report breaks down the open interest numbers into three categories—*large hedgers, large speculators,* and *small traders.* When commodity futures traders start dealing in large enough quantities to reach reportable levels in each market, these trades must be reported to the CFTC. The reported numbers are then used to compile the open interest statistics for large hedgers and traders. By subtracting those numbers from the total open interest, the resulting difference is presumed to be the small traders.

The value in having access to these numbers rests on the theory that large traders are presumed to represent "smart money." Let's say that small traders are considered to be less informed and not as astute at the skill of trading as are their larger counterparts. It is presumed that a small trader who gets smarter will cease being a small trader and will join the ranks of the larger traders. It is also presumed that any large trader who loses some of his or her smarts will cease being a large trader and will quickly become a small trader.

This type of analysis has long been performed by stock market technicians. Stock exchange specialists are presumed to usually be right on the market and their trading activity is closely monitored to see what they are doing. By contrast, the *odd lotters* (or the general public, often referred to smugly as the "little guy") supposedly have a history of being wrong most of the time on the direction of the market.

Some research done on the futures markets suggests that of the three categories, the large hedgers are the most successful in calling market turns. The next best group is the large speculator with the small traders coming in third. (See Figure 7.14.)

The correct way to use these statistics is to ally oneself with the "smart" money and to avoid doing what the less successful traders are doing. Figure 7.14 shows what the table looks like as it appears in the *CRB Futures Chart Service.* Notice the three categories along the top. Each category has four columns—% long, % short, net, and the delta symbol showing the % change from the previous month. In this table, for example, the live cattle market as of December 31, 1984 shows that large hedgers are 14% long and 43% short. The −29 in the third column means they are 29% net short (43% − 14%). The −2 in the fourth column means that the large hedgers in cattle are 2% more net short than they were the previous month.

The notations along the bottom of the table explain how to read the data in the table. Notice the caution that the positions do not always add up to 100% because intermarket spreading statistics are not included. Adding up the total long positions in cattle for all three categories—14% for large hedgers, 19% for large speculators, and 62% for small traders—we get a total of only 95%. Intermarket spreading accounts for the remaining 5%.

COMMITMENTS OF TRADERS—LARGE HEDGERS, SPECULATORS AND SMALL TRADERS											
Open Interest Positions Shown in Percent (Rounded) as of December 31, 1984											
MARKETS	LARGE HEDGERS				LARGE SPECULATORS				SMALL TRADERS			
	Long	Short	Net	△	Long	Short	Net	△	Long	Short	Net	△
Cattle (Live)	14	43	-29	-2	19	4	+15	+1	62	49	+13	-1
Cocoa	82	65	+17	+4	5	16	-11	+2	11	17	-6	-6
Coffee	51	70	-19	-2	16	5	+11	-1	29	21	+8	+3
Copper	42	76	-34	0	8	5	+3	+3	49	18	+31	-2
Corn	63	48	+15	-9	1	9	-8	0	34	42	-8	+7
Cotton	53	41	+12	-1	3	7	-4	+5	43	51	-8	-5
Crude Oil (N.Y.)	82	32	+50	+23	9	40	-31	-23	8	26	-18	+1
Gold (Comex)	73	59	+14	-1	3	11	-8	-1	13	19	-6	+2
Heating Oil #2	55	65	-10	-5	18	13	+5	+3	26	22	+4	0
Hogs	9	15	-6	-4	22	8	+14	-6	59	67	-8	+10
Leaded Gas (N.Y.)	83	72	+11	-3	2	14	-12	0	16	14	+2	+4
Lumber	21	36	-15	+8	11	5	+6	+2	63	54	+9	-9
Orange Juice	53	65	-12	+14	4	4	0	-5	39	27	+12	-10
Platinum	59	74	-15	+8	11	4	+7	-3	24	17	+7	-7
Pork Bellies	10	16	-6	-9	24	12	+12	-5	46	52	-6	+14
Silver (Comex)	47	57	-10	+1	6	9	-3	-1	34	21	+13	-1
Soybeans	32	45	-13	-4	5	6	-1	+1	56	41	+15	+5
Soybean Meal	50	29	+21	+15	3	8	-5	+3	34	50	-16	-17
Soybean Oil	48	41	+7	+1	2	4	-2	0	47	52	-5	0
Sugar "11"	34	64	-30	+8	15	7	+8	+1	51	28	+23	-7
Wheat (CHI)	32	38	-6	+3	7	12	-5	-7	54	43	+11	+5
Wheat (K.C.)	63	58	+5	-1	0	6	-6	-4	34	33	+1	+5
Wheat (Minn)	46	52	-6	0	0	0	0	+1	55	49	+6	-1
Euro $	70	64	+6	-1	7	8	-1	+4	18	23	-5	-2
T-Bills (90 Days)	40	63	-23	-3	15	1	+14	+3	37	29	+8	-2
T-Bonds	51	57	-6	-1	6	9	-3	-6	32	23	+9	+7
T-Notes	81	78	+3	+8	3	6	-3	-1	13	15	-2	+8
NYSE Composite	3	37	-34	-30	28	24	+4	+27	62	32	+30	+2
S&P 500	33	53	-20	-14	21	13	+8	+12	46	34	+12	+2
Value Line	8	28	-20	-15	14	26	-12	-3	77	45	+32	+18
British Pound	45	14	+31	+21	19	35	-16	-11	33	49	-16	-11
Deutsche Mark	32	62	-30	+1	26	9	+17	+9	42	29	+13	-9
Japanese Yen	24	28	-4	+5	34	28	+6	+10	40	44	-4	-17
Swiss Franc	20	42	-22	+23	20	18	+2	-14	60	40	+20	-10

△ Change in % Net from Previous Month (**PLUS** — increased long or decreased short.
MINUS — increased short or decreased long)   * Less than .05%
NOTE: Positions do not equal 100% because intermarket statistics are not included.

Figure 7.14 Table courtesy of the Commodity Research Bureau, a Knight-Ridder Business Information Service.

SEASONAL CONSIDERATIONS

Before inspecting the numbers in Figure 7.14 more closely, there is an important feature that must be taken into consideration and that is the seasonal movements in the statistics. Each group appears to follow certain seasonal trading habits. It is the departure from those normal seasonal trading habits that gives the real clues as to their trading attitudes. An article in the *1985 Commodity Year Book* by William L. Jiler (published by the Commodity Research Bureau, Jersey City, N.J., 1985) explains how that organization uses these statistics, and discusses some of the results of his own original research in this area.

> The differences between their current net open interest position and the seasonal norm supply us with a tangible percentage measure of the degree of bullishness or bearishness of each group towards a particular market to a certain extent. ("Analysis of the CFTC Commitments of Traders Reports Can Help You Forecast Futures Prices," Jiler, p. 52T.)

The article then goes on to present some general guidelines.

> The most bullish configuration would show large hedgers heavily net long more than normal, large speculators clearly net long, small traders heavily net short more than seasonal. The shades of bullishness are varied all the way to the most bearish configuration which would have these groups in opposite positions—large hedgers heavily net short, etc. Be wary of positions that are more than 40% from their long-term average and disregard deviations of less than 5%.

The results of the CRB research showed that while both categories of large traders had superior track records, the large hedgers outperformed the large speculators. The small traders had the worst performance of the three.

Figure 7.15 shows a sampling of some of the charts used by the CRB in tracking the seasonal habits of the three categories of traders (taken from the same article already cited). The trick is to compare the actual numbers in the table with the seasonal norms shown on the charts. Let's go back to the latest report and draw some conclusions.

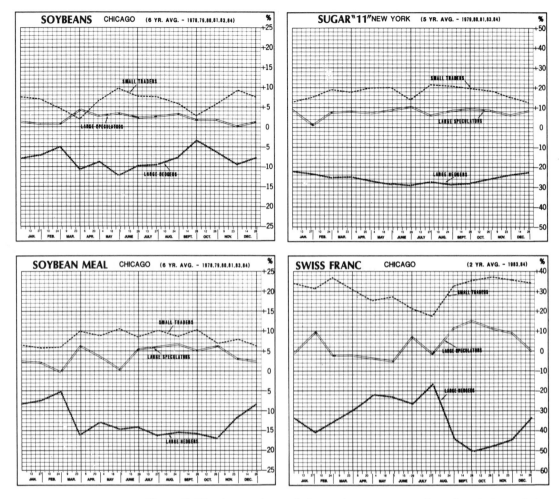

Figure 7.15 A sampling of charts showing seasonal trading habits of the three categories of traders. It's important to take these tendencies into consideration in tracking the attitude of each group. (Source: 1985 Commodity Year Book, Commodity Research Bureau, Jersey City, NJ.)

Take a look at the statistics for soybean meal. Quoting from the "Technical Comments" section in the January 18, 1985 issue of the *CRB Futures Chart Service* (written by the author), "The *Commitment of Traders Report* shows an unusually bullish configuration in that market." Let's see why. The report shows large hedgers 21% net long with an increase of 15% from the previous month. Small traders are 16% net short and 17% more short than the month before. Therefore, large hedgers are bullish and becoming more so. Small traders are bearish and becoming even more bearish.

Now look at the CRB seasonal chart for soybean meal. At the end of December, large hedgers are normally about 8% net short, while small traders are about 6% net long. This means that the actual numbers are even more bullish than they first appear. Large traders are 29% more bullish than normal (from -8% to $+21\%$) and small traders are 22% more bearish than usual ($+6\%$ to -16%). On the surface, the mere fact that the large hedgers are bullish and the small traders bearish is considered bullish. By netting out the seasonal tendencies, the numbers become even more bullish.

Just glancing at some of the other numbers, a few other things jump out. Scan the last columns of the three categories for any large changes. Notice the large positive changes in the large hedgers for crude oil ($+23$), orange juice ($+14\%$), British pound ($+21\%$) and Swiss franc ($+23\%$). Those markets might be watched for bullish developments. Small traders display a growing positive attitude for hogs ($+10\%$) and pork bellies ($+14\%$), which might be considered bearish for pork prices. Small traders show a strong negative bias towards orange juice (-10%) and the foreign currencies that might be taken as a bullish indication in those markets.

There's another way to view these numbers and that is to look for unusually large readings in the % long or short columns for small traders (above 70% would be considered large). Because this group is presumed to usually be wrong, a strong preference for one side of the market would be a warning that the market should go in the opposite direction (or so the theory goes).

In this report, some high readings in the % long column (potentially bearish) are cattle (62%) and lumber (63%). High numbers are also visible for the NYSE Composite Index (62%) and the Value Line Index (77%). Recent action appears to be supporting the judgment of the smaller traders in the stock indices. It should be noted here that most of the research in this area has been done on the traditional agricultural markets. Caution is advised in placing too much weight on an analysis of the *Commitments of Traders Report* in the newer financial futures markets until more research is done in that area.

A monthly analysis of the *Commitments of Traders Report* is another way to look at the open interest statistics by monitoring what the three major categories of market participants are doing. One major drawback of the approach is that the statistics are at least two weeks old before they can be analyzed and may have already lost some of their usefulness.

This is not an area of technical analysis that has received a great deal of attention in the commodity futures markets. It has been used extensively in stock market work, but has not attracted a wide following among futures chartists. It is an area, however, that would seem to lend itself to further investigation because of its potential for measuring market sentiment. (We'll have more to say on market sentiment during our discussion of *Contrary Opinion* in Chapter 10.) In any event, the *Commitments of Traders Report* is an area of technical analysis that the reader should at least be aware of and that can be monitored from time to time. A book that spends a good deal of time on the subject of "open interest mix" is *Charting Commodity Market Price Behavior*, 2nd edition, by L. Dee Belveal (Homewood, Ill: Dow Jones-Irwin, 1985).

CONCLUSION

Not only have we concluded our discussion of volume and open interest, but also a significant portion of the body of technical analysis of commodity futures markets. We've discussed the theory behind technical analysis, many of the building blocks used in that analysis, chart construction, and the study of price patterns. We've covered the three sources of data available to the technician—price, volume, and open interest.

But so far we've limited our coverage to the *daily* bar chart. The next step is to broaden our time horizon and to learn how to apply these valuable analytical aids to long-term weekly and monthly continuation charts for purposes of longer-range trend analysis. While we're at it, we'll also begin to include in our work a study of the broader commodity price indices and the indices of the various market groups. We'll accomplish all of this in the next chapter.

8
Long-Term Charts and Commodity Indices

INTRODUCTION

Of all the charts utilized by the market technician for forecasting and trading the commodity futures markets, the *daily* bar chart is by far the most popular. The daily bar chart usually covers a period of only six to nine months in the life of a futures contract. However, because most commodity futures traders and analysts confine their interest to relatively short-term market action, daily bar charts have gained wide acceptance as the primary working tool of the futures chartist. The relative ease in maintaining these charts and the fact that they are readily obtainable from commercial chart services also contribute to their popularity. (With recent improvements in computer technology and reporting capabilities, the intra-day chart is becoming more popular for even finer market inspection.)

The average commodity trader's dependence on these daily charts, however, and the preoccupation with short-term market behavior, cause many to overlook a very useful and rewarding area of price charting—*the use of weekly and monthly continuation charts for longer-*

range trend analysis and forecasting. The value of these charts is not limited to individual markets. These longer-range charts are also extremely helpful in studying the major trend performance of general commodity indices and the indices of various market groups.

The daily bar chart covers a relatively short period of time in the life of any market. A thorough trend analysis of a market, however, should include some consideration of how the daily market price is moving in relation to its long-range trend structure. In order to accomplish that task, *longer-range continuation charts are the tools that must be employed.* Whereas on the daily bar chart each bar represents one day's price action, on the weekly and monthly charts each price bar represents one week's and one month's price action, respectively. *The purpose of weekly and monthly charts is to compress price action in such a way that the time horizon can be greatly expanded and much longer time periods can be studied.*

THE IMPORTANCE OF LONGER-RANGE PERSPECTIVE

Long-range price charts provide a perspective on the market trend that is impossible to achieve with the use of daily charts alone. During our introduction to the technical philosophy in Chapter 1, it was pointed out that one of the greatest advantages of chart analysis is the application of its principles to virtually any time dimension, including long-range forecasting. We also addressed the fallacy, espoused by some, that technical analysis should be limited to short-term "timing" with longer-range forecasting left to the fundamental analyst.

I believe that the accompanying charts will amply demonstrate that the principles of technical analysis—including trend analysis, support and resistance levels, trendlines and channels, percentage retracements, and price patterns—lend themselves quite well to the analysis of long-range price movements. I'll go a step further here and state that *anyone who is not consulting these longer-range charts is missing an enormous amount of valuable price information.*

CONSTRUCTION OF CONTINUATION CHARTS

The average commodity futures contract has a trading life of about a year and a half before expiration. This *limited life* feature poses some obvious problems for the technician interested in constructing a long-range chart going back several years. Stock market technicians don't have this problem. Charts are readily available for individual common stocks and the market averages from the inception of trading. How then does the commodity futures technician construct longer-range charts for contracts that are constantly expiring?

The answer is the *continuation* chart. Notice the emphasis on the word "continuation." The technique most commonly employed is simply to link a number of contracts together to provide continuity. When one contract expires, another one is used. In order to accomplish this, the simplest method, and the one used by most chart services, is to *always use the price of the nearest expiring contract*. When that nearest expiring contract stops trading, the next in line becomes the nearest contract and is the one plotted.

The continuation charts used in this chapter are provided by the Commodity Research Bureau. That firm has a weekly publication, the *CRB Futures Chart Service*, which provides daily price charts on all the futures markets. As a supplement to the daily charts, weekly continuation charts are also made available. A set of monthly continuation charts is mailed quarterly. The weekly charts cover a period of four and a half years and the monthly charts go back twenty-two years.

Other Ways to Construct Continuation Charts

The technique of linking prices of the nearest expiring contracts is relatively simple and does solve the problem of providing price continuity. However, there are some minor problems with that method. Sometimes the expiring contract may be trading at a significant premium or discount to the next contract, and the changeover to the new contract may cause a sudden price drop or jump on the chart. Another potential distortion is the extreme volatility experienced by some *spot* contracts just before expiration.

Technicians have devised many ways to deal with these occasional distortions. Some will stop plotting the nearest contract a month or two before it expires to avoid the volatility in the spot month. Others will avoid using the nearest contract altogether and will instead chart the second or third contract. Another method is to chart the contract with the highest open interest on the theory that that delivery month is the truest representation of market value.

Continuation charts can also be constructed by linking specific calendar months. For example, a November soybean continuation chart would combine only the historic data provided by each successive year's November soybean contract. (This technique of linking specific delivery months was favored by W.D. Gann.) Some chartists go even further by averaging the prices of several contracts, or constructing indices that attempt to smooth the changeover by making adjustments in the price premium or discount.

THE PERPETUAL CONTRACT ™

An article in the March 1983 issue of *Commodities* (now *Futures*) Magazine, "Contracts That Don't Expire Aid Technical Analysis," describes an innovative solution to the problem of price continuity. Written by Robert Pelletier, president of Commodity Systems, Inc., a commodity and stock data service for microcomputer users, located in Boca Raton, Florida, the article introduced a new concept called the *Perpetual Contract* ™. ("Perpetual Contract ™" and "CSI Perpetual Contract ™" are registered trademarks of that firm.)

The purpose of the Perpetual Contract ™ is to provide years of futures price history in one continuous time series. That is accomplished by constructing a time series based on a constant forward time period. For example, the series would determine a value three months or six months into the future. The time period varies and can be chosen by the user. The Perpetual Contract ™ is constructed by taking a weighted average of two futures contracts that surround the time period desired. For example, if we are now in January and wish to construct a three-month Perpetual Contract ™, we first determine that three months forward in time would be April. Then choose the two active trading months surrounding April. Let's suppose that those two months are March and May. The actual technique for finding the weighted average is described in the article. If today is January 20, then take a price chart and mark a vertical line three months forward (on April 20). Then plot the closing prices for the two surrounding contracts on their respective expiration dates (let's say, for example, March 26 and May 28). Then draw a straight line connecting those two prices. Where that line crosses the vertical line at April 20 would be the correct value for the three-month Perpetual Contract ™.

The value for the Perpetual Contract ™ is not an actual price, but a weighted average of two other prices. For more information on the construction of the weighted average and its possible advantages, read the article or contact CSI. The main advantage of the Perpetual Contract ™, as stated by Pelletier, is that it eliminates the need for using only the nearest expiring contract and smooths out the price series by eliminating the distortions that can take place during the transition between delivery months.

THE PERPETUAL INDEX ™

Commodity Systems, Inc. recently announced an even newer concept called the *Perpetual Index* ™. While the Perpetual Contract ™ is based on the prices of futures contracts, the Perpetual Index ™ converts those values into an index. One of the obvious advantages of indexes is the ease in comparing the relative performance of different markets. CSI is also introducing Perpetual Indexes ™ on various market groups as well as a CRB look-alike index. That latter index will use the same markets as the CRB Futures Index, but with a different base year.

Whether or not these more sophisticated techniques prove themselves to be more valuable than the use of the nearest expiring contract remains to be seen. It should be emphasized that even with the relatively minor distortions in the latter technique, the method of construction that links the nearest contracts is still the most commonly used, being simple to maintain and, more importantly, having been proven to be quite effective over the years.

The Perpetual Contract™, by contrast, is cumbersome to construct each day for all the markets. The daily weighted averages can be obtained daily from CSI by the use of a computer and phone modem, but at much greater expense. The user must, therefore, balance the historical track record and simplicity of the older method against the possible benefits of the newer techniques with their difficulty in construction and greater expense.

CHARTING TECHNIQUES CAN BE APPLIED TO LONG-TERM CHARTS

It bears repeating that most of the charting techniques that are applied to daily bar charts can be applied to weekly and monthly charts as well. This claim might even be carried a step further by stating that long range trend forecasting can often be easier than short-term forecasting. Two of the basic tenets of technical analysis are: (1) that markets move in trends, and (2) that trends tend to persist. One of the most striking features of long-range charts is that not only are trends very clearly defined, but that long-range trends often last for years.

Imagine making a forecast based on one of these long-range trends, and not having to change that forecast for several years! By contrast, most technical market letters published today in the futures industry focus on the short-term and are often out of date before they reach their readers through the mail. This necessitates the use of electronic mail and telephone hotlines to keep them current until the next letter is sent.

The persistence of long-range trends raises another interesting question that should be mentioned—the question of *randomness*. While technical analysts do not subscribe to the theory that market action is random and unpredictable, it seems safe to observe that whatever randomness does exist in price action is probably a phenomenon of the very short term. *The persistence of existing trends over long periods of time, in many cases for years, is a compelling argument against the claims of Random Walk Theorists that prices are serially independent and that past price action has no effect on future price action.*

SUMMARY OF TECHNICAL PRINCIPLES

Before looking at the accompanying price charts, it might be useful to briefly recap some of the technical principles utilized in the examples. The cornerstone of the technical philosophy is that all of the relevant data that an analyst needs to forecast market direction is recorded on the price chart. Technical analysts believe that market price discounts (or reflects) all of the information that can ultimately affect that price. Rising prices are indicative of a bullish market psychology, while declining prices reflect a bearish psychology.

Technicians believe that the technical approach in a sense includes fundamental analysis, because the charts reflect the market's assessment of those fundamentals of supply and demand that cause bull and bear markets. Therefore, the chartist can conclude that, if prices are rising, demand must exceed supply and that the fundamentals must be bullish. The chartist, then, studies market action for clues as to which way prices are most likely to move. What he or she is attempting to do is to spot important trends in the price data as early as possible. As mentioned earlier, prices move in trends and these trends have a strong tendency to persist. Most technical *trend-following systems* do nothing more than identify existing trends in early stages of development. Then the systems take positions in the direction of those trends until some price evidence is given that the trend is ending or reversing.

TERMINOLOGY OF TECHNICAL ANALYSIS

Over the past 100 years, technicians have developed a terminology to describe different types of market action and a number of techniques to aid them in their forecasting. *Trend* is the general direction of the price move. The standard definition of an *uptrend* is a series of gradually ascending peaks and troughs. A *downtrend* is a series of descending peaks and troughs. In a sideways trend, these peaks and troughs are horizontal. Trends are usually classified as *major, intermediate,* or *minor.* Major trends often last for years. These major trends are the subject of this chapter.

Resistance is a price level (or zone) above the market where increased selling is expected. Most often, a previous peak represents resistance. *Support* is a price level (or zone) under the market where increased buying is expected. Usually, a *support level* is a previous reaction low. The presence of historic support and resistance levels going back for several years and their continuing ability to influence market action is probably the most striking feature of long-range charts. A support or resistance level, once penetrated by a reasonable margin, becomes its opposite. Once a support level is violated by a reasonable amount, it becomes a resistance level. In an uptrend, a penetrated resistance level becomes a new support level. An example of this phenomenon is seen on the cattle chart (Figure 8.7) where historic resistance levels at 35.00 and 56.00 later became support levels under the market.

Trendlines work especially well on these charts. In an uptrend, a basic *up trendline* is drawn under reaction lows. The uptrend is assumed to be in effect as long as that trendline is not violated. A *down trendline* slopes downward and to the right along the rally highs. Sometimes markets will form *price channels.* In a price channel, parallel trendlines are drawn over and under the price action. Figure 8.1 shows a ten-year price channel on the Commodity Research Bureau Futures Price Index.

Existing trends are often corrected by certain predictable percentages. The best-known percentage retracement is the 50% *retracement*. In an uptrend, for example, an intermediate correction may retrace approximately 50% of the previous advance before resuming its major uptrend. Minimum retracements are about a third of the previous trend, with two-thirds representing a maximum retracement. If a market retraces much more than two-thirds, a trend reversal is usually indicated. The two-thirds point, therefore, is especially critical. The sugar and gold charts in Figures 8.8 and 8.11a later in this chapter show examples of markets turning at about the two-thirds point.

PATTERNS ON CHARTS

Price patterns appear on the long-range charts, which are interpreted in the same way as on the daily charts. *Double tops and bottoms* are very prominent on these charts. A double top occurs when a market is unable to overcome a previous resistance peak and then turns down to violate the most recent reaction low. A double bottom is just the opposite. Major double tops show up on the corn and copper charts in Figures 8.5 and 8.12a, where the two peaks are almost seven years apart. Figure 8.10 shows a *head and shoulders bottom* that formed in the wheat market from 1964 to 1972. *Triangles,* which are usually continuation patterns, but sometimes act as reversal patterns, are very prominent. On the weekly chart of the CRB Futures Index in Figure 8.2 a *symmetrical triangle* can be seen clearly.

Another pattern that occurs quite frequently on these charts is the *weekly and monthly reversal.* For example, on the monthly chart, a new monthly high followed by a close below the previous month's close often represents a significant turning point, especially if it occurs near a major support or resistance area. Weekly reversals are quite frequent on the weekly charts. These patterns are the equivalent of the *key reversal day* on the daily charts, except that on the long-range charts these reversals carry a great deal more significance.

The best argument for using long-term charts for trend analysis is in the charts themselves. Several examples of weekly and monthly charts that cover the last 20 years are shown in the examples. It is hoped that the examples will largely speak for themselves and that the charts chosen will clearly demonstrate their usefulness and how well they lend themselves to trend analysis. If you haven't seen these charts before, you should be in for a pleasant surprise.

LONG-TERM TO SHORT-TERM CHARTS

It's especially important to appreciate the order in which price charts should be studied in performing a thorough trend analysis. The proper order to follow in chart analysis is to begin with the long range and gradually work to the near term. The reason for this should become apparent as one works with the different time dimensions. If the analyst begins with only the near-term picture, he or she is forced to constantly revise conclusions as more price data is considered. A thorough analysis of a daily chart may have to be completely redone after looking at the long-range charts. By starting with the big picture, going back as far as 20 years, all data to be considered are already included in the chart and a proper perspective is achieved. Once the analyst knows where the market is from a longer-range perspective, he or she gradually "zeroes in" on the shorter term.

The first chart to be considered is the 20-year continuation chart. The analyst looks for the more obvious chart patterns, major trendlines, or the proximity of major support or resistance levels. He or she then consults the most recent five years on the weekly chart, repeating the same process. Having done that, the analyst narrows his or her focus to the last six to nine months of market action on the daily bar chart, thus going from the "macro" to the "micro" approach. If the trader wants to proceed further, intra-day charts can then be consulted for an even more microscopic study of recent action.

COMMODITY INDICES: A STARTING POINT

In stock market analysis, the starting point of all market analysis is always the broad market averages, such as the Dow Jones Averages or the Standard & Poor's 500 Index, to determine the general direction of the market as a whole. A stock trader or investor wouldn't think of purchasing an individual common stock without first determining whether the stock market in general is in a bull or bear market. After looking at the broad market averages, the stock analyst then studies the various industry groups to isolate the strongest performers. The last step is to find the best performing stocks within the best performing industry groups. That process takes three distinct steps. The analyst begins with a very broad view and then gradually narrows his or her focus. This is the same process that should be followed by the futures trader.

Commodity Research Bureau Futures Price Index

The first logical step in the analysis of any commodity market is to determine the direction of the general commodity price level. This can be accomplished by studying the chart of the Commodity Research Bureau Futures Price Index, which is the most widely followed barometer of commodity prices. That index measures the trend performance of 27 commodity futures markets. Commodity markets tend to move in the same direction. Therefore, it is essential to determine as a starting point whether commodity markets in general are rising or falling and whether the individual markets are in a bullish or bearish environment.

CRB Group Indices

In the second step, the analyst should look at the various market groups for the strongest or weakest performers. If the CRB Futures Index is in an uptrend, for example, or in the process of turning up, the analyst could use the concept of *relative strength* to isolate those indices that have the strongest technical picture. Attention should then be concentrated on those stronger groups.

Individual Markets

The third step is to focus attention on the strongest group to determine the best performers in that group. (We're talking here about a bullish situation where the analyst is looking to operate from the long side.) During inflationary periods, with the CRB Futures Index trending higher (such as during the 1970s), the analyst should concentrate his or her attention on the strongest acting markets in the strongest groups for buying opportunities. During deflationary periods (since 1980) when the CRB Index is trending lower, the trader should look to the weakest markets in the weakest groups for possible shorting opportunities.

Before even looking at the charts of the market under consideration, therefore, the analyst should already have determined whether the commodity price level is bullish or bearish and whether the market group in which that market is included is in a bullish or bearish environment.

Putting all of this together, the correct order to follow in a thorough trend analysis is to begin with the 20-year monthly chart of the CRB Futures Price Index, then the five-year weekly chart, and then the daily chart. The next step is to consider the long range weekly and daily charts of the various CRB group indices (or the individual group the analyst is interested in). The final step is to study the monthly, weekly, and daily charts of the individual markets in that order. In accordance with that strategy, the first chart example in Figure 8.1 is the 20-year monthly continuation chart of the CRB Futures Price Index.

SHOULD LONG-RANGE CHARTS BE ADJUSTED FOR INFLATION?

Before concluding our discussion of these charts, a few final points deserve mention here. A question often raised concerning long-term charts is whether or not historic price levels seen on the charts should be adjusted for inflation. After all, the argument goes, given the tremendous inflationary bias since the early 1970s (and disinflationary tendencies during the 1980s), do these long-range peaks and troughs have any validity if not adjusted to reflect the changes in the value of the U.S. dollar? This is a point of some controversy among analysts.

I do not believe that any adjustment is necessary on these long range charts for a number of reasons. The main reason is my belief that the markets themselves have already made the necessary adjustments. A currency declining in value causes commodities quoted in that currency to increase in value. The declining value of the dollar, therefore, would contribute to rising commodity prices. There can be little doubt that much of the price increases on the long-range commodity charts during the 1970s were simply a reflection of a weaker dollar. On the other side of the coin, much of the decline in commodity prices over the past five years has been directly attributed to the stronger dollar.

Another point to ponder is that the tremendous price gains in commodity markets during the 1970s and declining prices in the 1980s are classic examples of inflation at work. To have suggested during the 1970s that commodity price levels that had doubled and tripled in price should then be adjusted to reflect inflation would make no sense at all. The rising commodity markets already were a manifestation of that inflation. Declining commodity markets during the 1980s are cited by economists as an indication that inflation is now under control. Should we take the price of gold, which is now worth less than half of its value in 1980, and adjust it to reflect the lower inflation rate? I think the market has already taken care of that.

The final point in this debate goes to the heart of the technical theory, which states that price action discounts everything eventually. The market itself adjusts to periods of inflation and deflation and to changes in currency values. The real answer to whether long-range charts should be adjusted for inflation lies in the charts themselves. The copper chart in Figure 8.12a shows the 1980 bull market high stopping right at the 1974 bull market high and then declining to the 1975-1977 bear market lows where it has stabilized. Many markets failed at historic resistance levels set several years earlier and then have declined to support levels not seen in several years. This type of action would not have happened if the chart levels needed to be adjusted for changes in the inflation rate.

LONG-TERM CHARTS NOT INTENDED FOR TRADING PURPOSES

Long-term charts are not meant for trading purposes. A distinction has to be made between market analysis for forecasting purposes and the timing of market commitments. Long-term charts are useful in the analytical process to help determine the major trend and price objectives. They are not suitable, however, for the timing of entry and exit points and should not be used for that purpose. For that more sensitive task, daily and intra-day charts should be utilized.

CONCLUSION

The techniques applied to the following examples are relatively basic and should be readily recognized by anyone familiar with elementary charting. Only the principles covered in Chapters 1 through 7 are used. There is no reason, however, why other charting techniques cannot be applied to weekly and monthly charts. For example, they are useful for determining long-range cycles. Elliott Wave analysis can be applied as well. Examples of five-wave bull markets are seen in the corn and cotton monthly charts.

An area where little work has been done is in the application of *long-range moving averages* to these charts. Some experimental work by the author several years ago revealed the value of using 10- and 30-week moving averages on the weekly charts to track long-range trends. These averages are similar to those used in stock market analysis, but have gone largely unnoticed in the futures markets.

Long-range charts only have to be studied in depth once in a while. Because long-range price patterns change very little over the short run, a glance at the charts for perspective, supplemented by an occasional in-depth analysis, seems to be all that is necessary.

The daily bar chart is and should remain the basic working tool of the futures trader. Intra-day charts are also highly recommended for shorter-term fine tuning. Nothing said in this chapter is meant to change that. However, this chapter is intended to impress upon the reader that an enormous amount of valuable price information is lost if long-range charts are not consulted to supplement the analysis of the shorter-term charts. The reader should be aware of the value of including a study of the broader commodity indices in the analytical process.

An increased awareness of the value of these long-term charts and indices, when used in conjunction with daily bar charts, can add an entirely new dimension to standard chart analysis, and greatly improve the application of technical principles to the commodity futures markets.

EXAMPLES OF WEEKLY AND MONTHLY CHARTS

The following pages contain several examples of long-term weekly and monthly charts. The charts pretty much speak for themselves and require little in the way of explanation. Except for one brief reference to Elliott Wave Theory and five-wave bull markets in Figures 8.5 and 8.6, only very basic concepts are applied. The drawings on the charts are limited to long-term support and resistance levels, trendlines, percentage retracements, weekly reversals, and an occasional price pattern.

Just glance through the charts and make note of the enormous amount of historical data that is totally missed on the daily charts. The daily charts exclude about 80% of the price data on the five-year weekly charts and about 95% of the data on the 20-year monthly charts. Hopefully, you'll begin to appreciate the value of that historical data and the importance of incorporating it into the analytical process.

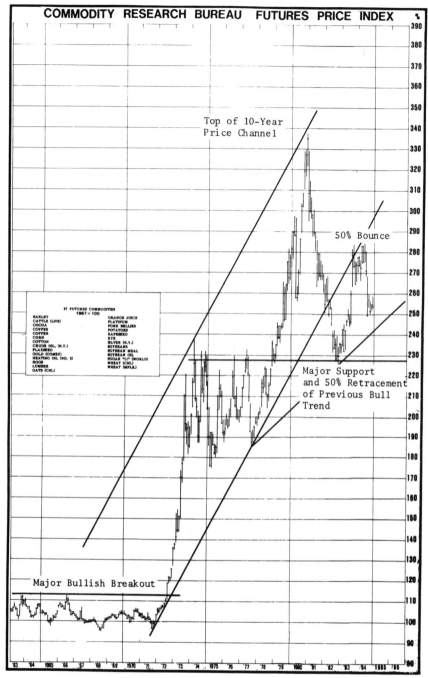

Figure 8.1 Monthly chart of the CRB Futures Price Index. (Chart courtesy of Commodity Research Bureau, a Knight-Ridder Business Information Service.)

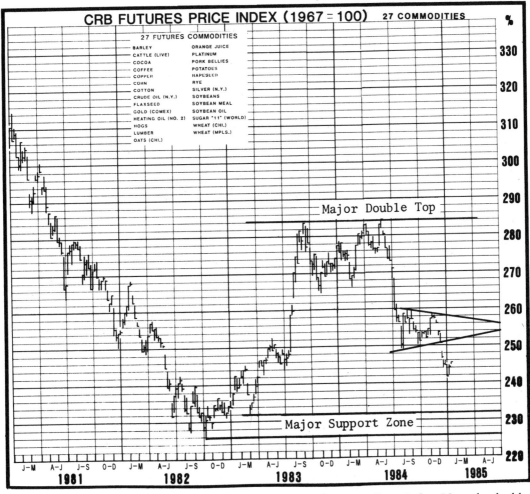

Figure 8.2 Weekly chart of the CRB Futures Price Index. Note the double top and symmetrical triangle. Prices are still in a downtrend, but have entered a potential support zone along 1982 lows. (Chart courtesy of Commodity Research Bureau, a Knight-Ridder Business Information Service.)

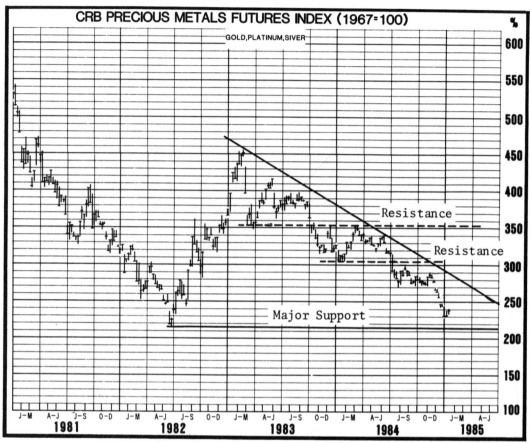

Figure 8.3 Weekly chart of the CRB Precious Metals Futures Index. Note the orderly downtrend with support levels later becoming resistance. The index is now in a major support zone. A study of this index would be helpful before an analysis of any individual precious metals market. (Chart courtesy of Commodity Research Bureau, a Knight-Ridder Business Information Service.)

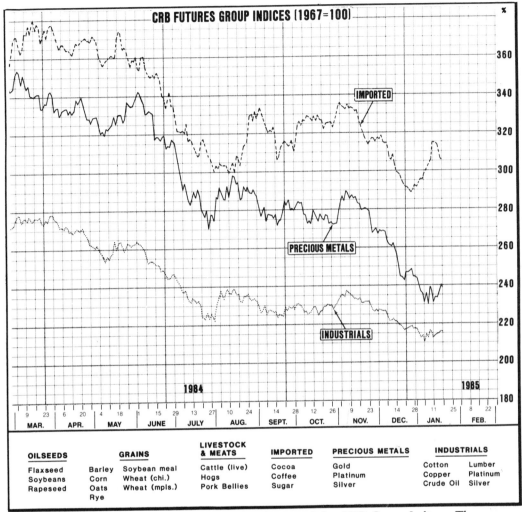

CRB FUTURES GROUP INDICES (1967=100)

IMPORTED

PRECIOUS METALS

INDUSTRIALS

1984   1985

| 9 | 23 | 6 | 20 | 4 | 18 | 1 | 15 | 29 | 13 | 27 | 10 | 24 | 14 | 28 | 12 | 26 | 9 | 23 | 14 | 28 | 11 | 25 | 8 | 22 |
| MAR. | | APR. | | MAY | | JUNE | | | JULY | | AUG. | | SEPT. | | OCT. | | NOV. | | DEC. | | JAN. | | FEB. | |

OILSEEDS		GRAINS		LIVESTOCK & MEATS	IMPORTED	PRECIOUS METALS		INDUSTRIALS	
Flaxseed		Barley	Soybean meal	Cattle (live)	Cocoa	Gold		Cotton	Lumber
Soybeans		Corn	Wheat (chi.)	Hogs	Coffee	Platinum		Copper	Platinum
Rapeseed		Oats	Wheat (mpls.)	Pork Bellies	Sugar	Silver		Crude Oil	Silver
		Rye							

Figure 8.4 An example of some of the CRB Group Indices. These group indices should be consulted before studying the individual markets. Notice here that the Imported Index is the strongest of the three shown. That would suggest that greater upside potential would be found in the cocoa, coffee, and sugar markets. Notice the various groups along the bottom of the chart. (Chart courtesy of Commodity Research Bureau, a Knight-Ridder Business Information Service.)

Figure 8.5 Notice how the 1980 top occurred at the same level as in 1974. Note the five-wave bull market. (Chart courtesy of Commodity Research Bureau, a Knight-Ridder Business Information Service.)

Figure 8.6 Notice the major resistance near $1.00 and support near 60¢. Notice the five-wave bull market from 1977 to 1980. (Chart courtesy of Commodity Research Bureau, a Knight-Ridder Business Information Service.)

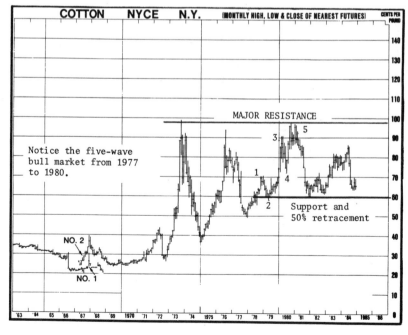

Figure 8.7 Notice how resistance levels at 35¢ and 56¢ became support once broken on the upside. Cattle prices have been in a 20¢ trading range since 1979. (Chart courtesy of Commodity Research Bureau, a Knight-Ridder Business Information Service.)

Figure 8.8 (Chart courtesy of Commodity Research Bureau, a Knight-Ridder Business Information Service.)

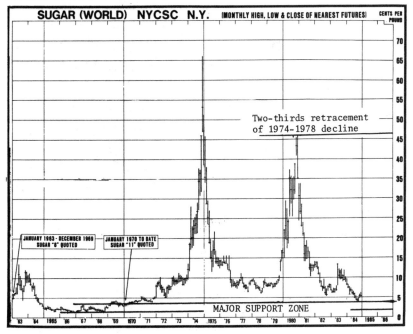

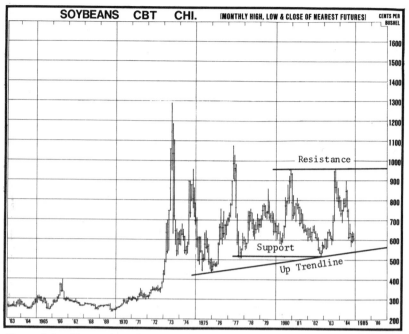

Figure 8.9 Notice how historic support and resistance levels influence the soybean market several years later. (Chart courtesy of Commodity Research Bureau, a Knight-Ridder Business Information Service.)

Figure 8.10 (Chart courtesy of Commodity Research Bureau, a Knight-Ridder Business Information Service.)

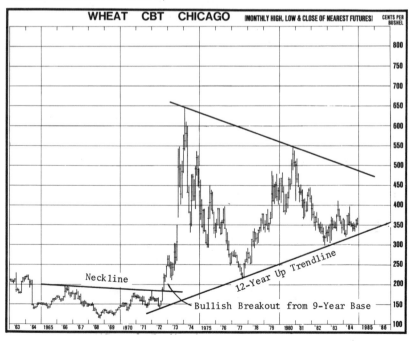

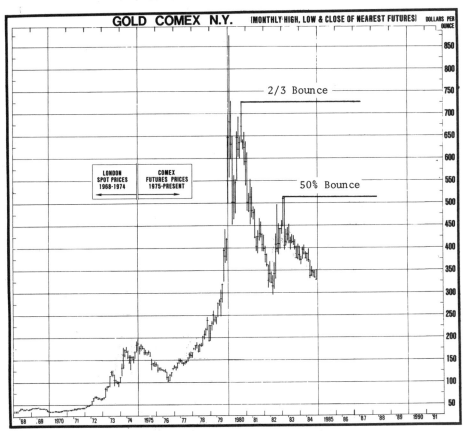

Figure 8.11a & b (Chart courtesy of Commodity Research Bureau, a Knight-Ridder Business Information Service.)

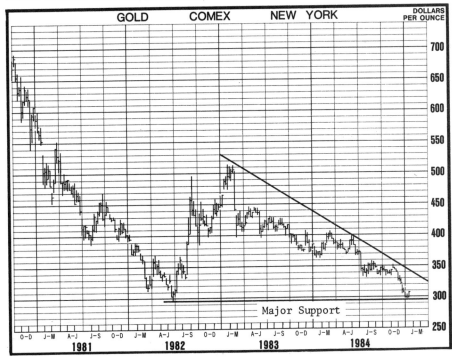

227

Figure 8.12a & b (Chart courtesy of Commodity Research Bureau, a Knight-Ridder Business Information Service.)

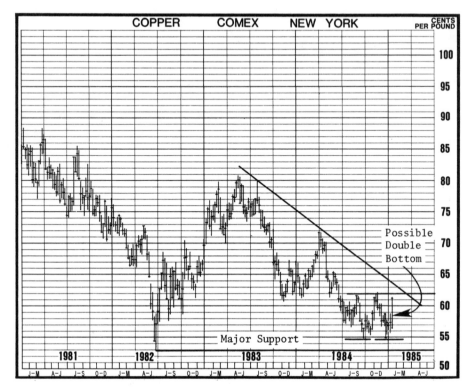

228

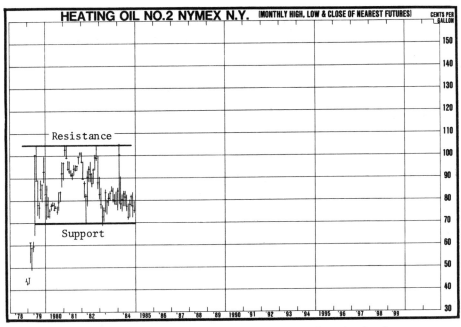

Figure 8.13a & b   On the long-term charts, the heating oil market has been in a six-year trading range between $1.05 and 70¢. (Chart courtesy of Commodity Research Bureau, a Knight-Ridder Business Information Service.)

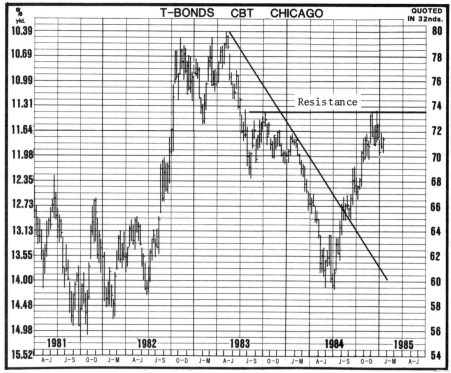

Figure 8.14a & b In the weekly chart (8.14a), bond prices are testing resistance near 73-16. In the monthly chart (8.14b), prices are also testing a long-term down trendline. (Chart courtesy of Commodity Research Bureau, a Knight-Ridder Business Information Service.)

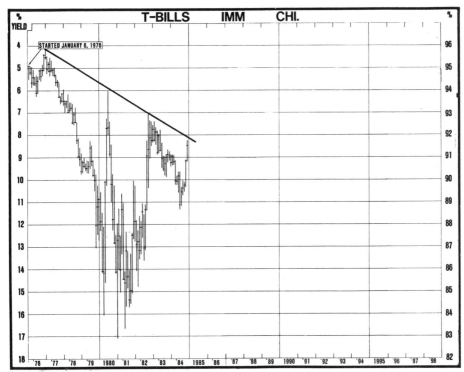

Figure 8.15a & b On the upper chart (8.15a), note the long-term down trendline. In the lower chart (8.15b), notice major resistance along 1982/1983 highs. (Chart courtesy of Commodity Research Bureau, a Knight-Ridder Business Information Service.)

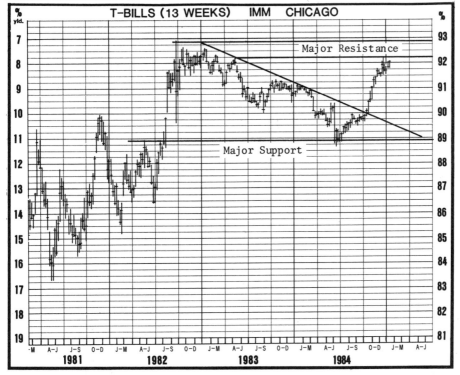

Figure 8.16a & b   None of these long-term support zones on the Swiss franc are visible on the daily chart. Notice the down trendline since 1979. (Chart courtesy of Commodity Research Bureau, a Knight-Ridder Business Information Service.)

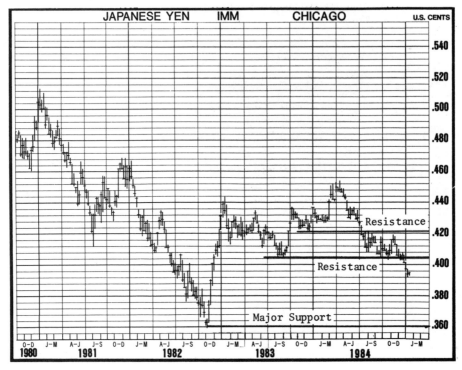

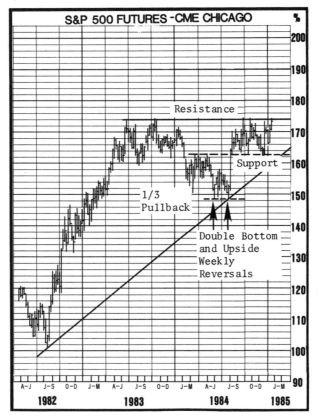

Figure 8.17 Weekly chart of the S&P 500 Futures Index. This chart gives a much better perspective than the daily chart. The 1983/84 decline retraced exactly a third of the 1982/83 bull trend. Note the double bottom in mid-1984 near 150 and the upside weekly reversals at both bottoms. Note that the late 1984 selloff to 163 found support along previous resistance at that level. Long-term charts usually provide a much better perspective on the long-term trend. This chart looks a good deal more bullish than the shorter-term charts. (Chart courtesy of Commodity Research Bureau, a Knight-Ridder Business Information Service.)

TECHNICAL INDICATORS

In the next chapter, we'll discuss one of the most widely used of all technical indicators and the workhorse of most trend-following systems—*the moving average.*

9

Moving Averages

INTRODUCTION

The *moving average* is one of the most versatile and widely used of all technical indicators. Because of the way it is constructed and the fact that it can be so easily quantified and tested, it is the basis for most mechanical trend-following systems in use today.

Chart analysis is largely subjective and difficult to test. As a result, chart analysis does not lend itself that well to computerization. Moving average rules, by contrast, can easily be programmed into a computer, which then generates specific buy and sell signals. While two technicians may disagree as to whether a given price pattern is a *triangle* or a *diamond*, or whether the volume pattern favors the bull or bear side, moving average trend signals are precise and not open to debate.

Let's begin by defining what a *moving average* is. As the second word implies, it is an *average* of a certain body of data. For example, if a 10-day average of closing prices is desired, the prices for the last ten days are added up and the total is divided by ten. The term *moving* is used because only the latest ten days' prices are used in the calculation. Therefore, the body of data to be averaged (the last ten closing prices) moves forward with each new trading day. The most common way to calculate the moving average is to work from the total of the last ten days' closing prices. Each day the new close is added to the total and the close 11 days back is subtracted. The new total is then divided by the number of days (ten).

The above example deals with a simple 10-day moving average of closing prices. There are, however, other types of moving averages that are not simple. There are also many questions as to the best way to employ the moving average. For example, how many days should be averaged? Should a short-term or a long-term average be used? Is there a *best* moving average for all markets or for each individual market? Is the closing price the best price to average? Would it be better to use more than one average? Which type of average works better—a simple, linearly weighted or exponentially smoothed? Are there times when moving averages work better than at others?

There are many valid questions to be considered when using moving averages. We'll address many of these questions in this chapter and show examples of some of the more common usages of the moving average. While there are no guaranteed right answers to the previous questions, we'll discuss the conclusions of some research done in this area.

THE MOVING AVERAGE: A SMOOTHING DEVICE WITH A TIME LAG

The moving average is essentially a trend-following device. Its purpose is to identify or signal that a new trend has begun or that an old trend has ended or reversed. Its purpose is to track the progress of the trend. It might be viewed as a curving trendline. It does not, however, predict market action in the same sense that standard chart analysis attempts to do. The moving average is a follower, not a leader. It never anticipates; it only reacts. The moving average follows a market and tells us that a trend has begun, but only after the fact.

The moving average is a smoothing device. By averaging the price data, a smoother line is produced, making it much easier to view the underlying trend. By its very nature, however, the moving average line also lags the market action. A shorter moving average, such as a five- or ten-day average, would hug the price action more closely than a 40-day average. The time lag is reduced with the shorter averages, but can never be completely eliminated. Shorter-term averages are more sensitive to the price action, whereas longer-range averages are less sensitive. In certain types of markets, it is more advantageous to use a shorter average and, at other times, a longer and less sensitive average proves more useful. (See Figures 9.1a and b.)

Which Prices To Average

We have been using the closing price in all of our examples so far. However, while the closing price is considered to be the most important price of the trading day and the price most commonly used in moving average construction, the reader should be aware that some technicians prefer to use other prices. Some prefer to use a *midpoint* value, which is arrived at by dividing the day's range by two.

Figure 9.1a The chart shows a simple 10- and 40-day moving average combination. Notice how much closer the shorter 10-day average follows the price trend. The 40-day average follows from a greater distance. Moving averages smooth the price trend, but always lag the price action. The solid line is the 10-day average and the dashed line, the 40-day average.

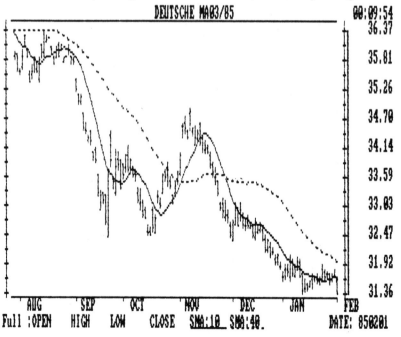

Others include the closing price in their calculation by adding the high, low, and closing prices together and dividing the sum by three. Still others prefer to construct a *price band* by averaging the high and low prices separately. The result is two separate moving average lines that act as a sort of volatility buffer or neutral band. We'll discuss the possible advantages of using a price band a bit later. Despite these variations, the closing or settlement price is still the price most commonly used for moving average analysis and is the price that we'll be focusing most of our attention on in this chapter.

The Simple Moving Average

The *simple moving average*, or the arithmetic mean, is the type used by most technical analysts. But there are some who question its usefulness on two points. The first criticism is that only the period covered by the average (the last ten days, for example) is taken into account.

Figure 9.1b   A simple 20-day average on the price chart. Traders use crossings of the average line to initiate trading signals. Prices are currently below the average, which means the trend is down. Notice that the 20-day line smooths the price action, but still lags behind.

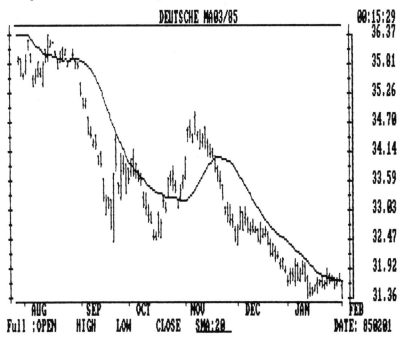

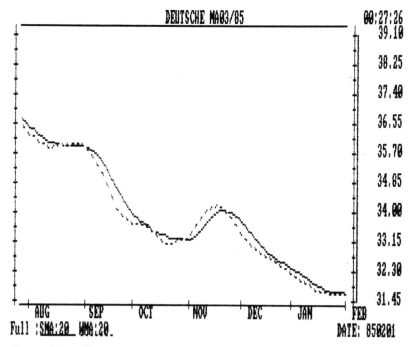

Figure 9.2a Comparison of a simple 20-day moving average (solid line) and a linearly weighted moving average (dotted line). Notice that the weighted (dotted) line tends to lead the simple average (solid) line. Weighted averages give more weight to recent price data.

The second criticism is that the simple moving average gives equal weight to each day's price. In a 10-day average, the last day receives the same weight as the first day in the calculation. Each day's price is assigned a 10% weighting. In a 5-day average, each day would have an equal 20% weighting. Some analysts believe that a heavier weighting should be given to the more recent price action.

The Linearly Weighted Moving Average

In an attempt to correct the weighting problem, some analysts employ a *linearly weighted moving average.* In this calculation, the closing price of the tenth day (in the case of a 10-day average) would be multipled by ten, the ninth day by nine, the eighth day by eight, and so on. The greater weight is therefore given to the more recent closings. The total is then divided by the sum of the multipliers (55 in the case of the 10-day average: $10 + 9 + 8 + . . . + 1$). However, the linearly weighted average still does not address the problem of including only

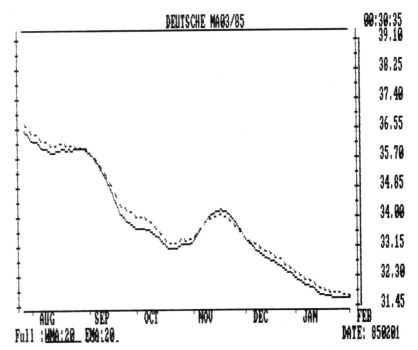

	39.10
	38.25
	37.40
	36.55
	35.70
	34.85
	34.00
	33.15
	32.30
	31.45

AUG   SEP   OCT   NOV   DEC   JAN   FEB

Full :MMA:20 DMA:20.   DATE: 850201

Figure 9.2b   Comparison of a 20-day linearly weighted moving average (solid line) and an exponentially smoothed average for the same period (dotted line). The exponentially smoothed line is also a weighted average, but includes all past action. Greater weight is still given to more recent price action.

the price action covered by the length of the average itself. (See Figures 9.2a and b.)

The Exponentially Smoothed Moving Average

A more sophisticated average that addresses both of the charges leveled against the simple moving average is called the *exponentially smoothed moving average*. First, the exponentially smoothed average assigns a greater weight to the more recent action. Therefore, it is a *weighted* moving average. But while it assigns diminished importance to past price action, it does include in its calculation all of the price data in the life of the futures contract. Needless to say, the formula for this average is complicated and requires the aid of a computer. It would seem then that the exponentially smoothed average solves both of the problems of the simple average, has the best of both worlds, and, being the most sophisticated of the three types of averages, would be the best of the three. Not necessarily. We'll come back to the relative merits of each technique a bit later in the chapter.

The Use of One Moving Average

The simple moving average is the one most commonly used by futures technicians, and is the one that we'll be concentrating on. Some traders use just one moving average to generate trend signals. The moving average is plotted on the bar chart in its appropriate trading day along with that day's price action. When the closing price moves above the moving average, a buy signal is generated. A sell signal is given when prices move below the moving average. For added confirmation, some technicians also like to see the moving average line itself turn in the direction of the price crossing.

If a very short-term average is employed (a 5- or 10-day), the average tracks closing prices very closely and several crossings occur. This action can be either good or bad. The use of a very sensitive average produces more trades (with higher commission costs) and results in many false signals (whipsaws). If the average is too sensitive, some of the short-term random price movement (or "noise") activates bad trend signals.

While the shorter average generates more false signals, it has the advantage of giving trend signals earlier in the move. It stands to reason that the more sensitive the average, the earlier the signals will be. So there is a trade-off at work here. The trick is to find that average that is sensitive enough to generate early signals, but insensitive enough to avoid most of the random "noise."

A Longer Versus a Shorter-Term Moving Average

A shorter term moving average generally works better when prices are in a sideways trading range. Because prices are essentially trendless in this type of situation, the shorter and more sensitive average allows the trader to capture more of the shorter swings. (See Figure 9.3.)

Once prices begin to trend, however—either up or down—the longer-range moving average becomes more advantageous. The less sensitive moving average (such as a 40-day) tracks the trend from a greater distance (because it has a longer time lag), does not get caught up in minor corrections or consolidations and, as a result, rides with the major trend a lot longer.

The shorter average, by contrast, gets stopped out of positions on minor trend reversals and may even signal trades against the prevailing trend. It was mentioned earlier that the trick was to know which average to use. It is now clear that no one average may be the best at all times. The correct approach would be to use a shorter average during nontrending periods and a longer average during trending periods. This approach is easier said than done.

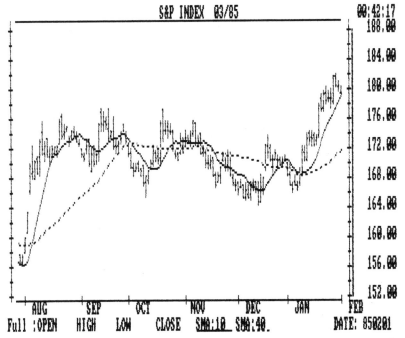

Figure 9.3a Comparison of 10- and 40-day moving averages. Notice that during the sideways period, the shorter average is more helpful in catching trading turns (solid line). The longer average is more helpful when markets are in a trending phase (dotted line).

Figure 9.3b Notice that during the downtrend, the longer 40-day average (dotted line) followed the trend at a safer distance and kept the trader on the short side throughout the entire decline. At the turn at the bottom, however, the shorter 10-day average gave an earlier exit signal.

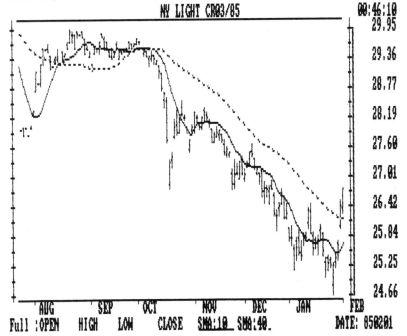

Let's carry the above comparison a step further. While the longer average performs better while the trend remains in motion, it "gives back" a lot more when the trend reverses. The very insensitivity of the longer average (the fact that it trailed the trend from a greater distance), which kept it from getting tangled up in short-term corrections during the trend, works against the trader when the trend actually reverses. Therefore, we'll add another corollary here: The longer averages work best as long as the trend remains in force; but a shorter average is better when the trend is in the process of reversing.

It becomes clearer, therefore, that the use of one moving average alone has several disadvantages. It might be more advantageous to employ two moving averages. Before we get to the use of two or even three moving averages, however, let's stay with the single moving average and discuss the use of filters and price bands.

Filters on a Single Moving Average

To reduce the number of whipsaws that occur when using a single moving average, technicians impose *filters* on the moving average signals. Following are some of those filters.

1. Besides requiring that prices must actually close beyond a moving average line, some technicians also require that the entire day's price range clear the average.

2. Another filter requires that the closing price penetrate the moving average by some predetermined amount—a penetration criterion. This amount could be a certain number of minimum fluctuations or a percentage amount. For example, a minimum fluctuation in the gold market on the Comex is ten cents (.10). A filter might require a closing penetration of the moving average by five minimum fluctuations, or 50 cents (.50). A percentage filter might require a closing penetration of the average by 1% (about $3.00 in today's market). Of course, the use of filters raises another dilemma. The smaller the filter, the less protection it provides. The larger the filter, the later the signal—another trade-off. The more insurance or protection provided by the filter, the greater the premium paid by a later entry into the market.

3. Some technicians require that a moving average signal be confirmed by some type of breakout on the chart. This renders a stronger signal and helps eliminate getting constantly whipsawed in a short-term trading range. A point and figure signal could be em-

ployed. Another possibility is the use of a weekly channel breakout. (We'll have more to say about weekly breakouts later on). The problem with these filters is that the more the trader relies on them, the further he or she gets from the original moving average signals.

4. *Time filters* are also employed by some traders who impose a one-to-three-day delay before taking action. Because most bad signals reverse themselves very quickly, the requirement that the signal remain in force an additional day or two helps weed out a fair amount of false signals. The price paid is later entry on the good signals.

5. The use of *percentage envelopes*, or *volatility bands*, is another popular filter. This is accomplished by the use of parallel lines at certain percentage points above and below the average. In other words, a line is plotted above and below the moving average line a certain percentage distance from the average line itself. For a buy signal to be given, prices would have to close not only above the moving average itself, but also above the upper envelope line. The basic moving average line then becomes the stop out point. (See Figures 9.4a and b.)

Figure 9.4a An example of the use of "envelopes" with moving averages. This example uses an envelope around a 40-day moving average of 1.5%. In other words, the upper and lower lines are each 1.5% away from the moving average line.

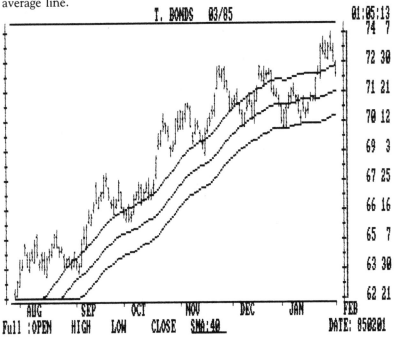

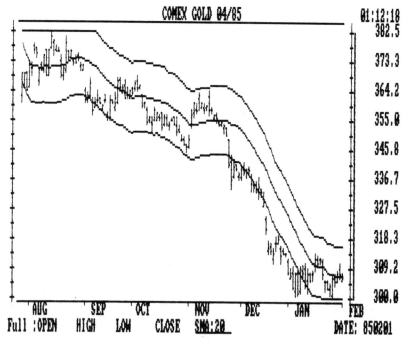

Figure 9.4b   Example of "envelopes" using a 3% filter around a 20-day moving average. The "envelope" technique creates a volatility zone around the average, which can be used to reduce whipsaws.

A *buffer zone* is created between the upper envelope line and the moving average. No action is taken between the two lines. A buy signal is generated above the upper line and the position is liquidated or stopped out on a close below the moving average.

A sell short signal requires a close below the lower envelope line, and a close back above the moving average line is required to cover or stop out the short position. One major advantage to the use of such filters is that a buffer or neutral zone is created where no positions are taken. This approach is superior to those techniques or systems that are always in the market.

6. The *high-low band* is constructed by applying the same moving average to the high and low prices instead of to the closing price. The result is two moving average lines—one of the highs and one of the lows. (See Figures 9.5a and b.)

To generate a buy signal, the closing price must close above the higher average. The lower line is then used to determine the stop out point. A sell short signal is given by a close beneath the lower line with the upper line becoming the line of defense for stoploss protection. The lower line is treated just like a bullish trendline in an uptrend with the upper line acting like a bearish trendline in a downtrend.

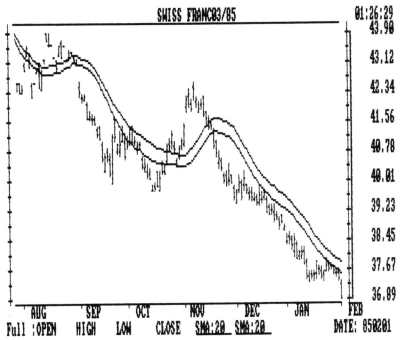

Figure 9.5a An example of a 20-day price band using highs and lows instead of closing prices. This technique reduces the amount of crossings and eliminates some false signals.

Figure 9.5b Another example of a high-low band, using a 20-day moving average of highs and lows.

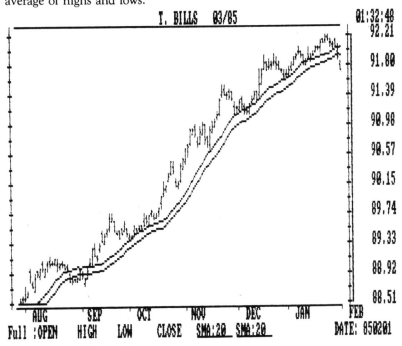

The Use of Two Moving Averages

In the previous section, it was stated that there were some advantages to using more than one average. At times, a shorter average worked better and, at others, a longer average was better. The use of a single average also produced an usually large number of whipsaws, necessitating the use of filters. To improve performance and reliability, many technicians prefer to use two or three moving averages together.

We're still talking primarily about the *simple* average as opposed to the *weighted* or *exponentially smoothed* variety (although we'll identify at least one technical system later on that uses two exponentially smoothed averages). Some research makes a compelling case for the use of two simple averages as perhaps the best of all possible combinations.

When two moving averages are employed, the longer one is used for trend identification, and the shorter one for timing purposes. It is the interplay between the two averages and the price itself that produces the trend signals.

Figure 9.6a Example of the double crossover method. A sell signal is given when the shorter 4-day average crosses below the longer 28-day average. These numbers were optimized. (See Table 9.5.)

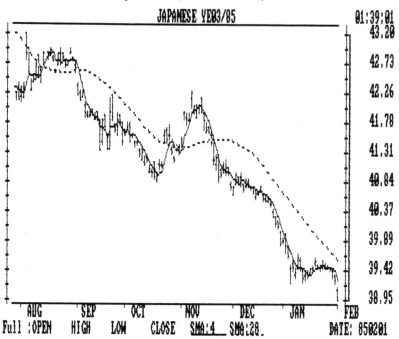

Moving Averages

How to Use Two Averages to Generate Signals

There are two ways to use the *double* moving average approach. (See Figures 9.6a to d.)

1. The first is called the *double crossover method*. This means that a buy signal is produced when the shorter average crosses above the longer. For example, two popular combinations are the 5- and 20-day averages and the 10- and 40-day averages. In the former, a buy signal occurs when the 5-day averages crosses above the 20, and a sell short signal when the 5-day moves below the 20. In this approach, the system is continuous, meaning that it is always in the market on the long or the short side. In the latter example, the 10-day crossing above the 40 signals an uptrend, and a downtrend takes place with the ten slipping under the 40. This technique of using two averages together lags the market a bit more than the use of a single average but produces fewer whipsaws. We'll continue the discussion of the double crossover method when we address the question of which averages work best in each market.

Figure 9.6b Another example of the double crossover method, using optimized averages. Notice that the shorter 14-day average crosses under the 40 back in October and is still in a downtrend.

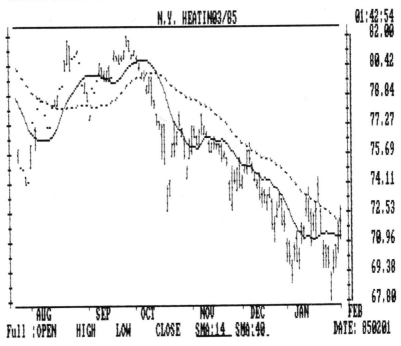

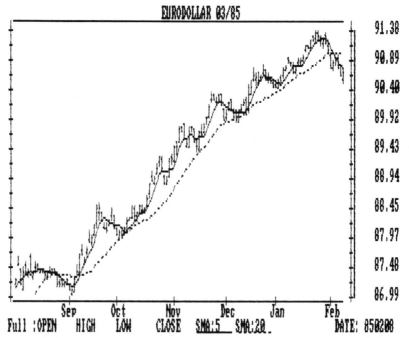

EURODOLLAR 03/85

Full :OPEN   HIGH   LOW   CLOSE   SMA:5   SMA:20   DATE: 850208

Figure 9.6c Example of a 5- and 20-day moving average combination. The 5-day average gave a "buy" signal in September when it moved above the 20. That was five months ago. Note that the five has just crossed below the 20, giving a "sell" signal.

2. A second way to use a combination of two averages is to use them as a sort of neutral zone. A close above both averages would be required for a buy signal, which would be cancelled if prices close back in the neutral zone. A close below the lower line would signal a sell short position. All short positions would be covered and a sidelines position maintained as long as prices are between the two averages. This system also has the advantage of not always being in the market. There are other variations of both of these approaches.

The Use of Three Averages, or the Triple Crossover Method

Operating on the premise that two moving averages seem to work better than one, then the use of three moving averages must be better than two. That brings us to the *triple crossover method.* The most widely used triple crossover system is the popular *4-9-18-day moving average combination.* This concept was first mentioned by R.C. Allen in his 1972 book, *How to Build a Fortune in Commodities* (Windsor Books,

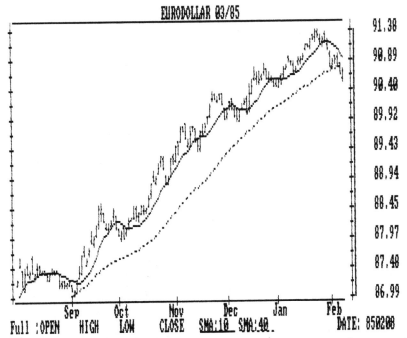

Full : OPEN   HIGH   LOW   CLOSE   SMA:10 SMA:40.   DATE: 850208

Figure 9.6d Example of a 10- and 40-day moving average combination. A "buy" signal was given last September when the ten crossed over the 40. Take note of the fact that for the first time in five months, actual prices have dipped below both averages. That could also be interpreted as a "sell" signal.

Brightwaters, N.Y.) and again later in a 1974 work by the same author, *How to Use the 4-Day, 9-Day and 18-Day Moving Averages to Earn Larger Profits from Commodities* (Best Books, Chicago). The 1974 book is also available through Traders Press, Inc., P.O. Box 10344, Greenville, South Carolina 29603. The 4-9-18-day system is a variation on the 5-, 10-, and 20-day moving average numbers, which are widely used in commodity circles. Many commercial chart services publish the 4-9-18-day moving averages as do many of the video retrieval systems.

How to Use the 4-9-18-Day Moving Average System

It's already been explained that the shorter the moving average, the closer it follows the price trend. It stands to reason then that the shortest of the three averages—the 4-day—will follow the trend most closely, followed by the the 9-day and then the 18. In an uptrend, therefore, the proper alignment would be for the 4-day average to be above the 9-day, which is above the 18-day average. In a downtrend, the order is reversed and the alignment is exactly the opposite. That is, the 4-day would be the lowest, followed by the 9-day and then the 18-day average. (See Figures 9.7a and b.)

A buying alert takes place in a downtrend when the 4-day crosses above both the 9 and the 18. A confirmed buy signal occurs when the 9-day then crosses above the 18. This places the 4-day over the 9-day which is over the 18-day. Some intermingling may occur during corrections or consolidations, but the general uptrend remains intact. Some traders may take profits during the intermingling process and some may use it as a buying opportunity. There is obviously a lot of room for flexibility here in applying the rules, depending on how aggressively one wants to trade.

When the uptrend reverses to the downside, the first thing that should take place is that the shortest (and most sensitive) average—the 4-day—dips below the 9-day and the 18-day. This is only a selling alert. Some traders, however, might use that initial crossing as reason enough to begin liquidating long positions. Then, if the next longer average—the 9-day—drops below the 18-day, a confirmed sell short signal is given. (See Figures 9.7a and 9.7b.)

Figure 9.7a Example of the 4-9-18-day moving average combination. The solid line is the 4-day, the dashed is the 9, and the dotted the 18.

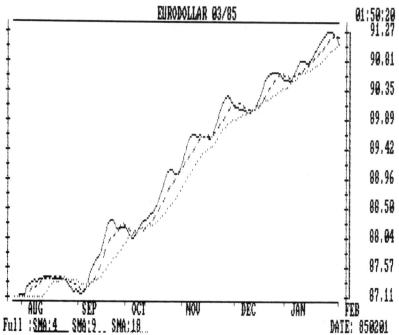

MOVING AVERAGE COMBINATIONS THAT WORK BEST

We've now considered the three different types of moving averages—the simple, linearly weighted, and the exponentially smoothed. We've looked at one, two, and three moving average combinations. We've raised a lot of questions. Let's try to find some answers.

To help find some of those answers, we're indebted to the Merrill Lynch research staff, led by Frank Hochheimer, which published a series of studies on computerized trading techniques from 1978 through 1982. This impressive body of work represents the most extensive published research on the subject of moving averages in the futures industry. In the studies, extensive testing of various moving average techniques was performed to find the best possible combinations in each market. Those moving average results were then compared to various other techniques, such as weekly price channels, inter-day and intra-day price channels, linear regression, and Welles Wilder's *Directional Movement System*.

Figure 9.7b A closer look at the same chart. Note here that the solid line (the 4-day) has just dipped below the 9 (dashed line). The uptrend is still intact, however.

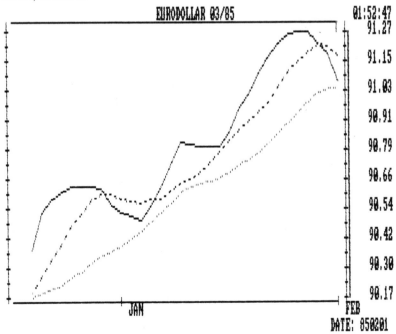

The purpose of the studies was to find the best (or optimized) result for each technique and then, by comparing the results of all the techniques together, to find the most consistent indicators in each market from among all of the possible methods.

Results of the Merrill Lynch Studies

Let's see what the results of those studies revealed and their particular application to the use of moving averages. Hochheimer presented some of the initial results of the studies in an article entitled "Computers Can Help You Trade the Futures Markets," which appeared in the *1978 Commodity Year Book* (published by the Commodity Research Bureau, Jersey City, N.J.). Moving average results for each contract month for 13 different commodities were tested from 1970 to 1976. The time span covered for the averages ranged from three to 70 days. The results of simple, linearly weighted, and exponentially smoothed averages were tabulated separately to find the optimum average for each market (see Tables 9.1 to 9.3). The results of those three studies were then compared in Table 9.4 to find the best from among the three types of averages.

To find the most *consistent* indicators, a weighting system was devised that took into account cumulative net profits or losses, largest string of losses, and a couple of profitability ratios. A number of interesting conclusions were drawn from the study.

1. For the first conclusion, let's quote Hochheimer himself: "It provides empirical evidence in support of the thesis that futures price movements are not strictly random. The fact that these trend-following techniques generated significant profits, even after commission charges, also lends support to the validity of technical analysis as a price forecasting method." (Hochheimer, p. 60)

2. No one moving average worked best in each market. Or, stated another way, each market seemed to have its own optimum moving average that worked best.

3. The longer-range moving averages outperformed the shorter averages. The cutoff point was around the 40-day average (eight weeks), with a surprising number of *best* averages in the 60- to 70-day range (around 13 weeks).

4. The simple moving average outperformed both the linearly weighted and exponentially smoothed averages. Of the 13 markets tested, Table 9.4 shows that the simple average worked best in ten cases, the linearly weighted in two cases, with exponential smoothing a dead last with only one (the cocoa market).

Table 9.1 Theoretical Trading Results from Simple Moving Averages

	Best Average	Cumulative Profits or Losses (Net)	Largest String of Losses	Number Trades	Number Profitable Trades	Number Losing Trades	Ratio: # Profits / # Trades
Cocoa	54	$ 87,957	$ − 14,155	600	157	443	.262
Corn	43	24,646	− 6,537	565	126	439	.223
Sugar	60	270,402	− 15,563	492	99	393	.201
Cotton	57	68,685	− 11,330	641	121	520	.189
Silver	19	42,920	− 15,285	1,393	429	964	.308
Copper	59	165,143	− 7,687	432	158	274	.366
Soybeans	55	222,195	− 10,800	728	151	577	.207
Soybean Meal	68	22,506	− 20,900	704	148	556	.210
Wheat	41	65,806	− 12,550	480	124	356	.258
Pork Bellies	19	97,925	− 9,498	774	281	493	.363
Soybean Oil	69	89,416	− 8,920	586	122	464	.208
Plywood	68	1,622	− 3,929	372	98	274	.263
Hogs	16	35,595	− 7,190	1,093	318	775	.291

Table 9.2 Theoretical Trading Results from Linearly Weighted Moving Averages

	Best Average	Cumulative Profits or Losses (Net)	Largest String of Losses	Number Trades	Number Profitable Trades	Number Losing Trades	Ratio: # Profits / # Trades
Cocoa	52	$ 74,450	$ − 8,773	796	206	590	.259
Corn	65	21,779	− 5,487	524	118	406	.225
Sugar	58	233,822	− 14,063	707	149	558	.211
Cotton	69	44,395	− 18,070	731	139	592	.190
Silver	45	− 34,435	− 20,930	1,036	297	739	.287
Copper	68	124,848	− 13,924	541	179	362	.331
Soybeans	42	178,261	− 19,100	892	213	697	.239
Soybean Meal	41	31,385	− 20,900	1,128	235	893	.208
Wheat	70	52,495	− 9,000	403	94	309	.233
Pork Bellies	28	81,625	− 9,222	815	267	548	.328
Soybean Oil	34	106,996	− 5,470	1,198	303	895	.253
Plywood	70	− 22,273	− 5,138	470	109	361	.232
Hogs	70	9,981	− 9,314	509	131	378	.257

Double Versus Triple Crossover Methods

Having determined that the simple average worked best, later studies tested the double crossover method (two moving averages) and the triple crossover (three averages) using just simple averages. Those results (from 1970 to 1976) were then compared to various other channel techniques already alluded to. In a 1979 study, of 17 markets tested, ten proved most consistently profitable using two averages.

Table 9.3 Theoretical Trading Results from Exponentially Smoothed Moving Averages

	Best Average	Cumulative Profits or Losses (Net)	Largest String of Losses	Number Trades	Number Profitable Trades	Number Losing Trades	Ratio: # Profits # Trades
Cocoa	57	$ 99,080	$ − 10,363	619	166	453	.268
Corn	68	15,119	− 4,901	471	98	373	.208
Sugar	59	172,985	− 15,921	591	105	486	.178
Cotton	70	35,855	− 15,075	605	113	492	.187
Silver	60	− 61,400	− 18,965	914	205	709	.224
Copper	68	136,130	− 5,886	450	150	300	.333
Soybeans	60	197,218	− 13,600	708	142	566	.201
Soybean Meal	62	− 8,486	− 18,200	840	162	678	.193
Wheat	70	13,570	− 11,150	421	75	346	.178
Pork Bellies	12	80,303	− 11,177	1,217	401	816	.329
Soybean Oil	66	82,904	− 6,730	677	160	517	.236
Plywood	69	− 24,526	− 5,002	467	104	363	.223
Hogs	67	− 11,834	− 11,863	504	112	392	.222

Source: "Computers Can Help You Trade The Futures Markets," by Frank L. Hochheimer, *1978 Commodity Yearbook,* Commodity Research Bureau, Jersey City, N.J.

Table 9.4 Most Consistent Indicators—Simple vs. Exponential vs. Linearly Weighted Moving Averages

Commodity	No. Days	Type of Average
Cocoa	57-day	Exponentially Smoothed
Corn	43-day	Simple
Sugar	60-day	Simple
Cotton	57-day	Simple
Silver	19-day	Simple
Copper	59-day	Simple
Soybeans	55-day	Simple
Soybean Meal	41-day	Linearly Weighted
Wheat	41-day	Simple
Pork Bellies	19-day	Simple
Soybean Oil	34-day	Linearly Weighted
Plywood	68-day	Simple
Hogs	16-day	Simple

Table 9.4 shows that of the 13 markets tested from 1970 to 1976, comparing the three types of averages, all but three showed the simple average to perform best.

(Source: Hochheimer, *1978 Commodity Year Book,* Commodity Research Bureau, Jersey City, N.J.)

Moving Averages

Using three averages worked best in only four cases. Various price channel techniques accounted for the remaining three markets. We'll discuss the *price channel* approach as an alternative to moving averages a bit later. (For more information on the above study, see "Computerized Trading Techniques," Merrill Lynch Commodity Division, February, 1979).

Another conclusion can be added to the list of four already mentioned concerning moving averages—the combination of two averages seems to be the best choice. It would seem, then, that the best

Table 9.5

Commodity	Consistent Weights	Cumulative Profits or Losses (Net)	Largest String of Losses	Number Trades	Number Profitable Trades	Number Losing Trades
British Pound	3,49	117,482	−7,790	160	68	92
Cocoa	14,47	160,226	−8,620	303	128	175
Corn	13,47	83,565	−3,890	258	114	144
Canadian Dollar	4,21	57,430	−13,560	286	124	167
Cotton	22,50	324,719	−7,910	371	176	195
Copper	14,33	254,744	−6,112	473	250	22
Deutsche Mark	4,40	78,631	−3,909	169	78	91
GNMA	17,43	94,476	−12,742	278	126	152
Gold	8,48	482,769	−7,932	334	184	152
Heating Oil	14,40	−4,721	−413	88	6	82
Japanese Yen	4,28	120,899	−4,367	131	74	57
Hogs	18,50	52,888	−8,710	409	182	227
Lumber	6,50	5,022	−10,054	368	127	241
Live Cattle	6,21	113,178	−10,410	936	385	551
Plywood	23,44	8,378	−17,350	436	132	304
Soybeans	20,45	393,390	−18,610	530	247	283
Swiss Franc	6,50	172,454	−7,467	148	66	82
Soybean Meal	22,47	187,264	−8,805	484	217	267
Soybean Oil	13,49	127,399	−6,573	527	206	321
Silver	7,29	386,557	−21,726	1213	478	735
Sugar #11	6,50	475,442	−13,399	500	181	319
Treasury Bills	6,18	74,933	−21,423	535	200	335
Treasury Bonds	25,50	184,487	−10,066	147	81	66
Wheat	11,47	169,640	−5,282	358	140	218

The above table shows the last Merrill Lynch update of the double crossover method. In the column under *consistent weights* are listed the moving average combinations. For example, the British pound shows a 3 and 49 day combination to be the best.

These numbers are meant for information purposes only and are now several years old. The reader is cautioned against using these numbers in current markets without further testing of their validity. Optimized averages must be retested and updated occasionally.

(Source: "Computerized Trading Techniques 1982," Merrill Lynch Commodities, Inc., Frank L. Hochheimer and Richard J. Vaughn.)

choice of all would be the combination of two simple moving averages that are optimized to fit each market.

The term *optimized* is used here because the one theme that runs throughout the entire series of studies was that each moving average (or technical indicator) could and should be optimized to fit the personality and character of each individual market.

Table 9.5 shows the last Merrill Lynch update of the double crossover approach ("Computer Trading Techniques 1982," Merrill Lynch Commodity Division). These latest results were updated through 1981 with several new futures markets added to the study.

Problems with Optimization

One problem with optimization is the need to constantly re-optimize every so often. Changing market conditions may cause these optimized numbers to change over time. Even though the Merrill Lynch studies seem to indicate that these numbers remain fairly constant over time, the reader is cautioned against placing too much importance on old optimized numbers. I should state here for emphasis that the optimized numbers in the accompanying tables are for information purposes only and are not meant to imply that they are the best averages to use in today's markets.

With the arrival of the personal computer, software programs are now available that can optimize with relative ease. Indeed, virtually any technical indicator can now be optimized to find the right time length to use in each market. The tough question remains, however, as to how often these parameters need to be redone. If they aren't retested often enough, the trader runs the risk of using obsolete parameters. If done too often, there are other problems. Not all technicians are believers in the value of optimization. Some believe that the entire optimization process is nothing more than back-fitting these parameters to past price action. These skeptics hold that optimized numbers are suspect since they're never actually tested under real market conditions.

The results of the preceding studies are not presented as the final answer in the never-ending quest for the best possible moving average methods to use in the futures markets. But the results do give us some guidelines to work with and provide an excellent starting point for additional research in this area.

PLACEMENT OF THE AVERAGES

The placement of the moving average in relation to the price data is another area open to question. *Most technicians place the latest moving average value on the last trading day.* Others, however, prefer to place the last moving average calculation a certain number of days ahead of the actual price data. The moving average is then said to be *leading* the prices by a certain time period. A moving average with a lead time will tend to follow the price action from a greater distance than if it were placed in the more conventional spot in the last trading day. *Plotting an average with a lead time means that more time is required to penetrate the average and results in fewer false signals.*

One novel approach employed by Arthur Sklarew in his book, *Techniques of a Professional Commodity Chart Analyst* (Commodity Research Bureau, New York, N.Y., 1980), is to advance the moving average by the number of days equal to the square root of the length of the average. For example, a 2- to 4-day average would be advanced two days; a 5- to 9-day average, three days; a 10- to 16-day average, four days, etc.

It must be remembered that when plotting the average at some point in the future, the last closing price is actually being compared to the point on the moving average line that lies in that day's column. In other words, if the average is plotted five days into the future, the last closing place is being compared to the moving average value five days before. That explains why crossings of the average line generally take longer. While varying the placement of the moving average opens an interesting set of possibilities, the most common practice is to place the average in the conventional spot, namely, in the same day as the last price bar.

Centering the Average

The more statistically correct way to plot a moving average is to *center* it. (See Figures 9.8a and b.) That means to place it in the middle of the time period it covers. A 10-day average, for example, would be placed five days back. A 20-day average would be plotted ten days back in time. *Centering* the average, however, has the major flaw of producing much later trend change signals. Therefore, moving aver-

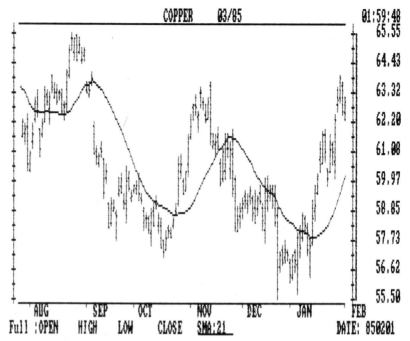

Figure 9.8a A simple 21-day moving average. The average did a reasonably good job of identifying trend changes.

ages are usually placed at the end of the time period covered instead of the middle. The centering technique is used almost exclusively by cyclic analysts to isolate underlying market cycles. We'll spend some time showing how centered averages are used in the detrending process in Chapter 14.

MOVING AVERAGES TIED TO CYCLES

Many market analysts believe that *time cycles* play an important role in market movement. Because these time cycles are repetitive and can be measured, it is possible to determine the approximate times when market tops or bottoms will occur. Many different time cycles exist simultaneously, from a short-term 5-day cycle to Kondratieff's long 54-year cycle. We'll delve more into this fascinating branch of technical analysis in a later chapter.

Moving Averages

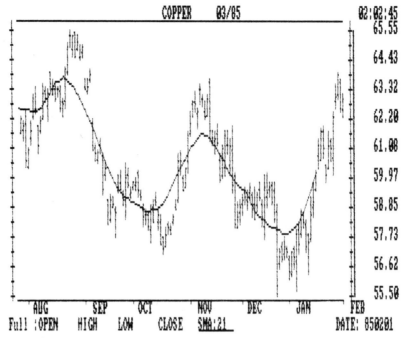

Figure 9.8b What the same 21-day average would look like if "centered." As you can see, the line loses most of its forecasting value. Centering is most useful in cycle analysis.

The subject of cycles is introduced here only to make the point that there seems to be a relationship between the underlying cycles that affect a certain market and the correct moving averages to use. In other words, the moving averages should be adjusted to fit the dominant cycles in each market.

There appears to be a definite relationship between moving averages and cycles. For example, the *monthly cycle* is one of the best known cycles operating throughout the commodity markets. A month has 20 to 21 trading days. Cycles tend to be related to their next longer and shorter cycles *harmonically*, or by a factor of two. That means that the next longer cycle is double the length of a cycle and the next shorter cycle is half its length.

The monthly cycle, therefore, may explain the popularity of the 5-, 10-, 20-, and 40-day moving averages. The 20-day cycle measures the monthly cycle. The 40-day average is double the 20-day. The 10-day average is half of 20 and the 5-day average is half again of ten.

Many of the more commonly used moving averages (including the 4-, 9-, and 18-day averages, which are derivatives of five, ten, and 20) can be explained by cyclic influences and the harmonic relationships of neighboring cycles. Incidentally, the four-week cycle may also help explain the success of the *four-week rule*, covered later in the chapter, and its shorter counterpart—the *two-week rule*.

FIBONACCI NUMBERS USED AS MOVING AVERAGES

We'll cover the Fibonacci number series in the chapter on Elliott Wave Theory. However, I'd like to mention here that this mysterious series of numbers—such as 13, 21, 34, 55, and so on—seem to lend themselves quite well to moving average analysis. This is true not only of daily charts, but for weekly charts as well. The *21-day moving average*, which we've already mentioned on the daily charts, is a Fibonacci number. On the weekly charts, the 13-week average has proven valuable in both stocks and commodities. We'll postpone a more in-depth discussion of these numbers until Chapter 13. (See Figures 9.9a to d.)

Figure 9.9a Examples of some Fibonacci numbers used as moving averages. The dotted line just broken is the 144-day average, the equivalent of the 30-week average. The two other averages shown here are the 13- and 34-day averages. The 13 (solid line) has crossed above the 34 (dashed line) giving a buy signal.

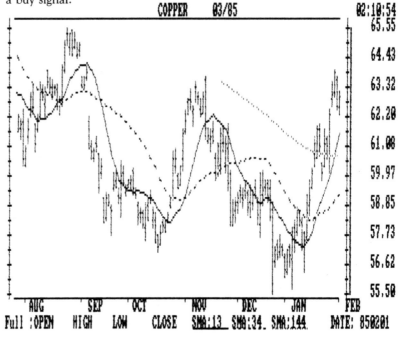

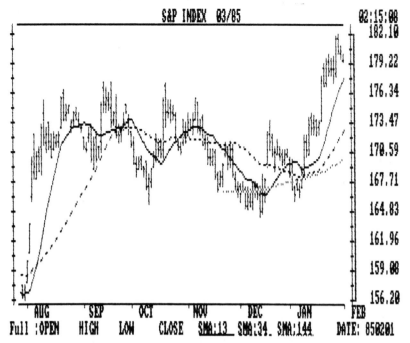

Full : OPEN   HIGH   LOW   CLOSE   SMA:13   SMA:34   SMA:144   DATE: 850201

Figure 9.9b   Another example of the 13-, 34-, and 144-day Fibonacci numbers. An excellent buy signal was given in late December when the 13 (solid line) crossed over the 34 (dashed line). Notice also that prices survived a test of the longer-term 144-day average (dotted line). Notice on both charts the number of whipsaws as prices traded sideways.

Figure 9.9c   Examples of the 13- and 34-day Fibonacci combinations. Notice how well they contained the uptrend since last July. Prices have just broken below both averages, giving an early warning of a possible trend change. The third line, well below the price action, is the 144-day (30-week) average.

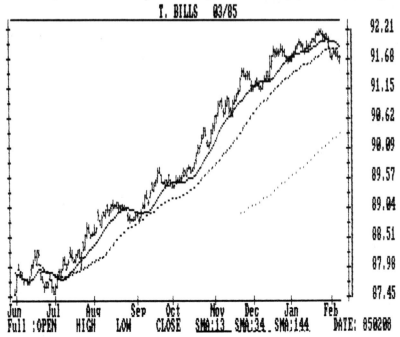

Full : OPEN   HIGH   LOW   CLOSE   SMA:13   SMA:34   SMA:144   DATE: 850208

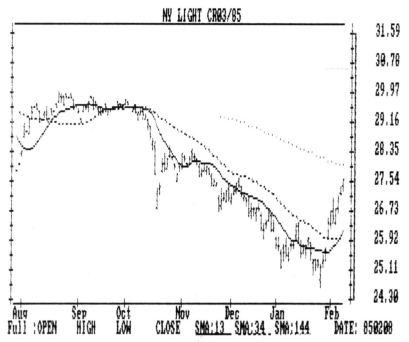

Figure 9.9d The 13- and 34-day Fibonacci numbers did a pretty good job containing the price decline. A "sell" signal was given in October when the 13 crossed under the 34. Prices recently crossed above both averages, which was confirmed when the 13 moved over the 34. A new uptrend has been signalled. Prices are now approaching the 144-day (30-week) average.

MOVING AVERAGES APPLIED TO ANY TIME DIMENSION

Moving average analysis is most commonly applied to daily bar charts. However, the reader should not overlook the possibility of applying this technique to longer-range trend analysis and also to very short-term trading. Longer-range moving averages, such as ten or 13 weeks, in conjunction with the 30-week average, have long been used in stock market analysis, but haven't been given much attention in the commodity futures markets. The 10- and 30-week moving averages can be used to help track the primary trend on weekly continuation charts going back several years. (See Figure 9.10.)

In the other direction on the time scale, moving averages are used on intra-day charts for short-term trading purposes. While the signals produced on these short-term charts are no doubt valid, the only question I would raise would be whether the lag time that is the nature of moving average analysis would diminish its usefulness in the day trading arena where quick response time is so crucial.

Moving Averages

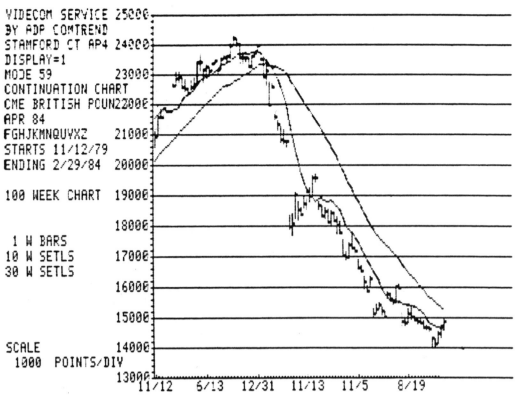

VIDECOM SERVICE
BY ADP COMTREND
STAMFORD CT AP4
DISPLAY=1
MODE 59
CONTINUATION CHART
CME BRITISH POUN
APR 84
FGHJKMNQUVXZ
STARTS 11/12/79
ENDING 2/29/84

100 WEEK CHART

1 W BARS
10 W SETLS
30 W SETLS

SCALE
1000 POINTS/DIV

Figure 9.10 Example of 10- and 30-week moving averages applied to a weekly continuation chart of the British pound. Notice how the crossing of the two averages over 2.30 at the end of 1980 accurately signalled the beginning of a major bear market. (Source: Automatic Data Processing, Inc., Comtrend Division, Stamford, CT.)

CONCLUSION

We've presented a lot of variations on the moving average approach in this chapter. In one sense, the very flexibility of this technique may present a problem, because the user is faced with a bewildering choice of possibilities. Let's try to simplify things a bit. Most technicians use a combination of two or three simple moving averages. These averages are applied to the closing prices and are plotted along with the last price bar, with no lead or lag time. The most commonly used averages are five, ten, 20, and 40 days or some variation of those numbers (such as four, nine, and 18). But feel free to do your own experimenting. The availability of microcomputers and optimization programs have made moving average analysis a good deal easier and a lot more fun.

Some Pros and Cons of the Moving Average

One of the great advantages of using moving averages, and one of the reasons they are so popular as trend-following systems, is that they embody some of the oldest maxims of successful futures trading. They trade in the direction of the trend. They let profits run and cut losses short. Sound familiar? Of course, every novice trader has read these old rules. The important point here is that the moving average system forces the user to obey those rules by providing specific buy and sell signals based on those principles.

Because they are trend-following in nature, however, moving averages work best when markets are in a trending period. They perform very poorly when markets get choppy and trade sideways for a period of time. And that might be anywhere from a third to a half of the time. Sometimes it seems like a lot more than that.

Figure 9.11a Notice the 5-day moving average applied to the volume bars. The use of averages can sometimes smooth the volume trend and make it simpler to follow. All kinds of trading signals can be devised by comparing different average lengths of the volume figures. Notice in this example that the volume average followed the price action pretty closely.

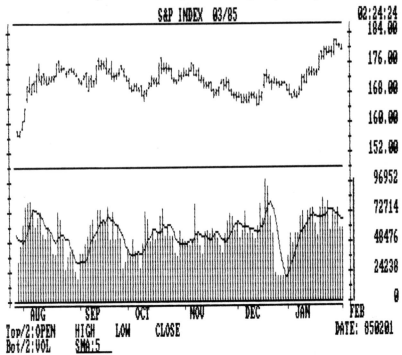

The fact that they do not work well for significant periods of time, however, is one very compelling reason why it is dangerous to rely too heavily on the moving average technique. It has been stressed time and time again that the technical trader must have at his or her disposal an arsenal of many different technical tools. In certain trending markets, the moving average can't be beat. Just switch the program to automatic and go fishing for awhile. At other times, a nontrending method like the overbought-oversold oscillator is more appropriate. And appropriately enough, we'll tackle the subject of *oscillators* in the next chapter.

Moving Averages as Oscillators

One way to construct an oscillator is to compare the difference between two moving averages. The use of two moving averages in the double

Figure 9.11b The upper half of this chart shows a 34-day average (Fibonacci number) applied to a price chart. The lower chart shows the same average applied to on balance volume (OBV).

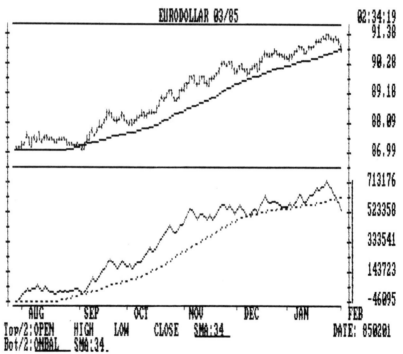

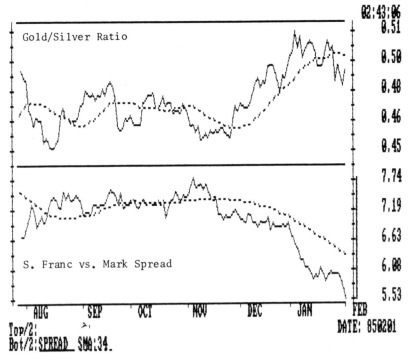

DATE: 850201

Figure 9.12a The upper chart shows a 21-day average used on a gold/silver ratio. The lower chart shows a 34-day average applied to a Swiss franc vs. a Deutsche mark spread chart.

crossover method, therefore, takes on greater significance and becomes an even more useful technique. We'll see how this is done in Chapter 10. Earlier in this chapter, mention was made of a method that compares two exponentially smoothed averages. That method is called the Moving Average Convergence/Divergence Trading Method (MACDTM). It is used primarily as an oscillator. Therefore, we'll postpone our explanation of that technique until we deal with the entire subject of oscillators in Chapter 10.

The Moving Average Applied to Other Technical Data

The moving average can be applied to virtually any technical data or indicator. It can be used on open interest and volume figures, including on balance volume. The moving average can be used on various indicators, spreads, and ratios. It can be applied to oscillators as well. Figures 9.11a and b and Figures 9.12a and b show some applications of this broader usage.

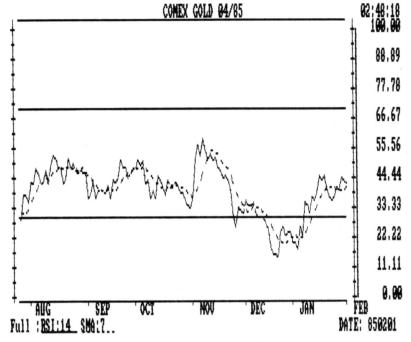

COMEX GOLD 04/85   02:48:18
100.00
88.89
77.78
66.67
55.56
44.44
33.33
22.22
11.11
0.00

AUG   SEP   OCT   NOV   DEC   JAN   FEB

Full :RSI:14 SMA:7..   DATE: 850201

Figure 9.12b   Example of a 7-day average used to help spot turns in the 14-day Relative Strength Index oscillator (RSI).

THE WEEKLY RULE

There are other alternatives to the moving average as a trend-following device. One of the best known and most successful of these techniques is called the *weekly price channel* or, simply, *the weekly rule*. This technique has many of the benefits of the moving average, but is less time consuming and simpler to use.

With the improvements in computer technology over the past decade, a considerable amount of research has been done on the development of technical trading systems for use in the commodity futures markets. These systems are mechanical in nature, meaning that human emotion and judgment are eliminated. These systems have become increasingly sophisticated. At first, simple moving averages were utilized. Then, double and triple crossovers of the averages were added. The averages were then linearly weighted and exponentially smoothed. More recently, advanced statistical methods, such as linear regression, have been applied. These systems are primarily trend-following, which means their purpose is to identify and then trade in the direction of an existing trend.

With the increased fascination with fancier and more complex systems and indicators, however, there has been a tendency to overlook some of the simpler techniques that continue to work quite well and have stood the test of time. We're going to discuss one of the simplest of these techniques—the weekly rule.

In 1970, a booklet entitled the *Trader's Notebook* was published by Dunn & Hargitt's Financial Services in Lafayette, Indiana. The best-known mechanical systems of the day were computer-tested and compared. The final conclusion of all that research was that the most successful of all the systems tested was *the four-week rule*, developed by Richard Donchian. Mr. Donchian, currently a Senior Vice President/Financial Consultant with Shearson Lehman American Express, has been recognized as a pioneer in the concept of commodity trend trading using mechanical systems. (In 1983, *Managed Account Reports* chose Donchian as the first recipient of the Most Valuable Performer Award for outstanding contributions to the field of commodity money management, and now presents The Donchian Award to other worthy recipients.)

The Four-Week Rule

The system based on the four-week rule is simplicity itself:

1. Cover short positions and buy long whenever the price exceeds the highs of the four preceding full calendar weeks.

2. Liquidate long positions and sell short whenever the price falls below the lows of the four preceding full calendar weeks.

The system, as it is presented here, is continuous in nature, which means that the trader always has a position, either long or short. As a general rule, continuous systems have a basic weakness. They stay in the market and get "whipsawed" during trendless market periods. It's already been stressed that trend-following systems do not work well when markets are in these sideways, or trendless phases.

The four-week rule can be modified to make it noncontinuous. This can be accomplished by using a shorter time span—such as a one- or two-week rule—for liquidation purposes. In other words, a four-week "breakout" would be necessary to initiate a new position, but a one- or two-week signal in the opposite direction would warrant liquidation of the position. The trader would then remain out of the market until a new four-week breakout is registered.

The logic behind the system is based on sound technical principles. Its signals are mechanical and clearcut. Because it is trend-following, it virtually guarantees participation on the right side of every important trend. It is also structured to follow the often quoted maxim of successful commodity trading—"let profits run, while cutting losses short." Another feature, which should not be overlooked, is that this method tends to trade less frequently, so that commissions are lower. This is one reason why this particular system (or some variation thereof) is popular among money managers, but not so popular among brokers. Another plus is that the system can be implemented with or without the aid of a computer.

The main criticism of the weekly rule is the same one leveled against all trend-following approaches, namely, that it does not catch tops or bottoms. But what trend-following system does? The important point to keep in mind is that the four-week rule performs at least as well as most other trend-following systems and better than many, but has the added benefit of incredible simplicity.

Adjustments to the Four-Week Rule

Although we're treating the four-week rule in its original form, there are many adjustments and refinements that can be employed. For one thing, the rule does not have to be used as a trading system. Weekly signals can be employed simply as another technical indicator to identify breakouts and trend reversals. Weekly breakouts can be used as a confirming filter for other techniques, such as moving average crossovers. One- or two-week rules function as excellent filters. Therefore, a moving average crossover signal would have to be confirmed by a two-week breakout in the same direction in order for a market position to be taken.

Weekly Rules Can Be Optimized

The length of the weekly rules can be adjusted to optimum lengths in different markets. Instead of applying a four-week rule to each and every market, the time span can be customized to each individual market. During our discussion of moving averges, reference was made to a series of Merrill Lynch studies. The Merrill Lynch Commodity Research Report, "Computerized Trading Techniques," dated February, 1979, did extensive testing of various weekly channel breakouts. Optimized results were then presented for each market. That study also suggested that trading performance could be further improved by altering the day on which the week ends. For example, the report claimed that the sugar market worked best with a five-week rule, with each week ending on Thursday. The best number for the soybean market was a two-week rule ending on Monday. Earlier Merrill Lynch studies tested various daily breakout parameters.

Shorten or Lengthen Time Periods For Sensitivity

The time period employed can be expanded or compressed in the interests of risk management and sensitivity. For example, the time period could be shortened if it is desirable to make the system more sensitive. In a relatively high-priced market, where prices are trending sharply higher, a shorter time span could be chosen to make the system more sensitive. Suppose, for example, that a long position is taken on a four-week upside breakout with a protective stop placed just below the low of the past two weeks. If the market has rallied sharply and the trader wishes to trail the position with a closer protective stop, a one-week stopout point could be used.

In a trading range situation, where a trend trader would just as soon stay on the sidelines until an important trend signal is given, the time period could be expanded to eight weeks. This would prevent taking positions on shorter-term and premature trend signals.

The Four-Week Rule Tied to Cycles

Earlier in the chapter reference was made to the importance of the monthly cycle in commodity markets. The four-week, or 20-day, trading cycle is a dominant cycle that influences all markets. This may help explain why the four-week time period has proven so successful and is probably the one best time period to employ. Notice that mention was made of one-, two-, and eight-week rules. The principle of *harmonics* in cyclic analysis holds that each cycle is related to its neighboring cycles (next longer and next shorter cycles) by two.

In the previous discussion of moving averages, it was pointed out how the monthly cycle and harmonics explained the popularity of the 5-, 10-, 20-, and 40-day moving averages. The same time periods hold true in the realm of weekly rules. Those daily numbers translated into weekly time periods are one, two, four, and eight weeks. Therefore, adjustments to the four-week rule seem to work best when the beginning number (four) is divided or multiplied by two. To shorten the time span, go from four to two weeks. If an even shorter time span is desired, go from two to one. To lengthen, go from four to eight. Because this method combines price and time, there's no reason why the cyclic principle of harmonics should not play an important role. The tactic of dividing a weekly parameter by two to shorten it, or doubling it to lengthen it, does have cycle logic behind it.

Keeping the Weekly Rule Simple

The problem with attempting to optimize the four-week rule, or adding some or all of the previously mentioned refinements, is that the user begins to lose the system's greatest strength, which is its simplicity.

Figure 9.13 Example of the four-week rule. The major "buy" signal, given in July when prices set new four-week highs, is still intact. The solid horizontal lines show where four-week rule signals would be activated. The dashed lines show where the two-week rule might have caused early liquidation. (Courtesy of Commodity Research Bureau, a Knight-Ridder Business Information Service.)

Figure 9.14 The solid lines show where four-week signals would be given. The "sell" signal given in October is still in effect. Note that prices have just moved above the dashed line, indicating a two-week high. That signal might have been used for liquidating shorts. A close over the solid line just under 74 is needed to give a "buy" signal. (Courtesy of Commodity Research Bureau, a Knight-Ridder Business Information Service.)

The four-week rule is a simple breakout system, which is based on the dominant monthly cycle. The original system can be modified by using a shorter time period—a one- or two-week rule—for liquidation purposes. If the user desires a more sensitive system, a two-week period can be employed for entry signals. Because this rule is meant to be simple, it is best addressed on that level. The four-week rule is simple, but it works. Add it to your checklist. (See Figures 9.13 to 9.16.)

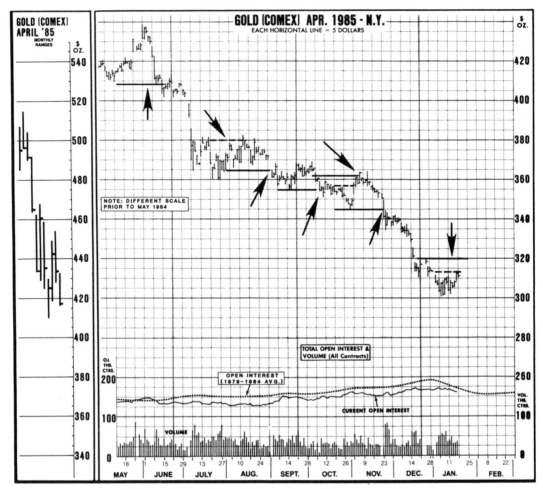

Figure 9.15 The solid lines show where four-week signals were given. One false buy signal was given in early November just above $360. Two-week rules (dashed lines) could have been used for earlier liquidation. To the right, a close above the dashed line is needed to cover shorts and a close over the solid line (at $320) is necessary to activate a new "buy" signal. (Courtesy of Commodity Research Bureau, a Knight-Ridder Business Information Service.)

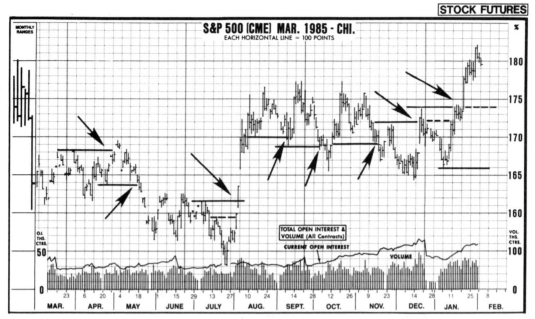

Figure 9.16 This chart shows both the good and bad elements of the weekly rule (and any trend-following system). Most of the downtrend from May to July was captured, the rally from July into August, and the January bullish breakout. This system guarantees participation in every important trend. Note, however, all of the false signals given while prices were trading sideways from September to January. By switching to an eight-week rule, some of the whipsaws might have been eliminated. Like all systems, the four-week rule has its periods of adversity. It functions best in a trend. (Courtesy of Commodity Research Bureau, a Knight-Ridder Business Information Service.)

ADDITIONAL REFERENCE MATERIAL

In addition to the sources mentioned in this chapter, the following two books contain additional information on moving averages and Donchian's weekly rules. Two chapters on "Moving Averages" and "Channels and Crossovers," by Frank Hochheimer, based on the earlier Merrill Lynch studies, appear in *Technical Analysis in Commodities,* edited by P.J. Kaufman, John Wiley & Sons, New York, 1980. The second book containing a discussion of various moving average techniques along with Donchian's weekly rules is *Technical Trading Systems for Commodities and Stocks,* by Charles Patel, Trading Systems Research, Walnut Creek, California, 1980.

10

Oscillators and Contrary Opinion

INTRODUCTION

Virtually every technical indicator discussed so far has been trend-following in nature. Their purpose has been to anticipate the beginning of new trends or to identify new trends as soon as possible after their inception. In this chapter, we're going to talk about an alternative to trend-following approaches—the *oscillator*. The oscillator is extremely useful in nontrending markets where prices fluctuate in a horizontal price band, or trading range, creating a market situation where most trend-following systems simply don't work that well. The oscillator provides the technical trader with a tool that can enable him or her to profit from these periodic sideways and trendless market environments.

The value of the oscillator is not limited to horizontal trading ranges, however. Used in conjunction with price charts during trending phases, the oscillator becomes an extremely valuable ally by alerting the trader to short-term market extremes, commonly referred to as *overbought* or *oversold* conditions. The oscillator can also warn that a trend is losing momentum before that situation becomes evident in the price action itself. Oscillators can signal that a trend may be nearing completion by displaying certain divergences.

We'll begin by explaining first what an oscillator is and the basis for its construction and interpretation. We'll then discuss the meaning of momentum and its implications for market forecasting. Some of the more common oscillator techniques will be presented from the very simple to the more complicated. The important question of divergence will be covered. We'll touch on the value of coordinating oscillator analysis with underlying market cycles. Finally, we'll discuss how oscillators should be used as part of the overall technical analysis of a market.

OSCILLATOR USAGE IN CONJUNCTION WITH TREND

The oscillator is only a secondary indicator in the sense that it must be subordinated to basic trend analysis. As we go through the various types of oscillators used by technicians, the importance of trading in the direction of the overriding market trend will be constantly stressed. The reader should also be aware that there are times when oscillators are more useful than at others. For example, near the beginning of important moves, oscillator analysis isn't that helpful and can even be misleading. Toward the end of market moves, however, oscillators become extremely valuable. We'll address these points as we go along. Finally, no study of market extremes would be complete without a discussion of Contrary Opinion. We'll talk about the role of the contrarian philosophy and how it can be incorporated into market analysis and trading.

Interpretation of Oscillators

While there are many different ways to construct momentum oscillators, the actual interpretation differs very little from one technique to another. Most oscillators look very much alike. They are plotted along the bottom of the daily price chart and resemble a flat horizontal band. The oscillator band is basically flat while prices may be trading up, down, or sideways. However, the peaks and troughs in the oscillator coincide with the peaks and troughs on the price chart. Some oscillators have a midpoint value that divides the horizontal range into two halves, an upper and a lower. Depending on the formula used, this midpoint line is usually a zero line. Some oscillators also have upper and lower boundaries ranging from 0 to 100 or -1 to $+1$, depending on the way they're constructed.

General Rules for Interpretation

As a general rule, when the oscillator reaches an extreme value in either the upper or lower end of the band, this suggests that the current price move may have gone too far too fast and is due for a correction or consolidation of some type. As another general rule, the trader should be buying when the oscillator line is in the lower end of the band and selling in the upper end of the range. The crossing of the zero line is often used to generate buy and sell signals. We'll see how these general rules are applied as we deal with the various types of oscillators.

The Three Most Important Uses for the Oscillator

There are three situations when the oscillator is most useful. You'll see that these three situations are common to most types of oscillators that are used.

1. The oscillator is most useful when its value reaches an extreme reading near the upper or lower end of its boundaries. The market is said to be *overbought* when it is near the upper extreme and *oversold* when it is near the lower extreme. This warns that the price trend is overextended and vulnerable.

2. A divergence between the oscillator and the price action when the oscillator is in an extreme position is usually an important warning.

3. The crossing of the zero line can give important trading signals in the direction of the price trend.

MEASURING MOMENTUM

The concept of *momentum* is the most basic application of oscillator analysis. Momentum measures the rate of change of prices as opposed to the actual price levels themselves. Market momentum is measured by continually taking price differences for a fixed time interval. To construct a 10-day momentum line, simply subtract the closing price ten days ago from the last closing price. This positive or negative value is then plotted around a zero line. The formula for momentum is:

$$M = V - Vx$$

where V is the latest closing price and Vx is the closing price x days ago.

If the latest closing price is greater than that of ten days ago (in other words, prices have moved higher), then a positive value would be plotted above the zero line. If the latest close is below the close ten days earlier (prices have declined), then a negative value is plotted below the zero line.

While the 10-day momentum is a commonly used time period for reasons discussed later, any time period can be employed. (See Figure 10.1a.) A shorter time period (such as five days) produces a more sensitive line with more pronounced oscillations. A longer number of days (such as 20 days) results in a much smoother line in which the oscillator swings are less volatile. (See Figure 10.1b.)

Figure 10.1a A 10-day momentum line compared to a bar chart of the Deutsche mark. The momentum line oscillates around a zero line. Extremes in either direction warn of oversold and overbought conditions. Signals are given by a crossing above or below the zero line in the direction of the price trend.

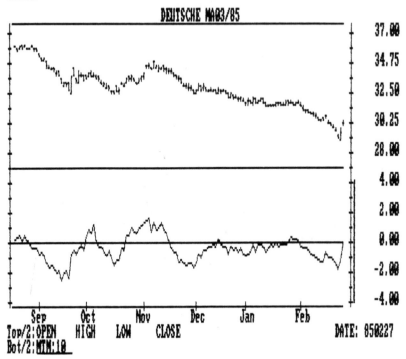

Oscillators and Contrary Opinion

Momentum Measures
Rates of Ascent or Descent

Let's talk a bit more about just what this momentum indicator is measuring. By plotting price differences for a set period of time, the chartist is studying rates of ascent or descent. If prices are rising and the momentum line is above the zero line and rising, this means the uptrend is accelerating. If the up-slanting momentum line begins to flatten out, this means that the new gains being achieved by the latest closes are the same as the gains ten days earlier. While prices may still be advancing, the rate of ascent (or the velocity) has leveled off. When the momentum line begins to drop toward the zero line, the uptrend in prices is still in force, but at a decelerating rate. The uptrend is losing momentum.

When the momentum line moves below the zero line, the latest 10-day close is now under the close of ten days ago and a near-term downtrend is in effect. (And, incidentally, the 10-day moving average also has begun to decline.) As momentum continues to drop farther

Figure 10.1b The sensitivity of the momentum line can be varied by changing the time period. The upper line is a more sensitive 5-day line. The lower line is a less sensitive 20-day.

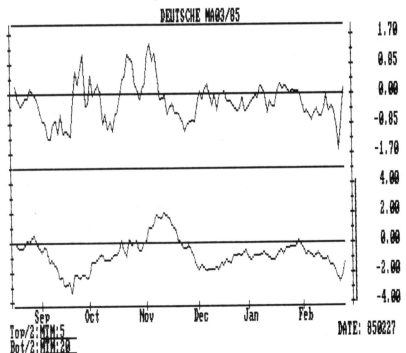

below the zero line, the downtrend gains momentum. Only when the line begins to advance again does the analyst know that the downtrend is decelerating.

It's important to remember that momentum measures the differences between prices at two time intervals. In order for the line to advance, the price gains for the last day's close must be greater than the gains of ten days ago. If prices advance by only the same amount as ten days ago, the momentum line will be flat. If the last price gain is less than that of ten days ago, the momentum line begins to decline even though prices are still rising. This is how the momentum line measures the acceleration or deceleration in the current advance or decline in the price trend.

The Momentum Line Leads the Price Action

Because of the way it is constructed, the momentum line is always a step ahead of the price movement. It leads the advance or decline in

Figure 10.2a Momentum line signals should be coordinated with the trend. The chart of the Deutsche mark shows a downtrend, identified by a falling 40-day moving average. In a downtrend, only the oscillator sell signals should be taken. Crossings over the zero line would not have been followed as long as the major price trend was down.

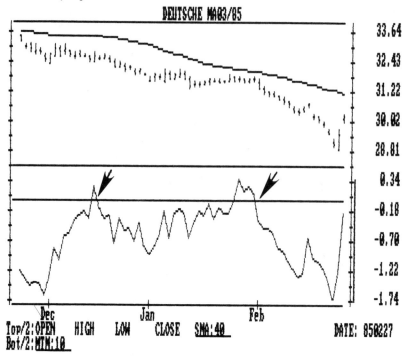

Oscillators and Contrary Opinion

prices by a few days, then levels off while the current price trend is still in effect. It then begins to move in the opposite direction as prices begin to level off.

The Crossing of
the Zero Line as a Trading Signal

The momentum chart has a zero line. Many technicians use the crossing of the zero line to generate buy and sell signals. A crossing above the zero line would be a buy signal, and a crossing below the zero line, a sell signal. It should be stressed here again, however, that basic trend analysis is still the overriding consideration. Oscillator analysis should not be used as an excuse to trade against the prevailing market trend. Buy positions should only be taken on crossings above the zero line if the market trend is up. Short positions should be taken on crossings below the zero line only if the price trend is down. (See Figures 10.2a and b.)

Figure 10.2b Throughout the uptrend in Treasury Bills, only the momentum buy signals (crossings above the zero line) should have been followed. Prices have now broken under the moving average, turning the trend lower. Oscillator sell signals would now be followed (crossings under the zero line).

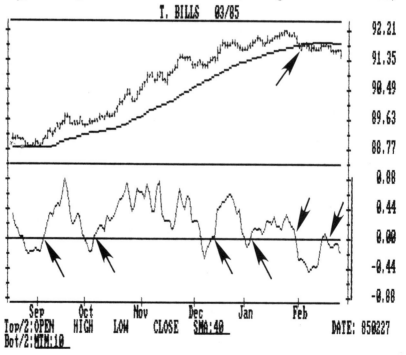

The Need for an Upper and Lower Boundary

One problem with the momentum line, as it is described here, is the absence of a prearranged upper and lower boundary. It was stated earlier that one of the major values of oscillator analysis is being able to determine when markets are in extreme areas. But, how high is too high and how low is too low on the momentum line? The simplest way to solve this problem is by visual inspection. Check the back history of the momentum line on the chart and draw horizontal lines along its upper and lower boundaries. These lines will have to be adjusted periodically, especially after important trend changes have occurred. But it is the simplest and probably the most effective way of identifying the outer extremities.

Another technique is to *normalize* the momentum line. This is accomplished by dividing the value of the momentum line by some constant divisor so that it will fall within a range of $+1$ and -1. The simplest way to do this is to divide the latest momentum value by the maximum possible price move for the time period being covered. For example, in a 10-day momentum line, calculate the momentum value by taking the difference between the last closing price and the price ten days ago. Then divide that difference by a limit move multiplied by ten (the length of the momentum line).

The final result will be some percentage of the maximum amount that a market can move, up or down, during the period of time and will fall within a range of $+1$ and -1. Once this has been achieved, the upper and lower boundaries are set and it becomes possible to identify beforehand where the "danger zones" are located. It also becomes easier to make historical comparisons with the same market or with other markets.

Once the extreme points of the band have been defined, the "danger zones" can be identified in various ways. One way would be to measure percentage moves above and below the zero line. Another would be to measure two standard deviations above and below the zero line so that 95% of all values fall within the upper and lower boundaries. Any move beyond those levels would warn of an extreme overbought or oversold condition. The intent in this exercise is to identify an upper and lower limit that contains most of the price oscillations in such a way that, when they are penetrated, a market extreme is identified and a warning of market vulnerability is given.

The use of a limit move as a divisor to normalize a momentum line has·some shortcomings. As a result, technicians have experimented with more sophisticated statistical devices to use as a divisor.

In the construction of his *Commodity Channel Index* (CCI), Donald R. Lambert uses the mean deviation as his divisor. (See "Commodity Channel Index," by Donald R. Lambert, *Commodities* [now *Futures*] *Magazine*, October, 1980, pp. 40-41.)

While Lambert's CCI was not developed primarily as an oscillator, the idea of using the mean deviation instead of the limit move as a divisor may also be applicable to oscillator analysis. Some technicians use the CCI as an oscillator even though that was apparently not its intended purpose. (See Figures 10.3a and b.) The problem of defining upper and lower boundaries is dealt with more effectively in some of the other oscillator formulas that we will deal with shortly—Welles Wilder's *Relative Strength Index* (RSI) and George Lane's *Stochastics*.

In our discussion of momentum, care has been taken not to use the term "oscillator" too loosely. While the original momentum line

Figure 10.3a A 5-day Commodity Channel Index (CCI) line applied to Treasury Bills. The intent of this indicator is to take long positions over the upper (+100) line and short positions below the lower (−100) line. All positions would be liquidated between the two lines. Many technicians, however, use the CCI as an oscillator.

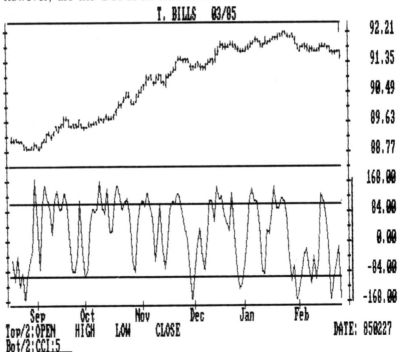

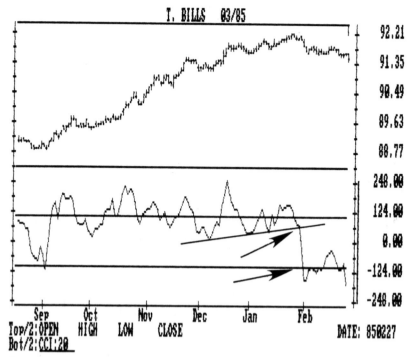

Figure 10.3b A smoother version of the CCI, using a 20-day period. Notice how the sharp break in the CCI line signalled a shift in the major trend.

is sometimes referred to as an oscillator, that usage is not totally correct. A simple momentum line is more correctly labelled "momentum." It is only when the momentum line is normalized that it is more correctly called an oscillator. Admittedly, the term "oscillator" generally includes all of the techniques used in this chapter. In order not to confuse anyone, we'll use more specific terminology when describing the various formulas for construction.

MEASURING RATE OF CHANGE (ROC)

In the previous discussion, price differences were taken between two time periods to determine market momentum. To measure the *rate of change*, a ratio is constructed of the most recent closing price to a price a certain number of days in the past. To construct a 10-day rate of change oscillator, the latest closing price is divided by the close 10 days ago. The formula is as follows:

Oscillators and Contrary Opinion

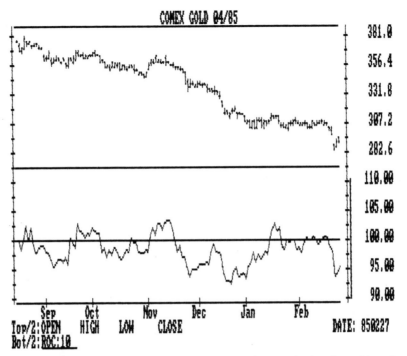

Figure 10.4a A 10-day rate of change (ROC) line applied to the gold market. The ROC is obtained by taking a ratio of the latest price to a price in the past. The ROC line oscillates above and below the 100 line.

Figure 10.4b A comparison of a 10-day momentum line (upper line) and a 10-day rate of change line (lower line). Although constructed differently, both lines look very similar and are interpreted the same way.

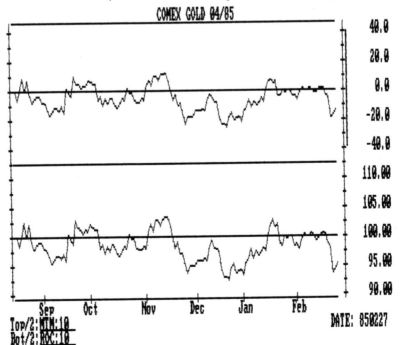

Rate of change $= 100 \; (V/Vx)$

where V is the latest close and Vx is the closing price x days ago.

In this case, the 100 line becomes the midpoint or zero line. (See Figures 10.4a and b.) If the latest price is higher than the price ten days ago (prices are rising), the resulting rate of change value will be above 100. If the last close is below ten days ago, the ratio would be below 100.

CONSTRUCTING AN OSCILLATOR USING TWO MOVING AVERAGES

Chapter 9 discussed two moving averages being used to generate buy and sell signals. The crossing of the shorter average above or below the longer average registered buy and sell signals, respectively. It was mentioned at that time that these double moving average combinations could also be used to construct oscillator charts. This can be done in two ways. The first, and most common, is to plot the difference between the two averages as a histogram. These histogram bars appear as a plus or minus value around a centered zero line. This type of oscillator has three uses:

1. To help spot divergences.

2. To help identify short-term variations from the long-term trend, when the shorter average moves too far above or below the longer average.

3. To pinpoint the crossings of the two moving averages, which occur when the oscillator crosses the zero line.

A second way to construct this type of oscillator is to plot the percentage difference between the two moving averages, instead of the point difference. (See Figures 10.5a and b.) To arrive at the percentage value, the shorter average is divided by the longer. In both cases, however, the shorter average oscillates around the longer average, which is in effect the zero line. If the shorter average is above the longer, the oscillator would be positive. A negative reading would be present if the shorter average were under the longer.

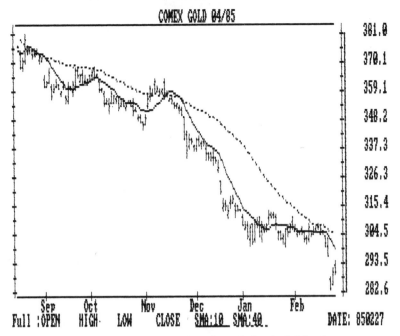

Full :OPEN HIGH· LOW   CLOSE   SMA:10 SMA:40 .   DATE: 850227

Figure 10.5a A bar chart of gold with a 10-day (solid line) moving average and 40-day moving average (dashed line).

Figure 10.5b The upper chart shows an oscillator that plots the point difference between the two averages. The lower chart shows an oscillator that plots the percentage differences. Both look very much alike and show basically the same thing. If the averages move too far apart, an oversold condition exists. The zero line acts as resistance in a downtrend and support in an uptrend. Moving average crossings are easier to spot.

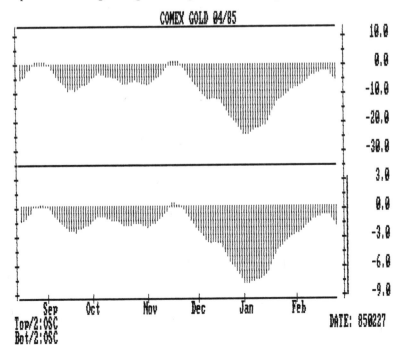

Top/2:OSC
Bot/2:OSC   DATE: 850227

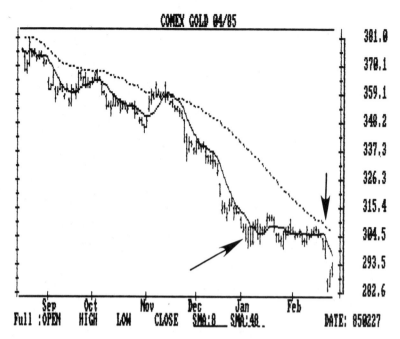

Figure 10.6a   The same gold chart as in Figure 10.5a with a couple of optimized moving averages. The shorter average (solid line) is eight days. The longer average (dashed line) is 48.

Figure 10.6b   The upper chart shows point differences and the lower shows percentage differences between the two averages. Notice that when the two averages got too far apart, the market traded sideways until the averages tested each other again near the zero line. The downtrend then resumed.

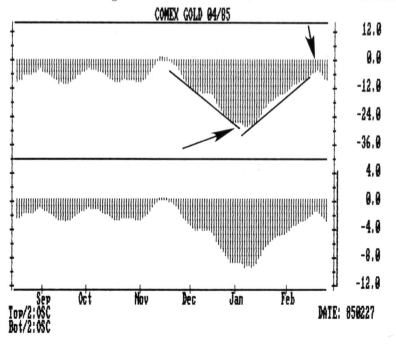

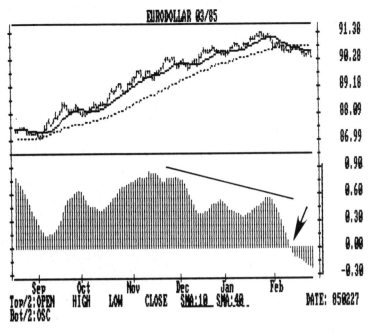

EURODOLLAR 03/85

91.38
90.28
89.18
88.09
86.99

0.90
0.60
0.30
0.00
-0.30

Sep   Oct   Nov   Dec   Jan   Feb
Top/2:OPEN   HIGH   LOW   CLOSE   SMA:10   SMA:40.   DATE: 850227
Bot/2:OSC

Figure 10.7a The upper chart shows 10- and 40-day averages on a bar chart of Eurodollars. The lower chart is an oscillator of the moving average differences. First, the last peak in the oscillator did not confirm the price move into new highs. Second, the crossing under the zero line gave a major sell signal.

Figure 10.7b Two Fibonacci moving averages (13 and 34 days) are applied to the crude oil market. See how the oscillator did not confirm the price move into new lows. A major buy signal was given when the oscillator moved over the zero line.

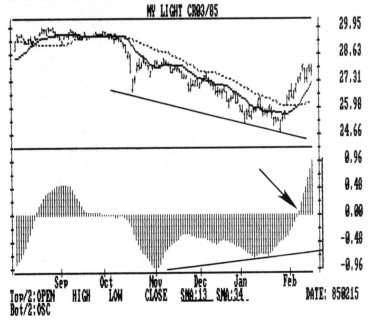

NY LIGHT CR03/85

29.95
28.63
27.31
25.98
24.66

0.96
0.48
0.00
-0.48
-0.96

Sep   Oct   Nov   Dec   Jan   Feb
Top/2:OPEN   HIGH   LOW   CLOSE   SMA:13   SMA:34.   DATE: 850215
Bot/2:OSC

When the two moving average lines move too far apart, a market extreme is created calling for a pause in the trend. (See Figures 10.6a and b.) Very often, the trend remains stalled until the shorter average line moves back to the longer. When the shorter line approaches the longer, a critical point is reached. In an uptrend, for example, the shorter line dips back to the longer average, but should bounce off it. This usually represents an ideal buying area. It's much like the testing of a major up trendline. If the shorter average crosses below the longer average, however, a trend reversal is signalled.

In a downtrend, a rise in the shorter average to the longer usually represents an ideal selling area unless the longer line is crossed, in which case a trend reversal signal would be registered. The relationships between the two averages can be used, therefore, not only as an excellent trend-following system, but also to help identify short-term overbought and oversold conditions. As a final note, the use of optimized moving averages should also be valuable in this type of oscillator construction and analysis. (See Figures 10.7a and b.).

OSCILLATOR INTERPRETATION

The three examples we've looked at so far—*momentum, rate of change*, and *moving average differences*—describe some of the simpler oscillator formulations. We're now about ready to investigate a couple of the more sophisticated oscillators—Welles Wilder's *Relative Strength Index* and George Lane's *Stochastics*. Before we get to them, however, let's discuss in more depth the interpretation of the oscillator, and introduce the important concept of *divergence*.

1. The Crossing of the Zero Line

The simplest way to utilize the oscillator is to use the midpoint value (or the zero line) as a signal generator. Buy when the oscillator moves above the zero line and sell when it moves below. This is the technique most commonly used on the momentum charts. As stated previously, this technique is most effective when trading signals are taken in the direction of the market trend.

The Commodity Research Bureau CRS Oscillator. An excellent example of the use of zero line crossing analysis is the Current Relative Strength (CRS) oscillator plotted in the Commodity Research Bureau's *CRB Futures Chart Service.* The CRB zero line functions as a support line in bull trends, much like a major up trendline. During bull market corrections, the oscillator (CRS) line usually declines to and bounces off the zero line. In bear trend rallies, the zero line acts as a solid resistance barrier like a major down trendline. Action can be taken as the zero line is approached from above or below.

The zero line represents a low-risk buying zone in an uptrend and a low-risk selling zone in downtrends. The crossing of the zero line constitutes an important trend signal that often remains in effect for several weeks to several months. Because the CRB oscillator is longer-term than most other oscillators, it can be used as both an oscillator and an important trend-following indicator.

Figure 10.8 The Current Relative Strength (CRS) line, plotted in the *CRB Futures Chart Service*, is used like an oscillator. Major trend signals are given when the CRS line crosses above and below the zero line. In major downtrends, the zero line acts as resistance. In uptrends, the zero line acts as support. (Charts courtesy of Commodity Research Bureau, a Knight-Ridder Business Information Service.)

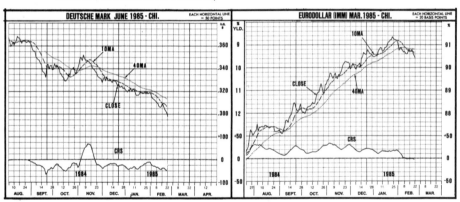

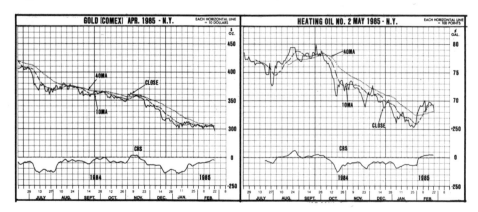

2. Edge Band Analysis, or the Study of Oscillator Extremes

The second way to use oscillators is *edge band* analysis, or the identification of extremes. In other words, the outer boundaries of the oscillator band are used to warn of market extremes. Most of the more sophisticated oscillators have an upper and lower zone that is considered overbought or oversold. The Relative Strength Index (RSI), for example, has a vertical scale from 0 to 100. Two horizontal lines appear on the oscillator at 70 and 30. A move above 70 would warn of an overbought condition, while a dip under 30 would constitute an oversold condition. (See Figures 10.9a and b.)

A trader could, for instance, take some profits on long positions when the oscillator is above 70, or lock up some short profits when the oscillator value is under 30. Crossings back below the 70 line from above or back above the 30 line from below can also be used to initiate new positions. But we'll defer our discussion of that point until we get into the individual oscillators themselves.

Figure 10.9a Some oscillators, like RSI, have an upper and lower band at 70 and 30. An overbought reading occurs when the value is over 70 and an oversold condition when the line is below 30.

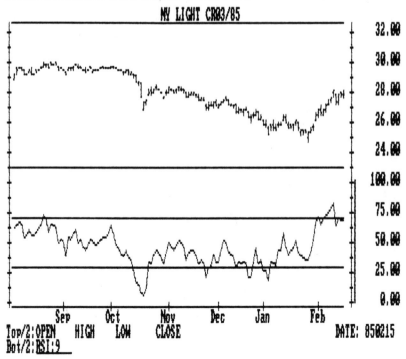

Oscillators and Contrary Opinion

3. The Importance of Divergence

The third, and possibly the most valuable, way to utilize oscillator analysis is to watch for *divergences*. A *divergence* describes a situation when the oscillator line and the price line diverge from one another and start to move in opposite directions. In an uptrend, the most common type of oscillator divergence, and the type we'll focus on in this discussion, occurs when prices continue to rise, but the oscillator fails to confirm the price move into new highs. This is often an excellent warning of a possible rally failure and is called a bearish, or a negative, divergence.

In a downtrend, if the oscillator fails to confirm the new low move in prices, a positive or bullish divergence exists and warns of at least a near-term bounce. The oscillator pattern in both cases often resembles a double top or double bottom. An important requirement for divergence analysis is that the divergence take place near the oscillator extremes. The divergence on the RSI, for example, is much more significant when the oscillator is over 70 or under 30 and already

Figure 10.9b Another example of RSI with 70 and 30 lines.

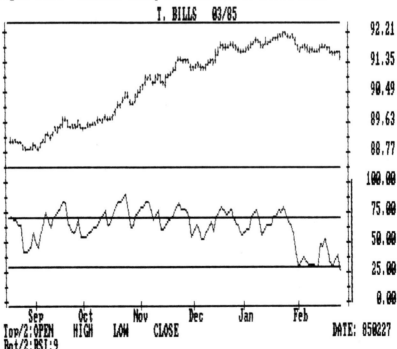

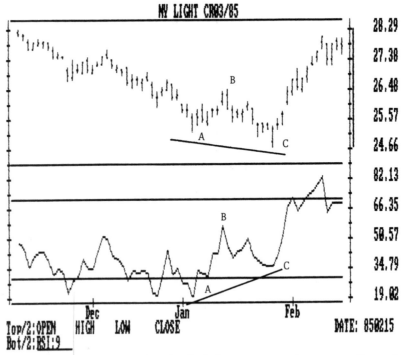

NY LIGHT CR03/85

```
28.29
27.38
26.48
25.57
24.66
82.13
66.35
58.57
34.79
19.82
```

B

A   C

B

C

A

Dec   Jan   Feb

Top/2:OPEN   HIGH   LOW   CLOSE   DATE: 850215
Bot/2:RSI:9

Figure 10.10a An example of a bullish or positive divergence. First, the oscillator dips under 30 into the oversold zone. Then, the oscillator second trough at point C stays above the previous trough at A, and does not confirm the price move into new lows at C. Some analysts then require the oscillator to cross above the peak at B to signal a turn to the upside. The important warning is the divergence itself.

in one of the danger zones. A bearish divergence with the oscillator over 70 or a bullish divergence under 30 can be an important warning and should be heeded. (See Figure 10.10a.)

A second form of divergence takes place when the oscillator line penetrates a significant peak or trough before prices do. There is a tendency for the oscillator scale to shift upward or downward, depending on the direction of the trend. In uptrends, the oscillator scale shifts a bit to the upside and in downtrends, to the downside. Peaks and troughs on the oscillator line usually coincide with peaks and troughs on the price chart. If prices are in an uptrend with the oscillator showing a pattern of rising peaks and troughs, and the oscillator suddenly drops through a significant previous trough, this is often a warning of a possible shift in trend from up to down. The penetration of a previous peak would, of course, warn of a possible bottom in a downtrend. (See Figure 10.10b.)

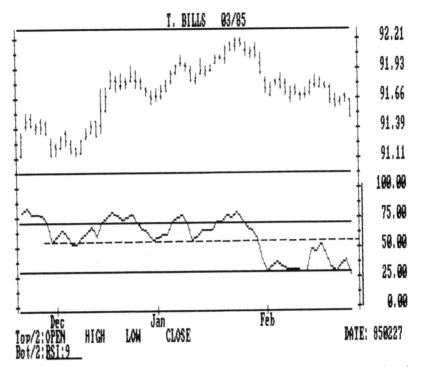

Figure 10.10b Another type of divergence occurs when the oscillator breaks an important shelf of support or resistance before prices do. In this example, the oscillator broke under several months of support, signalling an important shift in the trend to the downside.

In order to better demonstrate the application of divergence principles, let's turn our attention to what has become over the past few years the most widely followed oscillator among technical futures traders—Welles Wilder's *Relative Strength Index* (RSI).

THE RELATIVE STRENGTH INDEX (RSI)

The RSI was developed by J. Welles Wilder, Jr. and presented in his 1978 book, *New Concepts in Technical Trading Systems* (Greensboro, N.C.: Trend Research). We're only going to cover the main points here. A reading of the original work by Wilder himself is recommended for a more in-depth treatment. Because this particular oscillator is so popular among futures traders, we'll use it to demonstrate most of the principles of oscillator analysis.

As Wilder points out, one of the two major problems in constructing a momentum line (using price differences) is the erratic movement often caused by sharp changes in the values being dropped off. A sharp advance or a decline ten days ago (in the case of a 10-day momentum line) can cause sudden shifts in the momentum line even if the current prices show little change. Some smoothing is therefore necessary to minimize these distortions. The second problem is that there is the need for a constant band for comparison purposes. The RSI formula not only provides the necessary smoothing, but also solves the latter problem by creating a constant vertical range of 0 to 100.

The term "relative strength," incidentally, is a bit of a misnomer and often causes confusion among those more familiar with that term as it is used in stock market analysis. Relative strength generally means a ratio line comparing two different entities. A ratio of a stock or industry group to the S&P 500 Index is one way of gauging the relative strength of different stocks or industry groups against one objective benchmark. In commodity markets, a ratio can gauge the relative strength between different contract months or markets, or even against a more general measure such as the CRB Futures Price Index. Wilder's *Relative Strength Index* doesn't really measure the relative strength between different entities and, in that sense, the name is somewhat misleading. The RSI, however, does solve the problem of erratic movement and the need for a constant upper and lower boundary. The actual formula is calculated as follows:

$$RSI = 100 - \left[\frac{100}{1 + RS} \right]$$

$$RS = \frac{\text{Average of } x \text{ day's up closes}}{\text{Average of } x \text{ day's down closes}}$$

Suppose that a 14-day time period is used in the calculation. To find the average up value, add the total points gained on up days during the 14 days and divide that total by 14. To find the average down value, add the total number of points lost during the down days and divide that total by 14. Relative Strength (RS) is then determined by dividing the *up* average by the *down* average. That RS value is then

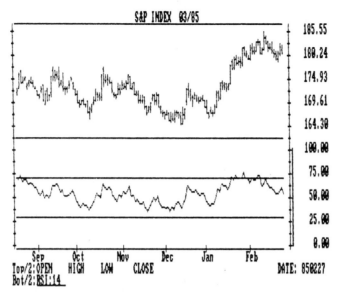

Figure 10.11a An example of a standard 14-day Relative Strength Index (RSI) oscillator (lower line) applied to an S&P contract. Notice here that during the sideways price action, the RSI line didn't reach the 70 or 30 lines for several months. This indicated that the 14-day period was too long.

Figure 10.11b The upper chart is a 9-day RSI oscillator and the lower chart, a more sensitive 5-day line of the same contract in Figure 10.11a. The amplitude of the oscillator can be widened by shortening the time period. The oscillator works better for shorter-term trading when the 70 and 30 lines are exceeded. Shorter-term traders use 5- or 7-day spans.

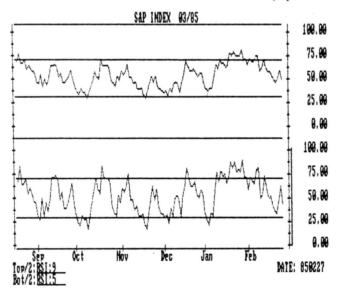

inserted into the formula for RSI. The number of days can be varied by simply changing the value of x.

Wilder originally employed a 14-day period. Some technical chart services, such as *Commodity Perspective* (a division of Commodity News Services, Inc., published in Chicago, IL.), use a 9-day period. *The shorter the time period, the more sensitive the oscillator becomes and the wider its amplitude.* RSI works best when its fluctuations reach the upper and lower extremes. Therefore, if the user is trading on a very short-term basis and wants the oscillator swings to be more pronounced, the time period can be shortened. The time period is lengthened to make the oscillator smoother and narrower in amplitude. The amplitude in the 9-day oscillator is therefore greater than the original 14-day. While 9- and 14-day spans are still the most common values used, technicians are experimenting with other periods, such as 5- and 7-day spans, to improve results. (See Figures 10.11a and b.)

The process of updating the RSI on a daily basis is not that difficult. The only back information the user needs is the latest up and down averages, which are provided by the chart services along with an explanation of how to construct and update the numbers. To update the 9-day formula, for example, multiply the previous up and down averages by eight, add the latest day's up or down value to the appropriate average and then divide the new total by nine. The new averages are then inserted into the formula. Performing these calculations by hand or even with a calculator does become a bit tedious if several markets are being followed. The chore of figuring the RSI on a daily basis has largely been eliminated by the fact that it is now available in most technical analysis software programs and on most video information retrieval systems. The computer now does the hard work of calculating the numbers and the analyst is freed up to do the more important task of interpreting.

Interpreting RSI

RSI is plotted on a vertical scale of 0 to 100. Movements above 70 are considered overbought, while an oversold condition would be a move under 30. Because the oscillator swings are wider on the 9-day formula, 80 and 20 are sometimes used in place of the 70 and 30 values. Also, because of the shifting that takes place in bull and bear markets, the 80 level usually becomes the overbought level in bull markets and the 20 level the oversold level in bear markets.

"Failure swings," as Wilder calls them, occur when the RSI is above 70 or under 30. A *top failure swing* occurs when a peak in the RSI (over 70) fails to exceed a previous peak in an uptrend, followed by a downside break of a previous trough. A *bottom failure swing* occurs when the RSI is in a downtrend (under 30), fails to set a new low, and then proceeds to exceed a previous peak. (See Figures 10.12a and b.)

Divergence between the RSI and the price line, when the RSI is above 70 or below 30, is a serious warning that should be heeded. Wilder himself considers divergence "the single most indicative characteristic of the Relative Strength Index [Wilder, p. 70]."

Figure 10.12a An example of a bottom failure swing in the RSI. If the RSI value is under 30, fails to confirm the price move into new lows at C, then exceeds the previous RSI peak at B, a bottom failure swing has been completed, which is a short-term buy signal. At a bottom, the RSI shows either a double bottom or two rising bottoms. This signal was actually the bottom of a 3-month secondary correction in a bull market.

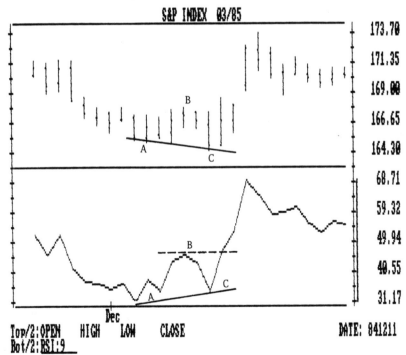

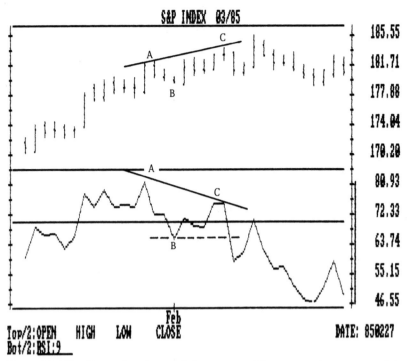

185.55

181.71

177.88

174.04

170.20

80.93

72.33

63.74

55.15

46.55

Feb

Top/2:OPEN   HIGH   LOW   CLOSE   DATE: 850227
Bot/2:RSI:9

Figure 10.12b Example of a top failure swing. This is just the reverse of the bottom. This near-term sell signal marked the beginning of an intermediate top. The sell signal has three parts: an RSI move above 70, a lower peak at C, then a violation of the previous low at B.

Various chart patterns show up on the RSI line as well as support and resistance levels. Trendline analysis can be employed to detect changes in the trend of the RSI. Moving averages can also be used for the same purpose. Several accompanying examples are shown to demonstrate how the previous points would look in real situations. (See Figures 10.13a and b.)

In my own personal experience with the RSI oscillator, its greatest value lies in failure swings or divergences that occur when the RSI is over 70 or under 30. Let's clarify another important point on the use of oscillators. Any strong trend, either up or down, usually produces an extreme oscillator reading before too long. In such cases, claims that a market is overbought or oversold are usually premature and can lead to an early exit from a profitable trend. In strong uptrends, overbought markets can stay overbought for some time. Just because the oscillator has moved into the upper region is not reason enough to liquidate a long position (or, heaven forbid, short into the strong uptrend).

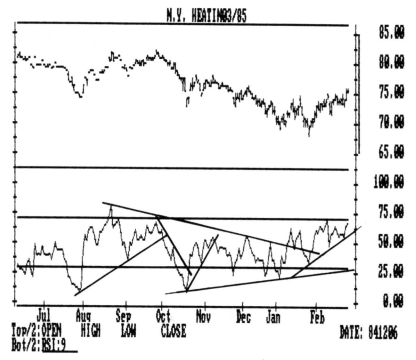

N.Y. HEATING 03/85

Top/2: OPEN   HIGH   LOW   CLOSE
Bot/2: RSI:9   DATE: 841206

Figure 10.13a Support and resistance levels can be seen on the RSI line. Trendline analysis can also be employed to help spot changes in the trend.

Figure 10.13b Moving averages can also be used on the RSI line. In this example, a 3-day average is used to smooth a 14-day RSI line.

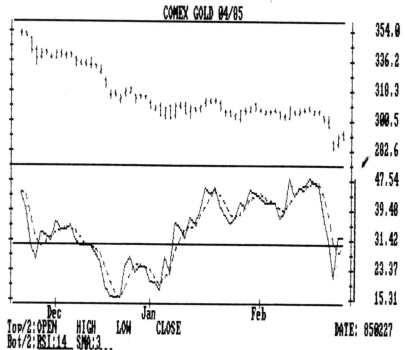

COMEX GOLD 04/85

Top/2: OPEN   HIGH   LOW   CLOSE
Bot/2: RSI:14 SMA:3   DATE: 850227

The first move into the overbought or oversold region is usually just a warning. The signal to pay close attention to is the second move by the oscillator into the danger zone. If the second move fails to confirm the price move into new highs or new lows (forming a double top or bottom on the oscillator), a possible divergence exists. At that point, some defensive action can be taken to protect existing positions. If the oscillator moves in the opposite direction, breaking a previous high or low, then a divergence or failure swing is confirmed.

Even then, however, market exit might prove premature until the price trend itself shows some signs of reversing. Tight protective stops are probably the most efficient way to handle such situations. The moral here is not to jump out of a profitable trade just because the oscillator reaches an extreme. Watch for the second move into the danger zone and only then begin to take some defensive action by partial profit-taking or the use of tighter protective stops.

USING THE 70 AND 30 LINES TO GENERATE SIGNALS

Horizontal lines appear on the oscillator chart at the 70 and 30 values. Traders often use those lines to generate buy and sell signals. We already know that a move under 30 warns of an oversold condition. Suppose the trader thinks a market is about to bottom and is looking for a buying opportunity. He or she watches the oscillator dip under 30. The hope, then, is that some type of divergence or double bottom will develop in the oscillator in that oversold region. A crossing back above the 30 line at that point is then taken by many traders as a confirmation that the trend in the oscillator has turned up. Accordingly, in an overbought market, a crossing back under the 70 line can often be used as a sell signal. Speaking of 70 and 30 lines, let's continue this discussion by looking at another oscillator formula that utilizes the same lines to help identify trend changes, but with same added wrinkles. (See Figures 10.14a and b.)

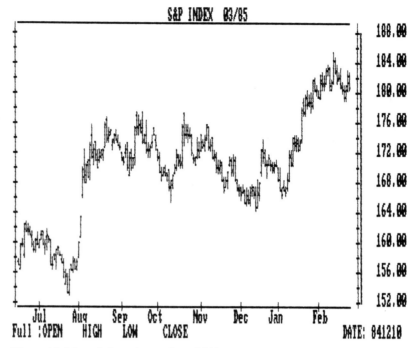

Figure 10.14a A bar chart of an S&P contract.

Figure 10.14b Crossings back below the 70 line can be used as a sell signal; crossings back above the 30 line can be used as a buy. This type of trading, using the 70 and 30 lines for signals, works better in the direction of the trend. In this example, a two-sided approach can be utilized to trade both sides of a trading range. This type of trading also works better if divergences are employed.

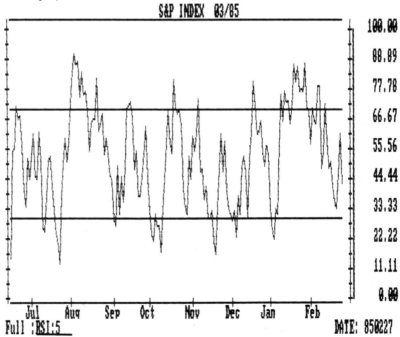

STOCHASTICS (K%D)

The *Stochastic Process* was invented by George Lane (president of Investment Educators, Inc., Des Plaines, IL, 60018) many years ago, but has attracted considerable attention in the futures markets in the past couple of years. It is based on the observation that as prices increase, closing prices tend to be closer to the upper end of the price range. Conversely, in downtrends, the closing price tends to be near the lower end of the range. Two lines are used in the Stochastic Process—the %K line and the %D line. The %D line is the more important and is the one that provides the major signals.

The intent is to determine where the most recent closing price is in relation to the price range for a chosen time period. Five days is the most common period used for this oscillator. To determine the K line, which is the more sensitive of the two, the formula is:

$$\%K = 100\,[\,(C - L5)\,/\,(H5 - L5)\,],$$

where C is the latest close, L5 is the lowest low for the last five days, and H5 is the highest high for the same five days.

The formula simply measures, on a percentage basis of 0 to 100, where the closing price is in relation to the total price range for a selected number of days. A very high reading (over 70) would put the closing price near the top of the range, while a low reading (under 30) near the bottom of the range.

The second line (%D) is just a 3-day smoothed version of the %K line. The formula for %D is as follows:

$$\%D = 100 \times (H3/L3)$$

where H3 is the 3-day sum of $(C - L5)$ and L3 is the 3-day sum of $(H5 - L5)$.

These formulas produce two lines that oscillate between a vertical scale from 0 to 100. The K line is a solid line, while the slower D line is a dashed line. The major signal to watch for is a divergence between the D line and the price of the underlying futures contract when the D line is in an overbought or oversold area. The upper and lower extreme zones are the same 70 and 30 values used in the RSI oscillator. Apparently, the best buy signals occur when the D value is in the 10 to 15 range and the best sell signals in the 85 to 90 overbought zone.

A bearish divergence occurs when the D line is over 70 and forms two declining peaks while prices continue to move higher. A bullish divergence is present when the D line is under 30 and forms two rising bottoms while prices continue to move lower. Assuming all of these factors are in place, the actual buy or sell signal is triggered when the solid K line crosses the slower dashed D line after the D line has already changed direction. In other words, the crossing should take place to the right of the peak or trough in the D line. At a bottom, for example, the buy signal is stronger if the K line crosses above the D line after the D line has already bottomed and turned up. At a top, the sell signal is stronger if the D line has already crested and turned down before it is crossed by the K line. The crossover is, therefore, stronger if both lines are moving in the same direction.

The importance of the right-sided crossover has been stressed in several articles on Stochastics. However, it is not as important a factor if the trade is in the direction of the original trend. If prices, for

Figure 10.15a Example of Stochastics. The oscillator uses two lines. The slower dashed line (%D) is the more important. The same 70 and 30 values are used to identify overbought and oversold boundaries. Divergences are used the same way as RSI. The strongest signal is given when the faster (solid %K) line crosses the %D line after the D line has already turned. Note the bullish divergence at the bottom in January and the recent bearish divergence at the top.

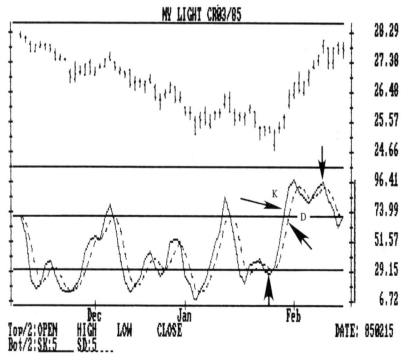

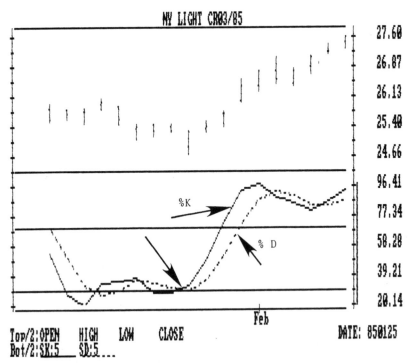

NY LIGHT CR03/85

27.60
26.87
26.13
25.40
24.66
96.41
77.34
58.28
39.21
20.14

%K

% D

Feb

Top/2:OPEN   HIGH   LOW   CLOSE   DATE: 850125
Bot/2:SK:5   SD:5 ...

Figure 10.15b A closer look at the two lines. The three requirements are fulfilled at the bottom. 1. The oscillator is oversold (under 30). 2. A bullish divergence is given. 3. The solid *K* line crosses over the dashed *D* line.

example, are only in a short-term corrective dip within an uptrend and register a buy signal from an oversold area, the right-sided crossover isn't that important. It becomes more significant, however, if the oscillator signal is indicating that a trend reversal is in progress. In all technical work, it always takes a stronger signal to reverse a trend than to resume one.

There are other refinements in the use of Stochastics, but this explanation covers the more essential points. (See Figures 10.15a and b.) Despite the higher level of sophistication, the basic oscillator interpretation remains the same. An alert or set-up is present when the %D line is in an extreme area and diverging from the price action. The actual signal takes place when the *D* line is crossed by the faster *K* line.

The Stochastic oscillator can be used on weekly and monthly charts for longer range perspective. In fact, Dr. Lane recommends plotting a weekly oscillator to help determine the overriding trend of the market. It can also be used effectively on intra-day charts for shorter term trading. (See Figures 10.16a and b.)

Oscillators and Contrary Opinion

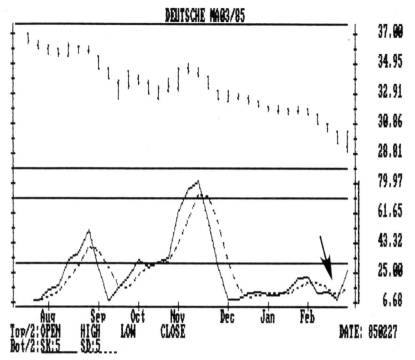

Figure 10.16a Stochastics can be applied to weekly charts for longer-range perspective. In this example, a 5-week Stochastic oscillator is used on a Deutsche mark contract. Notice the major divergence in February, warning of a possible bottom.

Figure 10.16b A 5-week Stochastics formula applied to an S&P 500 futures contract. Take note of the major buy signal in December under 30, and the major sell signal over 70 in August. The latest downturn is a warning of an overbought market condition.

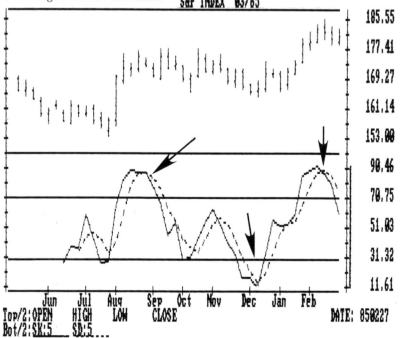

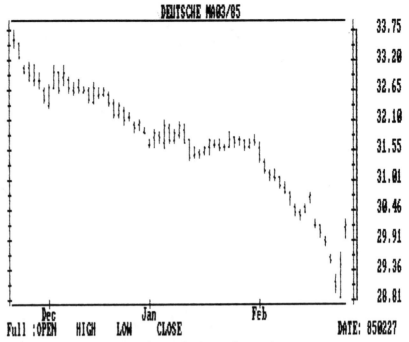

Figure 10.17a   Daily bar chart of a Deutsche mark contract.

Figure 10.17b   The upper chart is a regular 5-day Stochastic formula. The lower chart shows the slowed version. The slower version is easier to read and is considered to give better signals.

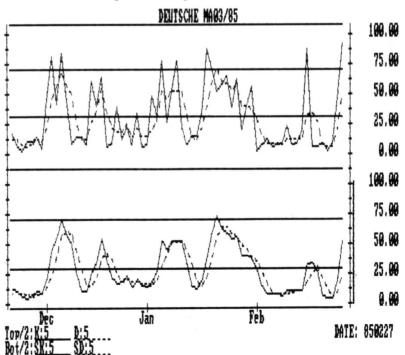

The Slowed Version of Stochastics

There is a slower version of the two lines, which seems to be preferred by most traders. In this formula, the more sensitive %K line is dropped. The original formula for the regular %D line becomes the new slow %K line. The new slow %D line is a 3-day moving average of the slow %K line. What we wind up with in the slowing process is the old %D line (now the %K line) and its 3-day moving average (now the %D line). It is believed that the slower version of the %D line gives better signals. (See Figures 10.17a and b.)

An article by George Lane, "Lane's Stochastics," appeared in the June, 1984 issue of the magazine, *Technical Analysis of Stocks & Commodities*, (P.O. Box 46518, Seattle, WA 98146). "Stochastics" by Dr. George C. Lane can also be found in *Trading Strategies*, published in 1984 by the Futures Symposium International, Tucson, Arizona 85719.

LARRY WILLIAMS %R

Larry Williams %R is based on a similar concept of measuring the latest close in relation to its price range over a given number of days. Today's close is subtracted from the price high of the range for a given number of days and that difference is divided by the total range for the same period. The scale in Williams' oscillator is reversed, however, so that an overbought reading is above 20 and an oversold reading is under 80. The concepts already discussed for oscillator interpretation are applied to %R as well, with the main factors being the presence of divergences in overbought or oversold areas. (See Figures 10.18a and b.)

Choice of Time Period Tied to Cycles

Another feature of Larry Williams %R is that it can be tied to underlying market cycles. A time period of $1/2$ the cycle length is used. The suggested time inputs are 5, 10, and 20 days based on calendar day periods of 14, 28, and 56 days. Wilder's RSI uses 14 days, which is half of 28. In the previous chapter, we discussed some reasons why the numbers 5, 10, and 20 keep cropping up in moving average and

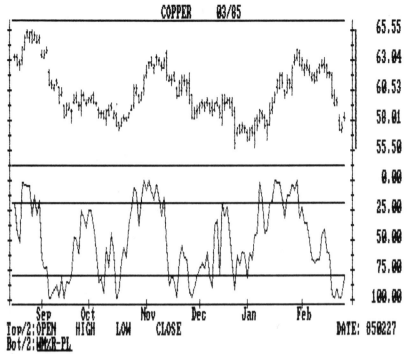

Figure 10.18a An example of Larry Williams %R oscillator. Notice here that the scale is reversed. An overbought reading is over 20 and oversold, under 80. The oscillator interpretation is similar to those already covered. Look for divergences in oversold and overbought extreme areas.

Figure 10.18b Another example of Williams %R applied to a Japanese yen contract.

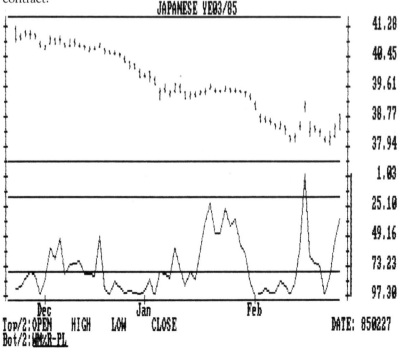

oscillator formulations, so we won't repeat them here. Suffice it to mention here that 28 calendar days (20 trading days) represent an important dominant monthly trading cycle and that the other numbers are related harmonically to that monthly cycle. The popularity of the 5-day Stochastic value, the 10-day momentum, and the 14-day RSI are based largely on the 28-day trading cycle and measure $1/4$ and $1/2$ of the value of that dominant trading cycle. We'll come back to the importance of cycles in Chapter 14.

THE IMPORTANCE OF TREND

In this chapter, we've discussed the use of the oscillator in market analysis to help determine near-term overbought and oversold conditions, and to alert traders to possible divergences. We started with the momentum line; then we normalized momentum to make it an oscillator. We discussed another way to measure rates of change (ROC) by using price ratios instead of differences. We then showed how two moving averages could be compared to spot short-term extremes and crossovers. Finally, we looked at RSI and the Stochastic Process and considered how oscillators should be synchronized with cycles.

Divergence analysis provides us with the oscillator's greatest value. However, the reader is cautioned against placing too much importance on divergence analysis to the point where basic trend analysis is either ignored or overlooked. Most oscillator analysts stress that oscillator buy signals work best in uptrends and oscillator sell signals are most profitable in downtrends. The place to start your market analysis is always by determining the general trend of the market. If the trend is up, then a buying strategy is called for. Oscillators can then be used to help time market entry. Buy when the market is oversold in an uptrend. Sell short when the market is overbought in a downtrend. Or, buy when the momentum oscillator crosses back above the zero line when the major trend is bullish and sell a crossing under the zero line in a bear market.

The importance of trading in the direction of the major trend cannot be overstated. The danger in placing too much importance on oscillators by themselves is the temptation to use divergence as an excuse to initiate trades contrary to the general trend. This action generally proves a costly and painful exercise. The oscillator, as useful as it is, is just one tool among many others and must always be used as an aid, not a substitute, for basic trend analysis.

WHEN OSCILLATORS ARE MOST USEFUL

There are times when oscillators are more useful than at others. During choppy market periods, as prices move sideways for several weeks or months, oscillators track the price movement very closely. The peaks and troughs on the price chart coincide almost exactly with the peaks and troughs on the oscillator. Because both price and oscillator are moving sideways, they look very much alike. At some point, however, a price breakout occurs and a new uptrend or downtrend begins. By its very nature, the oscillator is already in an extreme position just as the breakout is taking place. If the breakout is to the upside, the oscillator is already overbought. An oversold reading usually accompanies a downside breakout. The trader is faced with a dilemma. Should he or she buy the bullish breakout in the face of an overbought oscillator reading? Should the downside breakout be sold into an oversold market?

In such cases, the oscillator is best ignored for the time being and the position taken. The reason for this is that in the early stages of a new trend, following an important breakout, oscillators often reach extremes very quickly and stay there for awhile. Basic trend analysis should be the main consideration at such times, with oscillators given a lesser role. Later on, as the trend begins to mature, the oscillator should be given greater weight. (We'll see in Chapter 13, that the fifth and final wave in Elliott Wave analysis is often confirmed by bearish oscillator divergences.) Many dynamic bull moves have been missed by traders who saw the major trend signal, but decided to wait for their oscillators to move into an oversold condition before buying. To summarize, give less attention to the oscillator in the early stages of an important move, but pay close attention to its signals as the move reaches maturity.

MOVING AVERAGE CONVERGENCE/DIVERGENCE TRADING METHOD (MACDTM)

We mentioned in the previous chapter an oscillator technique that uses two exponential moving averages and here it is. The Moving Average Convergence/Divergence Trading Method (MACDTM) is attributed to Gerald Appel of Signalert Corporation (Great Neck, NY 11021). Although the study's formula suggests the periods to be used for the two averages, the user can experiment with different inputs. The results are two exponentially smoothed moving averages that revolve above and below a zero line. The most useful signals are given when the shorter (solid) line crosses the slower (dashed) line. A buy signal occurs when the shorter line crosses above the longer and a sell signal when it crosses below the slower line. (See Figures 10.19a and b.)

Divergences can also be spotted. The signal is confirmed on the crossing of the zero line. Trendlines can also be used to help spot turns in the trend. An ideal buy signal would be seen on a bullish divergence, accompanied by an upside crossing by the shorter average and then a crossing above the zero line by both averages. An ideal sell signal would be the reverse of the buy signal.

Figure 10.19a Example of Moving Average Convergence/Divergence Trading Method (MACDTM). It can be used either as an oscillator, a trend signal, or a combination of both. Buy and sell signals are given by the crossing of two exponentially smoothed averages. Crossings above and below the zero line can also be used as a signal activator. Divergences are also evident. Notice the excellent buy signal last December when the MACDTM lines broke a long-term downtrend line. The solid line crossed over the dotted and then crossed the zero line on the upside.

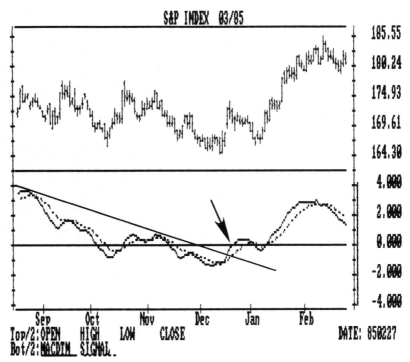

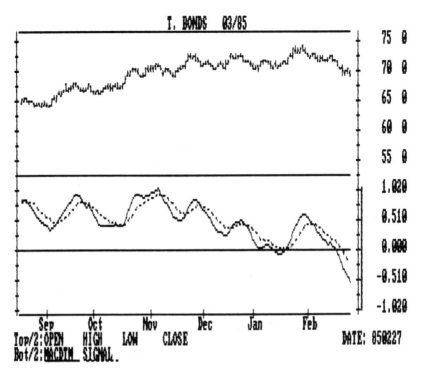

Figure 10.19b The failure to confirm the latest phase of the uptrend in bond prices and the crossing under the zero line gave early warnings of a reversal of trend to the downside.

VOLUME ACCUMULATION USED AS AN OSCILLATOR

In an earlier chapter, *volume accumulation* was given as an alternative to *on balance volume*. It was mentioned at the time that *volume accumulation* could also be plotted as an oscillator. Both the original *volume accumulation* formula and the oscillator formula were developed by Marc Chaikin of Drexel Burnham Lambert in New York. To plot the oscillator, two moving averages are constructed of the volume accumulation line and plotted as a histogram above and below a zero line. The suggested values are three and ten days. The oscillator is then interpreted in the same way as described earlier in the chapter when we discussed plotting moving average differences. The only difference here is that volume, not price, is being tracked. (See Figures 10.20a and b.)

Oscillators and Contrary Opinion

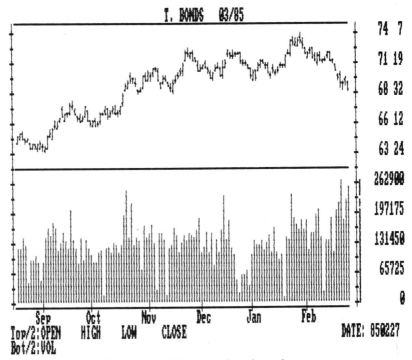

Figure 10.20a   A bar chart of bonds with volume bars.

Figure 10.20b   The upper line is the volume accumulation line covered in Chapter 7. The bottom histogram converts the volume accumulation line into an oscillator. The difference between the 3- and 10-day moving averages of the volume accumulation line is plotted around a zero line. This is just another way of studying short-term market extremes. Notice how well the volume accumulation line warned of the price downturn.

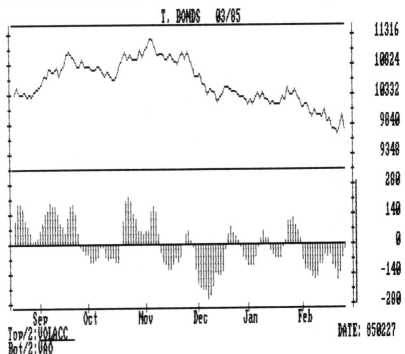

COMPU TRAC SOFTWARE FOR OSCILLATOR ANALYSIS

The most extensive software currently available for oscillator analysis is produced by Compu Trac, Inc. in New Orleans, LA 70175. Every oscillator mentioned in this chapter is included in Compu Trac's technical analysis program along with a few others not covered here. All of the charts are produced from that software.

THE PRINCIPLE OF CONTRARY OPINION

Oscillator analysis is the study of market extremes. One of the most widely followed theories in measuring those market extremes is the principle of Contrary Opinion. At the beginning of the book, two principal philosophies of market analysis were identified—fundamental and technical analysis. Contrary Opinion, although it is generally listed under the category of technical analysis, is more aptly described as a form of psychological analysis. Contrary Opinion adds the important third dimension to market analysis—the psychological—by determining the degree of bullishness or bearishness among speculators in the various futures markets.

The principle of Contrary Opinion holds that when the vast majority of people agree on anything, they are generally wrong. A true contrarian, therefore, will first try to determine what the majority are doing and then will act in the opposite direction.

Humphrey B. Neill, considered the dean of contrary thinking, described his theories in a 1954 book entitled, *The Art of Contrary Thinking* (Caldwell, OH: The Caxton Printers). Ten years later, in 1964, James H. Sibbet began to apply Neill's principles to commodity futures trading by creating the Market Vane advisory service, which includes the Bullish Consensus numbers. Each week a poll of market letters is taken to determine the degree of bullishness or bearishness among commodity professionals. The purpose of the poll is to quantify market sentiment into a set of numbers that can be analyzed and used in the market-forecasting process. The rationale behind this approach is that most futures traders are influenced to a great extent by market advisory services. By monitoring the views of the professional market letters, therefore, a resonably accurate gauge of the attitudes of the trading public can be obtained.

The Market Vane advisory service is published by Hadady Publications, Inc. in Pasadena, CA 91101. For a more thorough treatment of this subject, a book by R. Earl Hadady, *Contrary Opinion, How to Use It for Profit in Trading Commodity Futures* (Pasadena, CA: Hadady Publications, 1983) is highly recommended reading. Mr. Hadady is president of Hadady Publications, which publishes the Market Vane service.

Another service that provides an indication of market sentiment is the "Consensus Index of Bullish Market Opinion," published by *Consensus National Commodity Futures Weekly* (Kansas City, MO 64141). These numbers are published each Friday and use 75% as an over-bought and 25% as an oversold measurement.

A unique feature of Market Vane's Bullish Consensus numbers is a weighting formula applied to the various market letters. More weight is given to those letters with a larger following and, of course, less weight to those with fewer readers. The intention is to measure more accurately the degree of influence of each letter. The end result of this weekly poll is the Bullish Consensus numbers, published each Tuesday, based on market opinions as of the previous Friday. These numbers are presented as a percentage of bullishness and range from 0 to 100.

Interpreting Bullish Consensus Numbers

Most traders seem to employ a fairly simple method of analyzing these weekly numbers. If the numbers are above 80%, the market is considered to be overbought and means that a top may be near. (A bullish reading of 80% also means that only 20% of traders are bearish.) A reading below 30% (meaning that only 30% are bullish and 70% are bearish) is interpreted to warn of an oversold condition and the increased likelihood that a market bottom is near.

Even when used only in this way, the Bullish Consensus numbers can still prove very useful in helping to warn of danger areas. There is, however, a lot more to the correct and fuller use of these numbers. Let's take a closer look at the theory and discuss a few additional ways to use Contrary Opinion.

One commonly held notion is that the basis of Contrary Opinion is that professionals are usually wrong. While this may seem on the surface to be a logical implication, especially at market turning points, the principles of this theory are a good deal more subtle than that. The underlying philosophy actually has two parts.

Contrary Opinion Measures
Remaining Buying or Selling Power

Consider the case of an individual speculator. Assume that speculator reads his or her favorite newsletter and becomes convinced that a market is about to move substantially higher. The more bullish the forecast, the more aggressively that trader will approach the market. Once that individual speculator's funds are fully committed to that particular market, however, he or she is overbought—meaning there are no more funds to commit to the market.

Expanding this situation to include all market participants, if 80% to 90% of market traders are bullish on a market, it is assumed that they have already taken their market positions. Who is left to buy and push the market higher? This then is one of the keys to understanding Contrary Opinion. If the overwhelming sentiment of market traders is on one side of the market, there simply isn't enough buying or selling pressure left to continue the present trend.

Contrary Opinion Measures
Strong Versus Weak Hands

A second feature of this philosophy is its ability to compare strong versus weak hands. Futures trading is a zero sum game. For every long there is also a short. If 80% of the traders are on the long side of a market, then the remaining 20% (who are holding short positions) must be well-financed enough to absorb the longs held by the other 80%. The shorts, therefore, must be holding much larger positions than the longs (in this case, 4 to 1).

This means further that the shorts must be well-capitalized and are considered to be strong hands. The 80%, who are holding much smaller positions per trader, are considered to be weaker hands who will be forced to liquidate those longs on any sudden turn in prices. So, there is a lot more to this theory than the oversimplification that professionals are usually wrong. If this latter statement were true, they would cease to be professionals very quickly in the performance-oriented futures game.

Some Additional Features
of the Bullish Consensus Numbers

Let's consider a few additional points that should be kept in mind when using these numbers. The norm or equilibrium point is at 55%.

This allows for a built-in bullish bias on the part of the general public. The upper extreme is considered to be 90% and the lower extreme, 20%. Here again, the numbers are shifted upward slightly to allow for the bullish bias.

A contrarian position can usually be considered when the bullish consensus numbers are above 90% or under 20%. In these cases, the degree of unanimity is so extreme as to warrant immediate action opposite the current trend. Readings over 80% or under 30% are also considered warning zones and suggest that a turn may be near. However, in these less extreme areas, it is generally advisable to await a change in the trend of the numbers before taking action against the trend. A change in the direction of the Bullish Consensus numbers, especially if it occurs from one of the danger zones, should be watched closely. Generally, a change in direction by 5% during any given week is considered significant enough to warrant consideration of a contrarian trade.

The Importance of Open Interest

Open interest also plays a role in the use of Bullish Consensus numbers. In general, the higher the open interest figures are, the better the chance that the contrarian positions will prove profitable. A contrarian position should not be taken, however, while open interest is still increasing. A continued rise in open interest numbers increases the odds that the present trend will continue. Wait for the open interest numbers to begin to flatten out or to decline before taking action.

Study the Commitments of Traders Report to ensure that hedgers hold less than 50% of the open interest. Contrary Opinion works better when most of the open interest is held by speculators, who are considered to be weaker hands. It is also not advisable to trade against large hedging interests.

Watch the Market's Reaction to Fundamental News

Watch the market's reaction to fundamental news very closely. The failure of prices to react to bullish news in an overbought area is a clear warning that a turn may be near. The first adverse news is usually enough to quickly push prices in the other direction. Correspondingly, the failure of prices in an oversold area (under 20%) to react to bearish news can be taken as a warning that all the bad news has been fully discounted in the current low price. Any bullish news will push prices higher.

Combine Contrary Opinion with Other Technical Tools

As a general rule, trade in the same direction as the trend of the consensus numbers until an extreme is reached, at which time the numbers should be monitored for a sign of a change in trend. To repeat again, a change of direction by 5% is usually considered significant. It goes without saying that standard technical analytical tools can and should also be employed to help identify market turns at these critical times. The breaking of support or resistance levels, trendlines, or moving averages can be utilized to help confirm that the trend is in fact turning. Divergences on oscillator charts are especially useful when the Bullish Consensus numbers are overbought or oversold.

Retracements in Bullish Consensus Numbers

In addition to helping identify market extremes, retracements also occur in these numbers which can prove useful. The 50% area usually acts as a support area during uptrends and a resistance area during downtrends. In a strong uptrend, a downward reaction from an overbought region (over 80%) usually finds support near 50% if the uptrend is to be maintained. In a bear trend, a rally from a deeply oversold condition (under 20%) often carries close to the 50% level before turning lower again. A decisive breaking of the 50% area can often be a warning of a reversal in trend.

Conclusion

The preceding points are included here to alert the reader to the fact that the proper use of Bullish Consensus numbers can be a good deal more involved than at first realized. Whether or not the trader chooses to get that involved, it is strongly recommended that these published numbers be monitored on a weekly basis. They can alert the trader to dangerous market extremes and give an early warning of impending shifts in trend.

In keeping with the general philosophy espoused throughout this book, no one tool or method holds the key to successful trading. The philosophy of Contrary Opinion appears to hold a piece of the puzzle. It takes very little effort to glance at these numbers once in a while to derive some benefit from them. Its principles are respected and widely followed enough to warrant inclusion in the trader's growing collection of technical tools.

11

Intra-Day Point and Figure Charting

INTRODUCTION

Bar charts are the most popular type of charts in use today. However, considerable evidence indicates that the first charting technique used by stock market traders before the turn of the century was point and figure charting. The actual name "point and figure" has been attributed to Victor deVilliers in his 1933 classic, *The Point and Figure Method of Anticipating Stock Price Movements* (Brightwaters, NY: Windsor Books). The technique has had various names over the years. In the 1880s and 1890s, it was known as the "book method." This was the name Charles Dow gave it in a July 20, 1901 editorial of *The Wall Street Journal.* It was actually a variation of the old method of reading prices right off the tape (known appropriately enough as *tape reading*).

Dow indicated that the book method had been used for about 15 years, giving it a starting date of 1886. In 1933, deVilliers believed the technique to be over 50 years old, placing it in the early 1880s.

A sequential method of recording stock prices was also referred to in an 1898 work published by an anonymous writer using the name of Hoyle entitled *The Game in Wall Street* (publisher's information not available). While Hoyle's work may be the first actual reference to this charting method, Joseph M. Klein published a more comprehensive study in 1904 calling the technique the "Trend Register" method. Klein traced the beginnings of the technique to about 1881. The name "figure charts" was used from the 1920s until 1933 when "point and figure" became the accepted name for this technique of tracking market movement. R.D. Wyckoff also published several works dealing with the point and figure method in the early 1930s.

The Wall Street Journal started publishing daily high, low, and closing stock prices in 1896, which is the first reference to the more commonly known bar chart. Therefore, it appears that the point and figure method predates bar charting by at least 15 years. The origin of the term "point and figure" may be of interest to some readers. "Figure" charts, which were more popular in the 1920s, plotted the actual prices (figures) on the charts. In the 1930s, the use of x's (which deVilliers referred to as "points") were inserted in place of the actual figures. What deVilliers was really describing was two different methods by using the terms "point and figure." He also expressed his preference for the use of points instead of the older version of using figures. The term "point and figure," however, became identified with this method and is the name still used today.

We're going to approach point and figure charting in three steps. In this chapter, we'll look at the original method that relies on intra-day price moves. We'll discuss how these charts are constructed and then interpreted. Bar charts give a one-dimensional view of price action. The study of intra-day price movement reveals an enormous amount of price data that is completely missed with the use of bar charts alone. For example, the identification of hidden support and resistance levels becomes possible, congestion area analysis takes on a whole new meaning, and various price patterns can be seen. The use of the horizontal "count" will be discussed as a means of arriving at price objectives.

One of the major problems with constructing and following intra-day price charts is the difficulty in obtaining the intra-day data and the amount of time required to post the charts. It is possible to construct a point and figure chart using the high and low prices right out of the newspaper. Although this is a shortcut method and much of the important price data is lost, some of the benefits of point and figure charting can still be obtained. The most common use of this technique is the *three-point reversal method,* popularized by Abe Cohen and the *Chartcraft Chart Service,* which we'll tackle in the next chapter.

Finally, we'll take a look at *optimized* point and figure charting. Some research done in the early 1970s makes a case for varying the box and reversal sizes in chart construction to improve performance. We'll take a quick look at some of that research and see how optimized charts differ from the more traditional three-point reversal method.

It should be acknowledged before we begin that point and figure charting is a complex subject. We're only going to cover the more important elements of the technique here. Some additional recommended readings are given later for those readers who wish to pursue this very useful method in more depth.

THE POINT AND FIGURE VS. THE BAR CHART

Let's begin with some of the basic differences between point and figure charting and bar charting and look at a couple of chart examples.

The point and figure chart is a study of pure price movement. That is to say, it does not take time into consideration while plotting the price action. A bar chart, by contrast, combines both price and time. Because of the way the bar chart is constructed, the vertical axis is the price scale and the horizontal axis, a time scale. On a daily chart, for example, each successive day's price action moves one space or bar to the right. This happens even if prices saw little or no change for that day. Still, something must be always be placed in the next space. On the point and figure chart, only the price changes are recorded. If no price change occurs, the chart is left untouched. During active market periods, a considerable amount of plotting may be required. During quiet market conditions, little plotting will be needed. Some notations can be placed on the point and figure charts that give the user some time references (we'll talk about these notations a bit later when we treat chart construction), but these notations are only for convenience purposes and have nothing to do with the actual chart interpretation.

An important difference is the treatment of volume. Bar charts record volume bars under the day's price action. Point and figure charts ignore volume numbers, as a separate entity. This last phrase, "as a separate entity," is an important one. Although the volume numbers are not recorded on the point and figure chart, it does not necessarily follow that volume, or trading activity, is totally lost. On the contrary, since intra-day point and figure charts record all price change activity, the heavier or lighter volume is reflected in the amount of price changes recorded on the chart. Because volume is one of the more important ingredients in determining the potency of support and resistance levels, point and figure charts become especially useful in determining at which price levels most of the trading activity took place and, hence, where the important support and resistance numbers are. But we'll come back to this last point again when we address the subject of support and resistance.

Figures 11.1 and 11.2 compare a bar chart and a point and figure chart covering the same time span for an S&P 500 futures contract. In one sense, the charts look similar, but, in another sense, quite different. The general price and trend picture is captured on both charts, but the method of recording prices is different. Notice in Figure 11.2 the alternating columns of x's and o's. The x columns represent rising prices, while the o columns show declining prices. Each time a column of x's moves one box above a previous column of x's, an upside breakout occurs.

Figure 11.1   A bar chart of an S&P 500 futures contract.

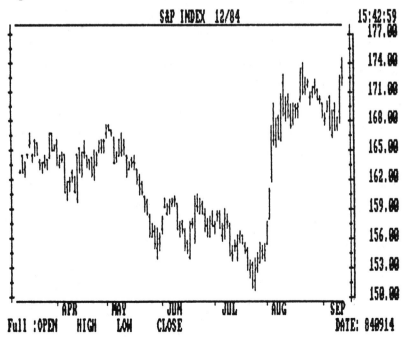

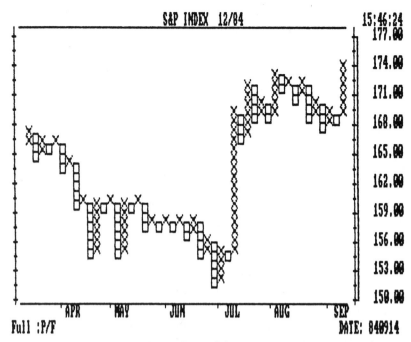

Figure 11.2 A point and figure chart of the same S&P 500 contract showing the same time period. Each box is 1.00 using a one-box reversal.

Correspondingly, when a column of o's declines one box under a previous column of o's, a downside breakout occurs. Notice how much more precise these breakouts are than those on the bar chart. These breakouts can, of course, be used as buy and sell signals. We'll have more to say on buy and sell signals a bit later. But the charts demonstrate one of the advantages of the point and figure chart, mainly the greater precision and ease in recognizing trend signals.

Figures 11.3 and 11.4 point up another major advantage of the point and figure chart—flexibility. All three point and figure charts (Figures 11.2 to 11.4) show the exact same price action. The box size in all three charts is 1.00, or one point. In Figure 11.2, however, the reversal criterion is only one box. This means every one box reversal is recorded. There are two ways to vary the point and figure chart—change the value of the box or change the reversal criterion (the number of boxes needed for a reversal). By changing the number of boxes required for a reversal, we have produced three different pictures. In Figure 11.2, notice that there are 47 columns. In Figure 11.3, we have switched from a one-box to a three-box reversal, resulting in a condensation of the price action. Notice that the number of columns has been reduced from 47 to 26. Figure 11.4 requires a five-box reversal and condenses the action even further. The number of columns is now almost cut in half to 14.

Intra-Day Point and Figure Charting

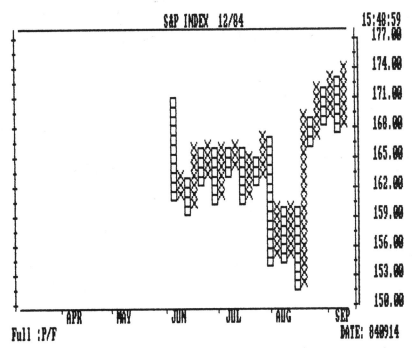

Figure 11.3 The same chart as in Figures 11.1 and 11.2, but using a three-box reversal.

Figure 11.4 The same chart as in Figures 11.1 to 11.3, but using a five-box reversal.

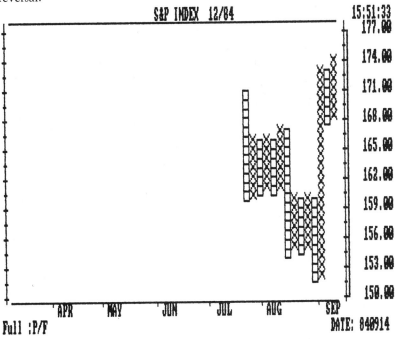

Therefore, point and figure charts can be made either more sensitive by using a smaller reversal number or less sensitive by using a larger reversal requirement. A one-box reversal could be used for a study of shorter-term market action, while a five-box reversal could be utilized to study longer-term trend action. The same goes for varying the size of the boxes themselves. These charts use a 1.00 box value. By using a smaller box value, such as .50, .20, or .10, the charts could be made increasingly sensitive to smaller market changes.

This tremendous flexibility, which allows the user to vary the chart parameters to suit his or her individual trading needs, is one of the major advantages of point and figure charting. Having already looked at some of the features of the point and figure chart (and having gotten a bit ahead of ourselves), let's go back to the beginning and discuss how the intra-day point and figure chart is constructed.

CONSTRUCTION OF THE INTRA-DAY POINT AND FIGURE CHART

We've already stated that the intra-day chart was the original type used by point and figure chartists. The technique was originally used to track stock market movement. The intent was to capture and record on paper each one-point move of the stocks under consideration. It was felt that accumulation (buying) and distribution (selling) could be better detected in this manner. Only whole numbers were employed. Each box was given a value of one point and each one-point move in either direction was recorded. Fractions were largely ignored. When the technique was later adopted to commodity markets, the value of the box had to be adjusted to fit each different commodity market. We'll spend more time on the determination of correct box size later. For now, let's construct an intra-day chart using some actual price data.

First, it helps to use the correct type of chart paper. A few years back, a special type of paper was readily available using a one-point reversal grid. Up until 1978, the firm of Morgan Rogers & Roberts supplied this type of paper along with the price data necessary to construct and update the charts. The paper was 11 inches in height and 17 inches in width, with green lines specifically geared for point and figure charts. Every fifth horizontal box was darkened. (The reason for this will soon become evident).

Unfortunately, the firm went out of business in 1978. Although the stock service was taken over by Muller Data, a division of Muller & Co. located in·New York, the paper is no longer supplied by them and the commodity data is no longer provided. To compensate for this loss, some of the large Wall Street brokerage firms actually publish their own point and figure paper. If you can obtain a supply, your task will be made easier. If not, the next best alternative is chart paper ten squares to the inch with darker lines every fifth box. There's no hard and fast rule as to box size, but the ten box to the inch size seems about right. Suit yourself. Just make sure the boxes are large enough to record the price action.

The next step is to determine the box size and the number of boxes needed to register a reversal. The box size means the value assigned to each box on the chart. For example, a gold chart could use a box size of $1.00. If the user wanted a less sensitive chart, a larger value of $2.00 or even $5.00 could be used. To obtain a more sensitive chart that captures more of the short-term price action, a box size of .50 could be used. For microscopic study, the minimum move of .10 could even be tried.

The *reversal criterion* means the number of boxes that the market must retrace to cause a reversal into the next column to the right. A one-box reversal means that each one-box move in either direction would be recorded. If a three-box reversal is used, then the market would have to retrace three full boxes before the next column would be started. The size of the box, then, and the reversal criterion are the only two ways to vary the point and figure chart. To construct the chart, the user must first decide on these parameters. Let's look at some examples.

The following numbers show the data needed to construct a very sensitive cotton chart using a box size of one point with a three-box reversal. A chart this sensitive would generally cover only one day's action and would only be appropriate for very short-term analysis or trading. But it will suffice here to demonstrate how to construct the chart. The numbers represent one actual day's trading activity.

8515	8525	8510	8515	8510	8515	8505	8515	8512	8515	8510	8516
8510	8515	8506	8510	8506	8510	8500	8514	8510	8517	8510	8519
8508	8515	8510	8525	8520	8525	8522	8525	8520	8525	8522	8525
8520	8523	8520	8523	8517	8525	8520	8528	8525	8539	8535	8538
8535	8545	8540	8544	8540	8545	8535	8544	8540	8545	8535	8538
_8532_	8538	8535	8543	8540	8543	8539	8549	8545	8550	8547	8554
8546	8563	8553	8565	8560	8563	8560	8563	8560	8563	8560	8563
8557	8560	8552	8555	8546	8550	8545	8550	8545	8550	8540	8560
8550	8553	8545	8555	8540	8548	8542	8545	8540	8545	8537	8540
8535	8550	8546	8555	8550	8558	8555	8565	8560	8570	8565	8570
8566	8575	8570	8580	8570	8580	8575	8585	8577	8585		

Now take a look at Figure 11.5. Notice the prices along the left vertical scale. The space in between every two lines represents one point. The bottom of the scale starts with 8500 and increases by one point per box. Note that every fifth box has a darker line. There are a couple of reasons for darkening every fifth line. One reason is that it makes the chart easier to plot. As you move further to the right, it's easy to lose your place on the chart. The darker lines help you keep track of where you are. Some chartists add another wrinkle here. Every fifth line ends with either a 0 or a 5. In order to help keep their place on the chart, they plot the 0's or 5's on those lines instead of the traditional x's or o's. Another reason for this refinement is that 0's and 5's represent natural support or resistance levels on the charts. In order not to confuse the issue here, we'll stick to our x's and o's.

Because the first number is 8515, place a dot in that box. We're not sure yet whether the column is up or down. Because the next number is 8525, prices are moving up and we put x's from 8515 up to 8525. The next number is 8510. This number represents at least a three-box reversal in the other direction, so we move one column to the right and put o's in each box all the way down to 8510. Remember that we use x's when moving up and o's when moving down. Because the next number is 8515, we move a column to the right and put x's all the way up to 8515. If it sounds complicated, it's really not. Always bear in mind that you must stay in the same column until a reversal occurs large enough to force a move to the next column. Because this is a three-box reversal chart, and each box represents only one point, then a three-point reversal would be enough to cause a reversal to the next column.

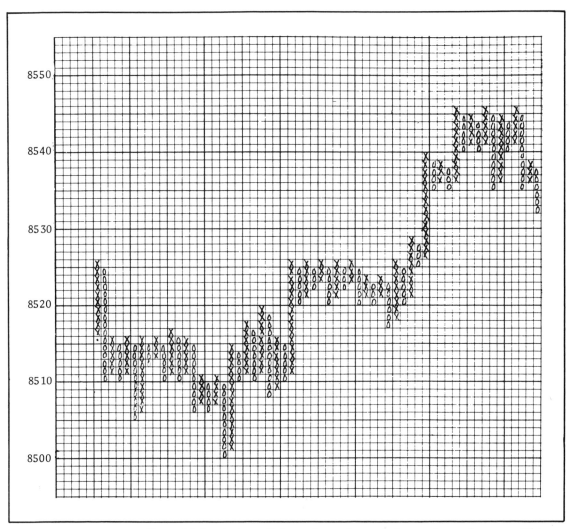

Figure 11.5 A 1 × 3 intra-day point and figure chart of cotton. This extremely sensitive chart covers only about half of one day's trading. It is probably too sensitive to be of any real value. Notice the tremendous detail that is obtained in studying very short-term market action.

If you feel like you need the practice, continue to follow the rest of chart to the number 8532, which is underlined. Notice that you have already reached the end of the chart. While you may be tired of plotting by now, you've only actually covered about half of the day's trading. In fact, the point where you just stopped was about 12:00 noon. There's another three hours to go in the day. Obviously, the one-point chart is too sensitive.

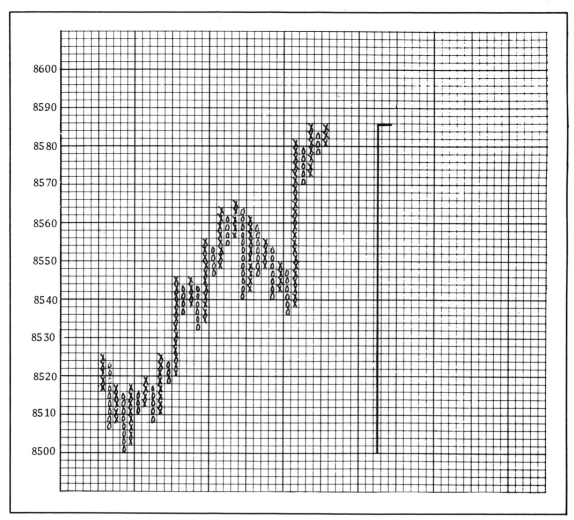

Figure 11.6 The same cotton chart used in Figure 11.5 except that each box is now valued at two instead of one points. Notice that the entire day's trading is now included by varying the box size. Compare the amount of price action on the point and figure chart with the day's high, low, and closing price bar on the right. Take note of how much data is lost on the bar chart.

Figure 11.6 takes the exact same figures, but this time makes each box two points instead of one. You can construct the two-point chart right from the one-point chart or go back to the original numbers. Because the second chart requires a six-point reversal before moving to the next column, a lot of the minor "noise" is left out and the chart is made smaller and more manageable. Figure 11.6 shows the entire day's trading activity. Just to contrast Figure 11.6 with the standard bar chart, look at the day's price bar just to the right. All it shows is the high, low, and last prices for the day. Compare this with the amount of data captured on the point and figure chart. Look at the areas of congestion during the day, the support and resistance levels that are now visible. It's easy to see why the point and figure chart is so popular with floor traders. This type of precision is simply not possible with the daily bar chart and an enormous amount of important price data is lost by relying on the bar chart alone.

So far we've looked at how to construct a three-box reversal intra-day chart. Now let's try a one-box reversal. The following numbers describe nine actual days of trading in a Swiss franc futures contract. The box size is five points. Therefore, every five-point swing in either direction is plotted.

```
4/29   4875  4880  4860  4865  4850  4860  4855

5/2    4870  4860  4865  4855  4860  4855  4860  4855  4860  4855  4865  4855

5/3    4870  4865  4870  4860  4865  4860  4870  4865

5/4    4885  4880  4890  4885  4890  4875

5/5    4905  4900  4905  4900  4905

5/6    4885  4900  4890  4930  4920  4930  4925  4930  4925

5/9    4950  4925  4930  4925  4930  4925  4935  4925  4930  4925  4935  4930  4940  4935

5/10   4940  4915  4920  4905  4925  4920  4930  4925  4935  4930  4940  4935  4940

5/11   4935  4950  4945  4950  4935  4940  4935  4945  4940  4965  4960  4965  4955  4960  4955  4965  4960  4970
```

Figure 11.7a is what the previously listed numbers would look like on the chart. Let's begin on the left side of the chart. First the chart is scaled to reflect a five-point increment for every box.

Column 1: Put a dot at 4875. Because the next number—4880—is higher, fill in the next box up to 4880.

Column 2: The next number is 4860. Move one column to the right, go down one box, and fill in all the o's down to 4860.

Column 3: The next number is 4865. Move one column to the right, move up one box and put an x at 4865. Stop here. So far you have only one x marked in column 3 because prices have only moved up one box. On a one-box reversal chart, there must always be at least two boxes filled in each column. Notice that the next number is 4850, calling for o's down to that number. Do you go to the next column to record the column of declining o's? The answer is *no* because that would leave only one mark, the x, in column

3. Therefore, in the column with the lone x (column 3) fill in o's down to 4850.

Column 4: The next number is 4860. Move to the next column, move one box up, and plot in the x's up to 4860.

Column 5: The next number is 4855. Because this is a move down, go to the next column, move down a box, and fill the o at 4860. Notice on the table that this is the last price of the day. Let's do one more.

Column 6: The first number on 5/2 is 4870. So far, you only have one o in column 5. You must have at least two marks in each column. Therefore, fill in x's (because prices are advancing) up to 4870. But notice that the last price on the previous day is blacked out. This is one of the conventions mentioned earlier to help keep track of time. By blacking in the last price each day, it's much easier to keep track of the separate days' trading.

Feel free to continue through the remainder of the chart to sharpen your understanding of the plotting process. Notice that this chart has several columns where both x's and o's are present. This situation will only develop on the one-point reversal chart and is caused by the necessity of having at least two boxes filled in each column. Some purists might argue with combining the x's and o's. Experience will show, however, that this method of plotting prices makes it much easier to follow the order of the transactions.

Figure 11.7b takes the same data from Figure 11.7a and transforms it into a three-box reversal chart. Notice that the chart is condensed and a lot of data lost. Figure 11.7c shows a five-box reversal. These are the three reversal criteria that have traditionally been used—the one-, three-, and five-box reversal. The one-box reversal is generally used for very short-term activity and the three-box for the study of the intermediate trend. The five-box reversal, because of its severe condensation, is generally used for the study of long-term trends. The correct order to use is the one shown here, that is, begin with the one-point reversal chart. The three- and five-box reversals can then be constructed right off the first chart. For obvious reasons, a one-point reversal chart could not possibly be constructed from a three- or five-box reversal.

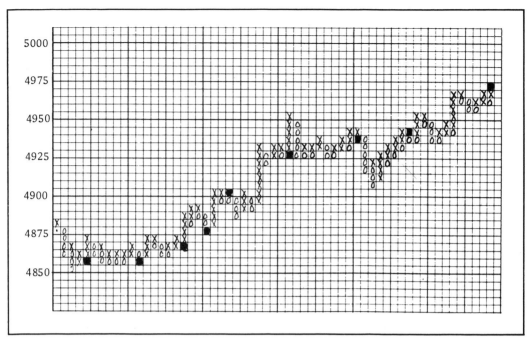

Figure 11.7a A 5 × 1 point and figure chart of a Deutsche mark contract is shown in the upper chart. The blackened boxes show the end of each day's trading. The bottom chart to the left shows the same price data with a three-box reversal. Notice the compression. The lower chart to the right shows a five-box reversal.

Figure 11.7b   *Figure 11.7c*

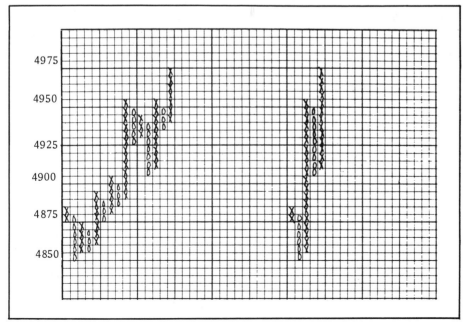

Gaps

Traditionally, gaps have been ignored on the point and figure chart. All the boxes must be filled in between successive prices. Some technicians, however, leave the gaps blank on the chart. Although this violates the strict rules for construction, it may actually be an improvement because gaps can act as important support and resistance levels. It's useful to know where they're located on the point and figure chart.

Time Reference Points

These reference points can be added at the chartist's discretion. A letter can be used for the first price of a new month. For example, a "J" for January or "F" for February can be used at the beginning of each month for purposes of keeping track of calendar time. If a new year is beginning, the year number (*e.g.*, 1985) can be placed at the bottom of the chart in the appropriate column. These calendar notations are solely for reference purposes and have little or nothing to do with the interpretation of the chart. They can be left off completely if desired. Personally, I prefer to use them.

CONGESTION AREA ANALYSIS

One of the most striking features of the intra-day one-box reversal charts is the presence of significant congestion areas. A congestion area is simply a period of horizontal or sideways price movement on the chart within a well-defined top and bottom. In fact, the visibility of these congestion areas may very well be the single most valuable feature of these charts.

Congestion area analysis can mean many different things. Its main purpose, however, is to help the analyst determine in advance the direction of the ultimate breakout. In an uptrend, for example, a congestion area or trading range could represent just a pause in that uptrend or it might be a reversal pattern signalling a major trend reversal to the downside. The secret is being able to tell the difference as soon as possible. Aside from the question of pattern analysis, which we'll treat later, there are some hints that can be gleaned from the congestion area itself.

The most important rule of thumb is where in the congestion area most of the trading activity has taken place. If most of the x's and o's are near the top of the trading range, this indicates significant supply over the market and probably represents distribution (selling). Trading activity that concentrates near the bottom of the range probably represents accumulation (buying). Also, it should be remembered that if the congestion area is large enough, the most recent action carries more weight. That is to say, if the earlier activity was near the top of the range, but the recent closer to the bottom, that pattern is more bullish than bearish.

THE HORIZONTAL COUNT

Another principal advantage of the intra-day one-box reversal chart is the ability to obtain price objectives through use of the *horizontal count*. If you think back to our coverage of bar charts and price patterns, the question of price objectives was discussed. However, virtually all methods of obtaining price objectives off bar charts were based on what we call *vertical measurements*. This meant measuring the height of a pattern (the volatility) and projecting that distance upward or downward. For example, the head and shoulders pattern measured the distance from the head to the neckline and swung that objective from the break of that neckline.

Point and Figure Charts
Allow Horizontal Measurement

The principle of the horizontal count is based on the premise that there is a direct relationship between the width of a congestion area and the subsequent move once a breakout occurs. If the congestion area represents a basing pattern, some estimate can be made of the upside potential once the base is completed. Once the uptrend has begun, subsequent congestion areas can be used to obtain additional counts which can be utilized to confirm the original counts from the base. (See Figure 11.8.)

The intent is to measure the width of the pattern. Remember we're talking here of intra-day one-box reversal charts. The technique requires some modifications for other types of charts that we'll come back to later. Once a topping or basing area has been identified, simply count the number of columns in that top or base. If there are 20 columns, for example, the upside or downside target would be 20 boxes from the measuring point. The key is to determine which line to measure from. Sometimes this is easy and, at other times, more difficult.

Usually, the horizontal line to count across is near the middle of the congestion area. A more precise rule is to use the line that has the least number of empty boxes in it. Or put the other way, the line with the most number of filled in x's and o's. Once you find the correct line to count across, it's important that you include every column in your count, even the ones that are empty. Count the number of columns in the congestion area and then project that number up or down from the line that was used for the count.

Figure 11.8 By counting the number of columns across the horizontal congestion area, price objectives can be determined. The wider the congestion area, the greater the objective.

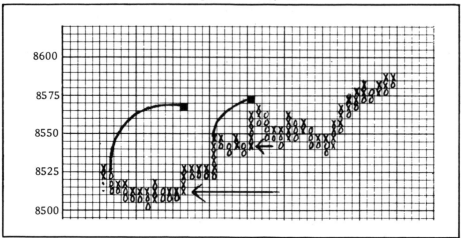

Intra-Day Point and Figure Charting

Some technicians use a compass to achieve this. The point of the compass is placed at the right extreme of the congestion area, then an arc is projected upward or downward once the width of the area has been measured. If the pattern is wide enough, it is possible to arrive at several objectives. Beginning at the right extreme, near-, intermediate-, and long-term objectives can be obtained by moving further to the left along the congestion area.

We've already mentioned that once the new trend has begun, subsequent congestion areas can be used to confirm the original counts. In an uptrend, for example, just measure across the congestion area, either by counting columns or using a compass, and project the measurement upward. These secondary counts can be used to confirm or modify the price objectives that were taken from the original basing or topping pattern. It's important to keep in mind that the count is only an approximation of the market potential. It would be unrealistic to expect an exact one-to-one relationship between the base width and the subsequent move. The main idea is to arrive at a best estimate of whether the move is minor in nature or has the potential for an important run.

PRICE PATTERNS

Pattern identification is also possible on point and figure charts. While the basic structure of price patterns is similar to that of the bar charts, there are some differences. For example, some of the patterns that are common to bar charts—such as gaps, flags, and pennants—are lost on the point and figure charts. The patterns on the intra-day point and figure charts look a bit different because of the presence of long congestion areas. Figure 11.9 shows the most common types of reversal patterns that show up on point and figure charts.

As you can see, they're not much different from ones already discussed on bar charting. Most of the patterns are variations on the double and triple tops and bottoms, head and shoulders, V's and inverted V's, and saucers. The term "fulcrum" shows up quite a bit in the point and figure literature. Essentially, the *fulcrum* is a well-defined congestion area, occurring after a significant advance or decline, that forms an accumulation base or a distribution top. In a base, for example, the bottom of the area is subjected to repeated tests, interrupted by intermittent rally attempts. Very often, the fulcrum takes on the

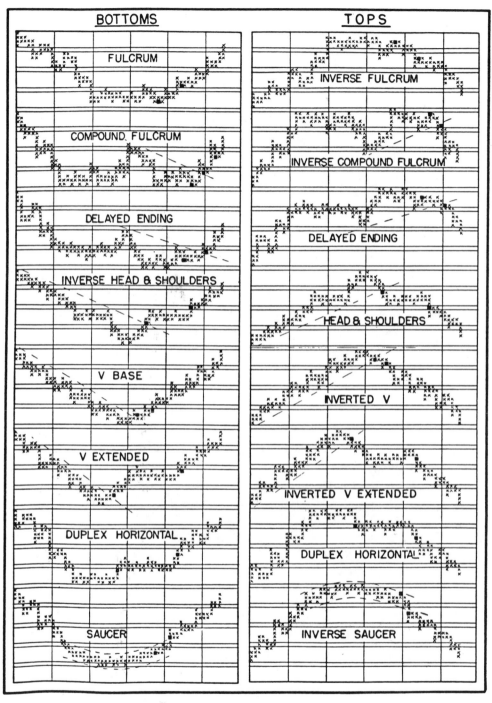

Figure 11.9 Reversal patterns. (Source: Alexander H. Wheelan, *Study Helps in Point and Figure Technique* [New York, NY: Morgan, Rogers and Roberts, Inc., 1954] p. 25.)

Intra-Day Point and Figure Charting

appearance of a double or triple bottom. The basing pattern is completed when a breakout (catapult) occurs over the top of the congestion area.

Those reversal patterns with the most pronounced horizontal ranges obviously lend themselves quite well to the taking of count measurements. The V base, in contrast, because of the absence of a significant horizontal price area, would not be amenable to the taking of a horizontal count. The blackened boxes in the chart examples in Figure 11.9 represent suggested buying and selling points. We'll have more to say about tactics a bit later. But notice here that those entry points generally coincide with the retesting of support areas in a base or resistance areas in a top, breakout points, and the breaking of trendlines.

Trend Analysis and Trendlines

The price patterns in Figure 11.9 show trendlines drawn as part of those patterns. Trendline analysis on intra-day charts is the same as that applied to bar charts. Up trendlines are drawn under successive lows and down trendlines are drawn over successive peaks. Parallel channel lines can also be utilized. Everything that has already been said concerning trendlines can be applied to the intra-day charts. This is not true of the modified point and figure chart, which we're going to study next. It utilizes 45-degree lines and plots them differently.

The basic concepts of trend analysis also apply. An uptrend is a series of ascending peaks and troughs. The failure of a price advance to reach or exceed a previous high is usually the first warning of a trend change. Correspondingly, when prices in a downtrend do not reach or fail to move below a previous low, this is the first warning of a possible bottom. All of these principles can be applied to point and figure analysis.

Support and Resistance

We're going to finish this section with what I consider to be the most important value in the point and figure chart—the identification of support and resistance levels or zones. The presence of these horizontal congestion areas, where significant price change activity has taken place, tells us where the potent support and resistance areas are located. In an earlier discussion of support and resistance, the point was made that the longer prices stay in a certain area, and the more trading activity that took place in that area, the more important that area became from the standpoint of providing support and resistance. Bar charts can help identify these areas, but a lot of data is excluded. Point and figure charts tell us not only where these areas are, but how much price change activity (volume) took place there.

In an uptrend, for example, the correct strategy would be to buy dips near support. But where is that support? Point and figure charts tell where these hidden congestion areas are located in a way that is practically impossible on the bar chart. In an uptrend, previous congestion areas act as support areas during price dips. In a downtrend, previous congestion areas act as resistance on rallies. Timing becomes a good deal easier. Figures 11.5 through 11.8 show intra-day activity for very short periods of time (one through nine days). Once a decision has been made to enter or exit a market, these very sensitive charts are indispensable in helping to pinpoint the best spot to get in or out. They permit the type of microscopic study that can dramatically improve trading performance.

Stops

Stop placement is one of the most essential aspects of successful commodity trading. Protective stops are a highly recommended trading technique. The problem is knowing where to place those stops. Placing them at obvious spots on the bar chart (under support, a gap, or a trendline) sometimes makes them too obvious and, therefore, vulnerable. Very often the stop has to be placed too far away from the entry point to coincide with a good chart point. The intra-day point and figure chart provides closer and less obvious protective stop points.

CONCLUSION

Let's conclude our treatment of the intra-day point and figure chart with a few general comments. These short-term charts are widely used by floor traders for obvious reasons. However, there is a misconception that this technique is only useful for very short-term trading. Not true. Sure, they are extremely helpful in that arena. But point and figure charting can be used in any time dimension. These charts can be used to show weeks and months of price action. All the user has to do is vary the box size and reversal requirement to look at longer time periods. It's even possible to construct long-term continuation charts going back several years. The method of interpretation is always the same. All that differs is how you choose to plot the data and which months you choose to employ. As a rule, for continuation charts, the most active month (highest open interest) is the best for analysis and counting purposes. You're limited only by your imagination and the amount of time you're willing to devote to the charts.

The question is often asked as to the correct box and reversal size for each commodity market. The question is difficult if not impossible to answer. The answer depends, to a large extent, on what the chart will be used for and what degree of sensitivity is desired. The user will have to determine these sizes after some experimentation. In the next chapter, we'll discuss the matter of box size and reversal criteria (including the question of optimization) as applied to a modified point and figure format.

WHERE TO OBTAIN
POINT AND FIGURE CHARTS AND DATA

When Morgan, Rogers & Roberts went out of business in 1978, it became extremely difficult to obtain the necessary intra-day price data to construct and update the charts. Not only was the data difficult to obtain, but no intra-day point and figure chart service was even available. Fortunately, that situation is being corrected. From the early 1970s, the only place to obtain intra-day charts and price data was the ADP Comtrend's Videcom System (Stamford, CT 06905). This data was available to most large brokerage firms, but probably too expensive for the individual trader. (See Figure 11.10.)

More recently, other services are doing more with point and figure charts. MarketVision Corp. (New York, NY 10006), as an example, has developed excellent intra-day point and figure charts, using the traditional x's and o's. Alternate days are shown in different colors (black and green) to dramatically improve the visual impact. Gaps are also visible on the charts. (See Figure 11.11.)

A newer chart service, *Quotron Futures Charts* (Racine, WI 53401), publishes the only intra-day charts available in printed format. What all of this means is that, while the data may be still hard to obtain, more attention is being paid to this neglected area. I strongly suspect that intra-day point and figure charting is on the verge of a comeback as more traders become aware of its potential. (See Figures 11.12 through 11.14.)

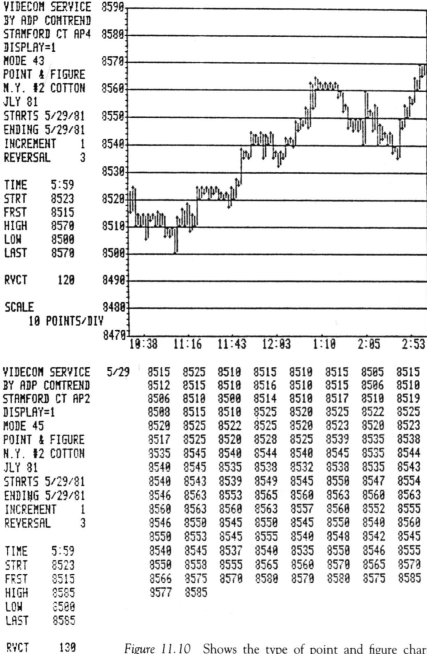

VIDECOM SERVICE	5/29	8515	8525	8510	8515	8510	8515	8505	8515
BY ADP COMTREND		8512	8515	8510	8516	8510	8515	8506	8510
STAMFORD CT AP2		8506	8510	8500	8514	8510	8517	8510	8519
DISPLAY=1		8508	8515	8510	8525	8520	8525	8522	8525
MODE 45		8520	8525	8522	8525	8520	8523	8520	8523
POINT & FIGURE		8517	8525	8520	8528	8525	8539	8535	8538
N.Y. #2 COTTON		8535	8545	8540	8544	8540	8545	8535	8544
JLY 81		8540	8545	8535	8538	8532	8538	8535	8543
STARTS 5/29/81		8540	8543	8539	8549	8545	8550	8547	8554
ENDING 5/29/81		8546	8563	8553	8565	8560	8563	8560	8563
INCREMENT 1		8560	8563	8560	8563	8557	8560	8552	8555
REVERSAL 3		8546	8550	8545	8550	8545	8550	8540	8560
		8550	8553	8545	8555	8540	8548	8542	8545
TIME 5:59		8540	8545	8537	8540	8535	8550	8546	8555
STRT 8523		8550	8558	8555	8565	8560	8570	8565	8570
FRST 8515		8566	8575	8570	8580	8570	8580	8575	8585
HIGH 8585		8577	8585						
LOW 8500									
LAST 8585									

RVCT   130

Figure 11.10 Shows the type of point and figure chart available on the Videcom System. Note the arrows instead of x's and o's. The actual numbers can be obtained at the bottom of the screen for manual plotting of the intraday numbers. (Source: Automatic Data Processing, Inc., Comtrend Division, Stamford, CT.)

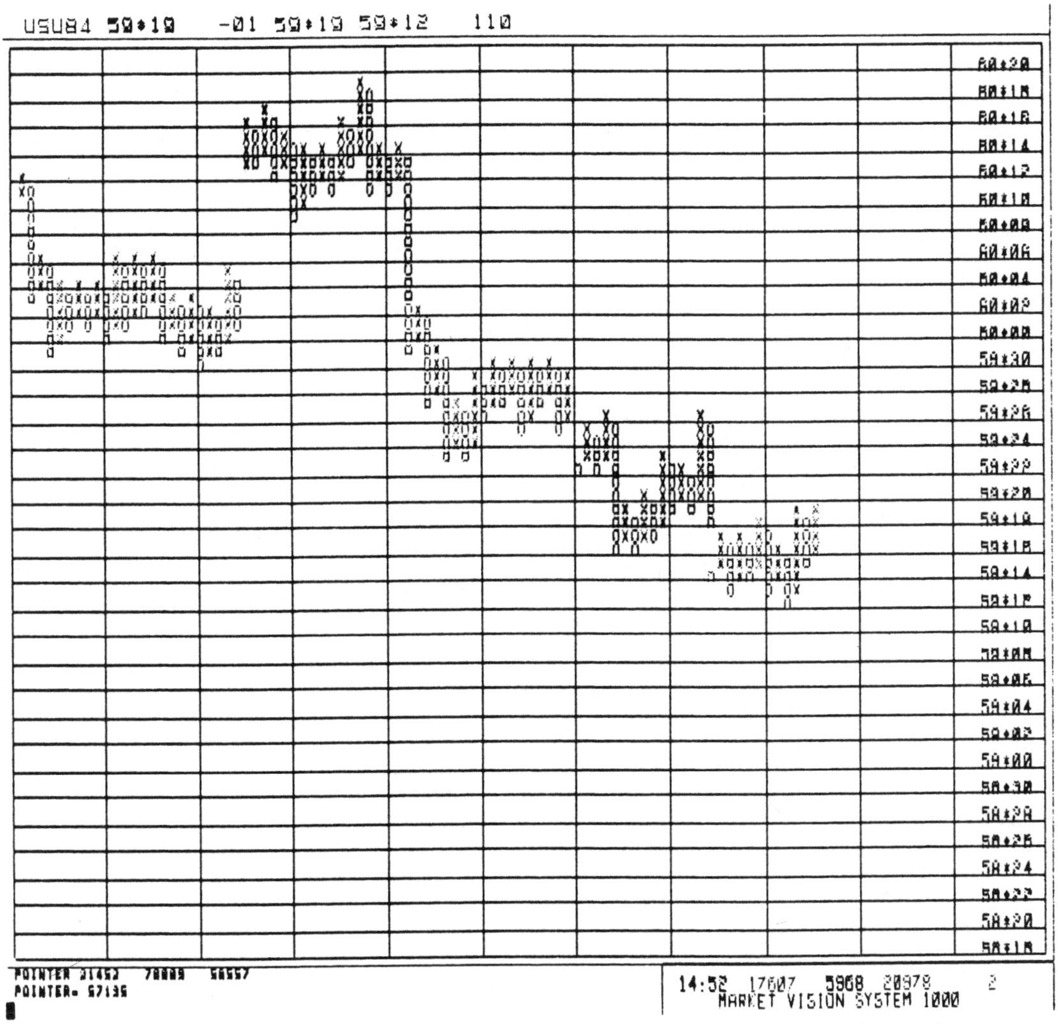

Figure 11.11 An intra-day point and figure chart using the Market Vision System. Notice the use of the more traditional x's and o's. Also notice the large price gap in the upper left of the chart, between two trading days. This chart shows five trading days of a September Treasury Bond contract. The actual screen display shows each day's activity by alternating green and black colors. (Source: Courtesy of MarketVision Corporation, New York, NY.)

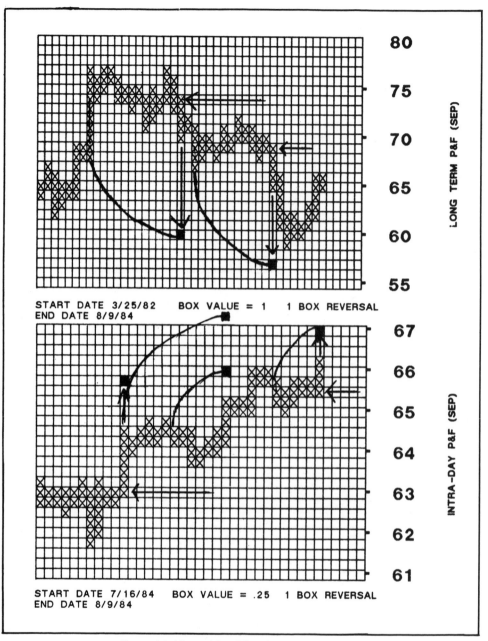

Figure 11.12a and b The chart on top is a long-term point and figure of a September Treasury Bond contract. By using a box value of one full point, it is possible to include over two years of price action. Notice the horizontal areas and the use of the "count" measuring technique to obtain the lower objectives. The bottom chart is a more sensitive value of eight basis points. Notice again how the congestion areas are visible and the use of the horizontal "count." Each congestion area allows the opportunity to take new counts. (Source: Courtesy of Quotron Futures Charts, Racine, WI.)

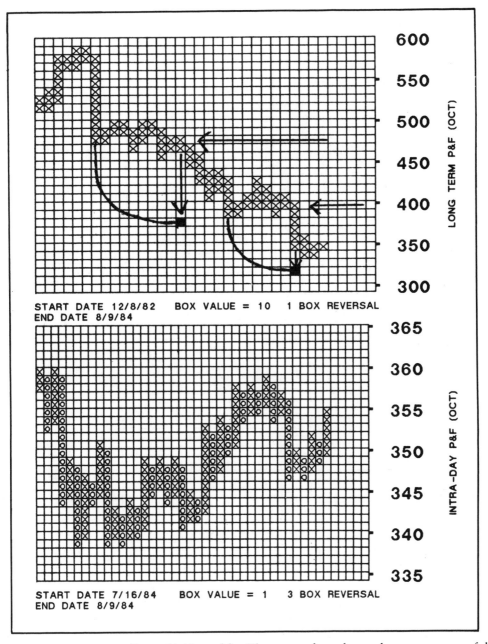

Figure 11.13a and b The upper chart shows almost two years of declining gold prices. Each box is worth $10. Notice the use of the count across the horizontal areas. The lower chart is a more sensitive $1 chart using a three-box reversal. This chart covers about a month's action. (Source: Courtesy of Quotron Futures Charts, Racine, WI.)

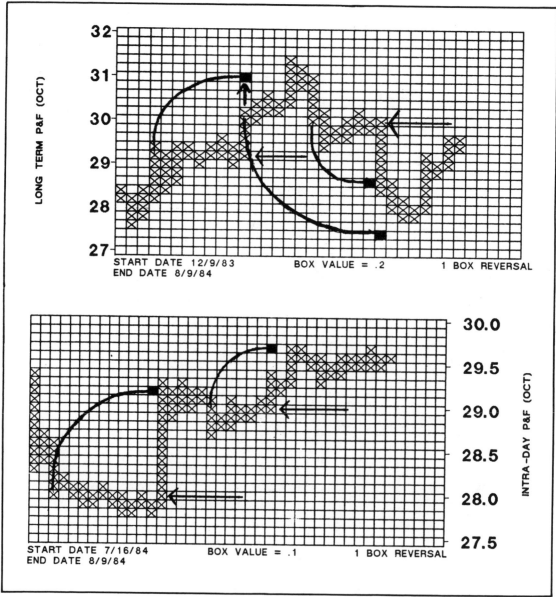

Figure 11.14a and b The upper chart covers almost a year of price action in a crude oil contract. Notice how the horizontal counts helped to determine price objectives. The lower chart covers only one month's action. Notice how much more sensitive the lower chart is by using a box value of 0.1 instead of the larger value of 0.2 used in the upper chart. (Source: Courtesy of Quotron Futures Charts, Racine, WI.)

Don't despair, however, if you have neither the inclination, the time, nor the access to the data to utilize intra-day charts. It is possible to obtain some of the benefits of point and figure charts with prices right out of the newspaper. Something is lost in the modified format, but much of the benefits are retained. To find out how it's done, let's move on to the next chapter.

12

Three-Box Reversal and Optimized Point and Figure Charting

INTRODUCTION

In 1947, a book on point and figure was written by A.W. Cohen entitled, *Stock Market Timing.* The following year, when the *Chartcraft Weekly Service* was started, the book's name was changed to *The Chartcraft Method of Point & Figure Trading.* Several revised editions have been published since then to include commodities and options. The soft-cover book is now available under the title of *How To Use The Three-Point Reversal Method Of Point & Figure Stock Market Trading* by A.W. Cohen, and is published by Chartcraft, Inc. in Larchmont, NY. This book is the authoritative source on the three-box reversal method of point and figure charting, requiring only prices out of the newspaper to construct and update.

The original one-box reversal method of plotting stocks required intra-day prices. The three-box reversal was a condensation of the one-box and was meant for intermediate trend analysis. Cohen reasoned that because so few three-box reversals occurred in stocks during the day that it was not necessary to use intra-day prices to construct the three-box reversal chart. Hence the decision to use only the high and low prices, which were readily available in most financial newspapers. This modified technique, which is the basis of the *Chartcraft* service, greatly simplified point and figure charting and made it accessible to the average trader.

CONSTRUCTION OF THE THREE-POINT REVERSAL CHART

The construction of the chart is relatively simple. First, the chart must be scaled in the same way as the intra-day chart. A value must be assigned to each box. These tasks are performed for subscribers to the *Chartcraft* service because the charts are already constructed and the box values assigned. The chart shows a series of alternating columns with x's representing rising prices and the o columns showing falling prices. (See Figure 12.1.)

The actual plotting of the x's and o's requires only the high and low prices for the day. If the last column is an x column (showing rising prices), then look at the high price for the day. If the daily high permits the filling in of one or more x's, then fill in those boxes and stop. That's all you do for that day. Remember that the entire value of the box must be filled. Fractions or partial filling of the box don't count. Repeat the same process the next day, looking only at the high price. As long as prices continue to rise, permitting the plotting of at least one x, continue to fill in the boxes with x's, ignoring the low price.

The day finally comes when the daily high price is not high enough to fill the next x box. At that point, look at the low price to determine if a three-box reversal has occurred in the other direction. If so, move one column to the right, move down one box, and fill the next three boxes with o's to signify a new down column. Because you are now in a down column, the next day consult the low price to see if that column of o's can be continued. If one or more o's can be filled in, then do so. Only when the daily low does not permit the filling in of any more o's do you look at the daily high to see if a three-box reversal has occurred to the upside. If so, move one column to the right and begin a new x column.

EXPLANATION of CHARTS

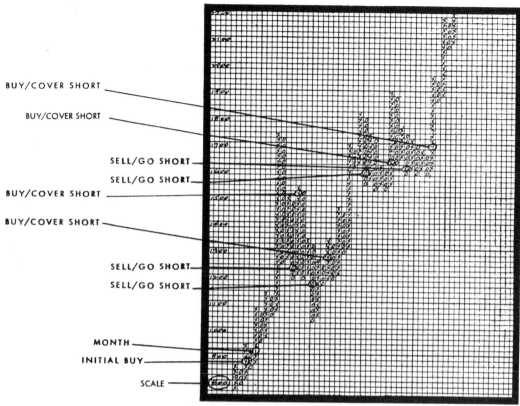

BUY/COVER SHORT

BUY/COVER SHORT

SELL/GO SHORT

SELL/GO SHORT

BUY/COVER SHORT

BUY/COVER SHORT

SELL/GO SHORT

SELL/GO SHORT

MONTH

INITIAL BUY

SCALE

POINT & FIGURE TECHNIQUES

BUY SIGNAL - Occurs when a column of Xs rises one box higher than the highest X of the prior X column. Since this point can be anticipated, a stop order to enter the position can be placed at the buy point.

SELL SIGNAL - Occurs when a column of Os declines one box below the lowest O on the prior O column.

COVER POINT FOR A SHORT - Exactly the same point as the buy signal. Since this point can be determined in advance, a stop-loss order to cover should be in the market.

CLOSEOUT OF A LONG - Exactly the same point as the sell signal.

ORDERS - Since all entry and stop-loss points can be determined prior to the occurrence, entry and closeout stop orders can be placed beforehand in the market. But remember, these signal points change and all orders should be periodically reviewed and adjusted.

TRADITIONAL ENTRY SIGNALS - The first buy signal following one or more sell-short signals and the first sell-short signal following one or more buy signals.

BULLISH - If the most recent signal was a buy signal, the position is bullish and remains bullish until a sell-short signal occurs.

BEARISH - If the most recent signal was a sell-short signal, the position is bearish and remains bearish until a buy signal occurs.

PULLBACKS - Rather than taking an immediate entry on a signal, if a reversal is anticipated after a signal, a strategy involving less risk is to take the position after the signal but at a price closer to the stop.

DAILY CHART UPDATING

IF THE CURRENT COLUMN IS AN X COLUMN - Look first at the daily high. If the daily high permits the drawing of one or more X's, draw them and ignore the daily low. If, and only if, no new Xs can be drawn, look at the daily low and determine whether a reversal has occurred. If a reversal has not occurred, make no entries at all.

IF THE CURRENT COLUMN IS AN O COLUMN - Look first at the daily low. If the daily low permits the drawing of one or more Os, draw them and ignore the daily high. If, and only if, no new Os can be drawn, look at the daily high to determine whether a reversal has occurred. If a reversal has occurred draw the appropriate number of Xs. If a reversal has not occurred, make no entries at all.

There can never be Xs and Os drawn on the same day. On a daily basis there is either a continuation of the current column, a reversal, or no new entries are made.

Figure 12.1 Source: Courtesy of Chartcraft, Inc., Larchmont, NY.

There will be days where no entries at all will be required. The daily price range will be small enough so that the current column can not be continued, but no three-box reversal is activated either. That's okay. Remember, the point and figure chart is meant to record pure price movement and ignores time. It's also important to remember that you cannot plot both x's and o's on the same day. If you do, you're not following the proper procedure. Either an x or o column can be filled in for one day, never both.

This last point raises an interesting dilemma. What about those days when, for example, the high price permits the filling of another one or more x's for that day and the low price also permits a three-box reversal to the downside. This usually occurs at wide-ranging reversal days where prices open higher and then trade sharply lower during the day. The rule says you should only plot the x column for that day and ignore the low. To do so, however, forces the trader to ignore what may be a significant turnaround. The correct way to handle this situation depends on the user. You may decide in such cases to plot first the higher x's and then the three-box reversal. You're taking liberties with the rules, but it may help your trading. My preference in such cases is to stick to the rules by plotting only the x's, but to use dots in the next column instead of o's to remind me that a significant downside reversal did occur during that day. I'll leave it to your discretion to handle this situation according to your needs.

Chart Patterns

Figure 12.2 shows 16 price patterns most common to this type of point and figure chart—eight buy signals and eight sell signals. These 16 entry points were tested by Robert E. Davis in his 1965 book, *Profit and Profitability* (West Lafayette, IN: R.E. Davis). Davis tested two common stocks from 1914 through 1964 and 1100 stocks from 1954 to 1964. The results of that study were impressive to say the least. Operating from both the long and short side, over 80% of all transactions were profitable, with average profits of about 25%. The study demonstrated that the traditional point and figure technique was quite successful when applied to common stock trading.

Of the individual patterns, the most frequent pattern (56.9%) was B-2, the simple buy signal with a rising bottom. A close second was S-2, the simple sell signal with a declining top (56.4%). The pattern that turned in the highest profitability ratio (percentage of times profitable) on the buy side was B-3, breakout of a triple top with

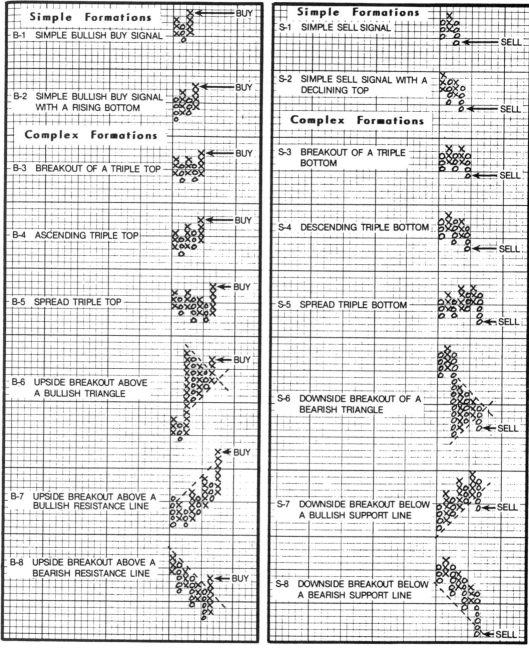

Figure 12.2 Source: K.C. Zieg, Jr., and P.J. Kaufman, *Point and Figure Commodity Trading Techniques* (Larchmont, NY: Investors Intelligence) p. 73.

Three-Box Reversal and Optimized Point and Figure Charting

87.9%. On the sell side, the corresponding S-3, breakout of a triple bottom, showed an even higher profitability ratio of 93.5%. Davis later did additional research on the commodity markets which we'll come back to when we discuss the topic of optimization.

Let's take a look at the patterns themselves. Since column 2, showing signals S-1 through S-8, is just a mirror image of column 1, we'll concentrate on the buy side. The first two signals, B-1 and B-2, are simple formations. All that is required for the *simple bullish buy signal* is three columns, with the second column of x's moving one box above the previous column of x's. B-2 is similar to B-1 with one minor difference—there are now four columns, with the bottom of the second column of o's higher than the first. B-1 shows a simple breakout through resistance. B-2 shows the same bullish breakout but with the added bullish feature of rising bottoms. B-2 is a slightly stronger pattern than B-1 for that reason.

The third pattern (B-3), *breakout of a triple top*, begins the complex formations. Notice that the simple bullish buy signal is a part of each complex formation. Also, as we move down the page, these formations become increasingly stronger. The triple top breakout is stronger because there are five columns involved and two columns of x's have been penetrated. Remember that the wider the base, the greater the upside potential. The next pattern (B-4), *ascending triple top*, is stronger than B-3 because the tops and bottoms are both ascending. The *spread triple top* (B-5) is even stronger because there are seven columns involved, and three columns of x's are exceeded.

The *upside breakout above a bullish triangle* (B-6) combines two signals. First, a simple buy signal must be present. Then the upper trendline must be cleared. (We'll cover the drawing of trendlines on these charts in the next section). Signal B-7, *upside breakout above a bullish resistance line*, is self-explanatory. Again, two things must be present. A buy signal must have already been given; and the upper channel line must be completely cleared. The final pattern, the *upside breakout above a bearish resistance line* (B-8), also requires two elements. A simple buy signal must be combined with a clearing of the down trendline. Of course, everything we've said regarding patterns B-1 through B-8 applies equally to patterns S-1 through S-8 except that, in the latter case, prices are headed down instead of up.

There is a difference between how these patterns are applied to commodity markets as opposed to common stocks. In general, all 16 signals can be used in stock market trading. However, because of the rapid movement so characteristic of the futures markets, the *complex* patterns are not as common in the commodity markets. Much greater emphasis is therefore placed on the *simple* signals. Many futures traders utilize the simple signals alone. If the trader chooses to wait for the more complex and stronger patterns, many profitable trading opportunities will be missed.

The problem with trading all of the simple signals, however, is their frequency. The trader who is following several different markets may find his or her funds depleted trying to follow all of the signals. For those who lack sufficient funds to follow all of the signals, or who find the simple signals too frequent, the complex patterns can be used as a filtering device. For example, the trader may choose to initiate new positions only if triple tops or ascending triple tops are present. This way the signals are fewer and the signals that do occur have a greater chance of working.

There is one very important distinction, however, that must be made. We've been talking here primarily of using simple or complex signals for the initiation of new commitments, either on the long or the short side. When we're discussing entry into the market, the trader can choose between the simple or the complex patterns. However, *all existing positions must be exited or closed out on all simple signals in the opposite direction.* That is to say, all long positions must be liquidated on any simple sell signal. All short positions must be covered on any simple buy signal. Whether the trader chooses to reverse the position or wait for a stronger signal before reentering the market is up to him or her, but the losing position must be closed out on the first simple signal in the direction opposite the current position.

THE DRAWING OF TRENDLINES

Another way to impose filters on the basic signals is the use of trend-lines. In our discussion of intra-day charts, it was pointed out that trendlines and channels were drawn in the conventional way. This is not the case on these three-point reversal charts. Trendlines on these charts are drawn at 45-degree angles. Also, trendlines do not necessarily have to connect previous tops or bottoms.

The Basic Bullish Support Line and Bearish Resistance Line

These are your basic up and down trendlines. Because of the severe condensation on these charts, it would be impractical to try to connect rally tops or reaction lows. The 45-degree line is, therefore, used. In

Three-Box Reversal and Optimized Point and Figure Charting

an uptrend, the *bullish support line* is drawn at a 45-degree angle upward to the right from under the lowest column of o's. As long as prices remain above that line, the major trend is considered to be bullish. In a downtrend, the *bearish resistance line* is drawn at a 45-degree angle downward to the right from the top of the highest column of x's. As long as prices remain below that down trendline, the trend is bearish. (See Figures 12.3 and 12.4.)

At times, those lines may have to be adjusted. For example, sometimes a correction in an uptrend breaks below the rising support line after which the uptrend resumes. In such cases, a new support line must be drawn at a 45-degree angle from the bottom of that reaction low. Sometimes a trend is so strong that the original up trendline is simply too far away from the price action. In that case, a tighter trendline should be drawn in an attempt to arrive at a "best fitting" support line.

Channel Lines

Parallel channel lines can also be drawn, but are considered to be much less reliable than the basic trendlines. In an uptrend, the channel line is called the *bullish resistance line*. A *bearish support line* describes the channel line in a downtrend. Once an uptrend has been established and the basic up trendline drawn, a rising channel line is drawn up to the right at a 45-degree angle, parallel to the basic up trendline. The resistance line is drawn from the first column of o's to the left of the pattern. That column of o's should have at least two exposed o's. Sometimes the new uptrend stalls at the resistance line.

If prices clear that line, a second resistance line should be drawn from the next column of o's further to the left. Prices may stall or halt their advance at that line. If not, a third line can be drawn. As already mentioned, these lines are considered secondary in importance, but sometimes can be helpful reference points in deciding where, for example, to take some profits. The ability of prices to move beyond that line can be viewed as a new buy signal with the next objective a move to the next channel line. That is the basis for B-7, the upside breakout above a bullish resistance line.

The *bearish channel line* in a downtrend, or the bearish support line, is drawn down to the right at a 45-degree angle parallel to the basic down trendline. The line is drawn from the first column of x's to the left of the pattern. To qualify, that column of x's should have at least two exposed x's. If that line is broken, which is usually the case, a second or even third support line can be drawn beginning from successive columns of x's to the left.

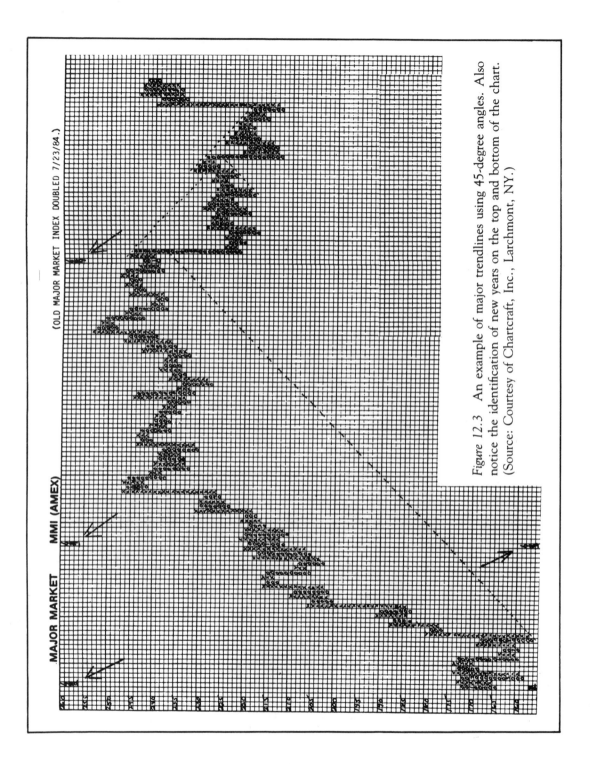

Figure 12.3 An example of major trendlines using 45-degree angles. Also notice the identification of new years on the top and bottom of the chart. (Source: Courtesy of Chartcraft, Inc., Larchmont, NY.)

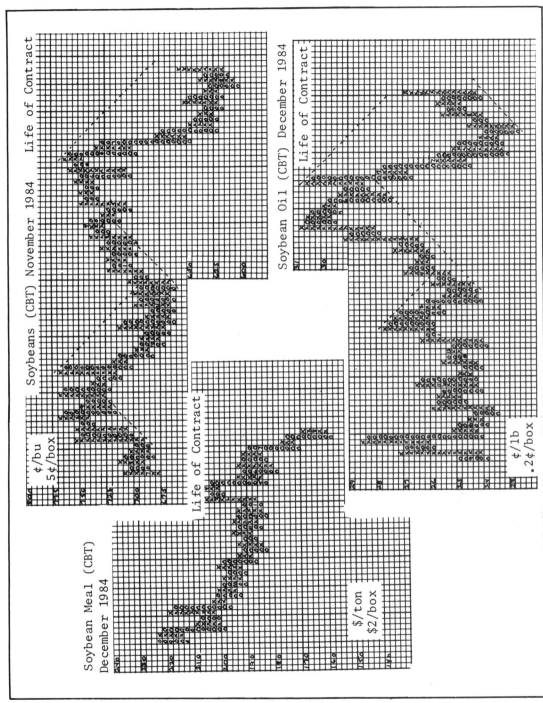

Figure 12.4 Examples of 45-degree trendlines. (Source: Courtesy of Chartcraft, Inc., Larchmont, NY.)

It's important to note that these trendlines must be completely cleared in order for a penetration to occur. An x or o that lands right on the trendline does not constitute a penetration. The channel lines are used mainly as timing aids. They can be helpful in knowing when to take some profits, but should not be used as an excuse to initiate positions against the prevailing trend. The major up and down trend-lines, however, can be an especially effective filtering device in determining when to initiate new positions. Their main function is to ensure that commitments are taken in the direction of the major trend.

In an uptrend, for example, point and figure buy signals would only be followed as long as prices are above the major up trendline. Any sell signals that occur would be used for liquidation purposes only. No short positions would be taken above the up trendline. When prices are in a downtrend, and below the major down trendline, only new short positions can be taken. Simple buy signals can be used as stopout points, but no long positions can be taken as long as prices remain below the down trendline.

MEASURING TECHNIQUES

The previous chapter showed how intra-day charts could be used to determine a horizontal "count" for finding price objectives. Modified charts allow the use of two different measuring techniques—the *horizontal* and the *vertical*. The *horizontal measurement* is similar to the count, but with a couple of minor changes. First, count the number of columns in a bottom or topping pattern. That number of columns must then be multiplied by the value of the reversal or the number of boxes needed for a reversal. For example, let's assign a $1.00 box value to a gold chart with a three-box reversal. We count the number of boxes across a base and come up with 10. Because we're using a three-box reversal, the value of that reversal is $3.00 (3 × $1.00). Multiply the ten columns across the base by $3 for a total of $30. That number is then added to the bottom of the basing pattern or subtracted from the top of a topping pattern to arrive at the price objective. Personally, I prefer to just count the number of boxes.

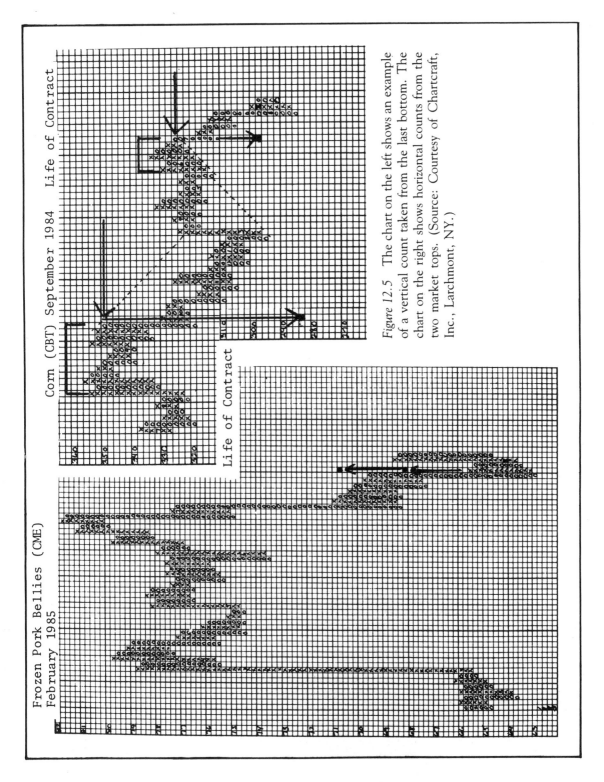

Figure 12.5 The chart on the left shows an example of a vertical count taken from the last bottom. The chart on the right shows horizontal counts from the two market tops. (Source: Courtesy of Chartcraft, Inc., Larchmont, NY.)

Others prefer to multiply the reversal criterion, in this case three boxes, by the actual dollar value of the box size. It really doesn't matter which way it's done. The reason for multiplying the width of the pattern by the reversal value is to compensate for the condensation that takes place when a reversal chart is used.

The *vertical* count is a bit simpler. (See Figure 12.5.) Measure the number of boxes in the first column of the new trend. In an uptrend, measure the first up column of x's. In a downtrend, measure the first down column of o's. Multiply that value by three, or the amount of the reversal, and add that total to the bottom or subtract it from the top of the chart. What you're doing in effect with a three-box reversal chart is tripling the size of the first leg. If a double top or bottom occurs on the chart, use the second column of o's or x's for the vertical count. Of these two techniques, the vertical is the easier and more reliable.

TRADING TACTICS

Let's look at the various ways that these point and figure charts can be used to determine specific entry and exit points.

1. A simple buy signal can be used for the covering of old shorts and/or the initiation of new longs.

2. A simple sell signal can be used for the liquidation of old longs and/or the initiation of new shorts.

3. The simple signal can be used only for liquidation purposes with a complex formation needed for a new commitment.

4. The trendline can be used as a filter. Long positions are taken above the trendline and short positions below the trendline.

5. For stop protection, always risk below the last column of o's in an uptrend and over the last column of x's in a downtrend.

6. The actual entry point can be varied as follows:

   a. Buy the actual breakout in an uptrend.

   b. Buy a three-box reversal after the breakout occurs to obtain a lower entry point.

   c. Buy a three-box reversal in the direction of the original breakout after a correction occurs. Not only does this require the added confirmation of a positive reversal in the right direction, but a closer stop point can now be used under the latest column of o's.

d. Buy a second breakout in the same direction as the original breakout signal.

As you can readily see from the list, there are many different ways that the point and figure chart can be used. Once the basic technique is understood, there is almost unlimited flexibility as to how to best enter and exit a market using this approach. There are two other points that should be touched on here—pyramiding and what to do after a prolonged move.

Pyramiding

Pyramiding refers to the adding of additional positions as the market continues to move in the right direction. The actual buy or sell signal occurs on the first signal. However, as the move continues, several other signals appear on the chart. These repeat buy or sell signals can be used for additional positions. Whether or not this is done, the protective stop point can be raised to just below the latest o column in an uptrend and lowered to just over the latest x column in a downtrend. This use of a *trailing stop* allows the trader to stay with the position and protect accumulated profits at the same time.

What To Do After a Prolonged Move

These intermittent corrections against the trend allow the trader to adjust stops once the trend has resumed. How is this accomplished, however, if no three-box reversals occur during the trend? The trader is then faced with a long column of x's in an uptrend or o's in a downtrend. This type of market situation creates what is called a *pole*, that is, a long column of x's and o's without a correction. The trader wants to stay with the trend but also wants some technique to protect profits. There is at least one way to accomplish this. After an uninterrupted move of ten or more boxes, place a protective stop at the point where a three-box reversal would occur. If the position does get stopped out, reentry can be done on another three-box reversal in the direction of the original trend. In that case, an added advantage is the placement of the new stop under the most recent column of o's in an uptrend or over the latest column of x's in a downtrend.

ADVANTAGES OF POINT AND FIGURE CHARTING

Let's briefly recap some of the advantages of point and figure charting.

1. By varying the box and reversal sizes, these charts can be adapted to almost any need. There are also many different ways these charts can be used for entry and exit points.

2. The modified type of chart described in this chapter is easy to plot and read. No more than 10 or 20 minutes a day is required to keep a complete library of all the futures markets.

3. Trading signals are more precise on point and figure charts than on bar charts.

4. Point and figure charts provide specific entry and exit points.

5. By following these specific point and figure signals, better trading discipline can be achieved.

OPTIMIZED POINT AND FIGURE CHARTS

Up until 1970, the three-box reversal method using traditional box sizes was the common way to use modified point and figure charts. The only real research that had been done to test that technique had been performed by Davis in his 1965 book, *Profit and Profitability*. But that book tested only common stocks. Davis teamed up with Charles C. Thiel, Jr. and produced another research work in 1970, entitled *Point and Figure Trading, A Computer Evaluation* (West Lafayette, IN: Dunn & Hargitt). Davis and Thiel tested two delivery months of 16 commodities from 1960-69. What made this study such a landmark, however, was that it represented the first attempt to find the best, or optimal, combination of box and reversal criteria.

A combination of 28 different box sizes and reversal values were tested. The results of the study demonstrated that the profitability of the traditional three-box reversal method could be greatly improved by optimizing the box sizes and the reversal values.

Two later researchers, Kermit C. Zieg, Jr. and Perry J. Kaufman, conducted further studies that were presented in their 1975 book, *Point and Figure Commodity Trading Techniques* (Larchmont, NY:

Investors Intelligence). Zieg and Kaufman performed three studies. The first study tested the traditional three-box reversal method for 135 days ending on May 17, 1974 and found it to be quite profitable. Two other studies were then done on another 135-day period ending June 28, 1974. The last two studies compared results for that time period using first the three-box reversal method and then optimized box and reversal values. That study showed that the results of the three-box reversal method were dramatically improved by using optimized box and reversal values. The profitability ratio (% of profitable trades) improved from 41% to 66% and the return on margin doubled from 100% to 199%.

The Need To Constantly Reoptimize

The question of optimization has been raised with virtually every other technique in this book. The computer has now enabled commodity researchers to take techniques that have proven themselves over time and improve performance by testing for optimal values. There's no reason to doubt the same is true with point and figure charts. One problem that does arise here, however, is the need to constantly reoptimize. How often do these values have to be retested and reoptimized—quarterly, semiannually, annually? The testing process can prove to be both timely and expensive. The trader must determine for himself or herself whether the benefits of optimizing point and figure charts justify the large expenditure in time and money needed to keep the optimal values current. (See Figures 12.6a to c.)

A Comparison of Three-Box Versus Optimized Reversals

	Traditional Three Boxes*	Optimized Values**
Cattle	20 × 3	20 × 5
Cotton	50 × 3	40 × 2
Hogs	20 × 3	40 × 5
Porkbellies	20 × 3	40 × 6
Soybeans	5 × 3	2 × 8
Soybean Oil	20 × 3	10 × 4
Wheat	2 × 3	1.5 × 5

*Source: Chartcraft, Inc., Larchmont, NY.
**Source: Commodity Price Charts, Cedar Falls, IA.

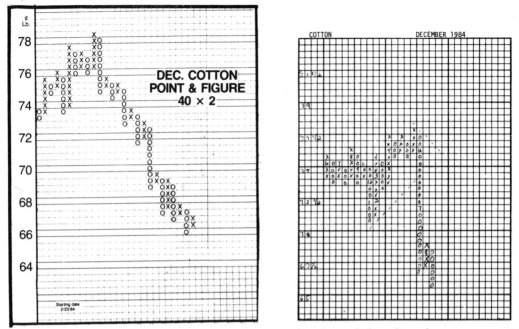

Figure 12.6a A comparison of traditional three-box chart on upper right and optimized chart on upper left. Notice that the optimized chart is much more sensitive, giving more signals. (Source: Courtesy of Commodity Price Charts, 219 Parkade, Cedar Falls, IA and Chartcraft, Inc., Larchmont, NY.)

SOURCES OF INFORMATION

For those who wish to obtain point and figure charts through the printed media, there are five current services available. For the traditional three-box reversal commodity charts, there is the *Chartcraft Commodity Service* at Larchmont, N.Y. An overseas chart service offering three-box reversal charts of the U.S. and U.K. markets is published by *Chart Analysis Ltd.* in London, England (See Figure 12.7). For optimized point and figure charts, there are two current sources: *Commodity Price Charts* in Cedar Falls, Iowa, and the *Dunn and Hargitt Advisory Service* in Lafayette, Indiana (See Figure 12.6c). For intraday point and figure charts, there is only one printed chart service on the market today, *Quotron Futures Charts*, in Racine, Wisconsin.

As for electronic media, the Videcom Comtrend service, located in Stamford, Connecticut, has been the standard in intra-day charts

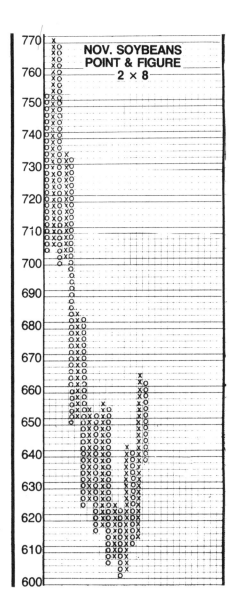

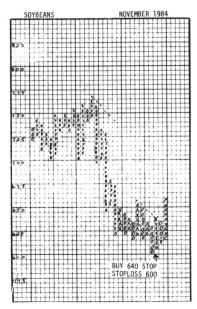

Figure 12.6b A comparison of the traditional three-box chart and optimized chart. Notice that in this case the three-box reversal chart (to the right) is more sensitive, giving earlier signals. (Source: Courtesy of Chartcraft, Inc., Larchmont, NY. and Commodity Price Charts, 219 Parkade, Cedar Falls, IA.)

for over a decade. Not only are the charts provided on the screen and available on a printout, but the actual price change data are provided for those wishing to plot their own point and figure charts. A newer service, mentioned in the previous chapter, is MarketVision in New York City. This new service does not provide the price change data for manual plotting, but produces attractive and highly visual point and figure charts, using different colors for alternate days. Compu Trac in New Orleans has point and figure capability, but only for the

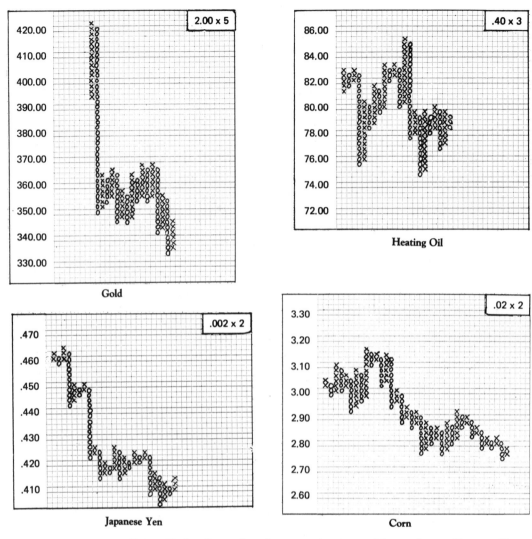

Figure 12.6c Examples of optimized point and figure charts. (Source: Courtesy of Dunn & Hargitt Commodity Service, Lafayette, IN.)

modified type of charts (See Figures 11.2 through 11.4 in Chapter 11). Other quote services are also beginning to provide more point and figure capability.

As for reading material, the best source for a thorough study of the intra-day point and figure method is Alexander Wheelan's *Study Helps in Point and Figure Technique* (New York, NY: Morgan, Rogers & Roberts, Inc., 1954). Wheelan wrote a more condensed version of his original work in an article entitled, "Point and Figure Procedure

Three-Box Reversal and Optimized Point and Figure Charting

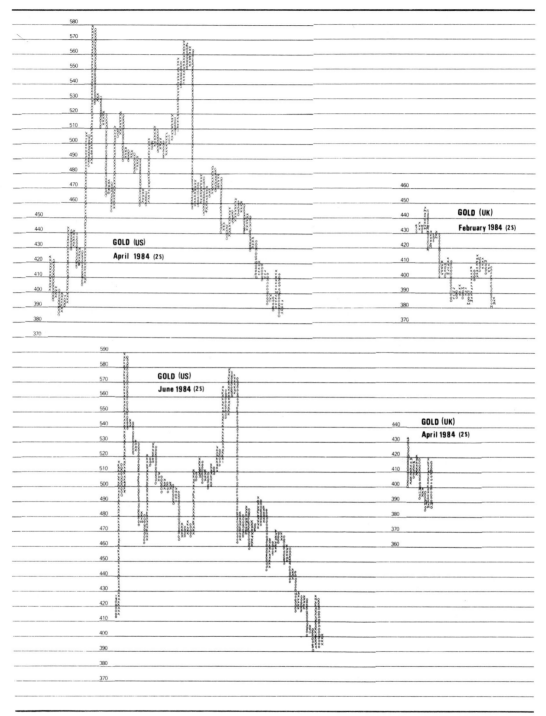

Figure 12.7 Examples of U.S. and U.K. gold charts. (Source: Courtesy of Chart Analysis Ltd., 7 Swallow St., London, W1R7HD.)

in Commodity Market Analysis" published in the *Guide to Commodity Price Forecasting* (Jersey City, NJ: Commodity Research Bureau, 1965). My recommendation for the three-box reversal method would be *The Three-Point Reversal Method of Point & Figure Stock Market Trading* (Larchmont, NY: Chartcraft, Inc., 1980). Zieg and Kaufman's *Point and Figure Commodity Trading Techniques* (Larchmont, NY: Investors Intelligence, 1975) should be consulted for a more in-depth treatment of optimized point and figure work.

CONCLUSION

This concludes a rather lengthy treatment of point and figure analysis. We've looked at the traditional intra-day method, the modified three-box reversal technique, and ended with a discussion of optimized point and figure charts. It should be stressed here that the bar chart should remain the basic working tool of the futures chartist. However, it would be foolhardy not to supplement bar chart analysis with some point and figure work. For very short-term traders, the intra-day point and figure chart is indispensable. Even for position traders, intra-day charts can be used to aid in timing of entry and exit points. Intra-day charts, however, should not be limited to just the short term, but also should be used for longer-range work. For those who lack the time and resources to take advantage of intra-day charts, there is the modified version using three-box reversals or optimized charting. Because of the tremendous flexibility in these charts, and the precision of the buy and sell signals, they provide an excellent adjunct to bar charting.

One final word should be mentioned here on the application of point and figure charts to technical indicators. There's no reason why point and figure charts cannot be used for standard technical indicators. Various oscillators, such as the *Relative Strength Index*, can be constructed using this technique. *On balance volume* could also be used. Breakouts or breakdowns on these various indicators show up with much greater clarity on point and figure charts. So once you've mastered the technique, use your imagination.

13

Elliott Wave Theory

HISTORICAL BACKGROUND

In 1938, a monograph entitled *The Wave Principle* was published. It was the first published reference to what has come to be known as the *Elliott Wave Principle*. The monograph was published by Charles J. Collins and was based on the original work presented to him by the founder of the Wave Principle, Ralph Nelson (R.N.) Elliott.

Elliott (1871–1948) had been an accountant by profession, specializing in restaurants and railroads. The latter activity took him to various railroad companies in Mexico and Central America. He retired in 1927 after contracting a serious illness in Guatemala and spent the next several years at his home in California struggling to regain his health.

It was during his long period of convalescence that he developed his theory of stock market behavior. He apparently was very much influenced by the Dow Theory, which has much in common with the Wave Principle. In a 1934 letter to Collins, then editor of a stock market service published by Investment Counsel Inc. in Detroit, Elliott mentioned that he had been a subscriber to Robert Rhea's stock market service and was familiar with Rhea's book on Dow Theory. Elliott goes on to say that the Wave Principle was "a much needed complement to the Dow Theory."

Elliott contacted Collins to inform him of his new discovery and in hopes of joining Collins' Firm. After much correspondence between the two men, Collins became impressed to the point that he helped Elliott get his start on Wall Street and agreed to publish *The Wave Principle* in 1938. Collins also introduced Elliott to the editors of *Financial World* magazine. As a result, Elliott wrote a series of 12 articles for that publication in 1939 in which he spelled out his theory. In 1946, just two years before his death, Elliott wrote his definitive work on the Wave Principle, *Nature's Law—The Secret of the Universe.*

If that title sounds a bit grandiose, that is because Elliott believed his stock market theory was part of a much larger natural law governing all of man's activities. While that broader aspect of his theory makes for interesting reading, we'll leave those larger questions for greater minds to ponder and concentrate our attention on his stock market work. Elliott's ideas might have faded from memory if A. Hamilton Bolton hadn't decided in 1953 to publish the first *Elliott Wave Supplement* to the *Bank Credit Analyst,* which he did annually for 14 years until his death in 1967. Bolton's 1960 work, *Elliott Wave Principle— A Critical Appraisal,* was the first major piece since Elliott's death. In 1967, A.J. Frost took over the Elliott Supplements and wrote his last major Elliott work for the *Bank Credit Analyst* in 1970.

Frost collaborated with Robert Prechter in 1978 on the *Elliott Wave Principle* (Gainesville, GA: New Classics Library), which is today considered the definitive text on the subject. Prechter went a step further and in 1980 published *The Major Works of R.N. Elliott* (Gainesville, GA: New Classics Library), making available the original Elliott writings that had long been out of print. Prechter is himself considered the leading Elliottician in the business and publishes a newsletter, "The Elliott Wave Theorist" out of Gainesville, Georgia—a monthly letter covering the stock market, interest rates, and precious metals. A second newsletter published by Prechter's New Classics Library, "The Elliott Wave Commodity Letter," is written by David Weis and deals exclusively with commodity futures markets. I would be remiss at this point if I did not acknowledge the generosity of Mr. Prechter in providing most of the diagrams used in this chapter.

INTRODUCTION TO THE THEORY

It's been my experience that most people find the Elliott Wave Principle difficult to grasp and somewhat intimidating. The principles behind the theory are actually relatively simple. The reader will notice before long that many of the points covered sound very familiar. This is because much of the Elliott material fits very nicely with the principles of the Dow Theory and traditional charting techniques. Elliott Wave Theory, however, goes beyond traditional charting by providing an overall perspective to market movement that helps explain why and where certain chart patterns develop and why they mean what they do. It also helps the market analyst determine where the market is in its overall cycle.

It's been said before that much of technical analysis is trend-following in nature. Dow Theory, despite all its merits, tends to give its signals well after a trend has been established. Elliott Wave Theory gives the analyst more advanced warning of tops and bottoms, which can then be confirmed by the more traditional approaches. As we go along, we'll try to point out the similarities between wave theory and the better known charting principles.

Our purpose here is to steer a middle course in the treatment of this subject. We'll cover the more important elements of the Elliott Wave Principle without going into all the fine points. For a more in-depth treatment, your best bet is Frost and Prechter's *Elliott Wave Principle*, published by New Classics Library.

BASIC TENETS OF THE ELLIOTT WAVE PRINCIPLE

There are three important aspects of wave theory—*pattern, ratio,* and *time*—in that order of importance. *Pattern* refers to the wave patterns or formations that comprise the most important element of the theory. *Ratio analysis* is useful in determining retracement points and price objectives by measuring the relationships between the different waves. Finally, time relationships also exist and can be used to confirm the wave patterns and ratios, but are considered by some Elliotticians to be less reliable in market forecasting.

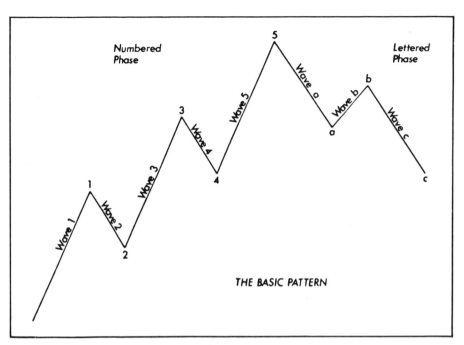

Numbered Phase

Lettered Phase

Wave 1

Wave 2

Wave 3

Wave 4

Wave 5

Wave a

Wave b

Wave c

THE BASIC PATTERN

Figure 13.1 The Basic Pattern. (A.J. Frost and Robert Prechter, *Elliott Wave Principle* [Gainesville, GA: New Classics Library, 1978], p. 20. Copyright © 1978 by Frost and Prechter.)

Elliott Wave Theory was originally applied to the major stock market averages, particularly the Dow Jones Industrial Average. In its most basic form, the theory says that the stock market follows a repetitive rhythm of a five-wave advance followed by a three-wave decline. Figure 13.1 shows one complete cycle. If you count the waves, you will find that one complete cycle has eight waves—five up and three down. In the advancing portion of the cycle, notice that each of the five waves are numbered. Waves 1, 3, and 5—called *impulse* waves—are rising waves, while waves 2 and 4 move against the up-trend. Waves 2 and 4 are called *corrective* waves because they correct waves 1 and 3. After the five-wave numbered advance has been completed, a three-wave correction begins. The three corrective waves are identified by the letters a, b, c.

Along with the constant form of the various waves, there is the important consideration of degree. There are many different degrees of trend. Elliott, in fact, categorized nine different degrees of trend (or magnitude) ranging from a *Grand Supercycle* spanning two hundred years to a *subminuette* degree covering only a few hours. The point to remember is that the basic eight-wave cycle remains constant no matter what degree of trend is being studied.

Each wave subdivides into waves of one lesser degree which, in turn, can also be subdivided into waves of even lesser degree. It also follows then that each wave is itself part of the wave of the next higher degree. Figure 13.2 demonstrates these relationships. The largest two waves—①and②—can be subdivided into eight lesser waves which, in turn, can be subdivided into 34 even lesser waves. The two largest waves—①and②—are only the first two waves in an even larger five-wave advance. Wave③of that next higher degree is about to begin. The 34 waves in Figure 13.2 are subdivided further to the next smaller degree in Figure 13.3, resulting in 144 waves.

The numbers shown so far—1,2,3,5,8,13,21,34,55,89,144—are not just random numbers. They are part of the *Fibonacci number sequence,* which forms the mathematical basis for the Elliott Wave Theory. We'll come back to them a little later. For now, look again at Figures 13.1 through 13.3 and notice a very significant characteristic of the waves. Whether a given wave divides into five waves or three waves is determined by the direction of the next larger wave. For example, in Figure 13.2, waves (1), (3), and (5) subdivide into five waves because the next larger wave of which they are part—wave ①—is an advancing wave. Because waves (2) and (4) are moving

Figure 13.2   (Frost and Prechter, p. 21. Copyright © 1978 by Frost and Prechter.)

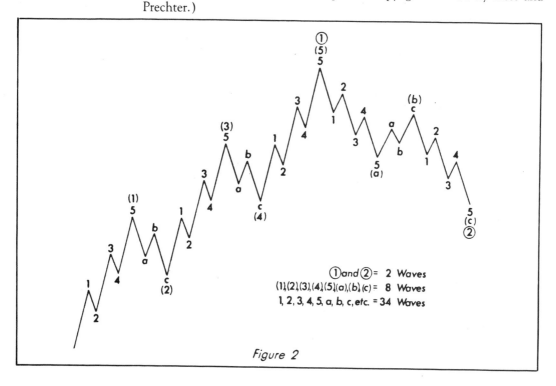

①and②= 2 Waves
(1),(2),(3),(4),(5),(a),(b),(c) = 8 Waves
1, 2, 3, 4, 5, a, b, c, etc. = 34 Waves

Figure 2

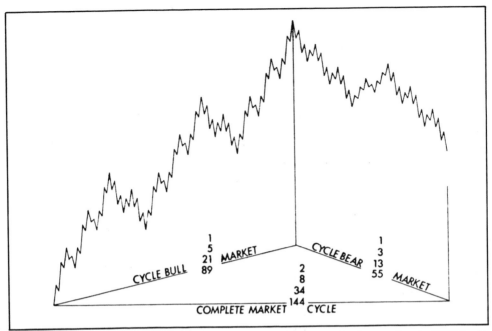

Figure 13.3 (Frost and Prechter, p. 22. Copyright © 1978 by Frost and Prechter.)

against the trend, they subdivide into only three waves. Look more closely at corrective waves (a), (b), and (c), which comprise the larger corrective wave ②. Notice that the two declining waves—(a) and (c)—each break down into five waves. This is because they are moving in the same direction as the next larger wave ②. Wave (b) by contrast only has three waves, because it is moving against the next larger wave ②.

Being able to determine between threes and fives is obviously of tremendous importance in the application of this approach. That information tells the analyst what to expect next. A completed five-wave move, for example, usually means that only part of a larger wave has been completed and that there's more to come (unless it's a fifth of a fifth). *One of the most important rules to remember is that a correction can never take place in five waves.* In a bull market, for example, if a five-wave decline is seen, this means that it is probably only the first wave of a three-wave (a-b-c) decline and that there's more to come on the downside. In a bear market, a three-wave advance should be followed by resumption of the downtrend. A five-wave rally would warn of a more substantial move to the upside and might possibly even be the first wave of a new bull trend.

CONNECTION BETWEEN
ELLIOTT WAVE AND DOW THEORY

Let's take a moment here to point out the obvious connection between Elliott's idea of five advancing waves and Dow's three advancing phases of a bull market. It seems clear that Elliott's idea of three up waves, with two intervening corrections, fits nicely with the Dow Theory. While Elliott was no doubt influenced by Dow's analysis, it also seems clear that Elliott believed he had gone well beyond Dow's theory and had in fact improved on it. It's also interesting to note the influence of the sea on both men in the formulation of their theories. Dow compared the major, intermediate, and minor trends in the market with the tides, waves, and ripples on the ocean. Elliott referred to "ebbs and flows" in his writing and named his theory the "wave" principle.

I'd like to digress here to interject an interesting piece of sea lore I ran across this summer while vacationing on Cape Cod that may have some bearing on Dow and Elliott. In his book, *The Outermost House* (New York, NY: Ballantine Books, 1928), Henry Beston describes a solitary year spent on a Cape Cod beach. While describing his observations of the ocean, he makes reference to a *triple rhythm* in the waves on the beach. He claims that the great waves reached the coast in threes: "Three great waves, then an indeterminate run of lesser rhythms, then three great waves again." (p.34). He further claims that, far from being some half-mystical fancy, this triple rhythm was well known to the local Coast Guard who took advantage of the lull after the third wave to launch their boats. Who knows? Maybe Dow and Elliott knew more about the sea than they let on.

Wave Personalities

Another area where the two theories overlap to some extent is in the description of the three phases of a bull market. Elliott said little about wave personalities. The question of the personalities of the different waves was discussed for the first time in Prechter's book and are based on his own original interpretation of Elliott's ideas. The three psychological "phases" of a bull market (covered in Chapter 2) are similar to the "personalities" of Elliott's three impulse waves. A knowledge of these wave personalities can be helpful, especially when wave counts are unclear. It's also important to remember that these wave personalities remain constant in all the different degrees of trend.

Wave 1.   About half of the first waves are part of the basing process and often appear to be nothing more than a rebound from very depressed levels. First waves are usually the shortest of the five waves. These first waves can sometimes be dynamic, especially if they occur from major base formations.

Wave 2.   Second waves usually retrace, or give back, all or most of wave 1. The ability of wave 2, however, to hold above the bottom of wave 1 is what produces many of the traditional chart patterns, such as *double* or *triple bottoms* and *inverse head and shoulders bottoms.*

Wave 3.   The third wave is usually the longest and the most dynamic, at least in the common stock area. The penetration of the top of wave 1 registers all kinds of traditional breakouts and Dow Theory buy signals. Virtually all technical trend-following systems have jumped on the bull bandwagon by this point. Volume is usually the heaviest during this wave and gaps become prevalent. Not surprisingly, the third wave is also the most likely to extend (see next section). Wave 3 can never be the shortest in a five-wave advance. By this time, even the fundamentals are looking good.

Wave 4.   The fourth wave is usually a complex pattern. Like wave 2, it is a corrective or a consolidation phase, but usually differs from wave 2 in its construction (see the section later in this chapter on the *rule of alternation*). Triangles usually occur in the fourth wave. One cardinal rule of Elliott analysis is that the bottom of wave 4 can never overlap the top of wave 1.

Wave 5.   In stocks, wave 5 is usually much less dynamic than wave 3. In commodities, wave 5 is often the longest wave and the one most likely to extend. It is during wave 5 that many of the confirming technical indicators, such as *on balance volume* (OBV), begin to lag behind the price action. It is also at this point that negative divergences begin to develop on various oscillators, warning of a possible market top.

Wave A.   Wave A of the corrective phase is usually misinterpreted as just a normal pullback in the uptrend. One dead giveaway that it's more serious than that is when wave A breaks down into five waves. Having already spotted several oscillator divergences on the prior advance, the alert technician may also notice a shift in the volume pattern at this point. Heavier volume may now have shifted to the downside, although that is not necessarily a requirement.

Elliott Wave Theory

Wave B. Wave B, the bounce in the new downtrend, usually occurs on light volume and usually represents the last chance to exit old long positions gracefully and a second chance to initiate new short sales. Depending on the type of correction taking place (see the section in this chapter on corrective waves), the rally may test the old highs (forming a double top) or even exceed the old highs before turning back down.

Wave C. Wave C leaves little doubt that the uptrend has ended. Again, depending on the type of correction in progress, wave C will often decline well below the bottom of wave A, registering all kinds of traditional technical sell signals. In fact, by drawing a trendline under the bottoms of wave 4 and wave A, the familiar head and shoulders top sometimes appears.

EXTENSIONS

While an ideal uptrend has five waves, it's not unusual for one of the impulse waves to extend. In other words, wave 1, 3, or 5 will take on an elongated form by breaking down into five additional waves. Figure 13.4 shows what the pattern would look like in each case. The first case, which is the most unusual, shows a wave 1 extension; the second case, the most common in stocks, shows a third-wave extension; the third case, most common in commodities, a fifth-wave extension. In the final example, it is difficult to discern which wave is extending because the five impulse waves are of equal length. In such a situation, it is sufficient to keep in mind that a nine-wave pattern, where all of the impulse waves are of equal proportion, carries the same significance as a completed five-wave advance.

The question of wave extensions carries some forecasting implications. First, only one impulse wave should extend. In addition, the two other impulse waves that do not extend tend toward equality in both time and magnitude. Therefore, if wave 3 extends, wave 5 does not and tends to resemble wave 1. If waves 1 and 3 are normal waves, wave 5 is the one most likely to extend. One final point to be mentioned here is the *double retracement* of extended fifth waves. That is, after a fifth-wave extension is completed, a three-wave decline takes place down to where the extension began. A rally back to the top of the extension then occurs. From that point, the uptrend either resumes or forms a top, depending on where it is in the longer-range cycle. Figure 13.5 demonstrates the double retracement in a bull market.

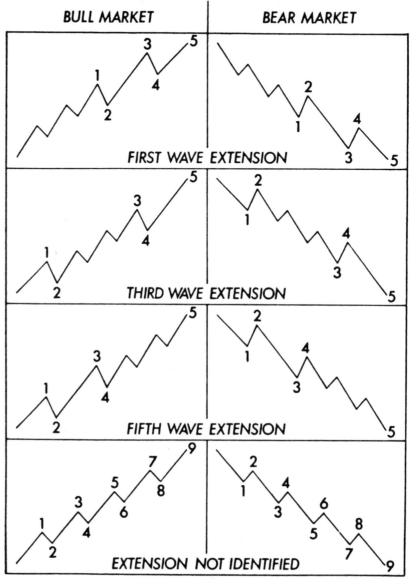

Figure 13.4 (Frost and Prechter, p. 26. Copyright © 1978 by Frost and Prechter.)

Diagonal Triangles and Failures

There are two other variations that take place in impulse waves—
diagonal triangles and *the failure*. Figures 13.6 and 13.7 show examples
of the diagonal triangle. The *diagonal triangle* usually shows up in the
fifth and final wave. It is, in effect, a wedge pattern. Remember in

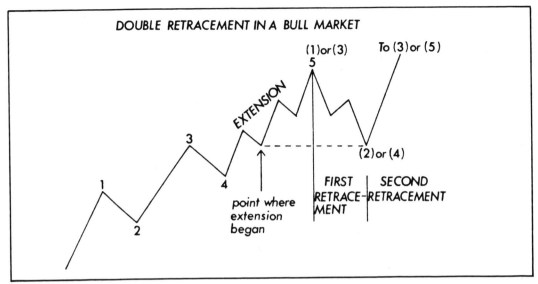

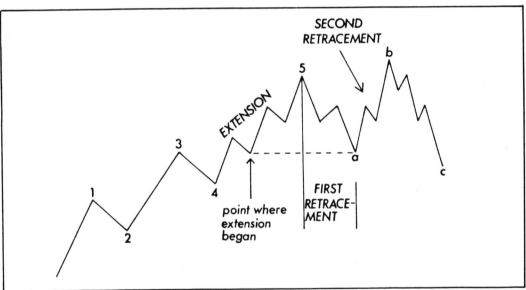

Figure 13.5   Double Retracement in a Bull Market. (Frost and Prechter, p. 29. Copyright © 1978 by Frost and Prechter.)

our earlier treatment of chart patterns (in Chapter 6) that a rising wedge is always bearish and a falling wedge, bullish. The pattern has five waves with each wave subdividing into three waves. Notice the converging trendlines. This type of pattern usually marks an important turn in the market when the steeper trendline is broken.

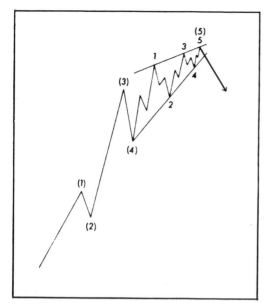

Figure 13.6 Diagonal Triangle (Rising Wedge). (Frost and Prechter, p. 31. Copyright © 1978 by Frost and Prechter.)

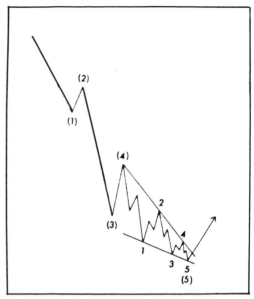

Figure 13.7 Diagonal Triangle (Falling Wedge). (Frost and Prechter, p. 31. Copyright © 1978 by Frost and Prechter.)

Figures 13.8 and 13.9 show what a failure looks like. The *failure* also shows up in the fifth and final wave. It shows a situation where, in a bull market for example, wave 5 breaks down into the required five waves, but fails to exceed the top of wave 3. In a bear market, wave 5 does not violate the low of wave 3. Notice that the Elliott failure pattern forms the more commonly known *double top or bottom*.

Figure 13.8 Bull Market Failure. (Frost and Prechter, p. 33. Copyright © 1978 by Frost and Prechter.)

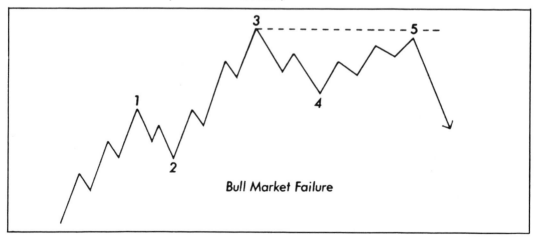

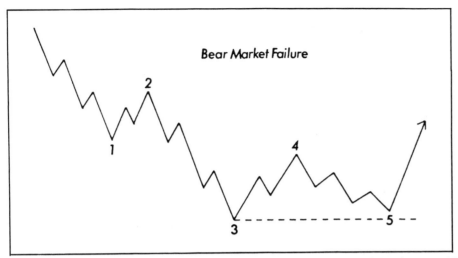

Figure 13.9 Bear Market Failure. (Frost and Prechter, p. 33. Copyright ©
1978 by Frost and Prechter.)

CORRECTIVE WAVES

So far, we've talked mainly about the impulse waves in the direction
of the major trend. Let's turn our attention now to the *corrective* waves.
In general, corrective waves are less clearly defined and, as a result,
tend to be more difficult to identify and predict. One point that is
clearly defined, however, is that corrective waves can never take place
in five waves. Corrective waves are threes, never fives (with the exception of triangles). There are four classifications of corrective waves—
zig-zags, flats, triangles, and the *double and triple threes.*

Zig-Zags

A zig-zag is a three-wave corrective pattern, against the major trend,
which breaks down into a 5-3-5 sequence. Figures 13.10 and 13.11
show a bull market zig-zag correction, while a bear market rally is
shown in Figures 13.12 and 13.13. Notice that the middle wave B
falls short of the beginning of wave A and that wave C moves well
beyond the end of wave A.

A less common variation of the zig-zag is the double zig-zag shown
in Figure 13.14. This variation sometimes occurs in larger corrective
patterns. It is in effect two different 5-3-5 zig-zag patterns connected
by an intervening a-b-c pattern.

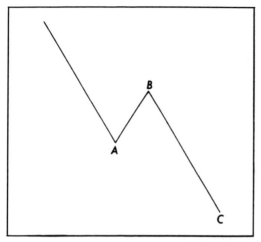

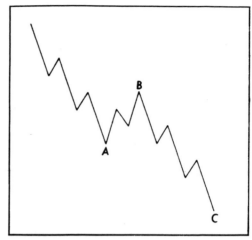

Figure 13.10   Bull Market Zig-Zag (5-3-5). (Frost and Prechter, p. 36. Copyright © 1978 by Frost and Prechter.)

Figure 13.11   Bull Market Zig-Zag (5-3-5). (Frost and Prechter, p. 36. Copyright © 1978 by Frost and Prechter.)

Flats

What distinguishes the flat correction from the zig-zag correction is that the flat follows a 3-3-5 pattern. Notice in Figures 13.16 and 13.18 that the A wave is a three instead of a five. In general, the flat is

Figure 13.12   Bear Market Zig-Zag (5-3-5). (Frost and Prechter, p. 36. Copyright © 1978 by Frost and Prechter.)

Figure 13.13   Bear Market Zig-Zag (5-3-5). (Frost and Prechter, p. 36 Copyright © 1978 by Frost and Prechter.)

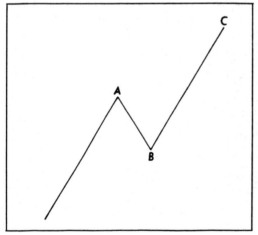

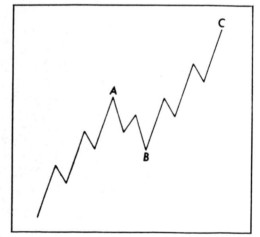

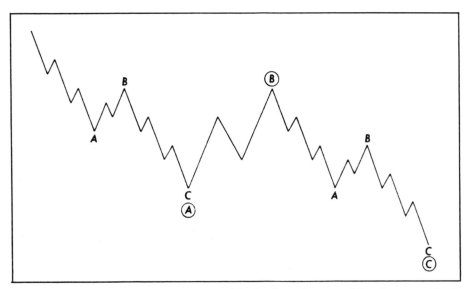

Figure 13.14 Double Zig-Zag. (Frost and Prechter, p. 37. Copyright ©
1978 by Frost and Prechter.)

more of a consolidation than a correction and is considered a sign of
strength in a bull market. Figures 13.15 through 13.18 show examples
of normal flats. In a bull market, for example, wave B rallies all the
way to the top of wave A, showing greater market strength. The final
wave C terminates at or just below the bottom of wave A in contrast
to a zig-zag, which moves well under that point.

There are two "irregular" variations of the normal *flat* correction.
Figures 13.19 through 13.22 show the first type of variation. Notice
in the bull market example (Figures 13.19 and 13.20) that the top of
wave B exceeds the top of A and that wave C violates the bottom of
A.

Another variation occurs when wave B reaches the top of A,
but wave C fails to reach the bottom of A. Naturally, this last pattern
denotes greater market strength in a bull market. This variation is
shown in Figures 13.23 through 13.26 for bull and bear markets.

The final variation on the flat correction denotes even greater
market strength and is called the running correction. Figure 13.27
shows a running correction in a bull market. Notice that wave b is
well above the top of a and that wave c is above the top of impulse
wave 1. This relatively rare variety of a corrective pattern shows a
situation where the market is so strong that the correction isn't able
to form properly.

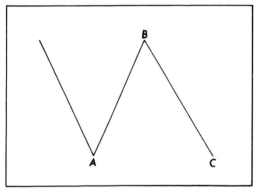

Figure 13.15 Bull Market Flat (3-3-5), Normal Correction. (Frost and Prechter, p. 38. Copyright © 1978 by Frost and Prechter.)

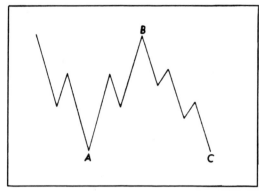

Figure 13.16 Bull Market Flat (3-3-5), Normal Correction. (Frost and Prechter, p. 38. Copyright © 1978 by Frost and Prechter.)

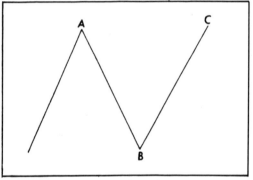

Figure 13.17 Bear Market Flat (3-3-5), Normal Correction. (Frost and Prechter, p. 38. Copyright © 1978 by Frost and Prechter.)

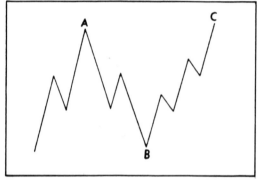

Figure 13.18 Bear Market Flat (3-3-5), Normal Correction. (Frost and Prechter, p. 38. Copyright © 1978 by Frost and Prechter.)

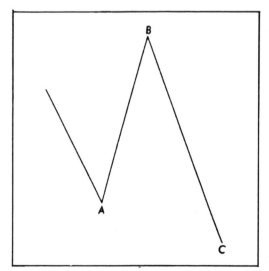

Figure 13.19 Bull Market Flat (3-3-5), Irregular Correction. (Frost and Prechter, p. 39. Copyright © 1978 by Frost and Prechter.)

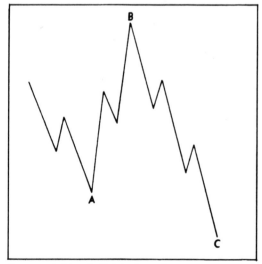

Figure 13.20 Bull Market Flat (3-3-5), Irregular Correction. (Frost and Prechter, p. 39. Copyright © 1978 by Frost and Prechter.)

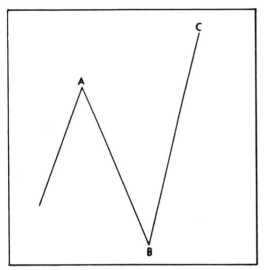

Figure 13.21 Bear Market Flat (3-3-5), Irregular Correction. (Frost and Prechter, p. 39. Copyright © 1978 by Frost and Prechter.)

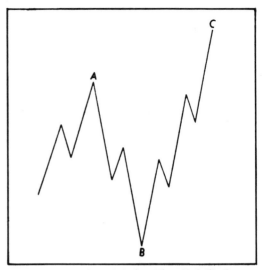

Figure 13.22 Bear Market Flat (3-3-5), Irregular Correction. (Frost and Prechter, p. 39. Copyright © 1978 by Frost and Prechter.)

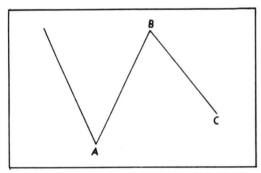

Figure 13.23 Bull Market Flat (3-3-5), Inverted Irregular Correction. (Frost and Prechter, p. 40. Copyright © 1978 by Frost and Prechter.)

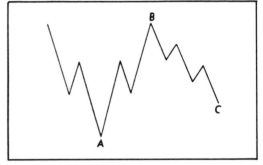

Figure 13.24 Bull Market Flat (3-3-5), Inverted Irregular Correction. (Frost and Prechter, p. 40. Copyright © 1978 by Frost and Prechter.)

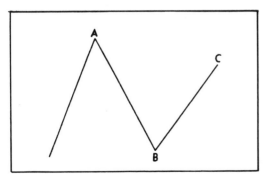

Figure 13.25 Bear Market Flat (3-3-5), Inverted Irregular Correction. (Frost and Prechter, p. 40. Copyright © 1978 by Frost and Prechter.)

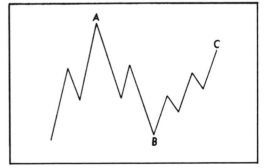

Figure 13.26 Bear Market Flat (3-3-5), Inverted Irregular Correction. (Frost and Prechter, p. 40. Copyright © 1978 by Frost and Prechter.)

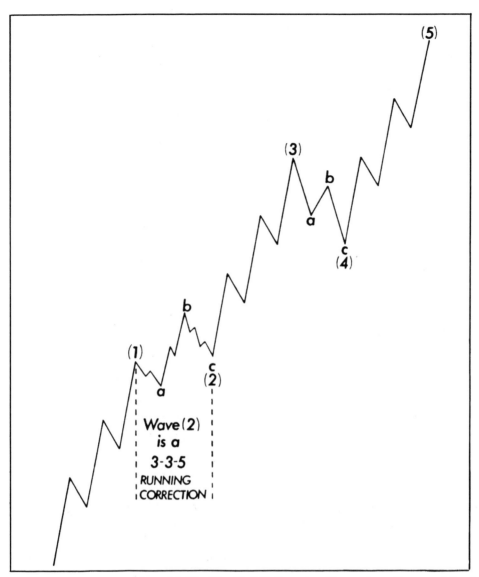

Figure 13.27 Flat (3-3-5) Running Correction. (Frost and Prechter, p. 42. Copyright © 1978 by Frost and Prechter.)

Triangles

Triangles usually occur in the fourth wave and precede the final move in the direction of the major trend. (They can also appear in the b wave of an a-b-c correction.) In an uptrend, therefore, it can be said that triangles are both bullish and bearish. They're bullish in the sense that they indicate resumption of the uptrend. They're bearish because they also indicate that after one more wave up, prices will probably peak. (See Figure 13.28.)

Figure 13.28 Corrective Wave (Horizontal) Triangles. (Frost and Prechter, p. 43. Copyright © 1978 by Frost and Prechter.)

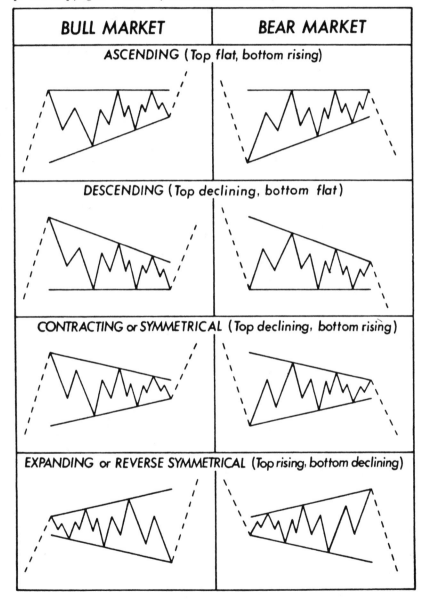

Elliott's interpretation of the triangle parallels the classical use of the pattern, but with his usual added precision. Remember from Chapter 6 that the triangle is usually a continuation pattern, which is exactly what Elliott said. Elliott's triangle is a sideways consolidation pattern that breaks down into five waves, each wave in turn having three waves of its own. Elliott also classifies four different kinds of triangles—*ascending, descending, symmetrical,* and *expanding*—all of which were seen before in Chapter 6. Figure 13.28 shows the four varieties in both uptrends and downtrends.

Because chart patterns in commodity futures contracts sometimes don't form as fully as they do in the stock market, it is not unusual for triangles in the futures markets to have only three waves instead of five. (Remember, however, that the minimum requirement for a triangle is still four points—two upper and two lower—to allow the drawing of two converging trendlines.) Elliott Wave Theory also holds that the fifth and last wave within the triangle sometimes breaks its trendline, giving a false signal, before beginning its "thrust" in the original direction.

Elliott's measurement for the fifth and final wave after completion of the triangle is essentially the same as in classical charting—that is, the market is expected to move the distance that matches the widest part of the triangle (its height). There is another point worth noting here concerning the timing of the final top or bottom. According to Prechter, the apex of the triangle (the point where the two converging trendlines meet) often marks the timing for the completion of the final fifth wave.

Double and Triple Threes

The final variation on the corrective waves is a less common complex pattern formed by combining two or three simpler patterns. Figures 13.29 and 13.30 demonstrate their appearance. In Figure 13.29, two a-b-c patterns are joined together to form seven waves. In Figure 13.30, three a-b-c patterns combine to form eleven waves. Notice how these patterns resemble the classical trading range or rectangular consolidation pattern.

This concludes our treatment of the basic wave forms that comprise Elliott Wave Theory. Let's take a quick look at a couple of associated guidelines—the *rule of alternation* and *channeling.*

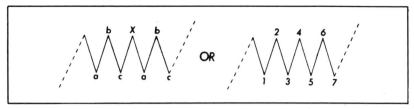

Figure 13.29 Double Three. (Frost and Prechter, p. 45. Copyright © 1978 by Frost and Prechter.)

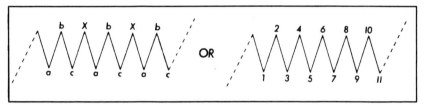

Figure 13.30 Triple Three. (Frost and Prechter, p. 45. Copyright © 1978 by Frost and Prechter.)

THE RULE OF ALTERNATION

In its more general application, this rule or principle holds that the market usually doesn't act the same way two times in a row. If a certain type of top or bottom occurred the last time around, it will probably not do so again this time. The rule of alternation doesn't tell us exactly

Figure 13.31 The Rule of Alternation. (Frost and Prechter, p. 50. Copyright © 1978 by Frost and Prechter.)

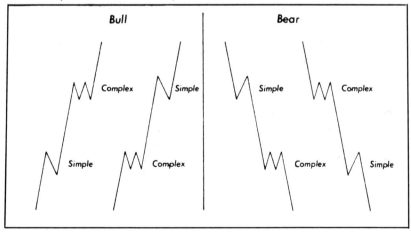

what will happen, but tells us what probably won't. In its more specific application, it is most generally used to tell us what type of corrective pattern to expect. Corrective patterns tend to alternate. In other words, if corrective wave 2 was a simple a-b-c pattern, wave 4 will probably be a complex pattern, such as a triangle. Conversely, if wave 2 is complex, wave 4 will probably be simple. Figure 13.3l gives some examples.

CHANNELING

Another important aspect of wave theory is the use of *price channels*. You'll recall that we covered trend channeling in Chapter 4. Elliott used price channels as a method of arriving at price objectives and also to help confirm the completion of wave counts. Once an uptrend has been established, an initial trend channel is constructed by drawing a basic up trendline along the bottoms of waves 1 and 2. A parallel channel line is then drawn over the top of wave 1 as shown in Figure 13.32. The entire uptrend will often stay within those two boundaries.

Figure 13.32 Old and New Channels. (Frost and Prechter, p. 62. Copyright © 1978 by Frost and Prechter.)

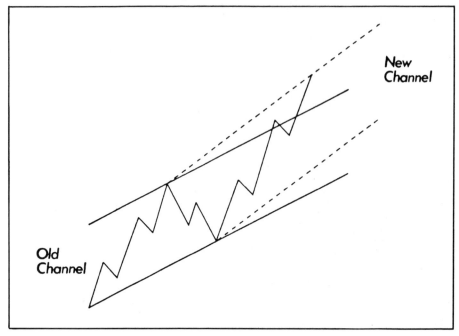

If wave 3 begins to accelerate to the point that it exceeds the upper channel line, the lines have to be redrawn along the top of wave 1 and the bottom of wave 2 as shown in Figure 13.32. The final channel is drawn under the two corrective waves—2 and 4—and usually above the top of wave 3 as shown in Figure 13.33. If wave 3 is unusually strong, or an extended wave, the upper line may have to be drawn over the top of wave 1. The fifth wave should come close to the upper channel line before terminating. For the drawing of channel lines on long-term trends, it's recommended that semi-log charts be employed along with arithmetic charts.

WAVE FOUR AS A SUPPORT AREA

In concluding our discussion of wave formations and guidelines, one important point remains to be mentioned, and that is the significance of wave 4 as a support area in subsequent bear markets. Once five up waves have been completed and a bear trend has begun, that bear market will usually not move below the previous fourth wave of one lesser degree; that is, the last fourth wave that was formed during the

Figure 13.33 Final Channel. (Frost and Prechter, p. 63. Copyright © 1978 by Frost and Prechter.)

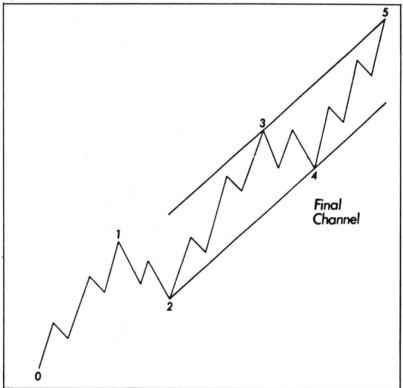

previous bull advance. There are exceptions to that rule, but usually the bottom of the fourth wave contains the bear market. This piece of information can prove very useful in arriving at a maximum downside price objective.

FIBONACCI NUMBERS AS THE BASIS OF THE WAVE PRINCIPLE

Most people who visit Pisa, Italy view the famous Leaning Tower, that less-than-perpendicular monument to its architect, Bonanna. What do Bonanna and the Leaning Tower have to do with the stock market and Elliott Wave Theory? Very little. But not far from the tower stands a small statue, unknown to most people, of another thirteenth century mathematician—Leonardo Fibonacci. What does Fibonacci have to do with the Elliott Wave Theory of stock market behavior? Everything. Elliott himself stated in *Nature's Law* that the mathematical basis for his Wave Principle was a number sequence discovered (or more accurately rediscovered) by Fibonacci in the thirteenth century. That number sequence has become identified with its discoverer and is commonly referred to as the *Fibonacci numbers*.

Fibonacci published three major works, the best known being *Liber Abaci* (Book of Calculations). That work introduced to Europe the Hindu-Arabic number system which gradually replaced the older Roman numerals. His work also contributed to later developments in mathematics, physics, astronomy, and engineering. In *Liber Abaci*, the Fibonacci sequence is first presented as a solution to a mathematical problem involving the reproduction rate of rabbits. The number sequence presented is 1, 1, 2, 3, 5, 8, 13, 21, 34, 55, 89, 144, and so on to infinity.

The sequence has a number of interesting properties, not the least of which is an almost constant relationship between the numbers.

1. The sum of any two consecutive numbers equals the next higher number. For example, 3 and 5 equals 8, 5 and 8 equals 13, and so on.

2. The ratio of any number to its next higher number approaches .618, after the first four numbers. For example, 1/1 is 1.00, 1/2 is .50, 2/3 is .67, 3/5 is .60, 5/8 is .625, 8/13 is .615, 13/21 is .619, and so on. Notice how these early ratio values fluctuate above and

below .618 in narrowing amplitude. Also, notice the values of 1.00, .50, .67. We'll comment further on these values when we talk more about ratio analysis and percentage retracements.

3. The ratio of any number to its next lower number is approximately 1.618, or the inverse of .618. For example, 13/8 is 1.625, 21/13 is 1.615, 34/21 is 1.619. The higher the numbers become, the closer they come to the values of .618 and 1.618.

4. The ratios of alternate numbers approach 2.618 or its inverse, .382. For example, 13/34 is .382, 34/13 is 2.615.

There are many other interesting relationships, but these are the best known and the most important. It was stated earlier that Fibonacci was really the rediscoverer of this number sequence. This is because the ratio of 1.618 or .618 was known to the ancient Greek and Egyptian mathematicians. The ratio was known as the Golden Ratio or Golden Mean. It is known to have application in music, art, architecture, and biology. The Greeks used the Golden Mean in constructing the Parthenon. The Egyptians used the Golden Ratio in building the Great Pyramid of Gizeh. The properties of the ratio were known to Pythagoras, Plato, and Leonardo da Vinci.

Some researchers have gone to great lengths to discover Fibonacci relationships. One actually measured the navel height of 65 women and found it averaged .618 of their total height. (We don't know whether the researcher measured from the top or bottom of the navel or, for that matter, why such a measurement would have occurred to anyone in the first place.) It should be sufficient to acknowledge here that Fibonacci relationships do seem to recur throughout nature and in virtually all areas of human activity.

THE LOGARITHMIC SPIRAL

It's beyond the scope of this chapter to get into a discussion of Golden Sections, Golden Rectangles, and Logarithmic Spirals, or even the mathematical basis of the wave theory and the Fibonacci sequence. It should probably be mentioned, however, that a logarithmic spiral can be constructed based on the Golden Ratio which, it is believed, describes part of the growth pattern seen throughout the entire Universe. It is further believed that this spiral maintains its constant form from the smallest to the largest elements of nature. Two such examples are the shell of the snail and the shape of the galaxy, both of which show the same logarithmic spiral. (The human ear is another example.) Finally, and more to the point, it is believed that the stock market should follow this same growth spiral because the market, besides representing an example of mass human behavior, is one manifestation of the natural growth phenomenon that characterizes all human progress.

FIBONACCI RATIOS AND RETRACEMENTS

It was already stated that wave theory is comprised of three aspects—wave form, ratio, and time. We've already discussed wave form, which is the most important of the three. Let's talk now about the application of the *Fibonacci ratios and retracements*. These relationships can apply to both price and time, although the former is considered to be the more reliable. We'll come back later to the aspect of time.

First of all, a glance back at Figures 13.1 and 13.3 shows that the basic wave form always breaks down into Fibonacci numbers. One complete cycle comprises eight waves, five up and three down—all Fibonacci numbers. Two further subdivisions will produce 34 and 144 waves—also Fibonacci numbers. The mathematical basis of the wave theory on the Fibonacci sequence, however, goes beyond just wave counting. There's also the question of proportional relationships between the different waves. The following are among the most commonly used Fibonacci ratios:

1. Because only one of the three impulse waves extends, the other two are equal in time and magnitude. If wave 5 extends, waves 1 and 3 should be about equal. If wave 3 extends, waves 1 and 5 tend toward equality.

2. A minimum target for the top of wave 3 can be obtained by multiplying the length of wave 1 by 1.618 and adding that total to the bottom of 2.

3. The top of wave 5 can be approximated by multiplying wave 1 by 3.236 (2 × 1.618) and adding that value to the top or bottom of wave 1 for maximum and minimum targets.

4. Where waves 1 and 3 are about equal, and wave 5 is expected to extend, a price objective can be obtained by measuring the distance from the bottom of wave 1 to the top of wave 3, multiplying by 1.618, and adding the result to the bottom of 4.

5. For corrective waves, in a normal 5-3-5 zig-zag correction, wave c is often about equal to the length of wave a.

6. Another way to measure the possible length of wave c is to multiply .618 by the length of wave a and subtract that result from the bottom of wave a.

7. In the case of a flat 3-3-5 correction, where the b wave reaches or exceeds the top of wave a, wave c will be about 1.618 the length of a.

8. In a symmetrical triangle, each successive wave is related to its previous wave by about .618.

Fibonacci Percentage Retracements

There are several other possible ratios, but the previously listed ones are the most commonly used. The ratios help to determine price objectives in both impulse and corrective waves. Another way to determine price objectives is by the use of *percentage retracements*. The most commonly used numbers in retracement analysis are 61.8% (usually rounded off to 62%), 38%, and 50%. Remember from Chapter 4 that markets usually retrace previous moves by certain predictable percentages—the best known ones being 33%, 50%, and 67%. The Fibonacci sequence refines those numbers a bit further. In a strong trend, a minimum retracement is usually around 38%. In a weaker trend, the maximum percentage retracement is usually 62%.

It was pointed out earlier that the Fibonacci ratios approach .618 only after the first four numbers. The first three ratios are 1/1 (100%), 1/2 (50%), and 2/3 (67%). Many students of Elliott may be unaware that the famous 50% retracement is actually a Fibonacci ratio, as is the two-thirds retracement. (The one-third retracement is also part of the Elliott picture, being an alternate Fibonacci ratio.) A complete retracement (100%) of a previous bull or bear market also should mark an important support or resistance area.

FIBONACCI TIME TARGETS

We haven't said too much about the aspect of time in wave analysis. There's no question that Fibonacci time relationships exist. It's just that they're harder to predict and are considered by some Elliotticians to be the least important of the three aspects of the theory. Fibonacci time targets are found by counting forward from significant tops and bottoms. On a daily chart, the analyst counts forward the number of trading days from an important turning point with the expectation that future tops or bottoms will occur on Fibonacci days—that is, on the 13th, 21st, 34th, 55th, or 89th trading day in the future. The same technique can be used on weekly, monthly, or even yearly charts. On the weekly chart, the analyst picks a significant top or bottom and looks for weekly time targets that fall on Fibonacci numbers.

COMBINING ALL THREE ASPECTS OF WAVE THEORY

The ideal situation occurs when wave form, ratio analysis, and time targets come together. Suppose that a study of waves reveals that a fifth wave has been completed, that wave 5 has gone 1.618 times the distance from the bottom of wave 1 to the top of wave 3, and that the time from the beginning of the trend has been 13 weeks from a previous low and 34 weeks from a previous top. Suppose further that the fifth wave has lasted 21 days. Odds would be pretty good that an important top was near.

A study of price charts in both stocks and futures markets reveals a number of Fibonacci time relationships. Part of the problem, however, is the variety of possible relationships. Fibonacci time targets can be taken from top to top, top to bottom, bottom to bottom, and bottom to top. These relationships can always be found after the fact. It's not always clear which of the possible relationships are relevant to the current trend.

FIBONACCI NUMBERS IN THE STUDY OF CYCLES

We'll have a lot more to say about the importance of time in market forecasting in the next chapter on *time cycles*. It suffices to state here that Fibonacci numbers keep cropping up, even in cycles analysis. As an illustration, one of the best known long-term economic cycles, the 54-year Kondratieff Cycle, is remarkably close to the Fibonacci number 55, and has a strong influence on most commodity markets. Before leaving this fascinating set of numbers, it should also be mentioned that they have proven useful in other areas of analysis. As an example, Fibonacci numbers are often used in moving average analysis. This shouldn't be surprising because the most successful moving averages are supposedly those that are tied into the dominant cycles of the various markets.

ELLIOTT WAVE APPLIED TO STOCKS VERSUS COMMODITIES

We've already touched on some of the differences in applying wave theory to stocks and commodities. For example, wave 3 tends to extend in stocks and wave 5 in commodities. The unbreakable rule that wave 4 can never overlap wave 1 in stocks is not as rigid in commodities. (Intra-day penetrations can occur on futures charts.) Sometimes charts of the cash market in commodities give a clearer Elliott pattern than the futures market. The use of continuation charts in commodity futures markets also produces distortions that may affect long-term Elliott patterns.

Possibly the most significant difference between the two areas is that major bull markets in commodities can be "contained," meaning that bull market highs do not always exceed previous bull market highs. It is possible in commodity markets for a completed five-wave bull trend to fall short of a previous bull market high. The major tops formed in many commodity markets in the 1980 to 1981 period failed to exceed major tops formed seven and eight years earlier. This difference has important implications because it calls into question the existence of the long-term growth spiral so critical to stock market analysis. As a final comparison between the two areas, it appears that the best Elliott patterns in commodity markets arise from breakouts from long-term extended bases.

It is important to keep in mind that wave theory was originally meant to be applied to the stock market averages. It doesn't work as well in individual common stocks. It's quite possible that it doesn't work that well in some of the more thinly traded futures markets as well because mass psychology is one of the important foundations on which the theory rests. Gold, as an illustration, is an excellent vehicle for wave analysis because of its wide following.

SUMMARY AND CONCLUSIONS

Let's briefly summarize the more important elements of wave theory and then try to put it into proper perspective.

1. A complete bull market cycle is made up of eight waves, five up waves followed by three down waves.

2. A trend divides into five waves in the direction of the next longer trend.

3. Corrections always take place in three waves.

4. The two types of simple corrections are zig-zags (5-3-5) and flats (3-3-5).

5. Triangles are usually fourth waves, and always precede the final wave. Triangles can also be B corrective waves.

6. Waves can be expanded into longer waves and subdivided into shorter waves.

7. Sometimes one of the impulse waves extends. The other two should then be equal in time and magnitude.

8. The Fibonacci sequence is the mathematical basis of the Elliott Wave Theory.

9. The number of waves follows the Fibonacci sequence.

10. Fibonacci ratios and retracements are used to determine price objectives. The most common retracements are 62%, 50%, and 38%.

11. The rule of alternation warns not to expect the same thing twice in succession.

12. Bear markets should not fall below the bottom of the previous fourth wave.

13. Wave 4 should not overlap wave 1 (not as rigid in futures).

14. The Elliott Wave Theory is comprised of wave forms, ratios, and time, in that order of importance.

15. The theory was originally applied to stock market averages and does not work as well on individual stocks.

16. The theory works best in those commodity markets with the largest public following, such as gold.

17. The principal difference in commodities is the existence of contained bull markets.

The Elliott Wave Principle may very well be the most comprehensive technical theory applied to the stock and futures markets. It builds on the more classical approaches, such as Dow Theory and traditional chart patterns. Most of those price patterns can be explained as part of the Elliott Wave structure. It builds on the concept of "swing objectives" by using Fibonacci ratio projections and percentage retracements. I mentioned in the introduction to this chapter that much of the material on the Elliott Wave Principle would sound familiar. The Elliott Wave Principle takes all of these factors into consideration, but goes beyond them by giving them more order and increased predictability.

Wave Theory Should Be Used in Conjunction with Other Technical Tools

No one theory, however, holds all the answers. I have used Elliott Wave Theory and Fibonacci numbers successfully for many years. My experience does not support the claim that all commodity market movement can be explained by precise Elliott patterns. There are times when Elliott pictures are clear and other times when they are not. When I see them, I use them. When I don't see them, I look elsewhere for clues. Trying to force unclear market action into an Elliott format, and ignoring other technical tools in the process, is an abuse of the theory and can lead to disaster. The key is to view Elliott Wave Theory as a partial answer to the puzzle of market forecasting. Using it in conjunction with all of the other technical theories in this book will, in my opinion, increase its value and improve your chances for success.

REFERENCE MATERIAL

The two best sources of information on Elliott Wave Theory and the Fibonacci numbers are *The Major Works of R.N. Elliott*, edited by Robert R. Prechter, Jr., and the *Elliott Wave Principle* by Frost and Prechter, both books published by New Classics Library, P.O. Box 1618, Gainesville, GA 30503. All of the diagrams used in Figures 13.1 through 13.33 are from the *Elliott Wave Principle* and are reproduced in this chapter through the courtesy of New Classics Library. Reference has already been made to the two newsletters published by New Classics Library, "The Elliott Wave Theorist" by Robert Prechter and "The Elliott Wave Commodity Letter" by David A. Weis.

A primer booklet on the Fibonacci numbers, *Understanding Fibonacci Numbers* by Edward D. Dobson, is available from Traders Press, P.O. Box 10344, Greenville, S.C. 29607. That work also includes an excellent bibliography of materials related to the application of the Fibonacci sequence.

In his book, *Commodity Trading Systems and Methods* (New York, NY: John Wiley & Sons, 1978, pp. 192-197), P.J. Kaufman contains some unique ideas on the Fibonacci numbers, including a discussion of how to increase their effectiveness by combining them with Lucas numbers.

Not all of the literature on Elliott Wave Theory is favorable. For a more negative review of Elliott's ideas, you might want to read "Who is R.N. Elliott and Why is He Making Waves?" by Fred Gehm, in the January/February 1983 issue of the *Financial Analysts Journal.*

EXAMPLES OF ELLIOTT WAVES IN ACTION

Figures 13.34 to 13.41 demonstrate some of the more important aspects of Elliott Wave Theory applied to the commodity futures markets.

Figure 13.34 An example of a five wave bull advance. Notice also how the top of wave 5 occurred at the first channel line. (Courtesy of Commodity Research Bureau, a Knight-Ridder Business Information Service.)

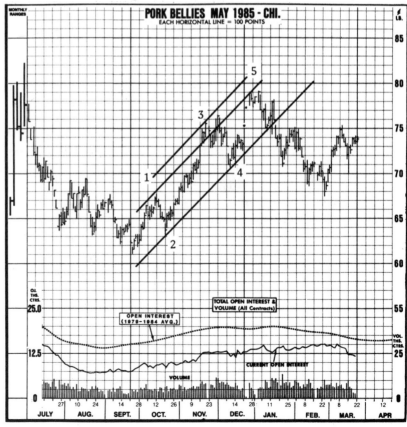

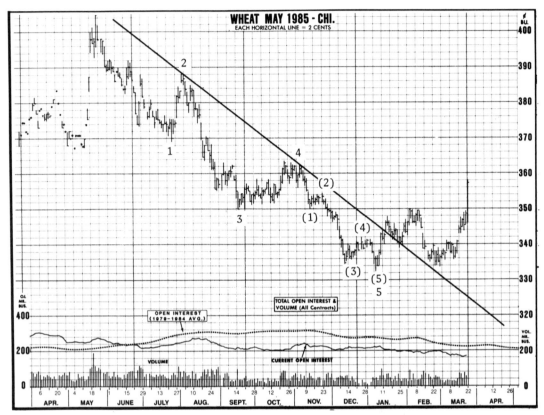

Figure 13.35 An example of a five wave decline. The top of wave 4 should not overlap the bottom of wave 1. If you look closely, you'll see that wave 5 itself is subdivided into five smaller waves. The best trendlines are often drawn connecting waves 2 and 4. (Courtesy of Commodity Research Bureau, a Knight-Ridder Business Information Service.)

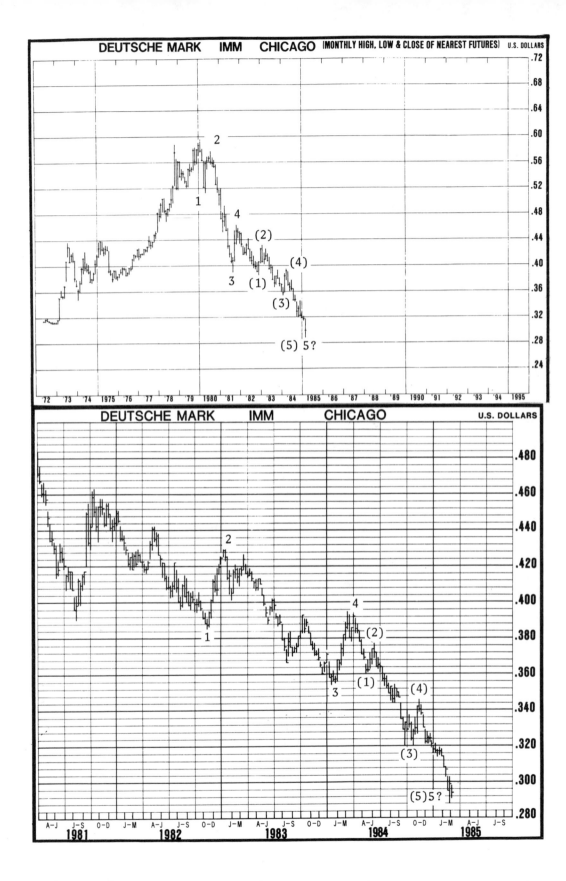

DEUTSCHE MARK   IMM   CHICAGO   (MONTHLY HIGH, LOW & CLOSE OF NEAREST FUTURES)   U.S. DOLLARS

DEUTSCHE MARK   IMM   CHICAGO   U.S. DOLLARS

Figure 13.36 (On page 404.) The upper monthly chart shows five major waves on the downside, with the last wave breaking down into five. The bottom weekly chart shows a further breakdown. Notice all of the five wave declines. The last decline from early 1984 also subdivided into five, suggesting a bottom may be near. (Courtesy of Commodity Research Bureau, a Knight-Ridder Business Information Service.)

Figure 13.37 Another example of a five wave advance. Notice the channel lines. Also, see how each of the impulse waves (upwaves) subdivide into five smaller waves. Wave 4 was a triangle consolidation which also subdivided into five waves. Triangles are usually wave 4. (Courtesy of Commodity Research Bureau, a Knight-Ridder Business Information Service.)

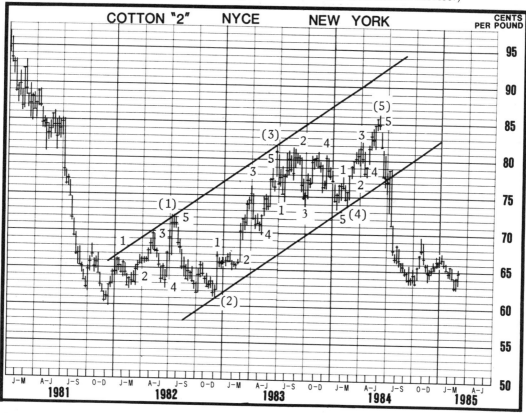

Figure 13.38 Another example of a five wave decline. Prices are now in a fifth wave decline from the early 1983 high over 14.00. Notice how major wave 3 subdivided into five waves. The fifth major wave beginning near 10.00 also appears to have broken down into five waves. Notice the triangle in wave 4 of the last wave. (Courtesy of Commodity Research Bureau, a Knight-Ridder Business Information Service.)

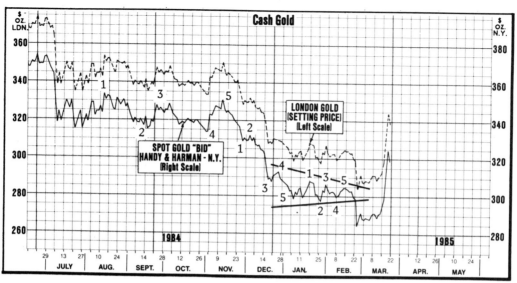

Figure 13.39   Notice in particular here how the consolidation patterns subdivided into five waves. The symmetrical triangle near the bottom of the
chart (Jan./Feb.) broke down into five waves. Triangles usually precede the
final wave. (Courtesy of Commodity Research Bureau, a Knight-Ridder Business Information Service.)

Figure 13.40   On this weekly chart, the entire 13-month correction (a Fibonacci number) retraced just a shade under 38% before turning back up
again. Take note of the classic A-B-C correction, with the C wave subdividing
into five waves. (Courtesy of Commodity Research Bureau, a Knight-Ridder
Business Information Service.)

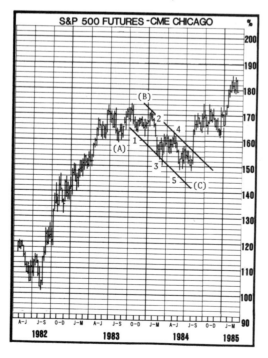

Figure 13.41 The correction from September to December also formed a classic A-B-C correction, with the C wave subdividing into five waves. The downside correction was a shade over 50%. Notice that the subsequent advance may also have completed five waves. (Courtesy of Commodity Research Bureau, a Knight-Ridder Business Information Service.)

Figures 13.42 through 13.49, however, use some advanced Fibonacci applications that require some brief explanation.

FIBONACCI FAN LINES, ARCS, AND TIME ZONES

Technical analysis software available from Compu Trac in New Orleans makes it possible to apply these three Fibonacci concepts—*fan lines, arcs,* and *time zones*. Time zones were explained earlier. These vertical lines on the charts appear by counting forward from significant tops or bottoms to identify Fibonacci time periods in the future. On these charts, a vertical bar is placed at period numbers 5, 13, 21, 34, 55, 89, 144, 233, and so on to the right of the starting point. Fibonacci numbers 1, 2, and 3 are skipped. The intention is to identify significant changes in trend or continued movement in the same direction as the current trend at or near the Fibonacci time targets.

Fibonacci fan lines are constructed much like speedlines (discussed in Chapter 4). Two extreme points are identified on the chart, usually an important top and bottom. A vertical line is then drawn from the second extreme to the beginning of the move. That vertical line is then divided by 38%, 50%, and 62% with lines drawn through each point from the beginning of the trend. These three lines should function as support and resistance points on subsequent reactions by measuring 38%, 50%, and 62% Fibonacci retracements.

Figure 13.42   Some examples of Fibonacci fan lines. These lines are drawn like speedlines but measure 38%, 50%, and 62% retracements. They can be used to determine support and resistance zones and to generate buy and sell signals on their penetration. The lines are drawn from an important market extreme at a top or bottom.

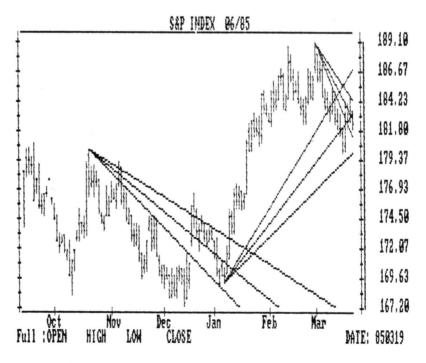

Fibonacci arcs incorporate the element of time. By using a retracement measurement similar to the fan lines, three arcs are drawn from a top or bottom based on 38%, 50%, and 62% Fibonacci parameters. These arcs identify the time as well as the place where support or resistance is likely to function. Fan lines and arcs are usually used together. Time zones can also be incorporated into the chart. Because all three tools measure important support or resistance areas, trend signals would be stronger in those situations where two or more of the lines coincide. A glance through the accompanying charts should give a better idea of what these concepts look like. Obviously, the user would have to do a fair amount of experimenting to determine the best way to incorporate these more advanced Fibonacci tools into his or her market analysis. The computer and Compu Trac software make that task possible and relatively painless. Figures 13.42 through 13.49 were generated using Compu Trac software.

Figure 13.43 Examples of Fibonacci arcs. Using a measuring concept similar to the fan lines, based on 38%, 50%, and 62% retracements, the arcs help determine time targets for support and resistance to function. These arcs were measured from the December bottom. Notice how prices paused at the upper two arcs.

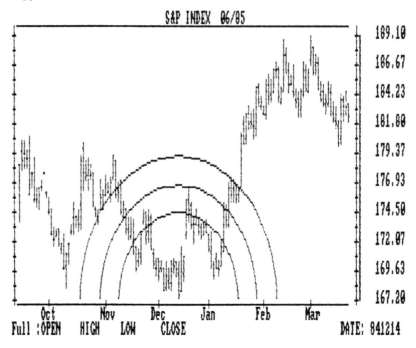

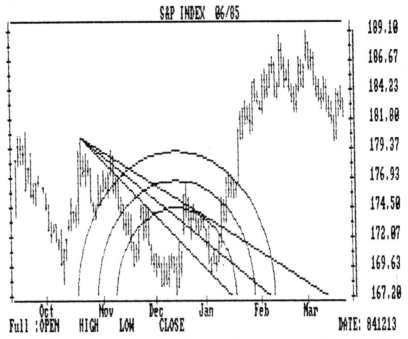

Figure 13.44 The Fibonacci fan lines and arcs can be used together. This chart shows both techniques used together. Wherever a fan line and arc meet, a stronger support or resistance area would be indicated.

Figure 13.45 Fibonacci time targets are found by counting forward from important tops and bottoms. In this example, Fibonacci time targets are taken from the October peak. The vertical lines indicate the 5th, 8th, 13th, 21st, 34th, 55th, and 89th trading days in the future. Those days may mark important turning points in the market.

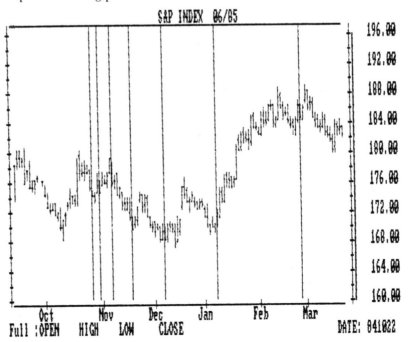

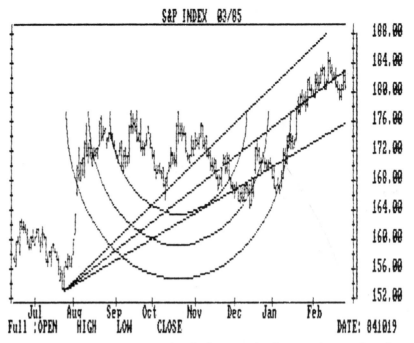

Figure 13.46 Another example of Fibonacci fan lines and arcs taken from the July 1984 low to the October high. Notice how the arcs provided support under the market and helped mark the time of the market turns.

Figure 13.47 Fibonacci time targets applied to the same chart. Notice how well the time targets called some of the market turns. These Fibonacci time targets were measured from the August bottom. Notice that the February top was about 144 days from the August bottom.

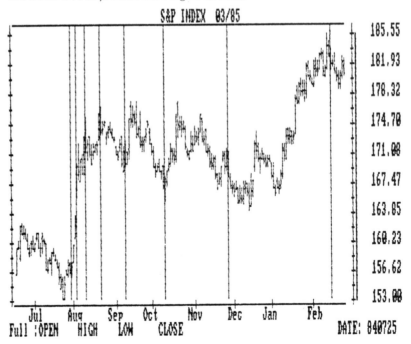

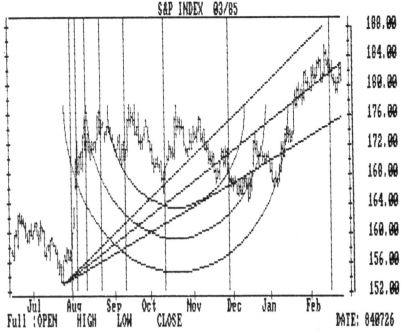

Figure 13.48 Fibonacci fan lines, arcs, and time target lines applied to the same chart. Stronger signals would obviously occur wherever more than one line come together.

Figure 13.49 Time targets applied to a weekly chart of the same futures contract. Virtually every vertical Fibonacci time target represented a market turn, measured from the summer bottom. Take particular notice of the fact that the December bottom was 21 weeks from the summer bottom.

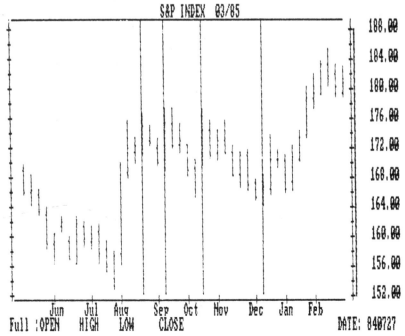

14
Time Cycles

INTRODUCTION

Our main focus up to this point has been on price movement, and not too much has been said about the importance of *time* in solving the forecasting puzzle. The question of time has been present by implication throughout our entire coverage of technical analysis, but has generally been relegated to secondary consideration. In this chapter, we're going to view the problem of forecasting through the eyes of cyclic analysts who believe that *time cycles* hold the ultimate key to understanding why markets move up or down. In the process, we're going to add the important dimension of time to our growing list of analytical tools. Instead of just asking ourselves *which way* and *how far* a market will go, we'll start asking *when* it will arrive there or even *when* the move will begin.

Consider the standard daily bar chart. The vertical axis gives the price scale. But that's only half of the relevant data. The horizontal scale gives the time horizon. Therefore, the bar chart is really a time and price chart. Yet, many traders concentrate solely on price data to the exclusion of time considerations. When we study chart patterns, we're aware that there is a relationship between the amount of time it takes for those patterns to form and the potential for subsequent market moves. The longer a trendline or a support or resistance level remains in effect, the more valid it becomes. Moving averages require input as to the proper time period to use. Even oscillators require some decision as to how many days to measure. In the previous chapter, we considered the usefulness of Fibonacci time targets.

It seems clear then that all phases of technical analysis depend to some extent on time considerations. Yet those considerations are not really applied in a consistent and dependable manner. That's where time cycles come into play. Instead of playing a secondary or supporting role in market movement, cyclic analysts hold that time cycles are the determining factor in bull and bear markets. Not only is time the dominant factor, but all other technical tools can be improved by incorporating cycles. Moving averages and oscillators, for example, can be optimized by tying them to dominant cycles. Trendline analysis can be made more precise with cyclic analysis by determining which are valid trendlines and which are not. Price pattern analysis can be enhanced if combined with cyclic peaks and troughs. By the use of "time windows," price movement can be filtered in such a way that extraneous action can be ignored and primary emphasis placed only on such times when important cycle tops and bottoms are due to occur.

CYCLES

I usually begin my lecture on cycles by asking the class if anyone can predict the future. The response is usually a strained silence. At that point, I pull out the day's local newspaper and begin to do some "predicting." Tomorrow's sunrise will take place at 6:47 A.M. with sunset at 4:35 P.M. High tide tomorrow at Montauk Point will be at 4:36 A.M. and 5:03 P.M. The next new moon will be on November 22 with a full moon on December 8. While ignoring all the smirks these predictions have provoked, I ask if anyone doubts any of them. The class response is always amusing. While no one doubts everything will happen on schedule, they act as if I've played some bad joke on them. After all, I wasn't really predicting the future. Or, was I?

The purpose of the exercise is to demonstrate a couple of points. First, that we do predict the future every day with astounding accuracy, at least in the area of natural or astronomical events. Second, that a high level of accuracy is possible because of the existence of certain clearly identified recurring cycles. Yet the reality of those cycles has become so much a part of our lives that we do not consider predictions based on those cycles as significant. All we're doing is projecting those cycles into the future and assuming they will continue to function.

But what if we could identify similar recurring cycles in other areas of human activity? What if it could be demonstrated that most areas of human existence show certain recurring cycles? Wouldn't it then be possible to predict the future by extrapolating those cycles into the future? What if it could be shown that business cycles, stock market cycles, and commodity futures market cycles also existed? Wouldn't it make sense to use those cycles to predict future market trends?

The most intriguing book I've ever read on the subject of cycles was written by Edward R. Dewey, one of the pioneers of cyclic analysis, with Og Mandino entitled *Cycles: The Mysterious Forces That Trigger Events* (Manor Books, Inc., New York, 1973). Thousands of seemingly unrelated cycles were isolated spanning hundreds and, in some cases, thousands of years. Everything from the 9.6-year cycle in Atlantic salmon abundance to the 22.20-year cycle in international battles from 1415 to 1930 was tracked. An average cycle of sunspot activity since 1527 was found to be 11.11 years. Several economic cycles, including the 18.33-year cycle in real estate activity and a 9.2-year stock market cycle, were presented. (See Figures 14.1 and 14.2.)

Two startling conclusions are discussed by Dewey. First, that many of the cycles of seemingly unrelated phenomena clustered around similar periods. On p. 188 of his book, Dewey listed 37 different examples of the 9.6-year cycle, including caterpillar abundance in New Jersey, coyote abundance in Canada, wheat acreage in the U.S., and cotton prices in the U.S. Why should such unrelated activities show the same cycles?

The second discovery was that these similar cycles acted in synchrony, that is, they turned at the same time. Figure 14.3 shows 12 different examples of the 18.2-year cycle including marriages, immigration, and stock prices in the U.S. Dewey's startling conclusion was that something "out there" in the universe must be causing these cycles; that there seemed to be a sort of *pulse* to the universe that accounted for the pervasive presence of these cycles throughout so many areas of human existence.

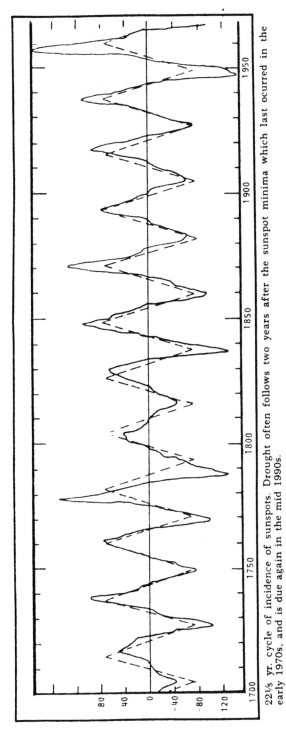

22⅕ yr. cycle of incidence of sunspots. Drought often follows two years after the sunspot minima which last occurred in the early 1970s, and is due again in the mid 1990s.

Figure 14.1 The 22.2-year cycle of incidence of sunspots. Drought often follows two years after the sunspot minima which last occurred in the early 1970s, and is due again in the mid 1990s. In the chart, the dotted line is the "ideal" cycle, and the solid line is the actual detrended data. (Courtesy of the Foundation for the Study of Cycles, Pittsburgh, PA.)

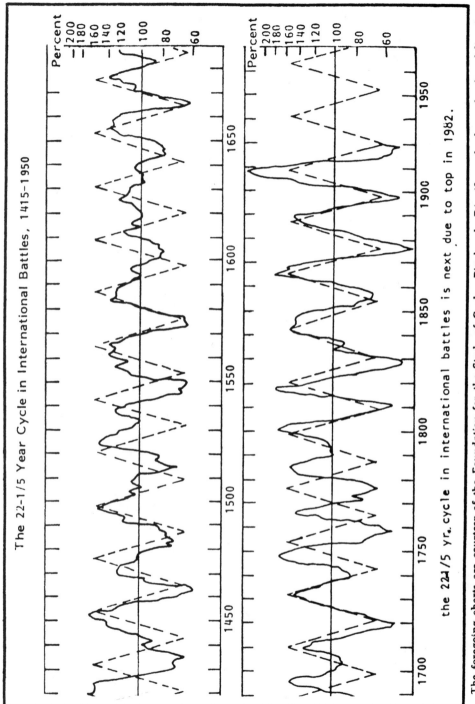

The 22-1/5 Year Cycle in International Battles, 1415–1950

Figure 14.2 The 22.2 year cycle in international battles was due to top in 1982. In the chart, the dotted line is the "ideal" cycle, and the solid line is the actual detrended data. (Courtesy of the Foundation for the Study of Cycles, Pittsburgh, P.A.)

The foregoing charts are courtesy of the *Foundation for the Study of Cycles*, Pittsburgh, PA. (In each chart, the dotted line is the "ideal" cycle, and the solid line is the actual detrended data.)

the 22-1/5 yr. cycle in international battles is next due to top in 1982.

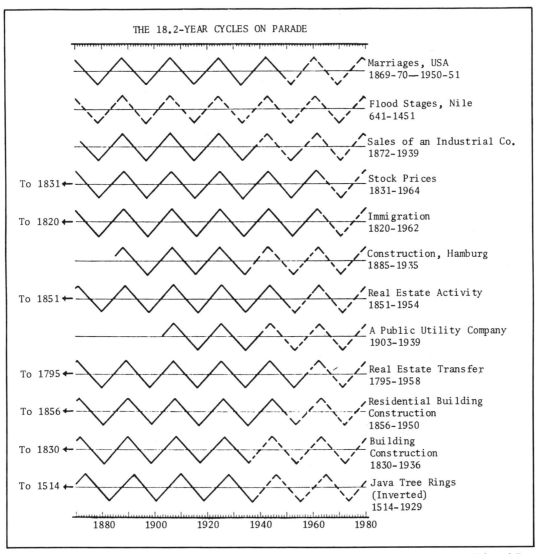

THE 18.2-YEAR CYCLES ON PARADE

Marriages, USA
1869-70—1950-51

Flood Stages, Nile
641-1451

Sales of an Industrial Co.
1872-1939

To 1831← Stock Prices
1831-1964

To 1820← Immigration
1820-1962

Construction, Hamburg
1885-1935

To 1851← Real Estate Activity
1851-1954

A Public Utility Company
1903-1939

To 1795← Real Estate Transfer
1795-1958

To 1856← Residential Building
Construction
1856-1950

To 1830← Building
Construction
1830-1936

To 1514← Java Tree Rings
(Inverted)
1514-1929

1880 1900 1920 1940 1960 1980

Figure 14.3 The 18.2-year cycles on parade. (Source: Dewey, Edward R., *Cycles: The Mysterious Forces That Trigger Events* (New York: Manor Books, 1973.)

In 1940, Dewey organized the Foundation for the Study of Cycles, located in Pittsburgh. It is the oldest organization engaged in cycles research and the recognized leader in the field. The Foundation publishes *Cycles* magazine, which presents research in many different areas including economics and business. Stock and commodity cycles are also covered.

Basic Cyclic Concepts

In 1970, J.M. Hurst authored *The Profit Magic of Stock Transaction Timing* (Prentice-Hall, Inc. Englewood Cliffs, N.J.). Although it deals mainly with stock market cycles, this book represents one of the best explanations of cycle theory available in print, and is highly recommended reading. Three years later a training course on cycles was published by Cyclitec Services, a division of Decision Models, Inc. (now owned by Cycle Sciences Corp., 718 B Street, Suite 2, San Rafael, CA 94901.)

Figure 14.4 Two cycles of a price wave. A simple, single price wave of the kind that combines to form stock and commodity price action. Only two cycles of this wave are shown, but the wave itself extends infinitely far to the left and to the right. Such waves repeat themselves cycle after cycle. As a result, once the wave is identified, its value can be determined at any past or future time. It is this characteristic of waves that provides a degree of predictability for equity price action. (Source: Cyclitec Services, a division of Decision Models, Inc., Marshalltown, IA.)

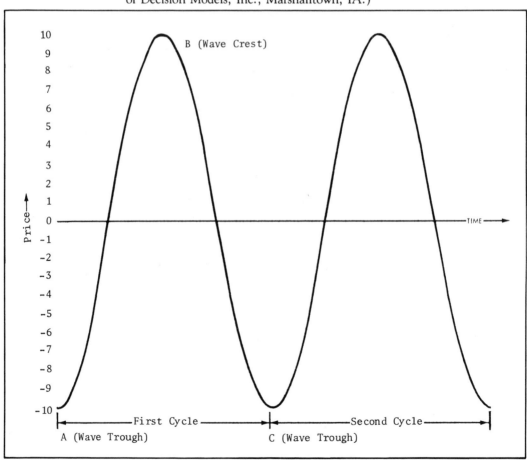

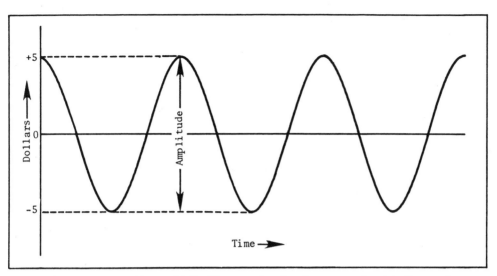

Figure 14.5 The amplitude of a wave. In this figure, the wave has an amplitude of ten dollars (from minus five dollars to plus five dollars). Amplitude is always measured from wave trough to wave crest. (Source: Cyclitec Services, a division of Decision Models, Inc., Marshalltown, IA.)

in Marshalltown, Iowa. That course of instruction built on Hurst's work and expanded the focus to include other investment vehicles, including commodity futures. The following brief explanation of basic cyclic concepts is drawn largely from those two sources.

First, let's see what a cycle looks like and discuss its three main characteristics. Figure 14.4 shows two repetitions of a price cycle. The cycle bottoms are called *troughs* and the tops referred to as *crests*. Notice that the two waves shown here are measured from trough to trough. *Cyclic analysts prefer to measure cycle lengths from low to low.* Measurements can be taken between crests, but they are not considered to be as stable or reliable as those taken between the troughs. Therefore, common practice is to measure the beginning and end of a cyclic wave at a low point, as shown in this example.

The three qualities of a cycle are *amplitude, period,* and *phase.* Amplitude measures the height of the wave as shown in Figure 14.5, and is expressed in dollars, cents, or points. The period of a wave, as shown in Figure 14.6, is the time between troughs. In this example, the period is 20 days. The phase is a measure of the time location of a wave trough. In Figure 14.7, the phase difference between two waves is shown. Because there are several different cycles occurring at the same time, *phasing* allows the cyclic analyst to study the relationships between the different cycle lengths. Phasing is also used to identify

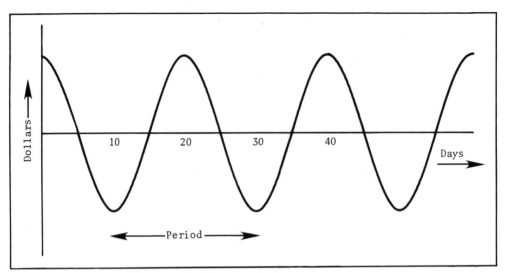

Figure 14.6 The period of a wave. In this figure, the wave has a period of 20 days, which is shown measured between two consecutive wave troughs. The period could just as well have been measured between wave crests. But in the case of price waves, the wave troughs are usually more clearly defined than the wave crests for reasons that will be discussed later. Consequently, price wave periods are most often measured from trough to trough. (Source: Cyclitec Services, a division of Decision Models, Inc., Marshalltown, IA.)

Figure 14.7 The phase difference between two waves. The phase difference between the two waves shown is six days. This phase difference is measured between the troughs of the two waves because, again, wave troughs are the most convenient points to identify in the case of price waves. (Source: Cyclitec Services, a division of Decision Models, Inc., Marshalltown, IA.)

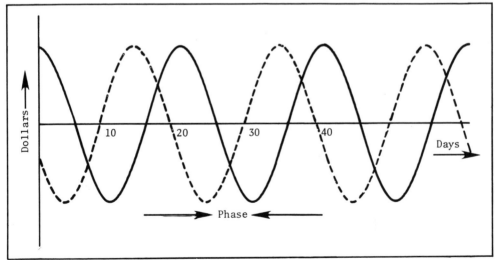

the date of the last cycle low. If, for example, a 20-day cycle bottomed ten days earlier, the date of the next cycle low can be determined. Once the amplitude, period, and phase of a cycle are known, the cycle can theoretically be extrapolated into the future. Assuming the cycle remains fairly constant, it can then be used to estimate future peaks and troughs. That is the basis of the cyclic approach in its simplest form.

Cyclic Principles

Let's take a look now at some of the principles that underlie the cyclic philosophy. The four most important ones are the Principles of Summation, Harmonicity, Synchronicity, and Proportionality.

The Principle of Summation holds that all price movement is the simple addition of all active cycles. Figure 14.8 demonstrates how the price pattern on the top is formed by simply adding together the two different cycles at the bottom of the chart. Notice, in particular, the appearance of the double top in composite wave C. Cycle theory holds that all price patterns are formed by the interaction of two or more different cycles. We'll come back to this point again. The Principle of Summation gives us an important insight into the rationale of cyclic forecasting. Let's assume that all price action is just the sum of different cycle lengths. Assume further that each of those individual cycles could be isolated and measured. Assume also that each of those cycles will continue to fluctuate into the future. Then by simply continuing each cycle into the future and summing them back together again, the future price trend should be the result. Or, so the theory goes.

The Principle of Harmonicity simply means that neighboring waves are usually related by a small, whole number. That number is usually *two*. For example, if a 20-day cycle exists, the next shorter cycle will usually be half its length, or ten days. The next longer cycle would then be 40 days. If you'll remember back to the discussion on the *four-week rule* (Chapter 9), the principle of harmonics was invoked to explain the validity of using a shorter two-week rule and a longer eight weeks.

The Principle of Synchronicity refers to the strong tendency for waves of differing lengths to bottom at about the same time. Figure 14.9 is meant to show both harmonicity and synchronicity. Wave B at the bottom of the chart is half the length of wave A. Wave A includes two repetitions of the smaller wave B, showing harmonicity between the two waves. Notice also that when wave A bottoms, wave

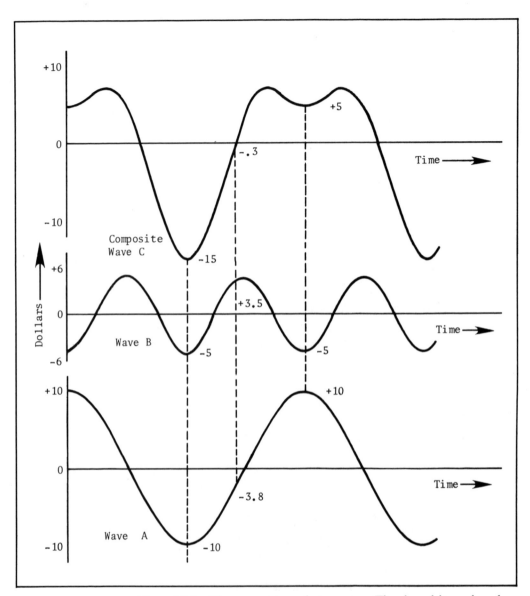

Figure 14.8 The summation of two waves. The dotted lines show how, at each point in time, the value of wave A is added to the value of wave B to produce the value of composite wave C. (Source: Cyclitec Services, a division of Decision Models, Inc., Marshalltown, IA.)

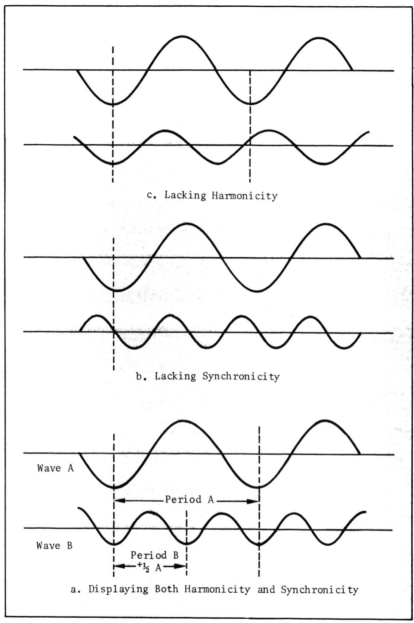

Figure 14.9 Harmonicity and synchronicity. (Source: Cyclitec Services, a division of Decision Models, Inc., Marshalltown, IA.)

B tends to do the same, demonstrating synchronicity between the two. Synchronicity also means that similar cycle lengths of different markets will tend to turn together.

The Principle of Proportionality describes the relationship between cycle period and amplitude. Cycles with longer periods (lengths) should have proportionally wider amplitudes. The amplitude, or height, of a 40-day cycle, for example, should be about double that of a 20-day cycle.

The Principles of Variation and Nominality

There are two other cyclic principles that describe cycle behavior in a more general sense—*The Principles of Variation and Nominality.*

The Principle of Variation, as the name implies, is a recognition of the fact that all of the other cyclic principles already mentioned—summation, harmonicity, synchronicity, and proportionality—are just strong tendencies and not hard-and-fast rules. Some "variation" can and usually does occur in the real world.

The Principle of Nominality is based on the premise that, despite the differences that exist in the various markets and allowing for some variation in the implementing of cyclic principles, there seems to be a nominal set of harmonically related cycles that affect all markets. And that nominal model of cycle lengths can be used as a starting point in the analysis of any market. Figure 14.10b shows a simplified

Figure 14.10a   The nominal cycle model.

Years	Months	Weeks	Days
18			
9			
	54		
	18	77.94	
	9	38.97	
		19.48	
		9.74	68.2
		4.97	34.1
			17.0
			8.5
			4.3

version of that nominal model. The model begins with an 18-year cycle and proceeds to each successively lower cycle *half* its length. The only exception is the relationship between 54 and 18 months which is a *third* instead of *half*.

When we discuss the various cycle lengths in the individual futures markets, we'll see that this nominal model does account for most cyclic activity. For now, look at the "Days" column. Notice 40, 20, 10, and 5 days. You'll recognize immediately that these numbers account for most of the popular moving average lengths. Even the well-known 4-, 9-, and 18-day moving average technique is a variation of the 5-, 10-, and 20-day numbers. Many oscillators use five, ten, and 20 days. Weekly rule breakouts use the same numbers translated into two, four, and eight weeks.

HOW CYCLIC CONCEPTS HELP EXPLAIN CHARTING TECHNIQUES

Chapter 3 in Hurst's book explains in great detail how the standard charting techniques—trendlines and channels, chart patterns, and moving averages—can be better understood and used to greater advantage when coordinated with cyclic principles. Figure 14.11 helps explain the existence of trendlines and channels. The flat cycle wave along the bottom becomes a rising price channel when it is summed

Figure 14.10b The simplified nominal model. (Source: Cyclitec Services, a division of Decision Models, Inc., Marshalltown, IA.)

Years	Months	Weeks	Days
18			
9			
	54		
	18		
		40	
		20	
			80
			40
			20
			10
			5

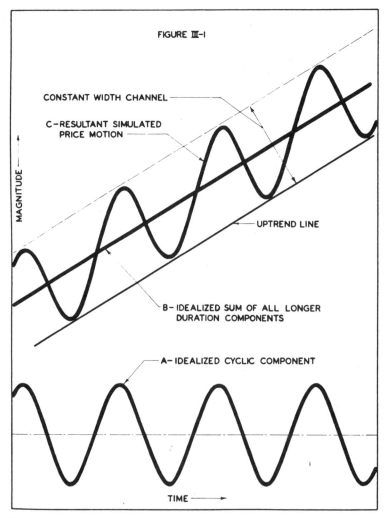

Figure 14.11 Channel formation. (Source: Hurst, J.M., *The Profit Magic of Stock Transaction Timing* [Englewood Cliffs, N.J.: Prentice-Hall, Inc., 1970].)

with a rising line representing the long-term uptrend. Notice how much the horizontal cycle along the bottom of the chart resembles an oscillator.

Figure 14.12 from the same chapter shows how a *head and shoulders* topping pattern is formed by combining two cycle lengths with a rising line representing the sum of all longer-duration components. Hurst goes on to explain double tops, triangles, flags, and pennants through the application of cycles. The "V" top or bottom, for example, occurs when an intermediate cycle turns at the exact same time as its next longer and next shorter duration cycles.

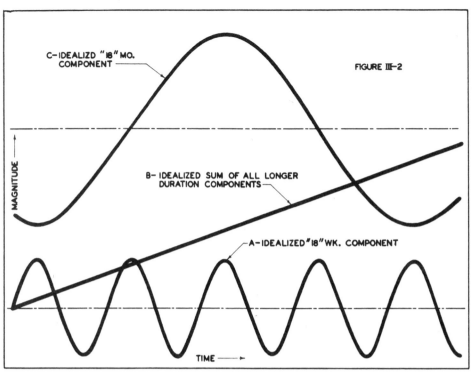

Figure 14.12a Adding another component. (Source: Hurst, J.M., *The Profit Magic of Stock Transaction Timing* [Englewood Cliffs, N.J.: Prentice-Hall, Inc., 1970].)

Figure 14.12b The Summation Principle Applied. (Source: Hurst, J.M., *The Profit Magic of Stock Transaction Timing* [Englewood Cliffs, N.J.: Prentice-Hall, Inc., 1970].)

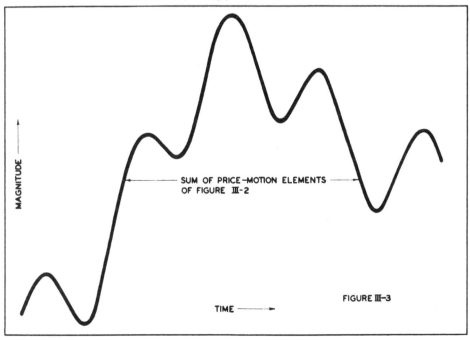

Hurst also addresses how moving averages can be made more useful if their lengths are synchronized with dominant cycle lengths. Students of traditional charting techniques should gain additional insight into how these popular chart pictures form and maybe even why they work by reading Hurst's chapter, entitled "Verify Your Chart Patterns."

DOMINANT CYCLES

There are many different cycles affecting commodity futures markets. The only ones of real value for forecasting purposes are the *dominant cycles*. Dominant cycles are those that consistently affect futures prices and that can be clearly identified. Most futures markets have at least five dominant cycles. In an earlier chapter on the use of long-term charts, it was stressed that all technical analysis should begin with the long-term picture, gradually working toward the shorter term. That principle holds true in the study of cycles. The proper procedure is to begin the analysis with a study of long-term dominant cycles, which can span several years; then work toward the intermediate, which can be several weeks to several months; finally, the very short-term cycles, from several hours to several days, can be used for timing of entry and exit points and to help confirm the turning points of the longer cycles.

Classification of Cycles

Cyclic analysts differ somewhat on the classification of cycle lengths and even in the cycle lengths themselves. (See Figure 14.13.) Taking this ambiguity into account, we'll attempt here to identify the major cycle categories. The general categories are: *long-term cycles* (two or more years in length), the *seasonal cycle* (one year), the *primary or intermediate cycle* (nine to 26 weeks), and the *trading cycle* (four weeks). These are the major cycles, but there are others as well. Some markets have a $\frac{1}{2}$ *primary cycle* in between the primary and the trading cycles. The trading cycle breaks down into two shorter *alpha* and *beta* cycles, which average two weeks each. (The labels Primary, Trading, Alpha, and Beta were first used by Walt Bressert of HAL Market Cycles to describe the various cycle lengths.)

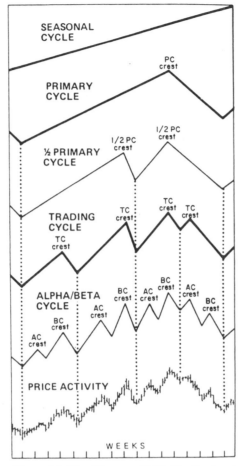

Figure 14.13   (Source: HAL Cyclic Analyst's Kit, p. 1-2.)

The Kondratieff Wave

There are even longer-range cycles at work. Perhaps the best known is the approximate 54-year Kondratieff cycle. This controversial long cycle of economic activity, first discovered by a Russian economist in the 1920s by the name of Nikolai D. Kondratieff, appears to exert a major influence on virtually all stock and commodity prices. In particular, a 54-year cycle has been identified in interest rates, copper, cotton, wheat, stocks, and wholesale commodity prices. Kondratieff tracked his "long wave" from 1789 using such factors as commodity prices, pig iron production, and wages of agricultural workers in Eng-

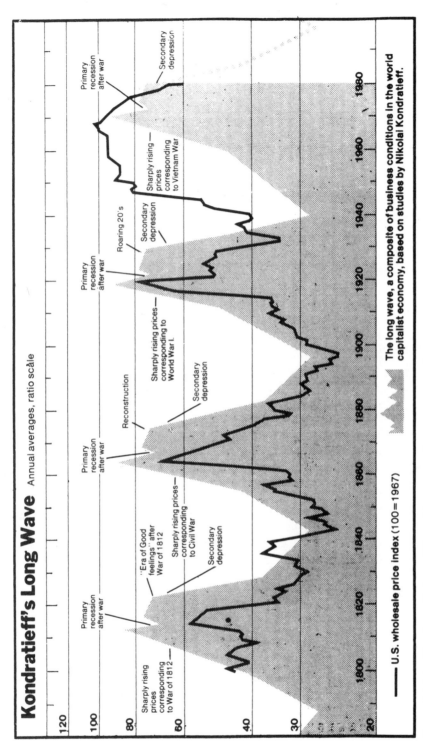

Figure 14.14 Kondratieff's Long Wave. For more information, see *The Long Wave Cycle* by Nikolai Kondratieff, translated by Guy Daniels (New York: Richardson and Snyder, 1984). That translation is the first ever from the original Russian text. (Copyright © 1984 by The New York Times Company. Reprinted by permission [May 27, 1984, p. F11.])

land. (See Figure 14.14.) The Kondratieff cycle has become a popular subject of discussion in recent years, primarily owing to the fact that its last top occurred in the 1920s, placing its next major top sometime in the 1980s. Kondratieff himself paid a heavy price for his cyclic view of capitalistic economies. He is believed to have died in a Siberian labor camp. For more information, see *The Long Wave Cycle* by Nikolai Kondratieff, translated by Guy Daniels (New York: Richardson and Snyder, 1984). That translation is the first ever from the original Russian text.

COMBINING CYCLE LENGTHS

As a general rule, long-term and seasonal cycles determine the major trend of a market. Obviously, if a two-year cycle has bottomed, it can be expected to advance for at least a year, measured from its trough to its crest. Therefore, the long-term cycle exerts major influence on market direction. Markets also have annual seasonal patterns, meaning that they tend to peak or trough at certain times of the year. Grain markets, for example, usually hit their low point around harvest time and rally from there. Seasonal moves usually last for several months.

For trading purposes, *the weekly primary cycle is the most useful.* The 3- to 6-month primary cycle is the equivalent of the intermediate trend, and generally determines which side of a market to trade. The next shorter cycle, the 4-week trading cycle, is used to establish entry and exit points in the direction of the primary trend. If the primary trend is up, troughs in the trading cycle are used for purchases. If the primary trend is down, crests in the trading cycles should be sold short. The 10-day *alpha* and *beta* cycles can be used for further fine tuning. (See Figure 14.13.)

THE IMPORTANCE OF TREND

The concept of trading in the direction of the trend is stressed throughout the body of technical analysis. In an earlier chapter, it was suggested that short-term dips should be used for purchases if the intermediate trend was up, and that short-term bulges be sold in downtrends.

In the chapter on Elliott Wave Theory, it was pointed out that five-wave moves only take place in the direction of the next larger trend. Therefore, it is necessary when using any short-term trend for timing purposes to first determine the direction of the next longer trend and then trade in the direction of that longer trend. That concept holds true in cycles. *The trend of each cycle is determined by the direction of its next longer cycle.* Or stated the other way, once the trend of a longer cycle is established, the trend of the next shorter cycle is known.

The 9- to 12-Month Cycle in the CRB Futures Price Index

Each individual futures market has its own unique set of cycle length combinations. However, there are certain general cycle lengths that seem to exert an influence on commodity markets as a whole. These cycles can best be seen on a general commodity price index, such as the *Commodity Research Bureau Futures Price Index.* (See Figure 14.15.) We've already mentioned the 54-year cycle. Some of the shorter cycles are $5^{1}/_{2}$ and 11 years. From a trading standpoint, however, the most useful cycle in the CRB Futures Index ranges from about 9 to 12 months. That averages out to a $10^{1}/_{2}$-month cycle, measured low to low.

In Chapter 8, we discussed the importance of following the CRB Futures Price Index to help determine the direction of commodity

Figure 14.15 Examples of the $10^{1}/_{2}$ month cycle in the CRB Futures Price Index. (Source: HAL Market Cycles, Tucson, AZ.)

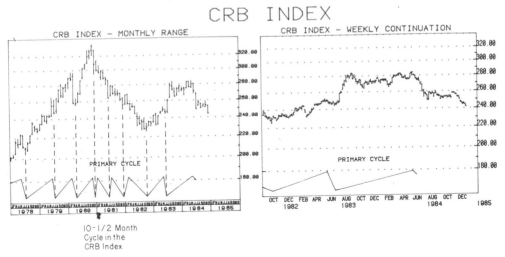

prices in general. An analysis of any commodity market must begin with a determination of which way commodity prices as a whole are moving. If commodity prices are advancing, this lends greater credence to an uptrend in any individual market. Therefore, the $10^1/_2$-month cycle in the CRB Index can be used to great advantage in any trading strategy. Because commodity markets do tend to move together, knowledge of when the next important cycle top or bottom will occur in the CRB Futures Index should have some influence on a trader's assessment of any individual market or group under consideration.

This $10^1/_2$-monthly cycle in the CRB Index has been tracked back to the 1950s. However, the cycle is not symmetrical, meaning the measurements from high to high are not as reliable as those from low to low. This is in keeping with general cyclic tendencies. There is an important implication here regarding the location of cycle highs. If the general trend of commodity prices is rising, the cycle high tends to occur later than expected. In a major downtrend, the peak tends to occur early. We'll cover this important aspect of cycle analysis in our section on *right and left translation*.

The 28-Day Trading Cycle

There is another important short-term cycle that tends to influence most commodity markets—*the 28-day trading cycle*. In other words, most markets have a tendency to form a trading cycle low every four weeks. One possible explanation for this strong cyclic tendency throughout all commodity markets is the *lunar cycle*. Burton Pugh studied the 28-day cycle in the wheat market in the 1930s (*Science and Secrets of Wheat Trading*, Lambert-Gann, Pomeroy, WA, 1978, orig., 1933) and concluded that the moon had some influence on market turning points. His theory was that wheat should be bought on a full moon and sold on a new moon. Pugh acknowledged, however, that the lunar effects were mild and could be overridden by the effects of longer cycles or important news events.

Whether or not the moon has anything to do with it, the average 28-day cycle does exist and explains many of the numbers used in the development of shorter-term indicators and trading systems. First of all, the 28-day cycle is based on calendar days. Translated into actual trading days, the number becomes 20. We've already commented on how many popular moving averages, oscillators, and weekly rules are based on the number 20 and its harmonically related shorter cycles, 10 and 5. The 5-, 10-, and 20-day moving averages are widely used along with their derivatives, 4, 9, and 18. The CRB *Futures Chart*

Service uses 10- and 40-day moving averages, with the number 40 being the next harmonically related longer cycle at twice the length of 20.

In Chapter 9, we discussed the profitability of the four-week rule developed by Richard Donchian. Buy signals were generated when a market set new four-week highs and a sell signal when a four-week low was established. Knowledge of the existence of a four-week trading cycle gives a better insight into the significance of that number and helps us to understand why the four-week rule has worked so well over the years. When a market exceeds the high of the previous four weeks, cycle logic tells us that, at the very least, the next longer cycle (the eight-week cycle) has bottomed and turned up.

LEFT AND RIGHT TRANSLATION

Many years ago as I was pursuing the study of cycles in the futures markets, I stumbled on the concept of *left and right translation*. I felt then, and I continue to feel now, that the concept of translation may very well be the most useful aspect of cycle analysis. Left and right translation refers to the shifting of the cycle peaks either to the left or the right of the ideal cycle midpoint. For example, a 20-day trading cycle is measured from low to low. The ideal peak should occur ten days into the cycle, or at the halfway point. That would allow for a ten-day advance followed by a ten-day decline. Ideal cycle peaks, however, rarely occur. Remember that most variations in cycles occur at the peaks (or crests) and not at the troughs. That's why cycle troughs are considered more reliable and are used to measure cycle lengths.

The cycle crests act differently depending on the trend of the next longer cycle. If the trend is up, the cycle crest shifts to the right of the ideal midpoint, causing right translation. If the longer trend is down, the cycle crest shifts to the left of the midpoint, causing left translation. Therefore, right translation is bullish and left translation is bearish. Stop to think about it. All we're saying here is that in a bull trend, prices will spend more time going up than down. In a bear trend, prices spend more time going down than up. Isn't that the basic definition of a trend? Only, in this case, we're talking about time instead of price.

Remember that an uptrend is defined as a series of successively rising peaks and troughs. A downtrend is a series of successively lower peaks and troughs. We can identify those peaks and troughs as cycle highs and lows. Now let's combine these two concepts of trend and translation. (See Figures 14.16 and 14.17.) As long as the peaks and troughs are moving higher, (that is, prices are in an uptrend) the cycle peaks should occur to the right of the ideal cycle midpoint. When the cycle peaks and troughs are declining (that is, prices are in a downtrend), the crests should occur earlier than the midpoint. The only time that the cycle crests occur at the midpoint is when no overriding trend influence is present, that is, in a sideways trading range when the bullish and bearish pressures are in balance.

Now let's consider the forecasting implications of right and left translation. At the very least, by observing where the midpoint occurs, we gain insight into whether the trend is up or down. As long as the peak occurs to the right, that is, as long as the time spent on the last upleg is greater than the last downleg, we can expect the uptrend to continue. When we see the crest shifting to the left, it's usually an early warning that the trend is about to change. On daily charts, this can be accomplished by simply comparing the number of days up versus the number down in the last cycle. The same can be down on weekly and monthly charts. (See Figures 14.18a to d.)

If, for example, the trend is down and the last downleg is 12 days, the next bear market rally shouldn't last for more than 12 days. This tells us two things of significance. First, if the rally is still in effect as the twelfth day approaches, the exact day of the turn can often be predicted if the downtrend is going to resume. If the rally goes beyond 12 days, then this says that a trend reversal is occurring.

The same can be done on weekly charts. Let's say, for example, that prices are in an uptrend. The last upleg takes seven weeks from bottom to top. This means that any downside correction or sideways consolidation shouldn't last more than seven weeks. This time boundary can be combined with certain price parameters. A maximum downside price retracement would normally be 50% to 66%. But there is also a maximum time retracement of seven weeks. Even as the correction is beginning, the trader not only has the maximum downside price parameters marked off on the chart, but he or she also has the seven-week maximum time parameter clearly identified.

This seven-week limit becomes especially valuable if the correction does in fact last into the seventh week. It's much like buying a market against a major up trendline. The reward/risk ratio is very

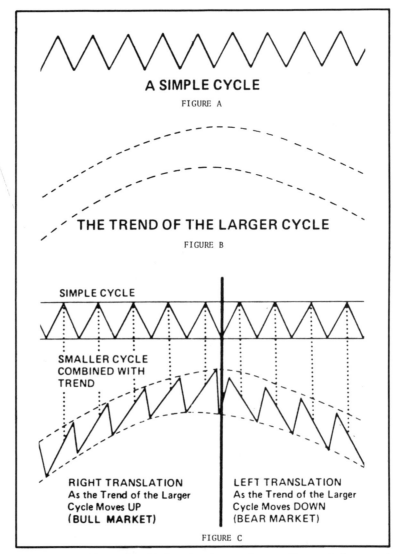

Figure 14.16 Example of left and right translation. Figure A shows a simple cycle. Figure B shows the trend of the larger cycle. Figure C shows the combined effect. When the longer trend is up, the midpeak shifts to the right. When the longer trend is down, the midpeak shifts to the left. Right translation is bullish, left translation is bearish. (Source: HAL Cyclic Analyst's Kit, p. 1-5.)

favorable. The trader can buy against the major up trendline with a tight stop. If the trendline is broken, he or she knows the trend has reversed and can now go the other way. The same is true in the time dimension. The trader has a low-risk entry point in the seventh week, knowing the trend must turn up at that point if it is going to do so. If it doesn't, he or she knows that the trend is turning and can consider reversing positions.

It was mentioned earlier that the four-week trading cycle divides into two shorter cycles of two weeks each, the *alpha* and *beta* cycles. The alpha cycle crest occurs in the first half, or the left side, of the trading cycle. The beta cycle takes place in the second, or right, half of the trading cycle. Therefore, in left translation, the trading cycle crest should coincide with the alpha crest. In right translation, the trading cycle crest usually occurs with the beta crest. It was also mentioned earlier that the use of alpha and beta cycles are part of the *HAL method* of cyclic analysis, developed by Walter Bressert.

The concept of left and right translation has proven an extremely useful ally over the years. It can be applied to virtually any trend or cycle length. Of course, like any other technical concept, it requires a fair amount of practice and experience before the user can fully grasp its significance and confidently incorporate it into his or her repertoire. If the reader comes away from a reading of this chapter with only one solid idea, I would recommend translation being that one.

Figure 14.17 The four-year "election year" cycle, measured from low to low. Notice the right translation from 1950 to 1968, a symmetrical pattern during the sideways pattern from 1968 to 1975, and right translation again as the major bull trend resumed from the 1975 bottom. Stock indices also have a consistent 20-week primary cycle. (Source: HAL Market Cycles, Tucson, AZ.)

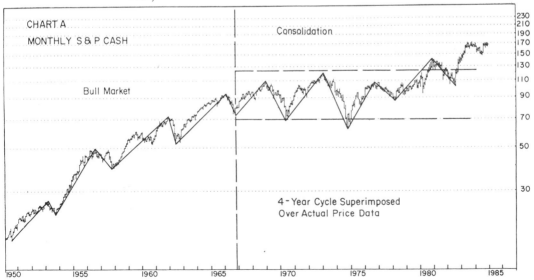

CHART A
MONTHLY S & P CASH

Consolidation

Bull Market

4 - Year Cycle Superimposed
Over Actual Price Data

MAR 85 T-BONDS

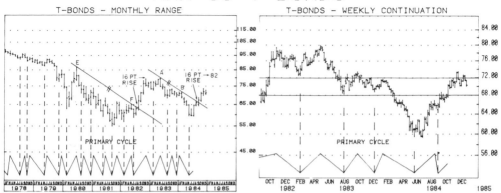

Figure 14.18a Examples of right and left translation of the primary cycle. Notice the shift from left to right translation in the middle of 1982 on the monthly chart as prices bottomed and again in June/August of 1984 on the weekly chart. Right and left translation tell us quite a bit about whether the trend is up or down. (Source: HAL Market Cycles, Tucson, AZ.)

MAR 85 SOYBEANS

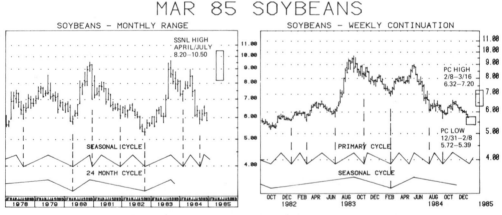

Figure 14.18b More examples of translation. Time and price windows, pioneered by HAL Market Cycles, are shown by boxes on the charts. (Source: HAL Market Cycles, Tucson, AZ.)

HOW TO ISOLATE CYCLES—DETRENDING

In order to study the various cycles affecting any given market, it is necessary to first isolate each dominant cycle. There are various ways of accomplishing this task. The simplest is by visual inspection. By studying daily bar charts, for example, it is possible to identify obvious tops and bottoms in a market. By taking the average time periods

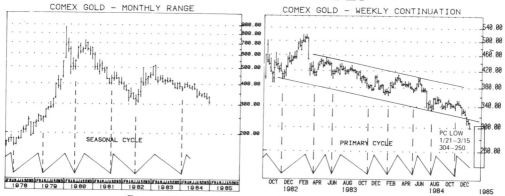

Figure 14.18c Notice on the monthly chart to the left, right translation into early 1980 as the bull market peaked. Left translation has characterized the subsequent bear market. (Source: HAL Market Cycles, Tucson, AZ.)

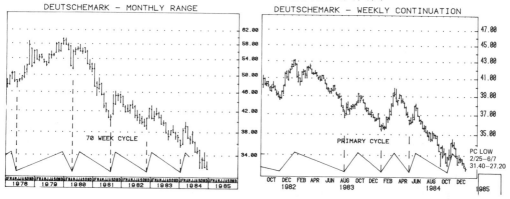

Figure 14.18d Notice on the monthly chart, right translation at the top, followed by left translation during the downtrend. The shifting of the midpeak can warn of shifts in trend. (Source: HAL Market Cycles, Tucson, AZ.)

between those cyclic tops and bottoms, certain average cycle lengths can be found.

There are tools available to make that task a bit easier. One such tool is the *Ehrlich Cycle Finder,* named after its inventor, Stan Ehrlich. The Cycle Finder is an accordion-like device that can be placed on the price chart for visual inspection. The distance between the points are always equidistant and can be expanded or contracted to fit any cycle length. By plotting a distance between any two obvious cycle lows, it can be quickly determined if other cycle lows of the same length exist.

There are also computer software programs available to help find cycles by visual inspection. (See Figures 14.19a to d.) The Compu Trac software has a Cycle Finder program to assist in isolating underlying cycles. The user first puts a price chart on the screen. The next step is to pick a prominent bottom on the chart as a starting point. Once that is done, vertical lines appear every ten days (the default value). By pressing a couple of keys, the cycle periods can be lengthened, shortened, or moved left or right to find the right cycle fit on the chart.

For the more mathematically inclined, there are a number of statistically advanced techniques for identifying cycles such as the *Box-Jenkins* technique, *spectral* and *Fourier analysis.* The Compu Trac program also includes a Fourier Analysis routine and has recently added a Fast Fourier Transform (FFT) program developed by Jack Hutson, editor of *Technical Analysis of Stocks and Commodities* magazine, and Anthony W. Warren, PhD. That magazine (Seattle, WA 98146) has published a considerable amount of work on cycle analysis including articles on Fourier Analysis and the *Maximum Entropy Method (MEM)* by Hutson and Warren. (Fourier Analysis, by identifying where dominant cycles are located, can be used as a starting point to shortcut the search for optimized moving averages and oscillators.)

There is another technique, however, which falls somewhere between visual inspection and the more advanced statistical techniques already mentioned—the process of *detrending.* One of the problems in trying to identify shorter time cycles is the presence of trend. Trend is caused by the existence of longer-range cycles. As a result, shorter cycles become much harder, if not impossible, to find on the price chart.

Moving averages have long been used as a smoothing device. Moving averages have the effect of smoothing or eliminating shorter-term cycles, while allowing longer-range cycles to come through. The process of detrending reverses that process by eliminating cycles longer than the length of the average while shorter-term cycles become more visible. This is accomplished in effect by eliminating the influence of trend.

The technique is relatively simple. (See figures 14.20a to d.) It can be done by hand, but is easier with a computer. First, a moving average length is chosen. The length of the average is determined by which cycle the user wishes to isolate. Let's construct a 40-day moving average for illustration purposes. The next step is to center the average. That is to say, the average is plotted on the 21st day of the data—or in the middle of the cycle length—instead of the last day, the more

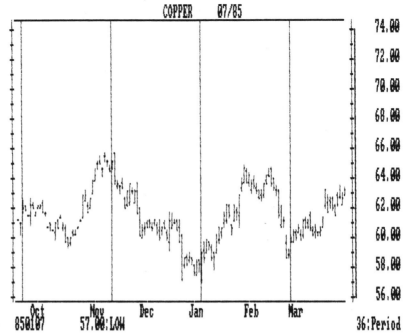

Figure 14.19a The Compu Trac Cycle Finder helped identify an apparent 36-day cycle on this copper chart. The vertical bars can be lengthened or shortened (distance between vertical bars) and can be moved either to the left or right. This tool makes visual inspection of cycle lows a good deal easier.

Figure 14.19b A shorter 18-day cycle also becomes visible on the same chart. Notice how the three major lows on the chart coincide with the vertical cycle bars 18 days apart. Note 18 days is also half of 36, meaning that the two cycles are harmonically related.

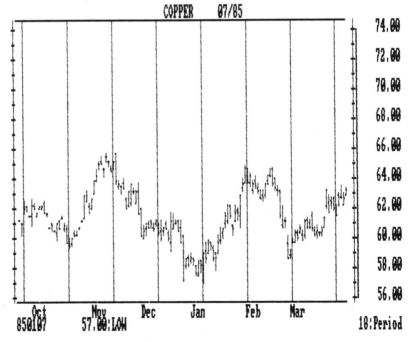

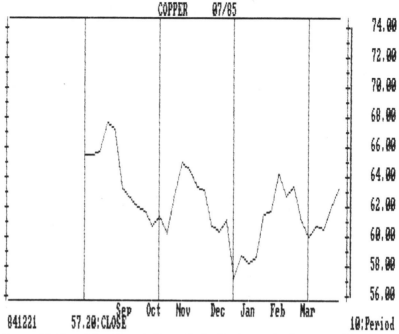

COPPER 07/85

74.00
72.00
70.00
68.00
66.00
64.00
62.00
60.00
58.00
56.00

Sep Oct Nov Dec Jan Feb Mar

841221   57.20:CLOSE   10:Period

Figure 14.19c The Compu Trac Cycle Finder applied to a weekly chart of the same copper contract shows a fairly obvious 10-week cycle from low to low. Notice that all three troughs in the apparent "head and shoulders" bottom were spaced ten weeks apart.

Figure 14.19d Using the same measuring technique, but doubling the cycle length, note that the two "shoulders" are 19 weeks apart. This can be useful information when trying to "time" entry into the market during the formation of the "right shoulder." Time as well as price targets become possible.

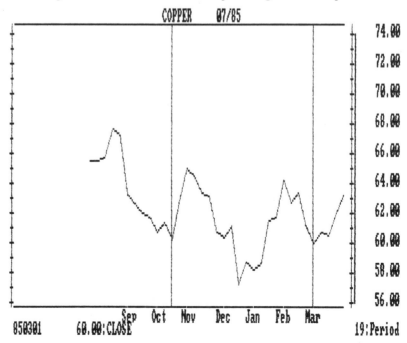

COPPER 07/85

74.00
72.00
70.00
68.00
66.00
64.00
62.00
60.00
58.00
56.00

Sep Oct Nov Dec Jan Feb Mar

850301   60.00:CLOSE   19:Period

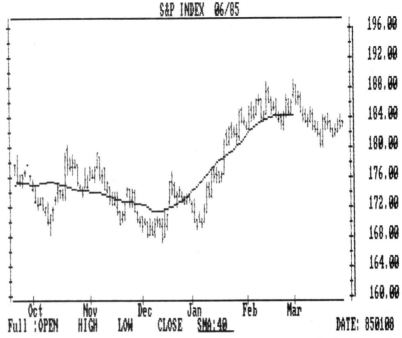

Figure 14.20a What a 40-day "centered" moving average looks like applied to an S&P stock index contract.

Figure 14.20b What the same contract looks like after being "detrended." Prices are plotted around the horizontal 40-day average, which is also centered. Shorter cycles become more visible once the trends longer than the length of the average are eliminated.

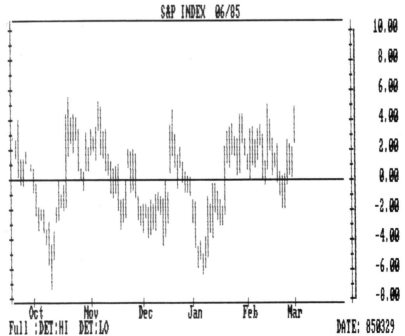

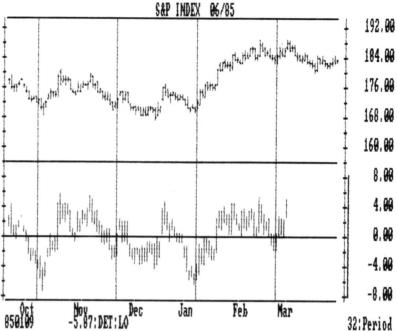

Figure 14.20c   A 40-day detrended moving average helped isolate an apparent 32-day cycle in the S&P futures contract. Note how much clearer the cycle lows are on the detrended chart on the bottom. The Compu Trac Cycle Finder can also be applied to detrended charts. The effects of longer range cycles are filtered out, allowing for closer study of shorter cycles.

Figure 14.20d   A 20-day centered average made the identification of a 16-day cycle much easier. The shorter the average, the more sensitive the detrended chart becomes. Cycles around the length of the moving average can be isolated in this fashion.

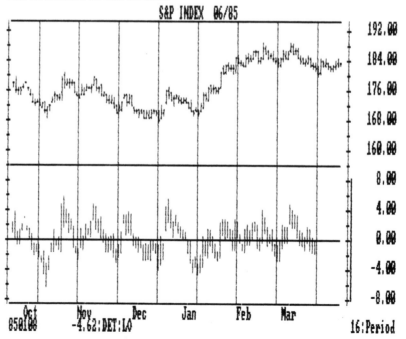

common placement for moving averages. The average is then plotted as a "zero line" on the bottom of the chart and prices are plotted above and below that zero centerline. The result is that cycles shorter than 40 days become much more pronounced and are easier to spot. The process can be continued for shorter and shorter periods until all dominant cycles have been found. A detrending program is available on Compu Trac software.

SEASONAL CYCLES

All commodity futures markets are affected to some extent by an annual seasonal cycle. This seasonal cycle or pattern refers to the tendency of markets to move in a given direction at certain times of the year. The most obvious seasonals involve the grain markets where seasonal lows usually occur around harvest time when supply is most plentiful. In soybeans, for example, 70% of all seasonal tops occur between April and July with seasonal bottoms taking place 75% of the time between August and November. Once a seasonal top or bottom has been formed, prices usually fall or rise for several months. Therefore, some knowledge of seasonal tendencies can be a valuable adjunct to other trading methods.

Although the reasons for seasonal tops and bottoms are more obvious in the agricultural markets, virtually all markets experience seasonal patterns. *One general seasonal pattern that seems to apply to all markets is that a penetration of the January high is considered bullish.* Examples of some other seasonal patterns can be seen in the metals markets. The copper market shows a strong seasonal uptrend from the January/February period with a tendency to top in March or April. The gold market also shows seasonal strength from January with another bottom in August. Silver has a low in January with higher prices into March.

Seasonal charts can be constructed by studying the frequency of seasonal moves in past years. (See Figures 14.21a and b.) It can then be determined what the percentage probabilities are for a seasonal move during each month and week of the year, depending on how many times such moves took place in the past during that same time period. A reading of 80% is considered a strong seasonal pattern. Anything under 65% is considered suspect.

Figure 14.21a   A seasonal chart of the copper market. Note the March/April high and the October/November low. (Source: MBH Commodity Advisors, Inc., P.O. Box 353, Winnetka, ILL 60093.)

There are a couple of caveats that must be considered when performing seasonal studies. Most cash seasonals are based on the average monthly price and sometimes show different seasonal patterns than the futures markets. Second, futures markets sometimes show two different seasonal patterns. The trader should be aware of both. The question of contra-seasonal moves must be considered. There will be years when prices will not follow the anticipated seasonal tendency. The trader must be on the alert for signs that something has gone wrong. Identifying a contra-seasonal move as soon as possible has obvious benefits and is extremely valuable information. Failure to conform to the normal seasonal pattern usually indicates a significant move in the other direction. Knowing when you're wrong early in the game is one of the most useful features of seasonal analysis in particular and of technical analysis in general.

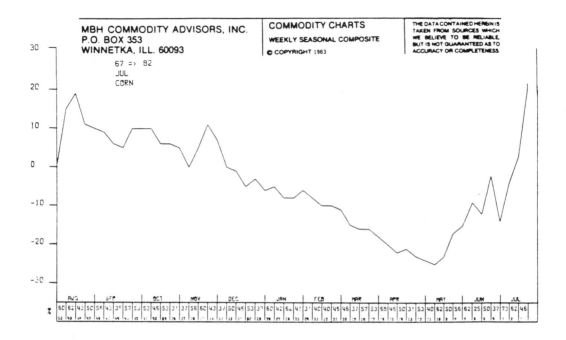

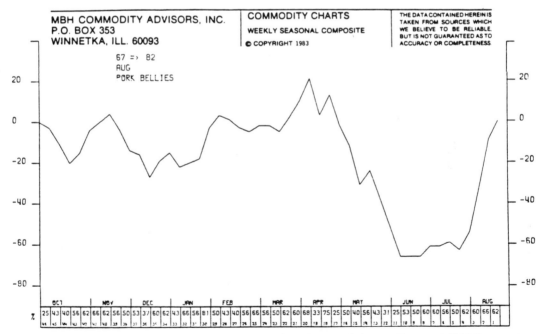

Figure 14.21b More examples of seasonal charts. (Source: MBH Commodity Advisors, Inc., P.O. Box 353, Winnetka, ILL 60093.)

COMBINING CYCLES
WITH OTHER TECHNICAL TIMING TOOLS

Cycle analysts stress that other technical timing tools must be combined with cyclic expectations to justify market entry. The use of *time windows* or *timing bands* alerts the analyst as to when cycles are due to turn. In this way, time considerations act as a filter on price action. Once the time window is entered, however, the trader must look to more conventional technical timing tools to confirm that a turn has occurred and to signal that action should be taken. Different analysts rely on their own favorite set of timing tools.

The two leading experts in the application of cycles to the commodity futures markets are Jake Bernstein of MBH Commodity Advisors in Winnetka, Illinois and Walter J. Bressert of HAL Market Cycles in Tucson, Arizona. While both firms produce highly regarded market letters based on cyclic principles, they differ somewhat in their timing approaches. For one thing, Bressert uses calendar days for shorter-term timing while Bernstein uses market days. The specific timing tools also differ somewhat.

In his highly acclaimed book, *The Handbook of Commodity Cycles: A Window on Time* (John Wiley & Sons, Inc., 1982), Bernstein stresses that *time windows* are meaningless if not combined with various timing signals. Among some of the signals he favors are breakouts through close only trendlines, key reversal days, and a closing above or below the close of the previous three time units. At a cycle bottom, for example, prices would have to close above the highest close of the previous three days. On a weekly chart, prices would have to set a three-week closing high.

Bressert's HAL Market Cycles uses a concept of time and price windows (identified by boxes on the price chart). The time targets are based on 70% timing bands, taken for each cycle length, meaning that cycle turns should occur within those bands 70% of the time. To aid in the process of locating those timing bands, a handy little device called the HAL Cycle Finder is made available to subscribers. The *HAL Cyclic Analyst's Kit Manual* describes the approach used by that firm.

Among the tools used by Bressert for combining price and time objectives are the *midcycle pause price objective* (similar to the swing objective technique covered in Chapter 4), 60-40% retracements (apparently a rounding off of the 38-62% Fibonacci retracements covered in the previous chapter), support and resistance levels, and trendlines.

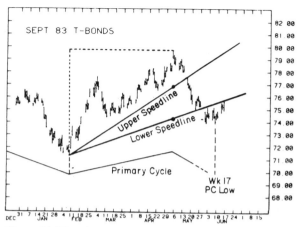

Figure 14.22 An example of using speedlines to catch the turn in the primary cycle top. Trendlines are more effective when combined with cyclic concepts. (Source: HAL Cyclic Analyst's Kit, p. 4-6.)

Bressert stresses that these tools must be combined with cyclic concepts. For example, the midcycle pause and 60% to 40% retracements are only valid for the cycle length to which they are applied, and work only when the trend of the next longer cycle continues.

Trendlines are most useful when they connect the tops or bottoms of the same cycle length. For example, trendlines should connect the crests or troughs of two trading cycles; or, adjoining alpha and beta cycles, which are usually the same length. The breaking of that trendline connecting two cycles of the same length is a signal that the next longer cycle has turned. For example, if a down trendline connecting the crests of the alpha and beta cycles is broken, this indicates that the next longer trading cycle has bottomed. Speedlines (covered in Chapter 4) are used within each individual cycle to confirm cycle turns. (See Figure 14.22.)

COMBINING CYCLES AND OSCILLATORS

One of the most intriguing areas of overlap between cycles and traditional technical indicators is in the use of oscillators. We covered the subject of oscillators in an earlier chapter to show how they were used to spot overbought/oversold areas and divergences. It is believed that the usefulness of oscillators can be enhanced if the time periods used in the calculations are tied to underlying cycles.

The Hal Blue Book by Walter J. Bressert and James H. Jones (HAL Market Cycles, 1981) discusses how cycles are combined with an overbought/oversold index and a momentum index. Both oscillators were derived from a 1973 work by Larry Williams, *How I Made One Million Dollars In The Commodity Market Last Year*, (Monterey, CA: Conceptual Management). The overbought/oversold index is a variation of Williams' %R oscillator, while the second is a simple momentum index obtained by measuring price differences between two time periods (see Chapter 10).

For purposes of explanation here, we'll concentrate on the simpler *momentum* oscillator. The formula for constructing the oscillator remains the same. The key is tying the time input to cycle lengths. The base starting point is the number of market days in the trading cycle. Assuming an average calendar day trading cycle of 28 days, we convert that number to 20 trading days. When using an oscillator to spot the turns in any cycle, it is necessary to use half the cycle length in the formula. In the above example, ten days would be used. In the momentum formula, then, the close ten days earlier would be subtracted from the latest close with the plus or minus number plotted above or below a zero line.

The Hal method is to construct three oscillators based on the length of the trading cycle (20 days), the alpha/beta cycles (ten days) and a long cycle (usually twice the trading cycle, or 40 days). These are average numbers, of course. Allowance must be made for the actual lengths in the individual markets. In constructing the three oscillators, half the cycle length is used in each case. The three numbers used in this example would therefore be 20, 10, and 5. These three oscillators can be plotted on the same chart or separately. The interaction of the various oscillator lengths can provide very useful information. (See Figures 14.23a and b.)

Another way to combine oscillators with cycles is to use *timing bands* as a filter. Be especially alert for a top or bottom in an oscillator when prices enter the *timing band* calling for a cycle peak or trough.

The concept of tying oscillators to cycle lengths can be used in virtually any oscillator formulation. The two mentioned here, the Hal Momentum Index and Williams' %R, are available in the Compu Trac software, making it extremely easy to experiment with different cycle combinations. Other oscillators available through Compu Trac are Sibbett's *Demand Index*, Wilder's *Relative Strength Index*, and Lane's *Stochastic*.

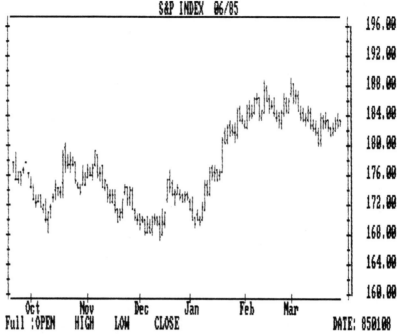

Figure 14.23a A bar chart of an S&P 500 futures contract.

Figure 14.23b The HAL Momentum Index, which tracks the alpha/beta, trading, and long-term cycles on the same oscillator chart. Each line is a momentum oscillator of a different cycle. Average user inputs are 5, 10, and 20 days, which are half the values of the cycles being tracked.

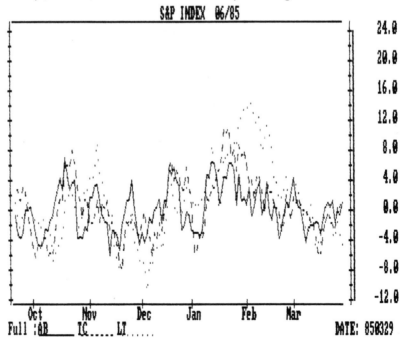

SUMMARY AND CONCLUSION

In this chapter, we've taken a close look at how time cycles bring the important dimension of time into market forecasting. A trader doesn't have to become an expert in cyclic analysis to recognize the benefits of incorporating some time elements into his or her work. It may even be that some technical tools already in use could be improved by combining them with cycles. Cyclic analysts believe that cycles hold the ultimate clue to market movement. Whether that's true or not, no one would dispute that cycles hold at least some of the clues.

In our coverage of the various technical disciplines, we've pointed out that some work better at certain times and not as well at others. Cycle analysis seems to work best in bull markets. By contrast, cyclic analysts have had their problems with bear markets. I have always suspected that this discrepancy arises from the nature of cycle theory and the emphasis placed on cycle troughs rather than crests. Because troughs are considered more reliable that crests, and cycles are measured from low to low, cyclic analysts focus their attention on the cycle low points. The unhappy result seems to be a strong tendency to "pick bottoms" rather than riding with the lower trend. Being aware of this tendency, it might be wise to pay less attention to cyclic analysis during bear markets, but follow it more closely during confirmed bull markets.

Hopefully, this relatively brief treatment of a complicated subject will awaken the reader's interest in exploring more deeply the world of cycles. Several respected works have already been mentioned, including those of Dewey and Hurst. More specifically related to commodity futures, there are the works by Walter J. Bressert and Jake Bernstein already mentioned. In addition to *The Handbook of Commodity Cycles*, Bernstein has published several other works including *How to Profit From Seasonal Commodity Spreads* (Wiley & Sons, 1983).

Reference has already been made to the Foundation for the Study of Cycles and its monthly publication, *Cycles* magazine. More information on the Foundation can be obtained at 124 South Highland Avenue, Pittsburgh, PA 15206. The Society for the Investigation of Recurring Events (SIRE) meets once a month in New York to hear speakers on all phases of cycle research. Their address is Drawer W, Downington, PA 19335.

The two most authoritative newsletters pertaining to cycles analysis of the commodity markets have been produced by Jake Bernstein of MBH Commodity Advisors in Winnetka, Illinois and Walter Bressert of HAL Market Cycles in Tucson, Arizona. Anyone interested in pursuing the study of cycles further might want to consult the work of those two experts. I would like to acknowledge the graciousness of both Bernstein and Bressert for allowing me to draw so heavily on their writings in the preparation of this chapter.

15
Computers and Trading Systems

INTRODUCTION

The computer has played an increasingly important role in the realm of technical analysis and commodity futures trading. In this chapter, we'll see how the computer can make the technical trader's task a good deal easier by providing quick and easy access to an arsenal of technical tools and studies that would have required an enormous amount of work just a few years earlier. This assumes, of course, that the trader knows how to use these tools, which brings us to one of the disadvantages of the computer.

The trader not properly schooled in the concepts that underlie the various indicators, and who is not comfortable with how each indicator is interpreted, may find him- or herself overwhelmed with the vast array of computer software currently available. Even worse, the amount of impressive technical data at one's fingertips sometimes fosters a false sense of security and competence. The trader comes to believe that he or she is a better technician and trader just because of access to a lot of fancy lines on the terminal screen.

The theme emphasized in this discussion is that the computer is an extremely valuable tool in the hands of a technically-oriented trader who has already done his or her basic homework. In fact, when we review many of the routines available in the computer, you'll see that a fair number of the tools and indicators are quite basic and have already been covered in previous chapters. There are, of course, more sophisticated tools that cannot be performed without the aid of a computer.

I've heard the claim by some newer computer-oriented traders that it is impossible to trade without the aid of a computer. I don't accept that. Traders were making money in the markets long before the computer was even a gleam in some scientist's eye. In truth, much of the work involved in technical analysis and trading is best performed without the computer. Certain functions can be more easily performed with a simple chart and ruler than with a computer printout. Certain types of longer-range analysis don't require a computer. As a matter of fact, a good deal of the technical analysis of a market should have already been performed before the computer is even turned on. As useful as it is, the computer is only a tool. It can make a good technical analyst even better. It won't, however, turn a poor technician into a good one.

Compu Trac Software

Several of the technical routines available in the Compu Trac software have been shown in previous chapters. The Compu Trac program is currently the best-known and most comprehensive technical analysis system available to futures traders. For that reason, we'll focus on that program to review what can be done with a computer. We'll begin by making a few general observations concerning the computer hardware and what is needed to use the system. Then we'll review the various tools and indicators currently available. We'll then address some additional features such as the ability to automate the various functions chosen by the user. In addition to providing us with the various technical studies, the computer also enables us to test various studies for profitability. This is where the ability to optimize one's work comes in, which may be the most valuable feature of the program. The user with some programming background can also go beyond the routines already available and construct his or her own indicators or systems.

Welles Wilder's
Directional Movement and Parabolic Systems

We'll take a close look at a couple of Welles Wilder's more popular systems, the *Directional Movement System* and the *Parabolic System*. We'll use those two systems in our discussion of the relative merits of relying on mechanical trading systems. It will be demonstrated that mechanical trend-following systems only work well in certain types of market environments. It will also be shown how a mechanical system can be incorporated into one's market analysis and used simply as a confirming technical indicator.

Artificial Intelligence Pattern Recognition

It may strike the reader as we look at the various menus that there are *too many* indicators from which to choose. Instead of simplifying our lives, has the computer only served to complicate things by giving us so much more to look at? Compu Trac, for example, has about 40 different studies that are available to the technician. How does one possibly reach any conclusions (and find the time to trade) with so much data to contend with? The answer as to how to deal with so many indicators may lie in the field of Artificial Intelligence and Pattern Recognition, which is a sophisticated attempt to use the logical powers of the computer to choose from among the many indicators to find the best combinations to utilize. We'll say a few words about some work being done in that direction.

SOME COMPUTER BASICS

Compu Trac can be applied to various financial vehicles including stocks, options, and futures. Our main interest is with futures. It can be used on the IBM-PC, XT, AT, IBM-PC compatibles, and the Apple. We'll be using the IBM-PC for examples. The system is user-friendly and menu-driven, meaning that it can be easily implemented by choosing from successive lists of available routines. The PC has two disk drives and therefore requires two separate diskettes to operate. The A disk drive (the source or left-handed disk drive) holds the Compu Trac program software. The B disk drive (the target or right-handed disk drive) holds the data files.

Compu Trac does not provide market data. The user must obtain that data elsewhere. Data can be entered to the data disk manually or collected automatically from a data service over telephone lines (requiring a phone modem). It is recommended that data collection be done automatically from a commercial data base. Compu Trac provides the names of various data vendors from which to choose. These data vendors provide all the software and instructions needed to set up and collect the data files on the disk.

When first starting out, the user must collect historical data going back for at least several months to have something to work with. After that, data should be collected daily. It is possible to analyze "on line" data during the trading day by hooking up to a quote service. However, in our use of daily data, we will be referring to end-of-day data, which is available after the markets close. The final piece of equipment needed is a printer to obtain a copy of whatever appears on the terminal screen. Color pictures can be obtained by using a plotter.

ANALYSIS TOOLS

Let's briefly review the types of choices and some of the analytical tools the user has available. Data can be displayed intra-day, daily, weekly, monthly, quarterly, and annually. For daily charts, three dif-

Figure 15.1   Menu 1. (Courtesy of Compu Trac.)

```
                              HELP Page

     Key   Function           Description

     F1 - Studies            Analytical calculations
     F2 - Window             Change current Display area
     F3 - Files              Change or Append data in memory
     F4 - Bar Cht            Draw a Bar Chart
     F5 - Output             Graphic or Tabular output to the Printer
     F6 - Tools              Interpretive aids
     F7 - Screen             Modify the Display format
     F8 - Zoom               Enlarge or Reduce the display


           Left or Right Arrow moves the Cursor
    <shift> Left or Right Arrow moves the Cursor 10 Days
    <ctrl>  Left or Right Arrow moves the Cursor to start/end of data
    <Home>  Erases the current window
    <rtn>   Large or Small cursor
    <esc>   Exit to the Main Menu


    <rtn> to Continue:
```

ferent formats are available. The standard Gann format, for example, places each price bar after the other with no spaces for holidays or weekends. A seven-day format is available for cycle analysts who leave space for both holidays and weekends. In the weekly format, the user can choose which day on which to end the week.

Let's take a quick tour through the various menus. Menu 1 is the main menu. (See Figure 15.1.) The figures in the far left column (F1 through F8) are function keys at the left of the IBM keyboard (remember we're looking at the Compu Trac/PC software). Each of those functions on the menu is activated by hitting the appropriate function key. The following is a brief explanation of each function.

- *F1—Studies:* These are the various technical analysis routines. We'll take a closer look at them later in Menu 4.

- *F2—Window:* The user can choose between two types of displays—a full screen or split screen. Some studies, like oscillators, require dividing the screen into two halves.

- *F3—Files:* Used to load the contract data into computer memory.

- *F4—Bar Cht:* Draws a bar chart in the "active" window. The "active" window means either the full screen or one of the two half windows of the user's choice.

- *F5—Output:* Used to obtain various types of hard copies from the printer. Copies can be obtained of the chart display or the underlying tabular data from the chart.

- *F6—Tools:* Various analytical tools available. We'll come back to this sub-menu of tools later in Menu 3.

- *F7—Screen:* Allows a variety of screen displays (Menu 2).

- *F8—Zoom:* Allows the user to magnify or condense the screen display. By "zooming in," the screen display is magnified for closer study. By "zooming out," more data can be included on the screen for longer-range study.

The instructions on the bottom of the menu refer to various functions, including the movement of the *cursor.* The cursor can be placed over any day on the screen. Data for that day can be displayed at the bottom of the screen. By moving the cursor forward or backward, data for any day can be viewed. *Scrolling* allows viewing of additional historic data by moving the cursor to the far left. Movement of the cursor is also necessary to implement some of the analytical tools, such as the drawing of trendlines. If the user prefers dates along the

Computers and Trading Systems

```
                            HELP Page

    Key   Function           Description

    F1 - Legend              Toggle: Dates or Data
    F2 - Rescale             Adjust scaling to your needs
    F3 - Log                 Semi-logarithmic scale
    F4 - Manip               Custom display & field Manipulation
    F5 - Data                Display Underlying data in Tabular form
    F6 - Grid                Vertical & Horizontal registration
    F7 - Mode                Medium or High resolution display


    <esc>   Exit to the Command Level
```

Figure 15.2   Menu 2. (Courtesy of Compu Trac.)

bottom of the chart instead of the price data, that can be done by pressing function key 7 (Screen).

Striking function key 7 on the previous main menu takes the user to Menu 2. (See Figure 15.2.) Again, by simply striking the function keys, various choices are available. F1 (Legend), for example, gives the user the choice of viewing data or dates along the bottom of the chart, as described previously. Data is the price, volume, open interest, and indicator data for the day on which the cursor is currently positioned. Notice that F3 (Log) gives the user the option of switching from arithmetic to semi-logarithmic scaling. Using a log instead of an arithmetic scale can make the viewing of bunched data easier to see and analyze. F7 (Mode) allows the user to "toggle" between medium or high resolution displays. Medium resolution is used for color displays.

Figure 15.3   Menu 3. (Courtesy of Compu Trac.)

```
                            HELP Page

    Key   Function           Description

    F1 - Trend               Set trend lines
    F2 - Env                 Enclose data within a channel
    F3 - Cyc                 Isolate underlying cycles
    F4 - %Retr               Percent retracement between moves
    F5 - Comp                Reload Daily as Weekly - etc.
    F6 - Profit              Calculate the P/L of a trading system
    F7 - Misc                Andrews & Fibonacci
    F8 - Fourier             Calculate & Display Fourier Transformation
    F9 - EqVol               Draw an Equivolume Chart on Screen


    <esc>   Exit to the Command Level
```

The Tools Menu

Striking the F6 key from the main menu takes us to the *tools* sub-menu. This menu (Menu 3) is where we begin to get into the guts of the technical analysis work.

- *F1—Trend:* Allows the drawing of trendlines and channels. By using the cursor, the user picks the points on the chart from where the lines are drawn.

- *F2—Envelope:* Allows the drawing of parallel envelopes above and below data, such as moving averages (see Chapter 9).

- *F3—Cycle:* Allows for the location and marking of cycles on charts (see Chapter 14).

- *F4—%Retrace:* Determines the percentage retracement between a high and low point. The user has to pick the spots. We'll take a closer look at this later.

- *F5—Compress:* Allows the user to switch from a daily to a weekly to a monthly format on the chart.

- *F6—Profit:* Runs a profitability test (must be predefined in another section of the program called the Profit Editor).

- *F7—Misc.:* A selection of sophisticated tools including Fibonacci arcs, zones, time zones (see Chapter 13), and Andrews Pitch Fork.

- *F8—Fourier:* Allows for operation of Fourier Analysis, an advanced statistical technique used in the identification of cycles (see Chapter 14).

- *F9—EqVol:* Equivolume price bars (or rectangles) have a vertical width in relation to each day's volume. The heavier the volume the wider the price box for that day. This is another way of viewing the impact of volume.

So far we've looked at various ways to plot data on the screen and some of the tools that can be applied to that data. You'll notice that many of the tools, such as trendlines and percentage retracements, are quite familiar. Others, such as Andrews Pitch Fork, Fourier Analysis, and Equivolume, may not be. (Figures 15.13a and b and 15.14a and b show what a couple of these newer indicators look like.) All the computer does is provide the capability of performing all of these routines quickly and with little or no effort. It's still up to the user to learn how to incorporate these tools into his or her work, if at all.

```
                        STUDY SELECTION
                        <esc> to Exit
                         Pg: 1 of 2

A - Advance-Decline              N - Moving Average
B - Commodity Channel Index      O - Open Interest
C - Commodity Selection Index    P - Oscillator
D - Demand Index                 Q - Parabolic (SAR)
E - Detrend                      R - Point & Figure
F - Directional Movement         S - Rate of Change
G - Hal Momentum                 T - Ratio
H - Haurlan Index                U - Relative Strength Index
I - Linear Regression            V - Short Term Trading Index
J - MA Convergence/Divergence    W - Spread
K - McClellan Oscillator         X - Stochastic (K%D)
L - Median Price                 Y - Swing Index
M - Momentum                     Z - Volatility


Your choice: A
                            PgDn for more
                        STUDY SELECTION
                        <esc> to Exit
                         Pg: 2 of 2


A - Volume
B - Weighted Close
C - Williams % R

Your choice: A
        PgUp for more
```

Figure 15.4   Menu 4. (Courtesy of Compu Trac.)

No one says that all of these tools have to be utilized. The user, however, by the process of elimination, can choose those that provide the most sense and that fit comfortably with the trader's style and philosophy. Let's turn our attention now to the studies themselves.

Study Selection

From the main menu (Menu 1), F1 takes us to the sub-menu for the analytical calculations, or the various technical studies. Menu 4 shows the sub-menu of technical studies. Altogether, there are 29 studies available on the menu. Each study is activated by touching the appropriate letter key which leads to another sub-menu where other choices are available. For example, *Volume* (A on page 2 of 2) leads to the following sub-menu:

A. Simple

B. Histogram

C. On Balance

D. Volume Accumulation

E. Volume Accumulation Oscillator

The user can choose between volume displayed as a solid line, a histogram (the usual format), on balance volume, volume accumulation, and the volume accumulation oscillator (all of which were discussed in Chapter 7).

The *Moving Average* choice (N) leads to another series of choices that the user must make.

A. Simple

B. Weighted

C. Exponential

In each case, the user must choose the data to be averaged (high, low, or close, for example). Moving averages can also be applied to any body of data or indicator that the user has already constructed, such as on balance volume, an oscillator, or even a spread. The user must also decide how many averages to use and the number of days for each one. Finally, a choice of whether the average should be "centered" is made. (Moving averages were discussed in Chapter 9.)

Most studies ask the user to input the number of days in the calculation. A "default" value is usually offered, which is the suggested time input for a given study. Stochastic, for example, has a default value of five and the Relative Strength Index (RSI) uses 14. That number appears on the screen and the user can accept it by simply hitting the "return" key. This default feature is especially helpful in those programs where the user is not familiar enough with the study to know which inputs are best. After some experimenting, the user can then customize or optimize the values to suit his or her own needs.

It's not our intention here to review all of the studies on the menu. Some of the studies—Advance-Decline, Haurlan Index, McClellan Oscillator, and Short-Term Trading Index (TRIN) are used for stock market studies (utilizing NYSE advance/decline figures) and need not concern us here. Most of the other studies have been mentioned in previous chapters. Commodity Channel Index (CCI) and the Demand Index are primarily oscillators (the latter utilizing volume figures). Detrend and HAL Momentum were mentioned in Chapter

14 on cycles. The MA Convergence/Divergence, momentum (price differences), oscillator (differences between two moving averages), rate of change (ROC), Relative Strength Index (RSI), Stochastic (K%D), and Williams %R were all discussed in Chapter 10 on oscillators. Moving average, open interest, and volume are self-explanatory, as are point and figure, ratios, and spreads. Some recent additions to the program are Commodity Selection Index, linear regression, median price, swing index, and volatility.

WELLES WILDER'S PARABOLIC AND DIRECTIONAL MOVEMENT SYSTEMS

Time and space don't permit an adequate explanation of each of the 29 studies. However, there are two studies on the menu that merit closer consideration. Both studies were developed by J. Welles Wilder Jr. and discussed in his book, *New Concepts in Technical Trading Systems*, published by Trend Research, Greensboro, NC in 1978. Three of Wilder's other studies included on the Compu Trac menu—Commodity Selection Index, Relative Strength Index, and the Swing Index—are also included in the same book.

Parabolic System (SAR)

Wilder's Parabolic system (SAR) is a time/price reversal system that is always in the market. The letters "SAR" stand for "stop and reverse," meaning that the position is reversed when the protective stop is hit. It is a trend-following system. It gets its name from the shape assumed by the trailing stops that tend to curve like a parabola. (See Figures 15.5 to 15.8.) Notice that as prices trend higher, the rising dots below the price action (the stop and reverse points) tend to start out slower and then accelerate with the trend. In a downtrend, the same thing happens but in the opposite direction (the dots are above the price action). The SAR numbers are calculated and available to the user for the following day.

Wilder built an acceleration factor into the system. Each day the stop moves in the direction of the new trend. At first, the movement of the stop is relatively slow to allow the trend time to become established. As the acceleration factor increases, the SAR begins to move faster, eventually catching up to the price action. If the trend falters, or fails to materialize, the result is usually a stop and reverse

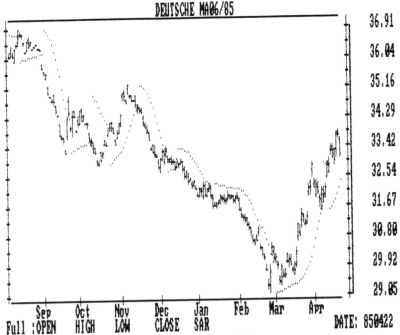

Figure 15.5 Welles Wilder's Parabolic system applied to a Deutsche mark contract. Dots below prices indicate a long position; dots above the price indicate a short position. The dots represent SAR, "stop and reverse" points. This system is always in the market. Like all trend-following systems, the Parabolic system works best in a trending market.

Figure 15.6 The Parabolic system applied to a crude oil contract. See how most of the trending moves were captured profitably.

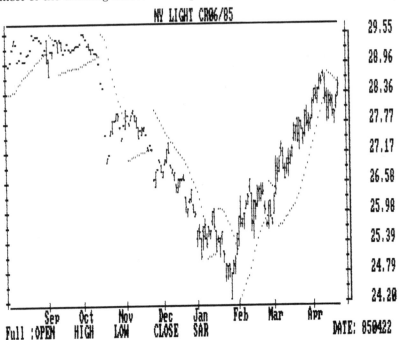

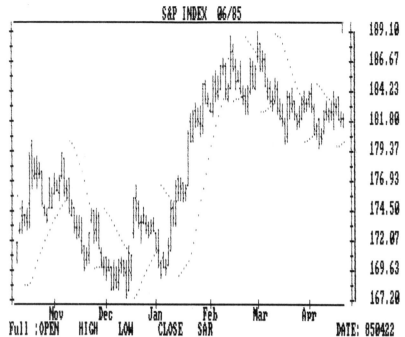

Figure 15.7 The Parabolic system used on an S&P 500 contract. Notice that most of the trending moves were captured. However, during the sideways periods, from Dec. to Jan. and then from March to April, the system got whipsawed quite a bit. Trend-following systems don't work as well in non-trending markets.

Figure 15.8 Notice that the Parabolic didn't work as well during the non-trending period in December and January. The Parabolic is a sensitive system, which means that it reacts to relatively minor market moves.

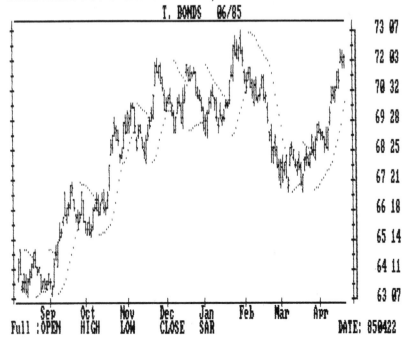

signal. As the accompanying charts show, the Parabolic system works extremely well in trending markets. Notice in Figures 15.5 and 15.6 how well the system followed the trends in the Deutsche mark and crude oil markets. The charts of the S&P 500 and Treasury Bond markets in Figures 15.7 and 15.8, however, give a slightly different story. Notice in both markets that while the trending portions were captured well, the system whipsawed constantly during the sideways, nontrending periods.

In the S&P contract (Figure 15.7), notice the whipsawing during the sideways period from December through January followed by the excellent buy signal in early January, only to be followed again by more whipsawing since February. That chart clearly demonstrates both the strength and weakness of most trend-following systems. They work well during strong trending periods, which Wilder himself estimates occur only about 30% of the time. If that estimate is even close to reality, then a trend-following system will not work well for about 70% of the time. How then does one deal with this dilemma?

Directional Movement Index (DMI)

One possible solution is to use some type of filter or a device to determine if the market is in a trending mode. That's where Wilder's Directional Movement system comes in. (See Figure 15.9.) The Directional Movement Index provides an indication of how much directional movement (trend) is present in each market and also provides a way to compare the trends in different markets. Wilder's ADXR line rates the directional movement of the various markets on a scale of 0 to 100. The higher the ADXR line the more the market is trending and the better candidate it becomes for a trend-following system. The ADXR line is seen in Figure 15.9 applied to the same S&P 500 and Deutsche mark contracts that we've already looked at. The Deutsche mark (lower chart) has shown strong trending characteristics since last November. A very low ADXR line (below 20) indicates a nontrending environment, which would not be suitable for a trend-following approach. The S&P 500 contract qualifies as a bad candidate for a trending system at this time.

If you'll look back at Figures 15.5 and 15.7, you'll see that the Parabolic system worked well in the Deutsche mark, but not so well recently in the S&P 500. The Directional Movement Index might have waved the trend trader off the stock indices and toward the foreign currency markets. Because the ADXR line is on a scale from 0 to 100, the trend trader could simply trade those markets with the

Computers and Trading Systems

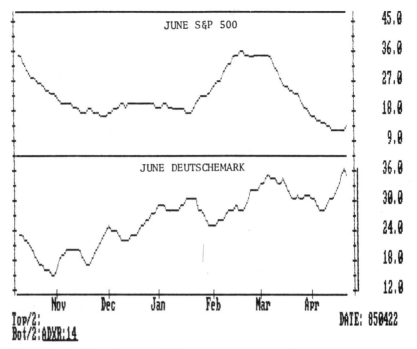

DATE: 850422

Figure 15.9 The Directional Movement system applied to two futures contracts. When the ADXR line is trending lower and below 20 (as in the case of the S&P contract) the market is not suitable for a trending system. A higher ADXR line (as in the case of the Mark) indicates a strong trending market. This type of market would lend itself well to a trend-following system.

highest trend ratings. Nontrending systems (oscillators, for example) could be utilized on markets with low directional movement.

Directional Movement can be used either as a system on its own or as a filter on the Parabolic or any other trend-following system. Two lines are generated in the DMI study, +DI and −DI. The first line measures positive (upward movement) and the second number, negative (downward movement). Figure 15.10 shows the two lines. The solid line is +DI and the dashed line −DI. A buy signal is given when the +DI (solid line) crosses over the −DI (dashed line) and a sell signal when it crosses below the −DI line.

Figure 15.11a and b show both the Parabolic and Directional Movement systems applied to the gold market. Notice in the upper chart that the Parabolic has given eight signals since late November, with a number of them being whipsaws. During that same period, the Directional Movement in the lower chart was short since November and then long from mid-March for a total of only two trades. The

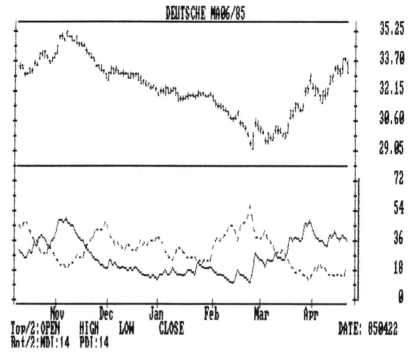

```
Top/2:OPEN    HIGH    LOW    CLOSE              DATE: 850422
Rnt/2:MDI:14  PDI:14
```

Figure 15.10 The bottom chart shows the +DI (solid line) and the −DI (dashed line) that make up the DMI system. A buy signal is given when the +DI line crosses over the −DI line. A sell signal would be a +DI line lower than the −DI. At present, the system is "long."

Parabolic is clearly a more sensitive system, meaning that more frequent and earlier signals are given. However, by using the Directional Movement as a filter, several of the bad signals in the Parabolic could have been avoided by following only those signals in the same direction as the Direction Movement lines. It appears then that the Parabolic and Directional Movement systems should probably be used together, with Directional Movement acting as a screen or filter on the more sensitive Parabolic.

Notice in the bottom chart in Figure 15.11b that the ADXR rating line shows strong directional movement from November to February (a rising line), a weaker trend from early February to early March (a declining line), and then stronger trend action since then. The best time to use a trending system is when the ADXR line is advancing. As demonstrated in the previous example, the Directional Movement system and the ADXR line are not that sensitive and are more appropriate for longer-term trend traders. Wilder developed another measure of market trend, which is more attuned to shorter-term action. That brings us to the Commodity Selection Index (CSI).

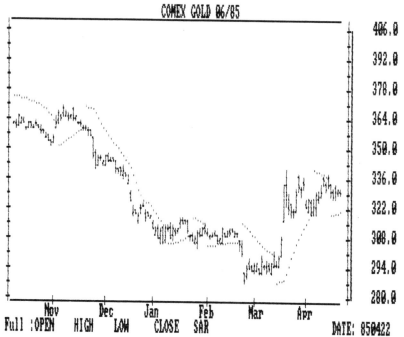

Figure 15.11a Wilder's Parabolic system applied to a gold contract. Although the major moves were traded profitably, several whipsaws took place during sideways periods and minor corrections to the trend.

Figure 15.11b The upper chart shows the DMI applied to the same gold contract. The Parabolic system might be improved by using the DMI system as a filter. The ADXR line on the bottom chart shows that gold has been trending better of late.

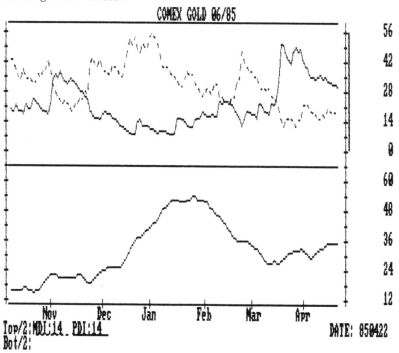

Commodity Selection Index (CSI)

Wilder's CSI uses the ADXR line from the Directional Movement system in its calculations, but also includes a volatility factor (Average True Range, or ATR), margin requirements, and commissions. While the DMI is meant more for longer-range trend-trading, the CSI is meant to identify the more volatile markets for shorter-term trading. The CSI identifies those markets that have both high directional movement and high volatility relative to their margin requirements and commission costs. Markets with a high CSI rating are considered good trading candidates both from the standpoint of strong trending characteristics and greater volatility.

This explanation should provide a basic understanding of a couple of Wilder's better known systems. For a more thorough study of the systems, along with the actual construction of the indicators, a reading of Wilder's book is highly recommended.

GROUPING TOOLS AND INDICATORS

It would be understandable if the reader felt a bit overwhelmed at this point at the number of studies and tools available. The following listing groups them into some order:

- *Basic Charts:* Bar, point and figure, spread, and ratio charts
- *Chart Scales:* Arithmetic and semi-logarithmic
- *Bar Chart:* Price, volume, and open interest
- *Volume:* Simple, histogram, on balance, volume accumulation, demand index, equivolume
- *Basic Tools:* Trendlines and channels, percentage retracements, moving averages, and oscillators
- *Moving Averages:* Reference envelopes
- *Oscillators:* Commodity Channel Index, momentum, oscillator, rate of change, MACD, Stochastic, Williams %R, RSI, volume accumulation, Demand Index, HAL Momentum Index
- *Cycles:* HAL Momentum, detrend, cycle finder, Fourier Analysis
- *Elliott Wave:* Fibonacci fan lines, arcs, and time zones

- *Misc.*: Andrews Pitch Fork, linear regression, weighted close, median price, volatility

- *Wilder*: RSI, Commodity Selection Index, Directional Movement System, Parabolic System, Swing Index

USING THE TOOLS AND INDICATORS

How does one cope with so much from which to choose? The answer is to first use the basic tools such as price, volume and open interest, trendlines, percentage retracements, moving averages, and oscillators. Point and figure, spreads, and ratio charts are useful, but are of secondary importance. Notice the large number of oscillators available. I think it would be a mistake to employ so many. Pick one or two that you are most comfortable with and go with them. Use such things as cycles and Fibonacci tools as secondary inputs unless you have a special interest in those areas. Fourier Analysis can be especially helpful in finding cycles, which in turn can help fine tune moving average and oscillator lengths, but is an advanced concept that requires study and practice. For mechanical system traders, Wilder's Parabolic and DMI are especially noteworthy. Users will have to decide for themselves the value of the remaining tools and options. My advice is to find those tools that work for you and concentrate on them. We'll come back to this point of how to deal with so many indicators later in the chapter. (See Figures 15.12 to 15.14.)

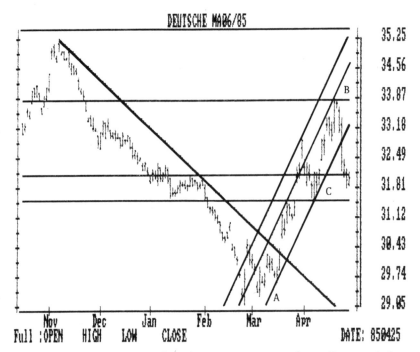

```
                                                                    35,25

                                                                    34,56
                                                              B
                                                                    33,87

                                                                    33,18

                                                                    32,49

                                                              C     31,81

                                                                    31,12

                                                                    30,43

                                                                    29,74
                                                    A
                                                                    29,05
     Nov      Dec      Jan      Feb      Mar      Apr
Full :OPEN   HIGH    LOW    CLOSE                        DATE: 850425
```

Figure 15.12a   Some examples of computer-generated trendlines and channels. The horizontal lines identify support and resistance levels.

Figure 15.12b   The program can identify percentage retracements. The decline from B to C on the upper chart retraced 40% of the advance from A to B. Notice that the computer also identified where the 33%, 40%, 50%, 60%, and 66% retracement levels are located.

```
% Retracement for CLOSE - <esc> to Exit
                    Base:   .01

Base Start:              29.31
Base End   :             33.79
Retrace to:              31.99
% Retrace  :       40.179

33-1/3%    :             32.30
40%        :             32.00
50%        :             31.55
60%        :             31.10
66-2/3%    :             30.80

<rtn> to Continue:
```

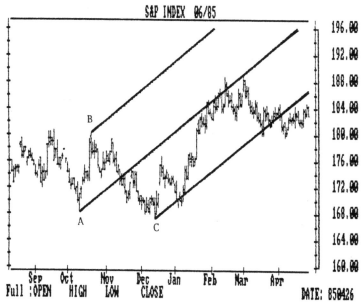

Figure 15.13a An example of Andrews Pitch Fork. Also known as the Median Line (ML) method, Andrews Lines, and Median Lines of Resistance (M.L.R. Lines). Three points are needed to draw the lines. The second two points (B and C) are connected by a straight line (not shown). That line is then bisected by a line drawn from the first point at A. The middle line is the median line. This is a channel technique, developed by Dr. Alan Andrews. The lines often act as support or resistance.

Figure 15.13b Andrews Lines applied to the copper market. Notice how the median line acted as a resistance barrier during the April rally.

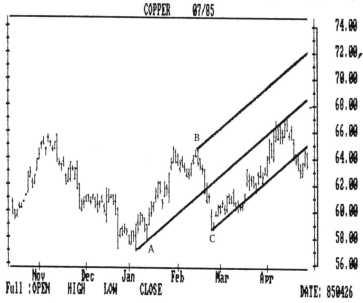

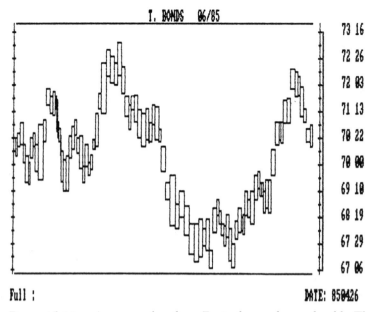

Figure 15.14a An example of an Equivolume chart of gold. The wider rectangles indicate heavier volume for that day. Notice the wider boxes (heavier volume) during the upside breakout. During the recent consolidation period, the boxes have gotten narrower (indicating light volume). Note how much more graphic the chart is and how much easier it is to identify the level of trading activity.

Figure 15.14b Another example of an Equivolume chart. This method is based on the original technique developed by Richard W. Arms, Jr. It is explained in his book, *Volume Cycles in the Stock Market: Market Timing Through Equivolume Charting* (Homewood, Il.: Dow Jones-Irwin, 1983).

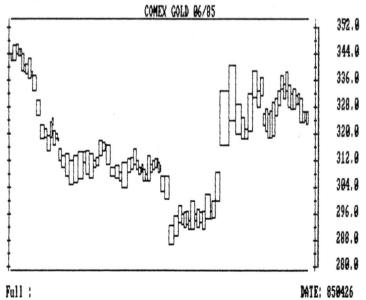

AUTOMATION, OPTIMIZATION, AND PROFITABILITY TESTING

After the user has decided on a package of studies to use on the various markets, it is possible to automate the procedure. The user can put together certain analytical procedures or tasks, which can then be tied to the various data files. The user is then free to do other things, while the computer does all the work. A Profitability Editor allows the user to test predetermined trading rules over historical data. It is also possible to test for optimized results. This ability to test any trading system or technical indicator over historical data and, at the same time, seek out the best parameters through the optimization process may prove to be the most valuable feature of the computer. Finally, a User Study section enables more ambitious users, with some background in computer programming, to write their own analysis routines.

PROS AND CONS OF MECHANICAL COMPUTERIZED SYSTEMS

The strong inflationary environment of the 1970s witnessed major bull trends in the commodity markets that lasted for several years. It was in that climate of strong and persistent bull trends that mechanical trend-trading came into its own. Technical trading systems proliferated and, for the most part, had extremely profitable track records. It was also during that time the public and private commodity funds became popular, which were the equivalent of stock market mutual funds. These large multimillion dollar pools of money relied heavily on technical trend-following systems. Everything went well as long as the bull trends continued. The systems continued to perform well, commodity funds prospered, and everyone was happy. Then something changed. Late in 1980, the inflationary bubble burst, ushering in five years of declining markets.

The 1980s have not been as kind to mechanical trend-following systems. Most of the large funds using these systems have been profitable, but have not been able to match the spectacular records of the 1970s. There may be several possible explanations for the poorer performance. For one, the systems were tested and developed during bull markets. They were never tested for bear markets. Second, trends haven't been as persistent nor widespread. Intermediate bear market rallies and consolidation patterns interrupted bear market strategies, often resulting in whipsawing. While trends have certainly been present, they have been more concentrated. As a result, profits in one or two trending markets were offset by losses in other nontrending markets.

Given the performance of the past few years, it's clear that the trend-following system that relies on automatic, computer-generated trading signals is not the Holy Grail. That doesn't mean, however, that these systems have no value or that they should be discarded. It's just that they must be placed in some perspective. Following are some advantages and disadvantages of these systems.

Advantages of Mechanical Systems

1. Human emotion is eliminated.

2. Greater discipline is achieved.

3. More consistency is possible.

4. Trades are taken in the direction of the trend.

5. Participation is virtually guaranteed in the direction of every important trend.

6. Profits are allowed to run.

7. Losses are minimized.

Disadvantages of Mechanical Systems

1. Most mechanical systems are trend-following.

2. Trend-following systems rely on major trends in order to be profitable.

3. Trend-following systems are generally unprofitable when markets are not trending.

4. There are long periods of time when markets are not trending and, therefore, not suitable for a trending approach.

Personally, I've used mechanical systems with great success at certain times. At other times, their performance has been disappointing to say the least. The major problem is the failure of the system to recognize when the market is not trending and its inability to turn itself off. The measure of a good system is not only its ability to make money in trending markets, but of more importance is its ability to preserve capital during nontrending periods. It is this inability of the system to monitor itself that is its greatest weakness. This is where some overriding filtering device, such as Welles Wilder's Directional Movement Index or Commodity Selection Index, could prove especially useful by allowing the trader to determine which markets are most suitable for a trending system.

Another drawback is that no allowance is generally made for anticipating market reversals. Trend-following systems ride with the trend until it turns. They don't recognize when a market has reached a long-term support or resistance level, when oscillator divergences are being given, or when an Elliott Wave fifth pattern is clearly visible. Most traders would get more cautious at that point, and begin taking some profits. The system, however, will stay with the position until well after the market has changed direction. Therefore, it's up to the trader to determine how best to employ the system. That is to say, whether it should be followed blindly or whether it should be incorporated into a trading plan with other technical factors. That brings us to our next section on how a mechanical system can be used as just another technical input into the forecasting and trading process.

INCORPORATING MECHANICAL SIGNALS INTO ANALYSIS

To illustrate how this can be done, I'm going to use the Electronic Futures Trend Analyzer (EFTA), marketed by the Commodity Research Bureau (Jersey City, NJ 07302). This is a mechanical, trend-following system that generates computer buy and sell signals. The system is based on a combination of technical factors, including three moving averages (10, 20, and 40 days), price volatility, momentum, and time cycles. The figures are available on a daily basis via a computer hookup. Those figures are modified for weekly use and are available on page 2 of the CRB *Futures Chart Service*, published each Friday. We'll focus on the weekly figures.

Figure 15.15 shows what the Computer Trend Analyzer looks like in the chart service. The first two columns give the commodity name and delivery month. The third column (Computer Trend) gives the trend direction and is the most important column on the page. The trend can either be up, down, or sideways. The fourth and fifth columns give the date and price when the current trend started. This

COMPUTER TREND ANALYZER

Commodity	Delivery	Computer Trend	Trend Started Date	Trend Started Price	Current Computer Support	Current Computer Resistance	Market Close 01/25/85	Week's Change
BARLEY (Wpg)	MAR. '85	DOWN	01/08/85	135.10		137.20	136.80	+ $.90
BRITISH POUND	MAR. '85	DOWN	11/26/84	1.1985		1.1360	1.1015	– $.0195
CATTLE (Live)	APR. '85	DOWN	01/09/85	66.02		68.00	67.37	– .08¢
COCOA	MAR. '85	UP	01/17/85	2186	2079		2215	+ $25
COFFEE "C"	MAR. '85	UP	11/07/84	137.98	146.90		151.11	+ 2.86¢
COPPER	MAR. '85	UP	01/17/85	60.15	57.35		61.10	– .10¢
CORN #	MAR. '85	SIDE FROM DOWN	01/21/85	273 3/4	267 1/2	274	271 1/2	– 1 1/4¢
COTTON #2 ##	MAR. '85	DOWN FROM UP	01/25/85	65.19		66.90	65.19	+ .78¢
CRUDE OIL (NY)	MAR. '85	DOWN	01/15/85	25.91		26.55	25.25	– $.50
DEUTSCHE MARK	MAR. '85	DOWN	11/26/84	.3299		.3205	.3168	– $.0004
EURODOLLAR	MAR. '85	UP	09/10/84	87.68	91.01		91.28	+ .15%
GOLD (Comex)	APR. '85	DOWN	11/23/84	350.50		314.00	303.90	– $7.10
HEATING OIL#2	MAR. '85	DOWN	01/16/85	70.99		74.05	69.65	– 3.03¢
HOGS *	JUNE '85	UP	12/24/84	54.12	52.80		53.62	– .43¢
JAPANESE YEN	MAR. '85	DOWN	11/23/84	.4093		.3985	.3946	– $.0003
LEADED GAS	MAR. '85	DOWN	10/12/84	75.40		66.05	65.31	– .18¢
LUMBER #	MAR. '85	DOWN FROM SIDE	01/21/85	154.30		166.30	159.90	+ $3.40
NYSE (NYFE)	MAR. '85	UP	12/19/84	99.20	99.05		103.60	+ 3.20%
ORANGE JUICE #	MAR. '85	UP FROM SIDE	01/21/85	169.55	161.80		179.25	+ 14.70¢
PLATINUM	APR. '85	DOWN	11/27/84	325.50		287.00	272.30	– $4.30
PORK BELLIES *	MAY. '85	SIDE	01/16/85	73.87	70.10	80.05	73.10	– .82¢
RAPESEED (Wpg) #	MAR. '85	SIDE FROM DOWN	01/25/85	394.70	381.60	395.00	394.70	+ $2.20
SILVER (N.Y.)	MAR. '85	DOWN	11/27/84	728.40		641.30	604.00	– 29.00¢
SOYBEANS	MAR. '85	SIDE	01/17/85	599 3/4	574	621	597	– 9¢
SOYBEAN MEAL	MAR. '85	DOWN	11/15/84	159.70		146.60	143.30	– $4.00
SOYBEAN OIL	MAR. '85	UP	01/17/85	25.80	25.05		26.69	+ .26¢
S&P 500	MAR. '85	UP	01/14/85	173.35	169.70		178.75	+ 5.35%
SUGAR "11"	MAR. '85	DOWN	01/17/85	4.23		4.70	4.54	+ .45¢
SWISS FRANC	MAR. '85	DOWN	11/23/84	.4034		.3825	.3769	– $.0015
T-BILLS (IMM)	MAR. '85	UP	07/13/84	88.21	91.97		92.15	+ .11%
T-BONDS (CBoT) #	MAR. '85	UP FROM SIDE	01/22/85	72-07	70-11		73-11	+ 1 30/32
T-NOTES (CBoT) #	MAR. '85	UP FROM SIDE	01/22/85	81-23	79-24		82-15	+ 1 15/32
WHEAT (Chi)	MAR. '85	UP	01/15/85	353 3/4	344		346 3/4	– 4¢
WHEAT (K.C.)	MAR. '85	DOWN	11/13/84	370 1/4		354	348 3/4	– 6¢
WHEAT (Mpls)	MAR. '85	DOWN	11/14/84	381 1/4		366	364 1/2	UNCH

Figure 15.15 (Source: Commodity Research Bureau, a Knight-Ridder Business Information Service.)

Computers and Trading Systems

particular table is dated January 25, 1985. Notice, for example, how long some of the trends have been in effect. The British pound, Deutsche mark, Japanese yen, and Swiss franc have been in down-trends since November. That means that a trader following this system would have been short for two months. Notice also that the Treasury Bill market has been "long" since the previous July—a trend lasting six months. Those are the kinds of markets that system traders dream of. We'll come back to the Treasury Bill market in a minute.

Columns 6 and 7 (Support and Resistance) contain valuable information. Those are the levels at which the current trend changes direction. If a trend is up, as in the case of cocoa, a support level is given. A close at or below the support level would turn the trend from up to side. If a trend is down, as in the case of the British pound, a resistance level is given. A close at or above the resistance level would turn the trend from down to side. If a trend is sideways, as in the case of corn, support and resistance levels are given. A close at or above resistance would turn the trend up, while a close at or below support would turn the trend down. A trend can never reverse from up to down or down to up in the same day. It must go to "side" first. From there, the trend either resumes or reverses. Therefore, this system makes allowances for times when there is no trend.

Making a System Continuous

Obviously, a trader following this system would go long when the trend is up, go short when the trend is down, and stay on the sidelines when the trend is sideways. If the trader wishes, the system can be adapted to make it continuous, that is, always in the market. This could be done in a number of ways. For longer-range trading, a long position could be held until the trend turns down. Conversely, a short position could be held until the trend turns up. The trader would hold previous positions even if the trend turns sideways. Of course, that strategy could entail sizeable losses.

Another way to make the system continuous would be to trade it more aggressively. A long position could reverse to the short side if the trend turns from up to sideways. More shorts could be added if and when the trend turns down. Conversely, all shorts could be covered and long positions taken if the trend turns from down to sideways, with more longs added if the trends turns up. Therefore, this system, or any system for that matter, can be adapted to a trader's own needs and preferences.

Using System Signals
as a Disciplining Device

The system signals can be used simply as a mechanical confirmation along with other technical factors. Even if the system is not being traded mechanically, and other technical factors are being employed, the signals could be used as a disciplined way to keep the trader on the right side of the major trend. No short positions would be taken as long as the computer trend was up. No longs would be taken in a computer downtrend. (This would be a simple way for fundamentally-oriented traders to use a technical device as a filter or trigger on their own trading ideas.) Trend direction is always a matter of judgement. The computer signals relieve the trader of some degree of uncertainty. They can prevent him or her from falling into the trap of "top and bottom picking."

I like to plot the computer-generated support and resistance levels right on my price chart. That way, I know where those critical levels are in advance and where the trend changes will occur. While I may be looking at many other technical factors, such as trendlines and chart support or resistance levels, I use the computer numbers as added confirmation of a trend change. As an example of this, let's return to the Treasury Bill market. On January 25, that market had been trending higher for six months. Prices turned lower the following week, violating tight up trendlines. On Friday, February 1, the "Technical Comments" portion of the CRB *Futures Chart Service* (written by the author), stated:

> This week's sharp selloff, from an area of long-term resistance . . ., has damaged the uptrend. Our computer trend in March Bills ("up" since July 13) turned "down" on Friday. March Eurodollars shifted to "sideways" after trending higher since Sept. 10. We're following our computer trend changes and are leaving the bull side for a neutral corner.

The point here is simply that computer trend signals can be especially valuable even when used only as another technical indicator. In the previous example, both short-term rate markets broke sharply to the downside for almost two months.

Using Signals as Alerts

The Computer Trend Analyzer can also be used as an excellent screening device to alert the trader to recent trend changes. Notice the trend changes that show up in Figure 15.15. At least seven markets changed trend direction in the third column. The trader sifting through the charts on a Monday morning can simply glance at the trend changes in the table and instantly has seven trading candidates. The same information could be found by studying all of the charts. The computer just makes that task quicker, easier, and more authoritative.

Using the Computer
for Broader Market Indicators

Before leaving this section, there is one other interesting group of numbers made available in the daily version of EFTA—market indicators. These include the number of contracts that advanced versus the number that declined for the day (from over 200 contracts), new highs versus new lows, and percentage of contracts in computer uptrends. The first two indicators are the commodity version of the same barometers used in stock market analysis. While advance/decline numbers and new highs/new lows measurements have not traditionally been applied to the commodity markets, it's an interesting area for further investigation and research to determine their value for forecasting purposes.

Percentage of Futures Contracts in Computer Uptrends.   This particular indicator has become a favorite of mine. The percentage figure is on a scale of 0 to 100. It functions as an oscillator and can be used to determine when commodity markets as a whole are overbought or oversold. Historically, when the figure exceeds 70%, commodity markets are overbought and due for a setback. A reading below 20% usually warns of an oversold condition and a market bottom. This broad gauge of market sentiment can be used effectively in tracking the movements in the *CRB Futures Index.*

ARTIFICIAL INTELLIGENCE PATTERN RECOGNITION

The computer has made the technician's task easier by providing quick and easy access to a vast array of technical tools and indicators. At the same time, the technician's work has been made more difficult. Whereas before the technical analyst only had to deal with handful of favorite tools, now he or she has to contend with as many as 40 different indicators at the same time. Based on research in cognitive psychology, it is believed that the human mind has difficulty inter-relating more than three separate variables at the same time. The analyst trying to assimilate four or more indicators simultaneoulsy may become overwhelmed. If the analyst decides to follow only three indicators, which three are the best?

The computer has been used almost exclusively in market analysis as a computational device. Its main function has been to calculate and present data, to save us time. A more important use for the computer, however, may be in the interpretation of all of the data it has calculated for us; that is, to use its *logical* powers along with its *computational.* That brings us to the subject of Artificial Intelligence (AI) and Pattern Recognition (PR).

Artificial Intelligence refers to the use of "heuristic" programs to solve problems in much the same way a person does. The computer actually performs in a way that would be described as "intelligent." The computer assesses situations, makes decisions, and learns from mistakes. Pattern Recognition enables the computer to learn how to make decisions and predictions based on classifications of different items or indicators. The term "pattern" used in this context is different from our earlier use of the term to describe various chart "patterns." The intent in Pattern Recognition is to produce a "synergistic" effect by combining all of the indicators instead of treating each one individually.

The first step in the process is to find the best single indicator from all of those available. The second step is to find the best pair of indicators. The third step is to find the best three indicators used together. That process is continued until the addition of a new indicator no longer improves the final combined result. In the testing process, two different sets of data are used: *learning* and *test* data. The results found in the learning data must then be confirmed on separate test data. This technique of using two different sets of data prevents "curve-fitting," a charge often leveled against the testing of other technical methods, in particular, testing for optimized results.

The use of Artificial Intelligence and Pattern Recognition may hold the answer as to how to contend with so much conflicting information. In dealing with conflicting information, the computer is asked to calculate all of the indicators and then to choose the best combination of those indicators to use in a given situation. Because that solution seems so obvious, why isn't more work being done in that direction? So far, this type of work has been applied mainly to academic situations and not to real world conditions. The cost is large and requires extensive computer power. Even when patterns in the market are identified, they tend to be unstable and require constant retesting. One group that appears to have gotten a head start along those lines is the Raden Research Group (located in New York City). The main spokesman for that group is its president, David Aronson.

SUMMARY AND CONCLUSIONS

We've taken a look at the role of the computer in the world of technical futures trading. A review of the Compu Trac software, currently the industry leader, provided some idea of what is currently available and how it might be used. We also considered some of the pros and cons of mechanical system trading, using computer-generated signals. System trading represents a "black box" approach to futures trading. The user doesn't have to get involved in the decision-making process or even, for that matter, know or understand what's in the system. Other computer users prefer to stay involved in the process and use computer-generated signals and indicators in the analytical process. But they reserve for themselves the right to make the final market decision. That is the Compu Trac philosophy.

There's no question that the growing dependence on computer trading systems, particularly by pooled private and public commodity funds, is having a greater influence on futures trading. The new game on the floor of the exchange is trying to outsmart the computer funds. The ability of those pooled funds to influence and even distort short-term market behavior is growing. The proliferation of microcomputers with easy access to technical analysis routines, including on-line data, has increased the general level of sophistication of the average trader and caused more shorter-term trading. Day trading has become more popular because of easier access to computer terminals that can chart intra-day data.

Where all this will lead is uncertain. However, it is clear that the computer is revolutionizing commodity futures trading. Not that the computer is making trading any easier. On the contrary, for reasons already alluded to in the chapter, the computer has in some ways made our task a good deal more difficult. One important fact emerges from all of this. The commodity futures trader who doesn't have access to some of this computer technology is placing him- or herself at a severe disadvantage. It's hard enough to beat the market and the other market participants when everyone is using the same information.

Operating without the aid of a computer is giving an unnecessary edge to one's competitors and placing oneself under a severe handicap. Computers are here to stay. They'll get better, easier to use, and cheaper to buy in the years to come. The present-day commodity trader, however, can't afford the luxury of waiting for that to happen.

SOURCES OF INFORMATION

The most comprehensive source of computer software for technical analysis is Compu Trac at 1021 9th Street, New Orleans, LA 70115. In addition to providing an excellent support network, annual seminars are held in various national locations to educate members on how to use the programs and to keep members informed on newer developments. (The term "Compu Trac" is a registered trademark of Compu Trac, Inc.)

Other services are of course available. The best single source of information to help one keep abreast of developments in this rapidly changing area is a computer-oriented magazine, *Technical Analysis of Stocks & Commodities* (published by Technical Analysis, Inc.: 9131 California Ave SW, Seattle, WA 98136). Besides publishing computer-oriented articles on technical analysis, the magazine reviews current literature along with computer software and hardware services available to the futures trader. *Futures* magazine (published by Oster Communications, Inc.: 219 Parkade, Cedar Falls, Iowa 50613) is another source of information, but is not as computer-oriented.

For system traders, Welles Wilder's book is must reading. Another book that might be of interest is *Technical Trading Systems For Commodities and Stocks* by Charles Patel (Walnut Creek, Ca.: Trading Systems Research, 1980). Patel's book lists 82 different trading methods, including 65 that are completely mechanical.

16

Money Management and Trading Tactics

INTRODUCTION

The previous chapters presented the major technical methods used to forecast and trade commodity futures markets. In this final chapter, we'll round out the trading process by adding to the task of *market forecasting* the crucial elements of *trading tactics* (or timing) and the often overlooked aspect of *money management*. No trading program can be complete without all three elements.

By way of pulling together the various technical methods, a checklist is included to help you "touch all the bases," which may prove helpful in the early stages of learning how to coordinate all of the technical information. We'll address the question of whether or not technical analysis should be coordinated with fundamental analysis and, if so, how that might be accomplished to benefit both the technician and the fundamentalist. Finally, some general observations will be offered on the role of technical analysis as a profession and the future of that profession.

THE THREE ELEMENTS OF
SUCCESSFUL COMMODITY FUTURES TRADING

Any successful trading program must take into account three important factors: price forecasting, timing, and money management.

1. *Price forecasting* indicates which way a market is expected to trend. It is the crucial first step in the trading decision. The forecasting process determines whether the trader is bullish or bearish. It provides the answer to the basic question of whether to enter the market from the long or short side. If the price forecast is wrong, nothing else that follows will work.

2. *Trading tactics*, or timing, determines specific entry and exit points. Timing is especially crucial in futures trading. Because of the low margin requirements and the resulting high leverage, there isn't much room for error. It's quite possible to be correct on the direction of the market, but still lose money on a trade if the timing is off. Timing is almost entirely technical in nature. Therefore, even if the trader is fundamentally oriented, technical tools must be employed at this point to determine specific entry and exit points.

3. *Money management* covers the allocation of funds. It includes such areas as portfolio makeup, diversification, how much money to invest or risk in any one market, the use of stops, reward-to-risk ratios, what to do after periods of success or adversity, and whether to trade conservatively or aggressively.

The simplest way to summarize the three different elements is that price forecasting tells the trader *what* to do (buy or sell), timing helps decide *when* to do it, and money management determines *how much* to commit to the trade. The subject of price forecasting has been covered in the previous chapters. We'll deal with the other two aspects here. We'll discuss money management first because that subject should be taken into consideration when deciding on the appropriate trading tactics.

MONEY MANAGEMENT

After having spent many years in the research department of a major brokerage firm, I made the inevitable switch to managing money. I quickly discovered the major difference between recommending trading strategies to others and implementing them myself. What surprised me was that the most difficult part of the transition had little to do with market strategies. The way I went about analyzing the markets and determining entry and exit points didn't change much. What did change was my perception of the importance of money management. I was amazed at the impact such things as the size of the account, the portfolio mix, and the amount of money committed to each trade could have on the final results.

Needless to say, I am a believer in the importance of money management. The industry is full of advisors and advisory services telling clients *what* to buy or sell and *when* to do it. Very little is said about how much of one's capital to commit to each trade.

Some traders believe that money management is the most important ingredient in a trading program, even more crucial than the trading approach itself. I'm not sure I'd go that far, but I don't think it's possible to survive for long without it. Money management deals with the question of survival in the futures markets. It tells the trader how to handle his or her money. Any good trader should win in the long run. Money management increases the odds that the trader will survive to reach the long run.

Some General Money Management Guidelines

Admittedly, the question of portfolio management can get very complicated, requiring the use of advanced statistical measures. We'll approach it here on a relatively simple level. The following are some general guidelines that can be helpful in allocating one's funds and in determining the size of one's trading commitments.

1. *Total invested funds should be limited to 50% of total capital.* The balance is placed in Treasury Bills. This means that at any one time, no more than half of the trader's capital should be committed to the markets. The other half acts as a reserve during periods of adversity and drawdown. If, for example, the size of the account is $100,000, only $50,000 would be available for trading purposes.

2. *Total commitment in any one market should be limited to 10 to 15% of total equity.* Therefore, in a $100,000 account, only $10,000 to $15,000 would be available for margin deposit in any one market. This should prevent the trader from placing too much capital in any one trade (and risking ruin in the process).

3. *The total amount risked in any one market should be limited to 5% of total equity.* This 5% refers to how much the trader is willing to lose if the trade doesn't work. This is an important consideration in deciding how many contracts to trade and how far away a protective stop should be placed. A $100,000 account, therefore, should not risk more than $5,000 on a single trade.

4. *Total margin in any market group should be limited to 20 to 25% of total equity.* The purpose of this criteria is to protect against getting too heavily involved in any one market group. Markets within groups tend to move together. Gold and silver are part of the precious metals group and usually trend in the same direction. Putting on full positions in each market in the same group would frustrate the principle of diversification. Market commitments in the same group should be controlled.

These guidelines are fairly standard in the industry, but can be modified to the trader's needs. Some traders are more aggressive than others and take bigger positions. Others are more conservative. The important consideration is that some form of diversification be employed that allows for preservation of capital and some measure of protection during losing periods.

Determining the Size of One's Positions

Once the trader has decided to take a position in a market, and the time is right, the next decision is how many contracts to trade. We'll use a 10% rule here. Just multiply the total equity ($100,000) by 10% to determine the amount available for a trade. In this case, 10% of $100,000 would be $10,000. Let's assume the margin requirement for a gold contract is $2500. By dividing $10,000 by $2500, the trader could trade four gold contracts. If the Treasury Bond margin is $5,000, two Treasury Bond contracts could be held. If the S&P 500 margin is $6,000, only one contract of that market could be taken. In that case, a judgment would have to be made whether or not to allow two contracts (for a total of 12%). Remember, these are only guidelines and sometimes situations require a degree of flexibility. The most important point is not to get oneself overcommitted in any one market or market group to the point that a series of bad trades would be devastating.

Diversification Versus Concentration

While diversification is one way to limit risk exposure, it can be overdone. If a trader has trading commitments in too many markets at the same time, the few profitable trades will be diluted by the larger number of losing trades. A tradeoff exists and the proper balance must be found. Some successful traders concentrate their trading in a handful of markets. That's fine as long as those markets are the ones that are trending at that time. There's no absolutely correct answer as to how to resolve the dilemma between too much and too little diversification. My experience suggests a reasonable balance would be to hold positions in no more than four to six unrelated markets at the same time. The key word here is "unrelated." The more negative correlation between the markets, the more diversification is achieved. Holding long positions in four foreign currency markets at the same time would not be a good example of diversification.

Using Protective Stops

I strongly recommend the use of protective stops. Stop placement, however, is an art. The trader must combine technical factors on the price chart with money management considerations. We'll show how this is done later in the chapter in the section on *tactics*. The trader must consider the volatility of the market. The more volatile the market is, the looser the stop that must be employed. Here again, a tradeoff exists. The trader wants the protective stop to be close enough so that losing trades are as small as possible. Protective stops placed too close, however, may result in unwanted liquidation on short-term market swings (or "noise"). Protective stops placed too far away may avoid the noise factor, but will result in larger losses. The trick is to find the right middle ground.

REWARD-TO-RISK RATIOS

The best traders make money on only about 40% of their trades. That's right. Most trades wind up being losers. How then do traders make money if they're wrong most of the time? Because futures contracts require so little margin, even a slight move in the wrong direction results in forced liquidation. Therefore, it may be necessary for a trader to probe a market several times before catching the move he or she is looking for.

Suppose a trader expects gold prices to rise from $300 to $500. He or she buys a contract at $300 and risks $10. The market declines to $290 and the trade is stopped out. Another long trade is attempted at $295, followed again by a small loss of $10. Finally, a third purchase at $305 is followed by the desired recovery to $500 resulting in a profit of $195. Three trades were done. The first two were small losses totalling $20. The third trade resulted in a profit of $195. While only one of the three trades was profitable, the net result was a profit of $175 ($195 − $20). That translates to $17,500 in actual dollar profits ($175 × $100).

This brings us to the question of reward-to-risk ratios. Because most trades are losers, the only way to come out ahead is to ensure that the dollar amount of the winning trades is greater than that of the losing trades. To accomplish this, most traders use a reward-to-risk ratio. For each potential trade, a profit objective is determined. That profit objective (the reward) is then balanced against the potential loss if the trade goes wrong (the risk). A commonly used yardstick is a 3 to 1 reward-to-risk ratio. The profit potential must be at least three times the possible loss if a trade is to be considered. If the pre-determined risk in the previous gold trade were $10, the potential profit would have to be at least $30.

Some traders include a probability factor into the reward/risk calculation. They claim that it's not enough to just determine profit and loss objectives. They believe that the potential profit and loss must be multiplied by the percentage probability that those profits or losses will occur. While that approach makes sense from a statistical standpoint, it assumes that the trader is able in advance to quantify the probabilities of a potential profit or loss.

"Letting profits run and cutting losses short" is one of the oldest maxims of futures trading and is related to the previous point. Large profits in commodity futures trading are achieved by staying with persistent trends. Because only a relative handful of trades during the course of a year will generate large profits, it's necessary to maximize those few big winners. Letting profits run is the way that is done. The other side of the coin is to keep losing trades as small as possible. You'd be surpised how many traders do just the opposite.

TRADING MULTIPLE POSITIONS: TRENDING VERSUS TRADING UNITS

Letting profits run isn't as easy as it sounds. Picture a situation where a market starts to trend, producing large profits in a relatively short period of time. Suddenly, the trend stalls. The oscillators show an overbought situation and there's some resistance visible on the chart. What to do? You believe the market has much higher potential, but you're worried about losing your paper profits if the market should fail. Do you take profits or ride out a possible correction?

One way to resolve that problem is to always trade in multiple units. Those units can be divided into *trading* and *trending* positions. The trending portion of the position is held for the long pull. Loose protective stops are employed and the market is given plenty of room to consolidate or correct itself. These are the positions that produce the largest profits in the long run.

The trading portion of the portfolio is earmarked for shorter-term in-and-out trading. If the market reaches a first objective, is near resistance and overbought, some profits could be taken or a close protective stop utilized. The purpose is to lock up or protect profits. If the trend then resumes, any liquidated positions can be reinstated. It's best to avoid trading only one unit or contract at a time. The increased flexibility that is achieved from trading multiple units makes a big difference in overall trading results.

MONEY MANAGEMENT: CONSERVATIVE VS. AGGRESSIVE TRADING

An excellent discussion on money management is included in *The Commodity Futures Game* by Teweles, Harlow, and Stone. In their chapter entitled "Money Management," the authors make a compelling case for trading conservatively as the way to achieve ultimate success.

> . . . a trader with less probability of success but trading conservatively can actually have a better chance of long-term success (winning the game) than a trader with a higher probability of success

who chooses to trade more aggressively. (*The Commodity Futures Game*, Richard J. Teweles, Charles V. Harlow, Herbert L. Stone, McGraw-Hill, New York, 1977, p. 263.)

My own experience supports the view that the conservative approach is best in the long run. The trader looking to get rich quick trades in an aggressive fashion. As long as the markets are going in the right direction, the profits are impressive. That same strategy, however, is usually devastating when things start to go bad. Personally, I prefer a smoother trading performance with less pronounced peaks and valleys. Each trader has to decide where he or she fits on the spectrum. Before you decide, you might want to carefully read the previously mentioned chapter.

WHAT TO DO AFTER PERIODS OF SUCCESS AND ADVERSITY

Here are a couple of tricky questions to think about that are related to money management. What does a trader do after a losing or a winning streak? Suppose your trading equity is down by 50%. Do you change your style of trading? If you've already lost half of your money, you now have to double what you have remaining just to get back to where you were in the first place. Do you get more selective choosing trades, start trading markets with smaller margin requirements, or keep doing the same things you were doing before? If you become more conservative, it will be that much harder to win back your losses.

A more pleasant dilemma occurs after a winning streak. What do you do with your winnings? Suppose you've doubled your money. The obvious answer is to put your money to maximum use by doubling the size of your positions. If you do that, however, what will happen during the inevitable losing period that's sure to follow? Instead of giving back 50% of your winnings, you'll wind up giving it all back. So the answers to these two questions aren't as simple or obvious as they might first appear.

Every trader's track record is a series of peaks and troughs, much like a price chart. The trend of the equity chart should be pointing upward if the trader is making money on balance. The worst time to increase the size of one's commitments is after a winning streak. That's much like buying into an overbought market in an uptrend. The wiser thing to do (which goes against basic human nature) is to begin increasing one's commitments after a dip in equity. This increases the odds that the heavier commitments will be made near the equity troughs instead of the peaks.

MONEY MANAGEMENT IS A TRICKY BUT CRUCIAL AREA

We've only scratched the surface of this important aspect of futures trading. My main purpose here has been to alert the reader to the importance of money management in a trading plan, suggest a few general guidelines, and raise some questions that few traders seem to think about. Hopefully, the right answers will flow from asking the right questions. I'd like to end this relatively brief discussion with another quote from the source cited previously:

> If money management now appears to be an area that requires considerable thought, full of dilemmas and contradiction, and generally quite frustrating to the reader, he has made real progress . . . Most of these rules for basic survival are to be found in the area of money management, in which few traders are especially interested, rather than in the area of trade selection, which is the basic interest of most of them. (Teweles, Harlow, and Stone, pp. 271-272.)

THE MONEY MANAGEMENT INDUSTRY

The term "money management" is also used in the futures industry with reference to the professional management of clients' funds. "Money management" in that broader context describes the performance of both private and public pools of money (funds) that are managed by professional traders (Commodity Trading Advisors and Commodity Pool Operators). As more private investors place their funds under the care of such traders, using the pooled concept similar to the mutual fund industry, this segment of the futures industry has grown steadily over the past decade. This other use of the term "money management" is mentioned here to prevent any confusion, but is outside our main area of interest in this discussion.

Reference Material

While money management hasn't been given as much attention as it deserves in futures literature, there have been a couple of books on the subject. *Commodity Market Money Management* by Fred Gehm (New York: Wiley, 1983) provides a thorough study of money management principles utilizing statistical methods. For more information on money management within the context of the managed account industry, *The Investor's Guide to Futures Money Management* by Morton S. Baratz (Columbia, Md.: Futures Publishing Group, 1984) is an excellent source. Mr. Baratz is editor of *Managed Account Reports* (5513 Twin Knolls Road, Columbia, MD 21045), a newsletter that monitors the performance of the various money managers and reports regularly on their published track records.

TRADING TACTICS

Upon completion of the market analysis, the trader should know whether he or she wants to buy or sell the market. By this time, money management considerations should have dictated the level of involvement. The final step is the actual purchase or sale of the futures contract. This can be the most difficult part of the process because the timing of entry and exit points must be extremely precise in futures trading. The final decision as to how and where to enter the market is based on a combination of technical factors, money management parameters, and the type of trading order to employ. Let's consider them in that order.

Using Technical Analysis in Timing

There's nothing really new in applying the technical principles discussed in previous chapters to the timing process. The only real difference is that timing covers the very short term. The time frame that concerns us here is measured in days, hours, and minutes as opposed to weeks and months. But the technical tools employed remain the same. Rather than going through all of the technical methods again, we'll limit our discussion to some general concepts.

1. Tactics on breakouts

2. The breaking of trendlines

3. The use of support and resistance

4. The use of percentage retracements

5. The use of gaps

Tactics on Breakouts: Anticipation or Reaction?

The trader is forever faced with the dilemma of taking a position in anticipation of a breakout, taking a position on the breakout itself, or waiting for the pullback or reaction after the breakout occurs. There are arguments in favor of each approach or all three combined. If the trader is trading several contracts, one unit can be taken in each instance. If the position is taken in anticipation of an upside breakout, the payoff is a better (lower) price if the anticipated breakout takes place. The odds of making a bad trade, however, are increased. Waiting for the actual breakout increases the odds of success, but the penalty is a later (higher) entry price. Waiting for the pullback after the breakout is a sensible compromise, providing the pullback occurs. Unfortunately, many dynamic markets (usually the most profitable ones) don't always give the patient trader a second chance. The risk involved in waiting for the pullback is the increased chance of missing the market.

This situation is an example of how trading multiple positions simplifies the dilemma. The trader could take a small position in anticipation of the breakout, buy some more on the breakout, and add a little more on the corrective dip following the breakout. If the trader is trading only a small position, the decision will largely be determined by how much can be risked on the trade and how aggressively he or she wants to trade. The most conservative approach would be to buy the pullback after the breakout. Each trader must decide these questions for him- or herself.

The Breaking of Trendlines

This is one of the most useful early entry or exit signals. If the trader is looking to enter a new position on a technical sign of a trend change or a reason to exit an old position, the breaking of a tight trendline is often an excellent action signal. Other technical factors must, of course, always be considered. Trendlines can also be used for entry points when they act as support or resistance. Buying against a major up trendline or selling against a down trendline can be an effective timing strategy.

Using Support and Resistance

Support and resistance are the most effective chart tools to use for entry and exit points. The breaking of resistance can be a signal for a new long position. Protective stops can then be placed under the nearest support point. A closer protective stop could be placed just below the actual breakout point, which should now function as support. Rallies to resistance in a downtrend or declines to support in an uptrend can be used to initiate new positions or add to old profitable ones. For purposes of placing protective stops, support and resistance levels are most valuable.

Using Percentage Retracements

In an uptrend, pullbacks that retrace 40% to 60% of the prior advance can be utilized for new or additional long positions. Because we're talking primarily about timing, percentage retracements can be applied to very short-term action. A 40% pullback after a bullish breakout, for example, might provide an excellent buying point. Bounces of 40% to 60% usually provide excellent shorting opportunities in downtrends. Percentage retracements can be used on intra-day charts also.

Using Price Gaps

Price gaps on bar charts can be used effectively in the timing of purchases or sales. After an upmove, for example, underlying gaps usually function as support levels. Buy a dip to the upper end of the gap or a dip into the gap itself. A protective stop can be placed below the gap. In a bear move, sell a rally to the lower end of the gap or into the gap itself. A protective stop can be kept over the gap.

Combining Technical Concepts

The most effective way to use these technical concepts is to combine them. Remember that when we're discussing timing, the basic decision to buy or sell has already been made. All we're doing here is fine-tuning the entry or exit point. If a buy signal has been given, the trader wants to get the best price possible. Suppose prices dip into the 40% to 60% buying zone, show a prominent support level in that zone, and/or have a potential support gap. Suppose further that a significant up trendline is nearby.

All of these factors used together would improve the timing of the trade. The idea is to buy near support, but to exit quickly if that support is broken. In a downtrend, sell as close to resistance as possible, exiting quickly if that resistance is broken. Violation of a tight down trendline drawn above the highs of a downside reaction could also be used as a buying signal. During a bounce in a downtrend, the breaking of a tight up trendline could be a shorting opportunity.

COMBINING TECHNICAL FACTORS AND MONEY MANAGEMENT

Besides using chart points, money management guidelines should play a role in how protective stops are set. Let's go back to our previous gold example. Suppose the trader has decided to buy gold near $300. Assuming an account size of $100,000, and using the 10% criteria for maximum commitment, only $10,000 is available for the trade. With margin requirements of $2500, only four contracts could be purchased. The maximum risk is 5%, or $5,000. Therefore, protective stops on the total position must be placed in such a way that no more than $5,000 would be lost if the trade doesn't work.

Where those stops are placed is a combination of money management limitations and the location of chart support or resistance levels. Suppose that the buy point is at $301. The chart shows that the nearest reliable support level is $11 below, at $290. Placing the protective sell stops at $289 (below support at $290) would result in a risk exposure of $1200 on each contract ($12 × $100). The total risk on all four contracts would be $4800 (4 × $1200) and would be within the $5,000 limitation set by the money management guidelines.

If the nearest support level were $15 away, requiring a total risk on each contract of $1600, only three contracts (3 × $1600) could be purchased instead of the original four in order to stay within the $5,000. A nicer choice occurs if a closer support level can be found. If a stop could be placed only $5 below (risking only $500 per contract), as many as ten contracts could be purchased and would not exceed the $5,000. Of course purchasing ten contracts would violate the 10% rule, but some tradeoff is possible here.

A closer protective stop would permit the taking of larger positions. A looser stop would reduce the size of the position. Some traders use only money management factors in determining where to place a protective stop. It's critically important, however, that the protective stop be placed over a *valid* resistance point for a short position or below a *valid* support point for a long position. The use of intra-day charts can be especially effective in finding closer support or resistance levels that have some validity.

TYPES OF TRADING ORDERS

Choosing the right type of trading order is a necessary ingredient in the tactical process. We'll concern ourselves only with some of the more common types of orders: market, limit, stop, stop limit, and market-if-touched (M.I.T.).

1. The *market order* simply instructs your broker to buy or sell a futures contract at the current market price. This is usually preferable in fast market conditions or when the trader wants to ensure that a position is taken and to protect against missing a potentially dynamic market move.

2. The *limit order* specifies a price that the trader is willing to pay or accept. A *buy limit* order is placed below the current market price and states the highest price the trader is willing to pay for a purchase. A *sell limit* order is placed over the current market price and is the lowest price the seller is willing to accept. This type of resting order is used, for example, after a bullish breakout when the buyer wants to buy a downside reaction closer to support.

3. A *stop order* can be used to establish a new position, limit a loss on an existing position, or protect a profit. A stop order specifies a price at which an order is to be executed. A *buy stop* is placed over the market and a *sell stop* under the market (which is the opposite of the limit order). Once the stop price is hit, the order becomes a *market* order and is executed at the best price possible. On a long position, a sell stop is placed below the market to limit a loss. After the market moves higher, the stop can be raised to protect the profit (a trailing stop). A buy stop could be placed above resistance to initiate a long

position on a bullish breakout. A sell stop under support would activate a new short position on a bearish breakout. Since the stop order becomes a market order, the actual "fill" price may be beyond the stop price, especially in a fast market.

4. A *stop limit order* combines both a stop and a limit order. This type of order specifies both a stop price where the trade is activated and a limit price. Once the stop is elected, the order becomes a limit order. This type of order is useful when the trader wants to buy or sell a breakout, but wants to control the price paid or received.

5. The *market-if-touched (M.I.T.) order* is similar to a limit order, except that it becomes a market order when the limit price is touched. An M.I.T. order to buy would be placed under the market like a limit order. When the limit price is hit, the trade is made at the market. This type of trade has one major advantage over the limit order. The buy limit order placed under the market does not guarantee a fill even if the limit price is touched. Prices may bounce sharply from the limit price, leaving the order unfilled. An M.I.T. order is most useful when the trader wants to buy the dip, but doesn't want to risk missing the market after the limit price is hit. In a bear trend, an M.I.T. order would be placed above the market.

Each of these orders is appropriate at certain times. Each has its own strong and weak points. Market orders guarantee a position, but may result in "chasing" the market. Limit orders provide more control and better prices, but risk missing the market. Stop limit orders also risk missing the market if prices gap beyond the limit price. Stop prices are strongly recommended to limit losses and protect profits. However, the use of a buy or sell stop to initiate new positions may result in bad fills. The market-if-touched order is particularly useful, but is not allowed on some exchanges. Familiarize yourself with the different types of orders and learn their strengths and weaknesses. Each of them has a place in your trading plan. Be sure also to find out which types of orders are permitted on the various futures exchanges.

FROM DAILY CHARTS
TO INTRA-DAY PRICE CHARTS

Because timing deals with very short-term market action, intra-day price charts are especially useful. Intra-day charts are indispensable for day-trading purposes, although that's not our focus here. We're mainly interested in how intra-day activity can be used to aid the trader in the timing of purchases and sales once the basic decision to enter or exit a market has been made.

It bears repeating that the trading process must begin with a long range view and then gradually work toward the shorter term. Analysis begins with monthly and weekly continuation charts for long-term perspective. Then the daily chart is consulted, which is the basis for the actual trading decision. The intra-day chart is the last one viewed for even greater precision. The long-term chart gives a telescopic view of a market. The intra-day chart allows more microscopic study. You'll see that the technical principles already discussed are clearly visible on these very sensitive charts.

Let's demonstrate the procedure to follow in a Standard & Poor's 500 futures contract. Figure 16.1 is a daily bar chart showing 90 days of price action. (These charts are taken from the ADP Comtrend Videcom System, located in Stamford, CT). Above the chart are six possible modes, each with a different level of sensitivity. We'll start with the daily chart and work toward shorter time dimensions.

Let's assume the trader has already consulted the monthly and weekly charts and has concluded the technical outlook is for higher prices. The daily chart in Figure 16.1 also shows prices trending higher. The trader is bullish on the market and wants to initiate a long position. The daily chart can be helpful by identifying underlying support areas where purchases are possible. But if more precision is desired, the daily chart isn't very helpful. (The "thrust" technique could be used as a way to buy the reaction on the daily chart. We'll discuss this technique shortly.) Notice the last five days of price action marked off in the box in Figure 16.1. It can be seen that prices backed off on Monday and Tuesday before setting new highs on Friday. Not enough detail is shown. Let's proceed to a more sensitive chart (Figure 16.2) showing the same five days outlined by the box in Figure 16.1. In this more sensitive chart (mode 37), each price bar represents 15 minutes.

Notice the much greater detail. The five days of price action take on a whole new dimension. Previously unseen support and resistance levels are now visible, trendlines can be drawn, and price patterns appear. The trader can see the selloff on Monday and Tuesday, the double bottom on Tuesday, the bullish ascending triangle on Thursday, and new highs on Friday. Purchases could have been made on the upside breakout on Tuesday, during the consolidation on Thursday, or the second upside breakout on Friday. Let's zero in even further. Since Tuesday is the day the correcton ended, it is the most crucial

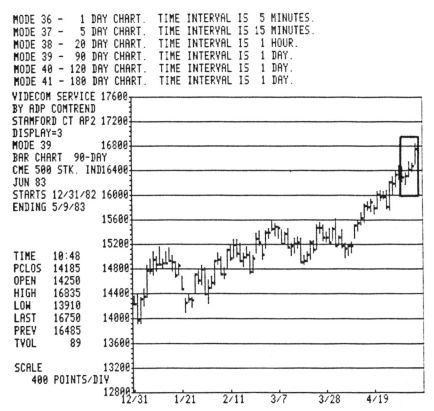

BAR CHARTS MODES 36-41

AP-6 DISPLAY=4

EACH BAR IS DEFINED AS THE HIGH, LOW AND LAST PRICE FOR THE
GIVEN TIME INTERVAL. IF THE TIME INTERVAL IS 1 DAY THE BAR WILL
REPRESENT THE DAILY HIGH, DAILY LOW, AND SETTLEMENT FOR THE DAY.
MODES 36-38 UPDATE AS NEW PRICES ARE REPORTED.

MODE 36 -   1 DAY CHART. TIME INTERVAL IS 5 MINUTES.
MODE 37 -   5 DAY CHART. TIME INTERVAL IS 15 MINUTES.
MODE 38 -   20 DAY CHART. TIME INTERVAL IS 1 HOUR.
MODE 39 -   90 DAY CHART. TIME INTERVAL IS 1 DAY.
MODE 40 - 120 DAY CHART. TIME INTERVAL IS 1 DAY.
MODE 41 - 180 DAY CHART. TIME INTERVAL IS 1 DAY.

VIDECOM SERVICE
BY ADP COMTREND
STAMFORD CT AP2
DISPLAY=3
MODE 39
BAR CHART 90-DAY
CME 500 STK. IND
JUN 83
STARTS 12/31/82
ENDING 5/9/83

TIME   10:48
PCLOS   14185
OPEN   14250
HIGH   16835
LOW   13910
LAST   16750
PREV   16485
TVOL   89

SCALE
   400 POINTS/DIV

Figure 16.1   Chart courtesy of Automatic Data Processing, Inc., Comtrend
Division, Stamford, CT.

day of the week. It would have been the best day to initiate new long
positions. Let's take a closer look at that day.

Figure 16.3 shows only Tuesday's price activity. Each price bar
shows five minutes of action (mode 36). Note the times of the day
along the bottom of the chart. Take special note of how well this
chart follows standard charting principles. See the double bottom that
was completed with the upside breakout above 162.50 around 2:15 in
the afternoon. An even earlier buy signal was given when prices broke
over resistance at 162.20. Notice the pullback around 3:15 which
retraced about 50% of the previous runup and stopped just above the

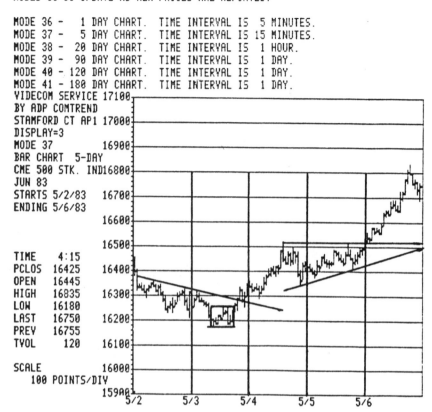

```
                                                AP-6 DISPLAY=3
EACH BAR IS DEFINED AS THE HIGH, LOW AND LAST PRICE FOR THE
GIVEN TIME INTERVAL.   IF THE TIME INTERVAL IS 1 DAY THE BAR WILL
REPRESENT THE DAILY HIGH, DAILY LOW, AND SETTLEMENT FOR THE DAY.
MODES 36-38 UPDATE AS NEW PRICES ARE REPORTED.

MODE 36 -    1 DAY CHART.  TIME INTERVAL IS  5 MINUTES.
MODE 37 -    5 DAY CHART.  TIME INTERVAL IS 15 MINUTES.
MODE 38 -   20 DAY CHART.  TIME INTERVAL IS  1 HOUR.
MODE 39 -   90 DAY CHART.  TIME INTERVAL IS  1 DAY.
MODE 40 -  120 DAY CHART.  TIME INTERVAL IS  1 DAY.
MODE 41 -  180 DAY CHART.  TIME INTERVAL IS  1 DAY.
VIDECOM SERVICE  17100
BY ADP COMTREND
STAMFORD CT AP1  17000
DISPLAY=3
MODE 37          16900
BAR CHART  5-DAY
CME 500 STK. IND 16800
JUN 83
STARTS 5/2/83    16700
ENDING 5/6/83

                 16600

                 16500
TIME    4:15
PCLOS  16425     16400
OPEN   16445
HIGH   16835     16300
LOW    16180
LAST   16750     16200
PREV   16755
TVOL     120     16100

SCALE            16000
   100 POINTS/DIV
                 15900
                     5/2    5/3     5/4     5/5     5/6
```

Figure 16.2 Chart courtesy of Automatic Data Processing, Inc., Comtrend Division, Stamford, CT.

162.50 breakout point—all standard chart analysis. Elliott Wave advocates should also notice a very clear five-wave advance from about 12:15 to the end of the day. All of this information could have been used by the trader. A buy could have been made on the breakout over 162.20, on the breakout over 162.50, or on the 50% pullback to support at 162.50. After the day's trading, a tight protective stop could have been placed under the low near 162.50.

People viewing these intra-day charts for the first time are often surprised at how well chart analysis works on such a short-term basis. In fact, if you didn't know in advance that Figures 16.2 and 16.3 were intra-day charts, you would never suspect it from the price action

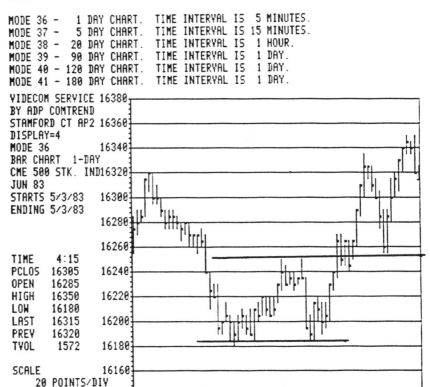

BAR CHARTS MODES 36-41

AP-6 DISPLAY=4

EACH BAR IS DEFINED AS THE HIGH, LOW AND LAST PRICE FOR THE
GIVEN TIME INTERVAL. IF THE TIME INTERVAL IS 1 DAY THE BAR WILL
REPRESENT THE DAILY HIGH, DAILY LOW, AND SETTLEMENT FOR THE DAY.
MODES 36-38 UPDATE AS NEW PRICES ARE REPORTED.

MODE 36 -   1 DAY CHART. TIME INTERVAL IS 5 MINUTES.
MODE 37 -   5 DAY CHART. TIME INTERVAL IS 15 MINUTES.
MODE 38 - 20 DAY CHART. TIME INTERVAL IS 1 HOUR.
MODE 39 - 90 DAY CHART. TIME INTERVAL IS 1 DAY.
MODE 40 - 120 DAY CHART. TIME INTERVAL IS 1 DAY.
MODE 41 - 180 DAY CHART. TIME INTERVAL IS 1 DAY.

Figure 16.3   Chart courtesy of Automatic Data Processing, Inc., Comtrend
Division, Stamford, CT.

alone, since these charts could just as easily be charts of six months
of action or six years. And that is precisely the point to be remembered
when market timing is attempted. The trader trying to fine-tune his
or her entry or exit point uses the exact same technical tools. The
difference lies only in the fact that these tools are being applied to
very short-term action.

Figures 16.4 through 16.7 show the same price action, but in
different formats. Figure 16.4 shows Tuesday's action on a "tic" chart.
Figures 16.5 and 16.6 show "trendline" charts, which draw an exponential smoothing curve through the tics. Figure 16.7 is an intra-
day point and figure chart of Tuesday's action. Point and figure charts

AP-5 DISPLAY=4
A TIC IS DEFINED AS THE NUMERICAL AVERAGE PRICE FOR ANY GIVEN TIME
INTERVAL. TIC CHARTS HAVE TIME INTERVALS FROM 1 MINUTE TO 1 DAY.
MODES 21-24 UPDATE AS PRICES ARE REPORTED.

MODE 21 -   1 DAY CHART. THE TIME INTERVAL IS 1 MINUTE.
MODE 22 -   5 DAY CHART. THE TIME INTERVAL IS 5 MINUTES.
MODE 23 -   20 DAY CHART. THE TIME INTERVAL IS 20 MINUTES.
MODE 24 -   60 DAY CHART. THE TIME INTERVAL IS 1 HOUR.
MODE 25 - 360 DAY CHART. THE TIC IS THE DAYS SETTLEMENT.

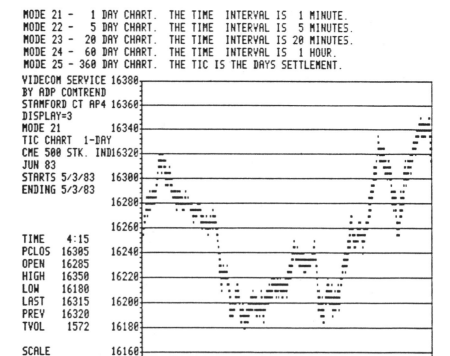

Figure 16.4   Chart courtesy of Automatic Data Processing, Inc., Comtrend Division, Stamford, CT.

lend themselves extremely well to short-term timing by identifying hidden support and resistance levels (see Chapter 11). Intra-day point and figure charts are especially popular among floor traders.

We've limited our chart examples to standard chart analysis. Virtually every method of technical analysis discussed in this book, including moving averages and oscillators, can be applied to intra-day charts. Moving averages are applied to a chosen number of tics or to intra-day time periods. In the latter case, for example, the last price for every five minutes could be averaged. Some of the more popular oscillators, such as the Relative Strength Index and Stochastics, are available on an intra-day basis. Compu Trac software, discussed at length in Chapter 15, is also available on an intra-day basis. That more sensitive version of its technical analysis routines is called the Intra-Day Analyst (IDA).

DUNNIGAN'S THRUST TECHNIQUE

The "thrust" technique, developed by William Dunnigan in the early 1950s, is one way to enter an existing trend on minor reactions using daily bar charts. The intention is to buy minor reactions against the

Figure 16.5 Chart courtesy of Automatic Data Processing, Inc., Comtrend Division, Stamford, CT.

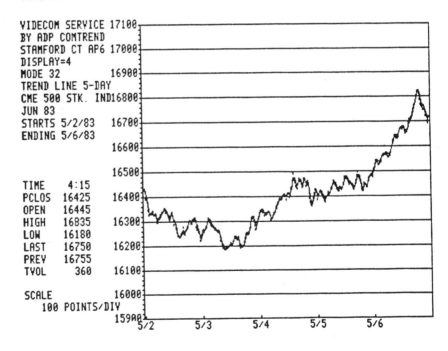

```
          TRENDLINE CHARTS  MODES 31-35
                                  AP-4 DISPLAY=4
A TRENDLINE CHART IS A TIC CHART WITH AN EXPONENTRAL SMOOTHING CURVE
DRAWN THROUGH THE TICS.  THE 5 DAY CHART DOES NOT HAVE THE SMOOTHING
CURVE DRAWN BETWEEN THE INTERDAY GAP.  THE OTHER MULTI-DAY CHARTS DO.
EACH TIC IS THE NUMERICAL AVERAGE PRICE FOR THE GIVEN TIME INTERVAL.
MODES 31-34 UPDATE AS PRICES ARE REPORTED.

MODE 31 -   1 DAY CHART.  TIME INTERVAL IS  1 MINUTE.
MODE 32 -   5 DAY CHART.  TIME INTERVAL IS  5 MINUTES.
MODE 33 -  20 DAY CHART.  TIME INTERVAL IS 20 MINUTES.
MODE 34 -  60 DAY CHART.  TIME INTERVAL IS  1 HOUR.
MODE 35 - 360 DAY CHART.  THE TIC IS THE DAYS SETTLEMENT.
```

AP-4 DISPLAY=4

A TRENDLINE CHART IS A TIC CHART WITH AN EXPONENTIAL SMOOTHING CURVE
DRAWN THROUGH THE TICS. THE 5 DAY CHART DOES NOT HAVE THE SMOOTHING
CURVE DRAWN BETWEEN THE INTERDAY GAP. THE OTHER MULTI-DAY CHARTS DO.
EACH TIC IS THE NUMERICAL AVERAGE PRICE FOR THE GIVEN TIME INTERVAL.
MODES 31-34 UPDATE AS PRICES ARE REPORTED.

```
MODE 31 -    1 DAY CHART.  TIME INTERVAL IS  1 MINUTE.
MODE 32 -    5 DAY CHART.  TIME INTERVAL IS  5 MINUTES.
MODE 33 -   20 DAY CHART.  TIME INTERVAL IS 20 MINUTES.
MODE 34 -   60 DAY CHART.  TIME INTERVAL IS  1 HOUR.
MODE 35 -  360 DAY CHART.  THE TIC IS THE DAYS SETTLEMENT.
```

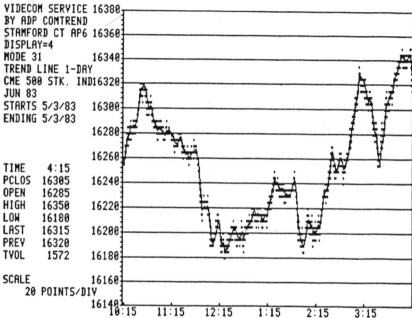

Figure 16.6 Chart courtesy of Automatic Data Processing, Inc., Comtrend Division, Stamford, CT.

trend. The minimum requirement in an uptrend is at least one down day. A more ideal situation would have three down days. A down day requires that both the high and low for the day be lower than the previous day. Inside and outside days don't count. Assuming at least one down day has occurred in the uptrend, the "thrust" signal to buy occurs when the high of the current day exceeds the high of the previous day by at least one tic. The long position is taken and a protective stop placed below the low of the day of entry.

This is the "thrust" technique in its simplest form. Some traders vary the amount of penetration needed for the actual buy or sell signal. In Figure 16.1, a strong uptrend is already in force. Both Monday and Tuesday of the final week were down days (both highs and lows lower than the previous day). A "thrust" signal to buy took place on Wednesday when prices exceeded Tuesday's high. This is a relatively simple technique that allows for entry into a strong trending market. The process is reversed in a downtrend. An up day would show the daily high and low higher than the previous day. The "thrust" signal to sell would take place on a violation of the previous day's low. A protective buy stop would be placed above the high point of the day of entry.

Figure 16.7 Chart courtesy of Automatic Data Processing, Inc., Comtrend Division, Stamford, CT.

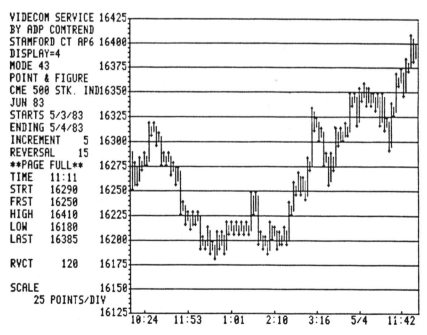

THE USE OF INTRA-DAY PIVOT POINTS

In order to achieve earlier entry with even tighter protective stops, some traders try to anticipate where a market will close by the use of pivot points. This technique combines seven key price levels with four time periods. The seven pivot points are the previous day's high, low, and close and the current day's open, high, low, and close. The four time periods are applied to the current trading day. They are the open, 30 minutes after the open, midday (about 12:30 New York time), and 35 minutes before the close.

These are average times and can be adjusted to the individual markets. The idea is to use pivot points only as a timing device when the trader believes a market is topping or bottoming. Buy or sell signals are given as the pivot points are broken during the day. The later in the day the signal is given, the stronger it is. As an illustration of a buy signal, if the market opens above the previous day's close, but is below the previous day's high, a buy stop is placed above the previous day's high. If the buy stop is elected, a protective sell stop is placed below the current day's low. At 35 minutes before the close, if no position has been taken, a buy stop is placed above the current day's high, with a protective stop under today's open. No action is generally taken during the first 30 minutes of trading. As the day progresses, the pivot points are narrowed as are the protective stops. As a final requirement on a buy signal, prices must close above both the previous day's closing price and today's opening price.

More detailed information on the use of pivot points can be found in a 40-page booklet by Walter J. Bressert, *Market Entry and Exit: How to Trade With the Professionals* (Tucson, Az.: Commodity Cycles, 1976). A shorter discussion is also included in the *HAL Cyclic Analyst's Kit* (HAL Market Cycles: Tucson, Az., 1984).

SUMMARY OF
MONEY MANAGEMENT AND TRADING GUIDELINES

The following list pulls together most of the more important elements of money management and trading.

1. Trade in the direction of the intermediate trend.

2. In uptrends, buy the dips; in downtrends, sell bounces.

3. Let profits run, cut losses short.

4. Always use protective stops to limit losses.

5. Don't trade impulsively; have a plan.

6. Plan your work and work your plan.

7. Use money management principles.

8. Diversify, but don't overdo it.

9. Employ at least a 3 to 1 reward-to-risk ratio.

10. When pyramiding (adding positions), follow these guidelines.

    a. Each successive layer should be smaller than before.

    b. Add only to winning positions.

    c. Never add to a losing position.

    d. Adjust protective stops to the breakeven point.

11. Never meet a margin call; don't throw good money after bad.

12. To prevent margin calls, make sure total equity is at least 75% of total margin requirements.

13. Close out losing positions before the winning ones.

14. Except for very short-term trading, make decisions away from the market, preferably when the markets are closed.

15. Work from the long term to the short term.

16. Use intra-day charts to fine-tune entry and exit.

17. Master inter-day trading before trying intra-day trading.

18. Try to ignore conventional wisdom; don't take anything said in the printed media too seriously.

19. Learn to be comfortable being in the minority. If you're right on the market, most people will disagree with you.

20. Technical analysis is a skill that improves with experience and study. Always be a student and keep learning.

21. Keep it simple; more complicated isn't always better.

Pulling It
All Together—A Checklist

As this book has demonstrated, technical analysis is a blend of many approaches. Each approach adds something to the analyst's knowledge of the market. Technical analysis is much like putting together a giant jigsaw puzzle. Each technical tool holds a piece of the puzzle. My approach to market analysis is to combine as many techniques as possible. Each works better in certain market situations. The key is knowing which tools to emphasize in the current situation. That comes with knowledge and experience.

All of these approaches overlap to some extent and complement one another. The day the user sees these interrelationships, and is able to view technical analysis as the sum of its parts, is the day that person deserves the title of technical analyst. The following checklist is provided to help the user touch all the bases, at least in the early going. Later on, the checklist becomes second nature. The checklist is not all-inclusive, but does have most of the more important factors to keep in mind. Sound market analysis seldom consists of doing the obvious. The technician is constantly seeking clues to future market movement. The final clue that leans the trader in one direction or the other is often some minor factor that has gone largely unnoticed by others. The more factors the analyst considers, the better the chances of finding that right clue.

TECHNICAL CHECKLIST

1. What is the direction of the *CRB Futures Price Index?*
2. What is the direction of the *group index?*
3. What are the *weekly* and *monthly* continuation charts showing?
4. Are the major, intermediate, and minor *trends* up, down, or sideways?
5. Where are the important *support* and *resistance* levels?
6. Where are the important *trendlines* or *channels?*
7. Are *volume* and *open interest* confirming the price action?
8. Where are the 33%, 50%, and 66% *retracements?*
9. Are there any price *gaps* and what type are they?
10. Are there any *major reversal patterns* visible?
11. Are there any *continuation patterns* visible?
12. What are the *price objectives* from those patterns?
13. Which way are the *moving averages* pointing?
14. Are the *oscillators* overbought or oversold?
15. Are any *divergences* apparent on the oscillators?
16. Are *contrary opinion* numbers showing any extremes?
17. What is the *Elliott Wave* pattern showing?
18. Are there any obvious *3- or 5-wave patterns?*
19. What about *Fibonacci* retracements or projections?
20. Are there any *cycle* tops or bottoms due?
21. Is the market showing *right or left translation?*
22. Which way is the *computer trend* moving: up, down, or sideways?
23. What are the *point and figure* charts showing?

After you've arrived at a bullish or bearish conclusion, ask yourself the following questions.

1. Which way will this market trend over the next one to three months?

2. Am I going to buy or sell this market?

3. How many contracts will I trade?

4. How much am I prepared to risk if I'm wrong?

5. What is my profit objective?

6. Where will I enter the market?

7. What type of order will I use?

8. Where will I place my protective stop?

Going through the checklist won't guarantee the right conclusions. It's only meant to help you ask the right questions. Asking the right questions is the surest way of finding the right answers. The keys to successful futures trading are knowledge, discipline, and patience. Assuming that you have the knowledge, the best way to achieve discipline and patience is doing your homework and having a plan of action. The final step is putting that plan of action to work. Even that won't guarantee success, but it will greatly increase the odds of winning in the futures markets.

HOW TO COORDINATE
TECHNICAL AND FUNDAMENTAL ANALYSIS

Despite the fact that technicians and fundamentalists are often at odds with one another, there are ways they can work together for mutual benefit. The technican often works in a vacuum. Many technicians don't want to be bothered with information that might cloud or influence the reading of their charts. Fundamental analysts often seem to perform their analysis with little or no consideration for technical factors.

Market analysis can be approached from either direction. While I believe that technical factors do lead the known fundamentals, I also believe that any important market move must be caused by underlying fundamental factors. Therefore, it simply makes sense for a technician to have some awareness of the fundamental condition of a market. If nothing else, the technician can inquire from his or her fundamental counterpart as to what would have to happen fundamentally to justify a significant market move identified on a price chart. In addition, seeing how the market reacts to fundamental news can be used as an excellent technical indication.

The fundamental analyst can use technical factors to confirm an analysis or as an alert that something important may be happening. The fundamentalist can consult a price chart or use a computer trend-following system as a filter to prevent him or her from assuming a position opposite an existing trend. Some unusual action on a price chart can act as an alert for the fundamental analyst and cause him or her to examine the fundamental situation a bit closer. During my years in the technical analysis department of a major brokerage firm, I often approached our fundamental department because of some market move that seemed imminent on the price charts. I never ceased to be amazed at how often I received responses like "that can never happen" or "no way." Very often, that same person was scrambling a couple of weeks later to find fundamental reasons to explain a sudden and unexpected market move. There's obviously room for much more coordination and cooperation in this area.

WHAT'S A TECHNICIAN ANYWAY?

This is a question the *Market Technicians Association* has been grappling with for the past couple of years. A lot of people use technical analysis. But what qualifications are required for a person to be called a professional technical analyst? Would a certain number of years in the business suffice, some type of identifiable product, or a written test? Should technical analysts be licensed or certified? Should some screening process be required similar to Chartered Financial Analysts (CFAs)? Whatever the outcome of those discussions, it's clear that the profession of technical analysis has reached a new level of maturity and recognition. This is true not only in the U.S., but worldwide as well.

The Market Technicians Association (MTA)

The *Market Technicians Association* (MTA) is the oldest and best known technical society in the world. It was founded in 1972 to encourage the exchange of technical information, educate the public and the investment community, and establish a code of ethics and professional standards among technical analysts. Membership includes full-time technicians and other users of technical analysis. Monthly meetings are held in New York, as well as an annual seminar at various locations. A monthly newsletter and a journal (published three times a year) are provided. The MTA is an organization that I would recommend to anyone seriously interested in technical analysis, either on the equity or futures side of the business. The MTA mailing address is 70 Pine Street, New York, N.Y. 10270.

THE GLOBAL REACH OF TECHNICAL ANALYSIS

Serious work is in progress to establish the International Federation of Technical Analysts. A meeting was held in the fall of 1985 in Japan, with representatives of several different countries, to draft a constitution. During 1985, new organizations were founded in Canada and Singapore. Technical organizations exist in several other countries, including England. (Each September, Investment Research [Cambridge, England] sponsors a conference on International Technical Analysis at that location.)

The catalyst in the international movement was the arrival of a delegation from the Nippon Technical Analyst Association (founded in 1978) at the 9th Annual MTA Seminar in Monterey, California in 1984. During that seminar, Japanese speakers reminded the audience that technical analysis was first used in the Japanese rice market in the 17th century, predating our usage by two centuries. The first written reference to technical methods in Japan was a collection of proverbs in the form of short poems (published in 1755) called "San-En-Kin-Sen-Roku" (Three Monkeys' Confidential Financial Documents). The 1985 MTA Annual Award was given to one of Japan's most respected technicians and marked the first time that award had been given to a non-American. Given this new technical link between the U.S. and Japan, it seems only fitting that the Chicago Mercantile Exchange recently obtained the right to trade futures and options on two major Japanese stock market averages, the Nikkei 225 and 500.

TECHNICAL ANALYSIS:
THE LINK BETWEEN STOCKS AND FUTURES

In addition to the growing international dimension, the universal language of technical analysis has provided a common bond between the different investment communities. Stock market technicians and commodity futures technicians had little contact in the past. With the popularity of stock index futures, and financial futures in general, the lines of division between the two groups are gradually disappearing. Stock market analysts are honing their tools to stock index and interest rate futures. Developments in foreign currency futures are being tracked closely. The direction of petroleum futures and the overall commodity price level have become important inputs into the analysis performed by equity technicians.

Various stock groups, such as copper and gold shares, are greatly influenced by those commodity markets, necessitating close monitoring of the futures markets. Futures technicians, in turn, might be well-advised to begin following movements in those stock groups for confirmation of their analysis in the futures markets or to uncover divergences. Both groups stand to benefit from greater contact and the sharing of ideas. Futures technicians, who have dealt mainly with the traditional commodities, can learn more about stock market analysis from their equity counterparts. The latter group must learn more about how technical analysis is performed in the futures markets if they're going to delve into that faster moving arena.

Because of the highly leveraged nature of the futures markets, technicians in that area have been forced to sharpen their timing tools to a fine edge. In my opinion, *most of the pioneering work in the area of market timing has been done in the futures area, not in stocks.* Stock market technicians are beginning to see this and have developed a new respect for futures traders, who in the past were relegated to the the status of second class citizens. In my contact with equity technicians, I have detected a growing interest in and respect for the work being done by technical analysts on the futures side.

I'd like to leave you with a couple of positive thoughts on the role of technical analysis as it applies to futures markets in general. The principles of technical analysis lend themselves to virtually any trading medium, either in stocks or futures, and to any time dimension as well. With the proper tools, and sharpened reflexes, the chartist in stocks should be able to make the necessary transition to futures trading. Second, because of the increased emphasis on timing in the trading of futures, which is purely technical in nature, *technical analysis is even more important in futures than it is in stocks.*

CONCLUSION

After a hundred years of use in this country (and over 300 in Japan), technical analysis has stood the test of time and has prospered. The growing worldwide interest in this subject speaks well of the discipline and the people who practice it. It's also interesting to note that, at a time when things seem to be changing so much in the marketplace, technical analysis is more popular than ever. With the proliferation of new products over the past couple of years, some have begun to question whether the traditional tools still apply. My answer to that question is that "the more things change, the more they stay the same." I believe that Charles Dow would still feel at home in today's markets. No discipline has adjusted to the new products as well as technical analysis. And, if the rules of the game ever do change, my hunch is that the technicians will be the first to know about it.

Appendix **1**

Spread Trading
and Relative Strength

This book has dealt mainly with the outright trading of commodity futures contracts. Spread trading, however, is another popular way to participate in the futures markets. *Outright trading* refers to the taking of long or short positions in anticipation of a price rise or decline. The trader stands to benefit from an absolute change in price. *Spread trading* refers to the simultaneous purchase and sale of two different futures contracts. Those contracts can be in the same commodity (intracommodity or interdelivery spreads), two different but related commodities (intercommodity spreads), or commodities on different exchanges (intermarket spreads).

When using spreads (also called *straddles*), the trader hopes to profit by changes in the spread (difference) between the two contracts. The trader is banking on either the widening or the narrowing of that spread relationship. Spread traders are not as concerned with the absolute price changes, up or down, as they are with the changing spread differentials. Spread trading is considered a less expensive and less risky way to participate in the futures markets. Margin requirements are lower in spreads than they are in outright positions. The risks are smaller since both a long and a short position are held at the same time. Since the risk is smaller, so is the profit potential.

Spread trading is more complicated than outright trading and requires a higher degree of sophistication. Other reference sources are available for an in-depth study of this type of trading. Our purpose is to briefly point out the application of technical analysis to spread trading. A secondary purpose is to discuss how spread or ratio relationships between different contracts (or markets) can be helpful in forecasting market direction, using the concept of *relative strength*.

THE APPLICATION OF
TECHNICAL ANALYSIS TO SPREAD CHARTS

Whether the trader is tracking the spread relationship between two contracts in the same market (July versus November soybeans or September versus December Treasury Bills) or contracts in two separate

Figure App. 1.1 The spread chart of leaded gas versus crude oil has strengthened since April. The spread trader should have bought leaded gas and sold crude oil futures contracts. The spread chart also reveals that leaded gas was a better candidate for an outright long position and crude oil a better shorting candidate. (Chart courtesy of Commodity Research Bureau, a Knight-Ridder Business Information Service.)

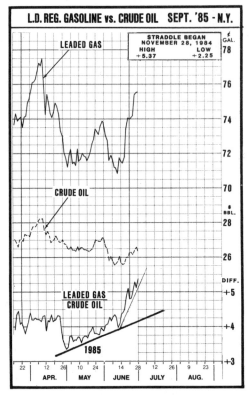

markets (December corn versus December wheat or September Value Line vs. September S&P 500), the spread is plotted on a chart. It can be seen that the spread relationship usually trends either upward or downward. It follows, therefore, that many of the technical tools applied to outright futures charts can also be used to track the trends

Figure App. 1.2 The platinum versus gold spread has been weakening. The trader should have been short platinum and long gold. A trader who is bearish on precious metals would have made more money by shorting platinum than gold in an outright trade. Platinum usually leads the precious metals group. This spread can also be used as a technical indication of the direction of the group as a whole. A weakening spread is bearish and a strengthening spread, bullish. (Chart courtesy of Commodity Research Bureau, a Knight-Ridder Business Information Service.)

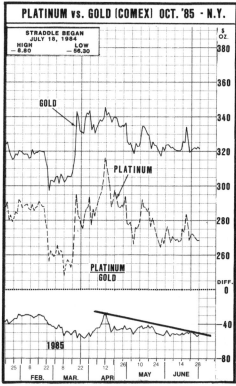

on the spread charts. Support and resistance are visible on the spread charts, and trendlines can be drawn. The breaking of valid trendlines can be used to spot shifts in the trend. Moving averages and oscillators can also be used. Point and figure spread charts can be constructed and utilized. The accompanying charts demonstrate some technical tools applied to spread charts. (See Figures App. 1.1 through 1.7.)

Figure App. 1.3   During the bull move in interest rate futures, T-Bills were weaker than Eurodollars. The spread trader should have been simultaneously short Bills and long Eurodollars. An outright trader would do better being long Eurodollars instead of Bills as long as the spread continues to move below the down trendline. During a banking crisis, government-backed debt, such as Treasury Bills, performs better than bank-related instruments, such as bank certificates of deposits (CDs) and Eurodollars. Eurodollars are dollar deposits in non-U.S. banks. The "flight to quality" spread takes place during a crisis of confidence in the banking system. Traders buy T-Bills and sell CDs and Eurodollars. (Chart courtesy of Commodity Research Bureau, a Knight-Ridder Business Information Service.)

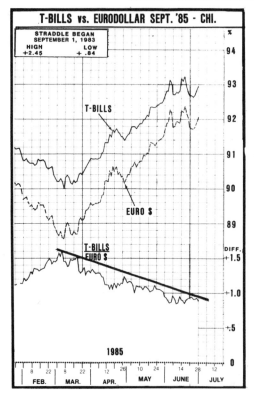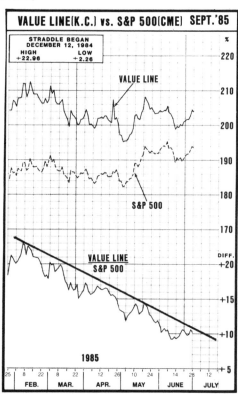

Figure App. 1.4   In the above example, the spreader should have been short the Value Line futures index and long the S&P 500. The breaking of the down trendline would be a signal to liquidate the spread position and maybe even reverse positions. This spread is also followed closely as a technical indication of market direction. A declining spread is bearish. A rising spread is bullish. (Chart courtesy of Commodity Research Bureau, a Knight-Ridder Business Information Service.)

Spread Trading and Relative Strength

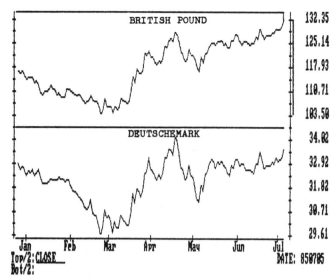

Figure App. 1.5 A comparison of two foreign currency charts. The upper chart is the British pound. The lower chart is the Deutsche mark. Both markets have been trending upward. However, the pound has been stronger than the mark. Notice that the pound has already set new 1985 highs.

Figure App. 1.6 These two charts show trendlines and moving averages applied to a spread chart of the pound versus the mark. The spread is trending upward showing that the pound has been stronger. The spread trader should have been long the pound and short the mark. An outright trader, looking to go long, could have used this chart as reason to buy the pound instead of the mark. Note the trendlines on the upper chart and the 10- and 40-day moving averages on the lower chart. Spread charts lend themselves well to most technical indicators.

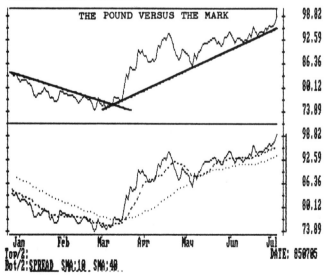

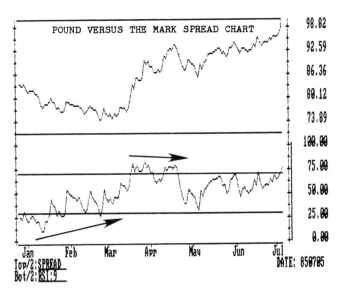

Figure App. 1.7 The lower chart is a nine-day Relative Strength Index (RSI) applied to the same spread chart. In that way, oscillator analysis can be used. Notice the bullish divergence in late February and the bearish divergence in April. The spread chart has just crossed the upper line and is becoming a bit overbought. Various types of oscillators can be used on spread charts.

RELATIVE STRENGTH
BETWEEN NEARBY AND DISTANT CONTRACTS

Besides being used for spread trading, tracking the spread relationships between different contracts in the same market or in different markets can provide useful clues about market direction. The relationships between the nearby and distant months in the same commodity often tell us something about the bullish or bearish nature of the market itself. In certain types of bull markets, caused by tightness in the supply/demand situation, the nearby months usually rise faster than the distant ones. *Bull spreading* is the purchase of a nearby contract and a short sale of a distant contract in such cases. In bear markets, caused by a relative overabundance in the supply/demand situation, the nearbys usually weaken more than the distant months. *Bear spreading* in such cases is the short sale of a nearby month and the purchase of a distant contract. (One notable exception to this principle in the traditional commodity markets is the precious metals group. Bull and bear markets in the gold, silver, and platinum markets are led by the distant months.)

By keeping an eye on the relationships between the nearby and distant months, the technical analyst can often get an early clue that a market is turning higher or lower. Whether or not the analyst actually does the spread trading, these relationships are useful to watch and can be used as another technical indication of market strength or weakness.

RELATIVE STRENGTH BETWEEN DIFFERENT MARKETS

Monitoring the spread relationships between different markets can also provide clues as to their relative strength or weakness. Suppose a trader is bullish on the foreign currency markets. By monitoring the spread relationships between the various currencies, long positions could be taken in the stronger markets. During downtrends, short positions could be taken in the weaker acting markets. Therefore, the concept of *relative strength* is much broader than the idea of spread trading itself. The ability to measure relative strength between various markets by tracking spread relationships can be helpful in deciding which markets to trade. (See Figure App. 1.8.)

Figure App. 1.8 A comparison of a spread and ratio chart. The upper chart is the same spread of the pound versus the mark. The lower chart is a ratio between the same two currencies. Ratio analysis is another way to determine relative strength between contracts. In this case, the ratio chart is even stronger than the spread chart. Note the 40-day moving average applied to both charts. Technical tools can also be used in ratio analysis.

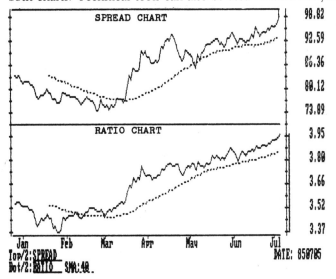

RATIO ANALYSIS

Ratio analysis can also be particularly valuable in the measurement of relative strength. *Spreads* refer to the actual price differences. *Ratios* refer to the price of one entity divided by another. Either concept can be utilized when comparing different contract months or markets. Ratios can be constructed between different contract months in the same market to identify the strongest or weakest months. In bull markets, long positions would be taken in the strongest month. In bear trends, the weakest month would be the best shorting candidate. In the analysis of various market groups, ratio analysis can be used to identify the strongest or weakest markets in the group. The strongest market would be the best candidate for a purchase and the weakest, for a short sale.

RELATIVE STRENGTH BETWEEN COMMODITY INDICES

So far, we've discussed how relative strength can be used to identify the best contract to trade in a given market, or to find the best market within a given group. Let's broaden the discussion to include identification of the best market group to trade. The basic principle we've been following is that the strongest contracts or markets are the best candidates for long positions and the weakest contracts or markets the best candidates for short positions. The trader could also use ratio analysis to compare various group indices to a broad index, such as the CRB *Futures Price Index.* That way, the strongest groups would be considered for long positions and the weakest groups for shorting purposes.

Suppose the trader believed that the CRB Futures Index was turning higher. That analysis would suggest a buying program. By applying ratio analysis between the CRB Index and the indices of the various markets groups, the strongest acting groups could be identified. Those groups would be the best candidates for new long positions. By then applying that same type of ratio analysis within each group, the strongest market in each group could be found. The final step would be to compare the different delivery months in the strongest market to find the strongest month to trade. The final goal would be to buy the strongest contract month in the strongest market in the strongest commodity group. In a bear market, the trader would be looking to short the weakest contract in the weakest market in the weakest group.

STOCK INDEX FUTURES VERSUS THE CASH INDEX: A MEASURE OF SHORT-TERM MARKET SENTIMENT

Arbitrage is the simultaneous purchase and sale of substantially identical entities. It's similar to spread trading with one major difference. Arbitrageurs move quickly to take advantage of situations where two entities are temporarily "out of line." A long position in one entity and a short position in the other are quickly taken on the expectation that a profit will be made when the two entities move closer together. This type of trading has become popular in stock index futures. The futures contracts are more volatile than the underlying cash indices and frequently move out of line with them. During market upmoves, the futures contract usually advances well ahead of the underlying instrument. Professional arbitrage programs will then be initiated to take advantage of the futures premium. The futures contract is sold short and a corresponding long position taken in a representative basket of common stocks. During market downmoves, the futures contract often moves to a discount. In that case, professionals will buy the futures contract and sell the basket of common stocks.

The spread relationship between the futures contract and the underlying cash index is watched closely as a short-term technical measure of bullish and bearish sentiment. When the futures contract moves too far above the cash index, a short-term overbought condition exists and a pullback is expected. When the futures contract moves too far below the cash index, an oversold condition exists and a technical bounce anticipated.

REFERENCE SOURCES

Most commercial chart services include some spread and ratio charts. One chart service that specializes in spread charts is *Spread Scope Inc.* (P.O. Box 5841, Mission Hills, CA 91345). There are several books on the subject. One is *Commodity Spreads, Techniques and Methods For Spreading Financial Futures, Grains, Meats, and Other Commodities* by Courtney Smith (New York, NY: John Wiley & Sons, Inc., 1982). Another book, already mentioned in Chapter 14, is *How to Profit from Seasonal Commodity Spreads: A Complete Guide* by Jacob Bernstein (New York, NY: John Wiley & Sons, Inc., 1983). Most books on commodity futures include a section on spread trading.

If the trader gets involved in spread trading, knowledge of technical analysis will prove valuable. Even if the trader doesn't do spread trading per se, some knowledge of the relationships between different contract months can provide useful insights into a market's strength and should be monitored. Knowledge of a market's relative strength vis a vis other markets can be useful information in the outright trading of commodity futures markets.

The Trading of Options

WHAT IS AN OPTION?

The use of *options* as an alternative way to participate in the futures markets has grown in popularity over the past couple of years. A *commodity option* gives the holder the right, but not the obligation, to purchase (a call) or sell (a put) on an underlying futures contract at a specific price within a specified period of time. The two types of options are *puts* and *calls*. In its most basic application, a trader who is bullish on a commodity market could simply purchase a *call* on the underlying futures contract instead of going long the futures contract itself. A bearish trader could simply purchase a *put* on the underlying futures contract instead of going short the futures market.

WHY PURCHASE AN OPTION
INSTEAD OF A FUTURES CONTRACT?

The basic advantage of purchasing an option on a futures contract, as opposed to the futures contract itself, is *limited risk*. When a trader takes a position in the futures market, initial margin money is required. That margin is relatively small and is usually only about 5% of the value of the futures contract. If the market moves against the trader's position, however, more margin money may be required to hold onto the position. In a fast moving market, the trader could lose more than the initial margin deposit. In options trading, however, the trader is required to pay only a *premium* to purchase the option. The size of the premium is determined on the floor of the exchange. That premium is the maximum amount the trader can lose if the market doesn't move as expected. If the market does trend as expected, the option holder still has unlimited profit potential (minus the premium cost).

Comparison of
Futures And Options Positions

Suppose a trader is bullish on gold and desires to benefit from the high leverage offered by participation in the futures market. The trader has two choices—to buy a futures contract or an option on the futures contract. Let's suppose the futures contract is bought. A long position is taken at $300. The initial margin requirement is $2,000. If the market goes up to $400, the trader has a profit of $10,000 ($100 × 100 oz.). As an alternative, suppose the trader chooses to buy a call option instead. A December gold call option is bought on the floor of the Comex at a strike price (exercise price) of $300. The premium paid for the option is $3,000 ($30 × 100 oz.). On a rally to $400, the option holder has a profit of $10,000 minus the $3,000 cost of the option (for a net profit of $7,000, compared to $10,000 for the futures trader). In this instance, the futures trader comes out ahead of the option trader because the latter has to pay the additional cost of the premium.

The Advantages of Limited Risk

But what if the price of gold dips to $250 instead of going up? The futures trader, who went long at $300, has a loss of $5,000 ($50 × 100 oz.). Most futures traders would probably have liquidated the long position before the loss became that large. In that case, however, the futures trader could no longer profit if the price did in fact turn higher (since the long futures position has been liquidated). This situation illustrates two advantages the option trader has: *limited risk* and *staying power*. If the price does start to fall and continues to move lower, the holder of a call option simply chooses not to exercise the call. The most that can be lost is the original premium of $3,000 ($30 × 100 oz.). There are no margin calls for the holder of an option. (The absence of margin calls makes options particularly attractive for hedging purposes.)

The Advantage of Staying Power

The second advantage of options trading is *staying power*. Whereas the holder of the futures long position may be forced to liquidate the position, the option holder has bought time. He or she has until the expiration date of the option to profit from a price increase. If the expiration date of the option is six months away, then the option holder can profit from a price increase during that period of time. The option holder can ride out adverse price moves. This reduces the need to closely monitor positions and reduces much of the stress of futures trading. The option buyer has the same unlimited profit potential as the futures trader and the same high leverage, but with the advantages of predetermined risk and greater staying power.

HOW OPTIONS AND FUTURES CAN BE USED TOGETHER

Most commodity options are never exercised. If a paper profit results from a price move in the underlying futures contract, the put or call option is simply offset on the floor of the exchange and the profit taken. That way, the options trader doesn't even have to take a position in the futures market. There are ways, however, that futures and options trading can be combined.

1. An option can be used to limit losses on a futures contract. If a trader takes a long position in the futures market, a put option can also be bought and used as a protective sell stop.

2. An option can be used as a trailing stop on a futures contract. If the market moves in the expected direction and a paper profit is achieved on a futures contract, an opposite option position could be assumed and used as a trailing stop. A put option could be bought to protect long futures profits, and a call option to protect short profits in the futures market.

3. An option could also be bought to add to a profitable position in the futures market. Suppose a long position is held in the futures market and a trader wants to utilize a low-risk method of adding to the long position. A call option could be purchased. If the market continues higher, the trader would profit from any gains in excess of the cost of the option. If the market turns down, all that would be lost on the option would be the premium. A put option would be utilized to add to a profitable short position in the futures market.

WHAT DETERMINES PREMIUM VALUE?

Options trading is a very complex subject, requiring careful study before it should be attempted. We're just touching on basic concepts in this discussion. The reader should become familiar with the terminology of options strategies and the factors that help determine a fair premium value. The two basic determinants of the premium are intrinsic value and time value.

Intrinsic value refers to the amount the option is already "in the money." If the price of the futures contract is already above the exercise price of a call option, a built-in profit already exists. The buyer of the option has to pay at least the amount of that built-in profit.

Time value varies with the amount of time left in the option before expiration. A six-month option has more time value than a three-month option. Time value drops as the option approaches expiration. (Hence the term "wasting asset.") Other factors that determine the size of the premium are market volatility, interest rates, and the demand for the option itself. The demand for the option itself is determined by the market's evaluation of price direction. During periods of rising futures prices, call premiums will be higher and put options lower (since there's a greater demand for call options). With falling futures prices, put premiums are higher and call premiums lower.

TECHNICAL ANALYSIS AND OPTION TRADING

Our main concern here is the relevance of technical analysis in the trading of options on futures contracts. Bear in mind that put and call options can be viewed simply as surrogate futures positions. A call option is similar to a long position and a put option the same as a short position. An option trader can therefore read through the technical principles described in this book and simply insert the phrase "call option" in place of "a long futures position" and replace "short futures position" with "put option." By making that simple mental adjustment, technical analysis can be viewed through the eyes of an option trader.

Option strategies generally require a market view. The buyer of a call option is bullish on a market. A buyer of a put option expects prices to fall. Even an option writer (the seller or grantor) bases that strategy on his or her opinion of the underlying market. The option writer usually sells call options in flat to slightly bearish markets. Put options are usually sold in neutral to slightly bullish markets. An option writer receives the premium paid by the option buyer. In return for absorbing the risk that the option buyer is avoiding, the writer is paid the premium. Writing options is one way of profiting from sideways market moves when no trend is apparent or expected. Option writing is a risky business and is best left to more experienced market participants.

TECHNICAL ANALYSIS APPLIED TO THE UNDERLYING FUTURES MARKET

In determining option strategy, the option trader does not apply the principles of market analysis to the option itself. *Technical analysis must be performed on the underlying futures market.* Once that is done, and the option trader has developed a market view, the appropriate bullish, bearish, or neutral option strategies can be developed and implemented. Remember that an option is just another way of trading or investing in the futures markets. The major factor determining the value of that option, as well as the appropriate option strategy to follow, is the performance of the underlying futures market. Therefore, the first and most important step in developing option strategies is the analysis of the futures market itself. For that important task, technical analysis is highly recommended. And that's what this book is all about.

RECOMMENDED READING

The reader wishing to pursue option trading in the futures markets should consult other texts that deal specifically with that subject. One such text is *Commodity Options: A User's Guide to Speculating and Hedging* by Terry S. Mayer (New York, NY: The New York Institute of Finance, 1983). Another is *Inside the Commodity Option Markets* by John W. Labuszewski and Jeanne Cairns Sinquefield (New York, NY: John Wiley & Sons, Inc., 1985).

PUT/CALL RATIOS AS A MEASURE OF MARKET SENTIMENT

An option trader with a bullish attitude toward a market buys call options. A market bear buys put options. If most option buyers are bullish, that bias is reflected in a higher level of call activity. Correspondingly, a greater bearish consensus is manifested in higher put activity. Volume figures for put and call options are reported daily in the financial press. It is therefore possible, by monitoring the respective put and call volume levels, to determine whether option buyers are predominantly bullish or bearish and whether that relative bias is intensifying or diminishing.

Technicians have developed a variety of put/call ratios that are used as a measure of market sentiment. The most common ratio is based on the volume figures. The number of put options traded is divided by the number of call options. A rising ratio suggests a bearish attitude (more puts are being purchased than calls). A falling ratio indicates a bullish attitude (more calls are being purchased than puts). The greatest value of a put/call ratio is at extremes, similar to an overbought/oversold oscillator. It is then used as a contrary indicator. An extremely high reading usually signals a market bottom. An ex-

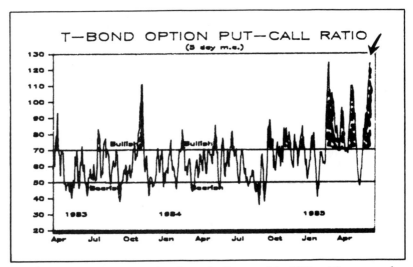

Figure App. 2.1   An example of a put/call ratio of the T-Bond futures market. An usually high reading (using a 5-day moving average) shows put activity much higher than call activity. This is considered a bullish reading. A high put/call ratio is bullish. A low ratio is considered bearish. (Chart courtesy of *Marketrend*, Butcher & Singer, Inc., Manhasset, NY.)

tremely low reading would be interpreted as a warning of an impending market top. The technician can also interpret divergences between the ratio line and the price action as another warning that the price trend may be near a turn. (See Figure App. 2.1.)

Stock market technicians have been trading listed options on the Chicago Board Options Exchange (CBOE) since the early 1970s and have developed a number of technical indicators based on option activity. Listed options on futures exchanges are a phenomenon of the 1980s. No doubt futures technicians, with more experience and research in this area, will also find option trading statistics a fertile ground for a new generation of technical indicators.

W.D. Gann: Geometric Angles and Percentages

INTRODUCTION

William D. (W.D.) Gann (1878-1955) was a legendary stock and commodity trader during the first half of the century. During his fifty-year career, he developed a unique combination of precise mathematical and geometric principles, which he applied successfully in his trading. During the second half of his career, he began to write about and teach his methods. Most of his work was out of print during the 1950s and '60s, and public knowledge of his writing suffered accordingly. In 1976, Billy Jones, a wheat farmer and cattle rancher, purchased the Lambert-Gann Publishing Company from Gann's former partner, Edward Lambert. Jones has reprinted much of Gann's original work and has been largely responsible for the renewed interest in Gann's methods over the past decade.

Gann's approach is extremely complicated and not easy to grasp. Gann analysts have spent years pouring over old charts and writings, spanning a period of 25 years, to decipher his many insights. Much of Gann's work is based on traditional charting concepts. He placed tremendous importance on historic highs and lows as future resistance and support areas, respectively. He stressed that a broken resistance level became support and that former support became resistance. He was a firm believer in the 50% retracement. Some of his more original ideas include cardinal squares, the squaring of price and time, and geometric angles.

The *cardinal square* is a method of arriving at future support or resistance levels by counting forward from the all-time low price of a commodity. The beginning price is placed in the center of the square, and each higher price increment is entered in a clockwise fashion. Numbers that fall in the *cardinal-cross* portion of the square (on the vertical and horizontal lines that cross at the center) are the most likely future support or resistance levels. (See Figure App. 3.1.)

Figure App. 3.1   Gann square of cycle size 12, starting at 400 with step size 5. (Source: Compu Trac.)

```
F1                               C2                                    F2

     1060 1065 1070 1075 1080 1085 : 1090 : 1095 1100 1105 1110 1115 1120

     1055  850  855  860  865  870 :  875 :  880  885  890  895  900 1125

     1050  845  680  685  690  695 :  700 :  705  710  715  720  905 1130

     1045  840  675  550  555  560 :  565 :  570  575  580  725  910 1135

     1040  835  670  545  460  465 :  470 :  475  480  585  730  915 1140

     1035  830  665  540  455  410 :  415 :  420  485  590  735  920 1145
     -------------------------------------------------------------------
C1   1030  825  660  535  450  405 :  400 :  425  490  595  740  925 1150   C3
     -------------------------------------------------------------------
     1025  820  655  530  445  440 :  435 :  430  495  600  745  930 1155

     1020  815  650  525  520  515 :  510 :  505  500  605  750  935 1160

     1015  810  645  640  635  630 :  625 :  620  615  610  755  940 1165

     1010  805  800  795  790  785 :  780 :  775  770  765  760  945 1170

     1005 1000  995  990  985  980 :  975 :  970  965  960  955  950 1175

     1240 1235 1230 1225 1220 1215 : 1210 : 1205 1200 1195 1190 1185 1180

F4                               C4                                    F3
```

The *geometric forms* that most influenced him are the circle, triangle, and square. The 360 degrees that make up a circle feature prominently in his work. Gann used harmonics of 360 to arrive at time targets for future market turning points. One way of arriving at Gann calendar day counts for future market turns is to count forward from significant tops and bottoms by 30, 90, 120, 180, and 360. Those forward calendar days earmark possible market turns. An anniversary date (one year forward) of a prominent top or bottom is an especially potent time target. Gann also attached special significance to time periods coinciding with the number 7.

Combining *time* and *price* forms the basis for much of his theory. Gann saw a definite proportional relationship between the two. One of his methods for finding tops or bottoms is based on *the squaring of price and time*—that is, when a unit of price equals a unit of time. For example, Gann would take a prominent high in a market, convert that dollar figure into a calendar unit (days, weeks, months, or years), and project that time period forward. When that time period is reached, time and price are squared and a market turn due. As an illustration, if a market hit a prominent high at $100, Gann counted 100 days, weeks, months, or years forward. Those future dates identified possible turning points. Gann's proportional relationship between time and price is the basis for his theory of *geometric angles*, which is our main concern in this discussion.

GEOMETRIC ANGLES AND PERCENTAGES

Our purpose is to discuss one of Gann's simpler and, in the opinion of some prominent Gann users, one of his most valuable techniques— *geometric angles*. We're also going to include in the discussion another relatively simple concept—percentage retracements—which can be utilized effectively in conjunction with the angle lines.

Let's begin with the Gann percentages. In Chapter 4, during our coverage of percentage retracements, it was mentioned that Gann divided price action into eighths: $1/8$, $2/8$, $3/8$, $4/8$, $5/8$, $6/8$, $7/8$, $8/8$. He also divided price movement into thirds: $1/3$ and $2/3$. The following table breaks those fractions down into their percentage equivalents. Notice that the $1/3$ and $2/3$ percentage parameters are inserted in their proper place along with the divisions into eighths.

$^1/_8 = 12.5\%$
$^2/_8 = 25\%$
$^1/_3 = 33\%$

$^3/_8 = 37.5\%$
$^4/_8 = 50\%$
$^5/_8 = 62.5\%$
$^2/_3 = 67\%$

$^6/_8 = 75\%$
$^7/_8 = 87.5\%$
$^8/_8 = 100\%$

You'll notice immediately that the five middle numbers—33%, 37.5%, 50%, 62.5%, and 67%—are quite familiar. The 50% retracement is the most important to Gann. This is also the best known of all percentage retracements. Expanding outward from 50%, the next two in order of importance are 37.5% and 62.5%, which also happen to be the equivalent of the Fibonacci retracements discussed in Chapter 13. Therefore, we're now combining Gann and Elliott Wave Theory. Continuing outward, the next two are 33% and 67%, identified in Chapter 4 as Dow Theory minimum and maximum retracement benchmarks.

Gann believed that the other percentage numbers were also present in market action, but with diminishing importance. Gann fans would also be alert to retracements of 75% and 87.5% as possible market turning points. For smaller retracements, 12.5% and 25% might also play a role. These last four numbers are, however, beyond the 33% and 67% boundaries generally used by most market technicians.

Gann's geometric angles are trendlines drawn from prominent tops or bottoms at certain specific angles. Those angles are determined by the relationship between price and time. Gann's most important angle is 45 degrees. In an uptrend, that line is drawn upward to the right from a market low. In a downtrend, it is drawn down to the right from a market high (similar to the 45-degree lines presented in Chapter 12 on modified point and figure charting). The line is based on a one-to-one relationship between units of time and price. In other words, prices advance or decline at the rate of one price unit (or box on the chart) per time unit (usually a week on the daily bar chart). To draw the line on the bar chart from a bottom, move one box (a week) to the right and one price box upward. Continue the process for each week and the result will be a 45-degree line. A protractor would accomplish the same task.

THE IMPORTANCE OF THE 45-DEGREE LINE

The 45-degree line represents Gann's major up and down trendline. A bull market is in force as long as prices are above the rising line. A bear market is in force as long as prices remain below the declining line. The breaking of the 45-degree line usually indicates a major trend reversal. It can be seen that the 45-degree line represents a perfect balance of price and time. When prices in an uptrend decline to the 45-degree line, time and price are in perfect balance and a state of equilibrium exists. The breaking of the trendline therefore indicates a shift in that relationship and a possible change in the trend. Channel lines can also be drawn, using 45-degree angles, from prominent highs and lows that are parallel to the basic trendline.

Steeper or flatter geometric trendlines can be drawn combining time and price units by a factor of 2. A 1×1 line would be the 45-degree line. A 1×2 line would be the next steeper line above the 45-degree line, showing an increase of two price units for each unit of time. That means that prices are increasing at twice the rate of time. The next steeper line would be 1×4, showing four units of price advance per unit of time. These steeper lines can be continued up to 1×8, although the use of the steeper numbers is not as common. (See Figure App. 3.2.)

Below the 45-degree up trendline, the next flatter line is 2×1, showing one unit of price advance per two units of time (or $^1/_2$ price unit change per week). An even flatter line would be 4×1, showing four units of time per unit of price change (or only $^1/_4$ unit of price change per week). The following table shows the various angle lines in descending order with their degree equivalents. The first number represents time and the second is price. Read as time × price:

$1 \times 8 = 82\ ^1/_2$ degrees
$1 \times 4 = 75$ degrees
$1 \times 3 = 71\ ^1/_4$ degrees

$1 \times 2 = 63\ ^3/_4$ degrees
$1 \times 1 = 45$ degrees
$2 \times 1 = 26\ ^1/_4$ degrees
$3 \times 1 = 18\ ^3/_4$ degrees

$4 \times 1 = 15$ degrees
$8 \times 1 = 7\ ^1/_2$ degrees

W.D. Gann: Geometric Angles and Percentages

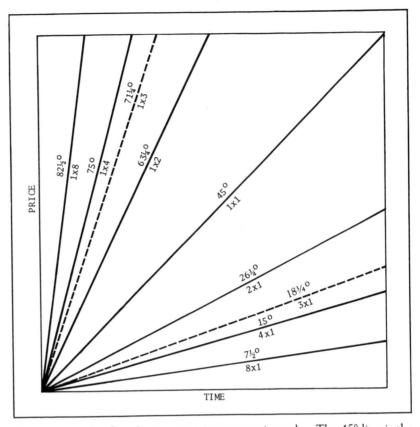

Figure App. 3.2 Gann's time × price geometric angles. The 45° line is the most important trendline, showing that time and price are in perfect balance. When the 45° line reaches the upper right corner of the square, time and price are equal and are said to be *squared*. That often marks a change in trend. These trendlines are used to indicate support and resistance levels. When one line is broken (by the entire day's price range), prices should move to the next line. These lines are drawn from a market bottom. Geometric angle trendlines are also drawn downward from market tops. At important tops and bottoms, Gann also believed in drawing 45° lines upward to the right from a zero line.

Notice that 1 × 3 and 3 × 1 lines are included in the table. Gann apparently felt that these particular lines, dividing price movement into thirds, were more useful on weekly and monthly charts. Gann's geometric lines are used in much the same way as speedlines and Fibonacci fan lines. In an uptrend, these lines are support lines; in a downtrend, resistance lines. During an uptrend, the breaking of one line would suggest a further price drop to the next lower line. Correspondingly, if prices break above one line, they would be expected to rally to the next higher one.

COMBINING GEOMETRIC
ANGLE LINES AND PERCENTAGE RETRACEMENTS

These two techniques are more effective if used together. Once an important market move has occurred, the entire price range can be divided into eighths. This can be accomplished by drawing eight horizontal lines at the appropriate percentage points. In an uptrend, these lines should provide support on dips. During a downtrend, they would represent possible resistance. By inserting these lines on the chart, the Gann follower knows in advance exactly where the important percentage retracements are located. While Gann used eight different numbers, the most important are located near the center at $^3/_8$, $^4/_8$, and $^5/_8$. These include the 50% retracement and the two Fibonacci numbers. The remaining parameters become less important, but at least the trader knows where they are.

Then draw in the Gann geometric angles from the prominent low, the prominent high, or both. The three most important angles are the 45-degree line (1 × 1), the $63^3/_4$ degree line (1 × 2), and the $26^1/_4$ line (2 × 1). These three lines (together with the middle three percentage retracements of 37.5%, 50%, and 62.5%) define the center of gravity of the chart. The other lines, from the steeper to the flatter ones, can also be drawn, but are of diminishing importance.

The user then looks for coincidence or confirmation between the two techniques. The best example would be a 50% pullback in an uptrend to the 45-degree line. That would represent an excellent support area. Another example would be a corrective dip in an uptrend to the 37.5% Fibonacci retracement level and the $63^3/_4$ (1 × 2) angle line. The idea is have a situation where prices decline to a prominent geometric angle and a significant percentage retracement parameter at the same time.

Gann geometric angles should be drawn from both prominent peaks and troughs. Therefore, the chart can show rising and declining lines at the same time. These lines can be used in conjunction with one another. When a declining angle line (drawn from a top) crosses a rising geometric angle line (drawn from a bottom) at a 90-degree angle, that point of intersection carries more weight. If that point of intersection also coincides with a horizontal percentage retracement level, that price level takes on even more importance. In addition to drawing geometric angle lines from prominent tops and bottoms, Gann also favored drawing 45-degree lines from 0. In other words, at the time point on the chart where a prominent top or bottom is seen, a 45-degree up trendline is drawn not only from that top or bottom, but also from the price on the chart corresponding to zero. Gann believed that lines drawn from zero had future significance. Gann had many other ways of drawing these lines that are beyond the scope of this discussion.

The accompanying charts give a demonstration of these geometric lines and angles in action. For purposes of simplicity and clarity, however, the examples focus on the more important lines and angles. (See Figures App. 3.3 through 3.7.)

Figure App. 3.3 The chart shows how well the 1 × 1 basic trendline and a 1 × 1 channel line define the trend action. During the March/April rally, a steeper 1 × 2 trendline worked better. Notice that the pullback from April to May fell to the 45° (1 × 1) up trendline and retraced just about 50 percent (4/8) of the February/April advance. Combining geometric trendlines with percentage retracements improves the overall results. When drawing the lines, simply count the numbers of boxes to the right and then up. A 1 × 1 line means one box to the right and 1 box up. 2 × 1 (time × price) means 2 boxes to the right and 1 box up. A steeper line, 1 × 2, means 1 box to the right and 2 boxes up. (Chart courtesy of Commodity Research Bureau, a Knight-Ridder Business Information Service.)

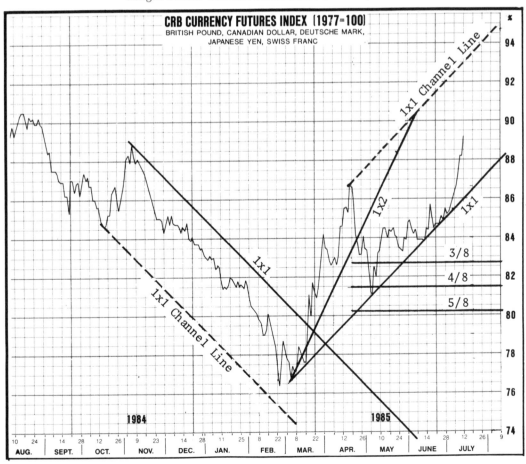

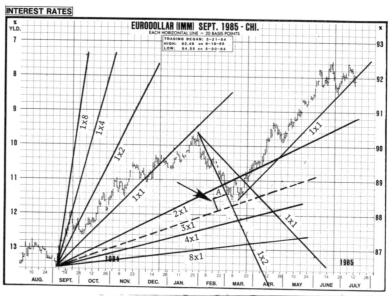

Figure App. 3.4 An example of all the Gann lines in action during the September/February advance in Eurodollars. The basic 1 × 1 line contained most of the uptrend. Notice, however, that the 3 × 1 up trendline contained the selloff in March. At Angle A, the rising 3 × 1 line and the declining 1 × 2 line meet at a near 90° angle. That usually marks an important support area. The 1 × 1 trendline worked pretty well also during the February/March decline and the March/June uptrend. (Chart courtesy of Commodity Research Bureau, a Knight-Ridder Business Information Service.)

Figure App. 3.5 Gann lines applied to the copper market. Notice how the various lines provided support during the April/July selloff. The downtrend was well contained by the 1 × 1 (45°) line and the 45° channel line drawn from the May bottom. (Chart courtesy of Commodity Research Bureau, a Knight-Ridder Business Information Service.)

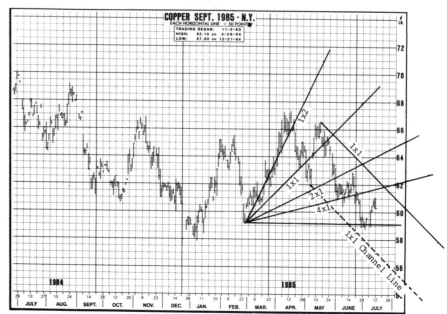

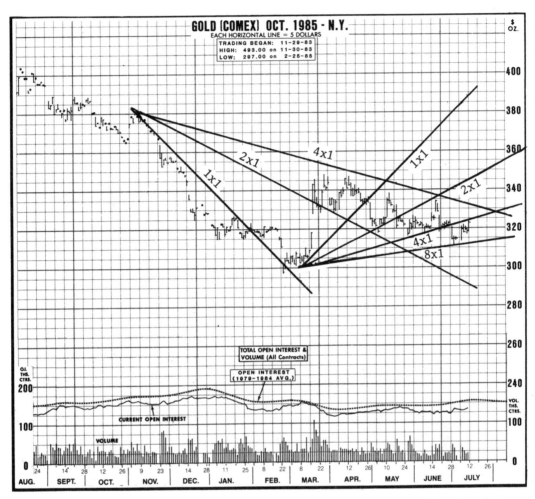

Figure App. 3.6 The February/March rally was contained by the declining 4 × 1 trendline from the November peak. Notice how the 4 × 1 and 8 × 1 rising Gann lines supported the gold market during the May/June decline. (Chart courtesy of Commodity Research Bureau, a Knight-Ridder Business Information Service.)

Figure App. 3.7 Notice during the steep January/March advance, the 1 × 4 up trendline defined the trend very well. That steep a trend usually doesn't last very long. Prices will usually retrace back to a more sustainable 45° rate of advance. Notice along the right margin that the price range from the December low to the March highs can be divided into eighths. The center of gravity on the chart is in the 3/8 to 5/8 zone in the vicinity of the 45° (1 × 1) line. In this case, prices retraced about half. The 90° angle formed by the crossing of the rising and falling (1 × 1) lines also marked an important support area (point A). (Chart courtesy of Commodity Research Bureau, a Knight-Ridder Business Information Service.)

W.D. Gann: Geometric Angles and Percentages

REFERENCE SOURCES

Our purpose has been to present a couple of Gann's simpler and more useful techniques. The reader should consult other sources for a fuller explanation of Gann's ideas. The best single source of information is the Lambert-Gann Publishing Company (P.O. Box O, Pomeroy, WA 99347). That organization publishes several Gann books including his best known work, *How to Make Profits in Commodities* (originally written in 1942, revised in 1951, and reprinted in 1976). In addition to marketing two of Gann's courses, (the *W.D. Gann Stock Market Course* and the *W.D. Gann Commodities Course*,) Lambert-Gann publishes a newsletter called the "W.D. Gann Technical Review," holds occasional seminars on Gann's techniques, and even sells chart paper most useful for that type of analysis.

Some market letters specialize in Gann analysis. One of the best known is "Gann Angles," written by Phyllis Kahn, president of Gannworld, Inc. (245-A Washington St., Monterey CA 93940). Another newsletter, "Precision Timing," is produced by Donald R. Vodopich (Box 11722, Atlanta, GA 30305) and applies a unique combination of Gann analysis and Elliott Wave Theory. Mr. Vodopich explains his technique in his book entitled, *Trading for Profit With Precision Timing* (Atlanta, GA: Precision Timing, Inc., 1984). Vodopich's major approach is to combine Elliott Wave analysis with Gann angles, particularly the three major Gann angles—1×1, 1×2, and 2×1.

Computer software is available to assist the Gannophile. "Ganntrader 1" (copyright 1983 by Peter Pich) is marketed by the same Lambert-Gann Publishing Company and is the most ambitious program, producing charts with some of Gann's more intricate routines, including the "Master Price and Time Calculator." The Pardo Corporation (Evanston, IL 60201) markets a technical analysis software program, the "Advanced Chartist," that draws the Gann angles (geometric trendlines) and Gann lines (horizontal percentage lines) right on the computer-generated chart. CompuTrac has a Gann (Cardinal) Square routine (See Figure App. 3.1) and provides the numbers necessary for the drawing of the geometric lines.

For those who still like to do things by hand, the Kansas City Board of Trade (Kansas City, MO 64112) has made available, for a nominal fee, a handy little transparent plastic device, called the "Opportunity Angles" tool, that is used to draw Gann angles.

Bibliography

Allen, R.C. *How to Use the 4 Day, 9 Day and 18 Day Moving Averages to Earn Larger Profits from Commodities.* Chicago: Best Books, 1974.

Arms, Richard W. *Volume Cycles in the Stock Market: Market Timing Through Equivolume Charting.* Homewood, IL: Dow Jones-Irwin, 1983.

Belveal, L. Dee *Charting Commodity Market Price Behavior,* 2nd edition. Homewood, IL: Dow Jones-Irwin, 1985.

Bernstein, Jacob *The Handbook of Commodity Cycles: a Window on Time.* New York: Wiley, 1982.

Bolton, A. Hamilton *The Elliott Wave Principle: a Critical Appraisal.* Hamilton, Bermuda: Monetary Research, 1960.

Blumenthal, Earl *Chart for Profit Point & Figure Trading.* Larchmont, NY: Investors Intelligence, 1975.

Bressert, Walter J. and James Hardie Jones *The HAL Blue Book: How to Use Cycles With an Over-bought/Oversold and Momentum Index For More Consistent Profits.* Tucson, AZ: HAL Market Cycles, 1984.

Cohen, A.W. *How to Use the Three-Point Reversal Method of Point & Figure Stock Market Trading,* 8th revised edition. Larchmont, NY: Chartcraft, 1982.

Cootner, Paul H. (editor) *The Random Character of Stock Market Prices.* Cambridge, MA: MIT Press, 1964.

de Villiers, Victor *The Point and Figure Method of Anticipating Stock Price Movements: Complete Theory and Practice:* Brightwaters, NY: Windsor Books, orig. 1933, reprinted in 1975.

Dewey, Edward R. with Og Mandino *Cycles, the Mysterious Forces That Trigger Events.* New York: Manor Books, 1973.

Dunn & Hargitt *Point and Figure Commodity Trading: a Computer Evaluation.* Lafayette, IN; Dunn & Hargitt, 1971.

Dunn & Hargitt *Trader's Notebook: Trading Methods Checked by Computer.* Lafayette, IN: Dunn & Hargitt, 1970.

Edwards, Robert D. and John Magee *Technical Analysis of Stock Trends.* 5th edition, Boston, MA: John Magee, 1966.

Elliott, Ralph N. (edited by Robert Prechter) *The Major Works of R.N. Elliott.* Chappaqua, NY: New Classics Library, 1980.

Emery, Walter L. (editor) *Commodity Year Book* (published annually). Jersey City, NJ: Commodity Research Bureau.

Frost, Alfred J. and Robert R. Prechter *Elliott Wave Principle, Key to Stock Market Profits.* Chappaqua, NY: New Classics Library, 1978.

Gann, W.D. *How to Make Profits in Commodities,* revised edition. Pomeroy, WA: Lambert-Gann Publishing, orig. 1942, reprinted in 1976.

Hadady, R. Earl *Contrary Opinion: How to Use it For Profit in Trading Commodity Futures.* Pasadena,

TELEPHONE   001   504   8951474

COMPA TRAC
1021 9TH STREET
NEW ORLEANS
LA   70115

TELEPHONE   001   504   8951474
FAX

TECHNICAL AN

153

JOHN

CA: Hadady Publications, 1983.

Hurst, J.M. *The Profit Magic of Stock Transaction Timing*, Englewood Cliffs, NJ: Prentice-Hall, 1970.

Jiler, Harry (editor) *Guide to Commodity Price Forecasting*. New York, NY: Commodity Research Bureau, 1971.

Jiler, William L. *How Charts Can Help You in the Stock Market*. New York: Trendline, 1962.

Kaufman, Perry J. *Commodity Trading Systems and Methods*. New York: Wiley, 1978.

Kaufman, Perry J. *Technical Analysis in Commodities*. New York: Wiley, 1980.

Patel, Charles *Technical Trading Systems for Commodities and Stocks*. Walnut Creek, CA: Trading Systems Research, 1980.

Pring, Martin *Technical Analysis Explained*, 2nd edition. New York: McGraw-Hill, 1985.

Schultz, John W. *The Intelligent Chartist*. New York: WRSM Financial Services, 1962.

Schwager, Jack D. *A Complete Guide to the Futures Markets: Fundamental Analysis, Technical Analysis, Trading, Spreads, and Options*. New York: Wiley, 1984.

Sklarew, Arthur *Techniques of a Professional Commodity Chart Analyst*. New York: Commodity Research Bureau, 1980.

Teweles, Richard J., Charles V. Harlow and Herbert L. Stone *The Commodity Futures Game—Who Wins?—Who Loses?—Why?*, 2nd edition. New York: McGraw-Hill, 1974.

Vodopich, Donald R. *Trading For Profit With Precision Timing*. Atlanta, GA: Precision Timing, 1984.

Wheelan, Alexander H. *Study Helps in Point and Figure Technique*. Morgan Rogers, 1966.

Wilder, J. Welles *New Concepts in Technical Trading Systems*. Greensboro, NC: Trend Research, 1978.

Williams, Larry R. *How I Made $1,000,000 Trading Commodities Last Year*, 3rd edition. Monterey, CA: Conceptual Management, 1979.

Zieg, Kermit C., Jr. and Perry J. Kaufman *Point and Figure Commodity Trading Techniques*. Larchmont, NY: Investors Intelligence, 1975.

Futures Chart Services

Chart Analysis Ltd., 7 Swallow St., London W1R7HD.

Chartcraft Commodity Service, 1 West Avenue, Larchmont, NY 10538.

Commodity Perspective, 30 S. Wacker Dr., Chicago, IL, 60606.

Commodity Price Charts, 219 Parkade, Cedar Falls, IA 50613.

Commodity Trend Service, 1224 U.S. Hwy. 1, N. Palm Beach, FLA 33408.

CRB Futures Chart Service, Commodity Research Bureau, 75 Montgomery St., Jersey City, NJ 07302.

Dunn & Hargitt, Inc., 22 N. Second St., Lafayette, IN 47902.

Financial Futures, 200 W. Monroe St., Chicago, IL 60606.

Quotron Futures Charts, P.O. Box 1424, Racine, WISC 53401.

The Professional Chart Service, 61 S. Lake Ave., Pasadena, CA 91109.

Security Market Research Inc., P.O. Box 14088, Denver, CO 80214.

Spread Scope Inc., P.O. Box 5841, Mission Hills, CA 91345.

Futures Periodicals

Consensus, P.O. Box 19086, Kansas City, MO 64141.

Cycles, Foundation for the Study of Cycles, 124 S. Highland Ave., Pittsburgh, PA 15206.

Futures, the Magazine of Commodities and Options, 219 Parkade, Cedar Falls, IA 50613.

Intermarket Magazine, 175 W. Jackson Blvd., Chicago, IL 60604.

Journal of Commerce, 110 Wall St., New York, NY 10005.

Technical Analysis of Stocks and Commodities, P.O. Box 46518, Seattle, WA 98146.

The Journal of Futures Markets, John Wiley & Sons, 605 Third Ave., New York, NY 10158 (in affiliation with the Center for the Study of Futures Markets, Columbia University Business School).

Technical Organizations

COMPU-TRAC (The Technical Analysis Group—TAG) 1021 9th St., New Orleans, LA 70115.

Foundation for the Study of Cycles, 124 S. Highland Ave., Pittsburgh, PA 15206.

Market Technicians Association, 70 Pine St., New York, NY 10270.

Society for the Investigation of Recurring Events (S.I.R.E.), Drawer W, Downington, PA 19335.

Index

550